DESIGNS UPON NATURE

FIGURE 0.1. An old stagecoach road at Yellowstone Lake (2015).
Photograph © Janet L. Pritchard, from her book, *More than Scenery: Yellowstone, an American Love Story* (George F. Thompson Publishing, 2022), 133. Courtesy of the artist.

DESIGNS UPON NATURE

THE CULTURAL LANDSCAPE HISTORY OF YELLOWSTONE NATIONAL PARK SINCE 1872

EDITED BY

William K. Wyckoff and Karl Byrand

GEORGE F. THOMPSON PUBLISHING
Staunton, Virginia

UNIVERSITY OF WYOMING PRESS
Laramie, Wyoming

in association with
THE FOUNDATION FOR LANDSCAPE STUDIES

Published by George F. Thompson Publishing and University of Wyoming Press

George F. Thompson Publishing
217 Oak Ridge Circle
Staunton, Virginia 24401-3511
www.gftbooks.com

University of Wyoming Press
An imprint of University Press of Colorado
1580 North Logan Street, Suite 660
PMB 39883
Denver, Colorado 80203-1942

Printed in the United States of America

The University Press of Colorado is a proud member of the Association of University Presses.

The University Press of Colorado is a cooperative publishing enterprise supported, in part, by Adams State University, Colorado School of Mines, Colorado State University, Fort Lewis College, Metropolitan State University of Denver, University of Alaska Fairbanks, University of Colorado, University of Northern Colorado, University of Wyoming, Utah State University, and Western Colorado University.

∞ This paper meets the requirements of the ANSI/NISO Z39.48-1992 (Permanence of Paper).

ISBN: 978-1-64642-768-0 (hardcover)
ISBN: 978-1-64642-769-7 (ebook)
DOI: https://doi.org/10.5876/9781646427697

The DOI (digital object identifier) provides a permanent link to information about this content's location and availability.

Cataloging-in-Publication data for this title is available online at the Library of Congress

EDITOR AND PUBLISHING CONSULTANT:
George F. Thompson
EDITORIAL AND RESEARCH ASSISTANT:
Mikki Soroczak
MANUSCRIPT EDITORS: Purna Makaram and Carolyn Elerding
BOOK DESIGN: Kristina Kachele
PRODUCTION: Dan Pratt

Cover image: Vintage Haynes postcard (28478), "Old Faithful Inn and Geyser, Yellowstone National Park." Source: private collection of William K. Wyckoff.

FIGURE 0.2. Artist Point, overlooking Lower Falls of the Yellowstone River (2010). Photograph © Janet L. Pritchard, from her book, *More than Scenery: Yellowstone, an American Love Story* (George F. Thompson Publishing, 2022), 6. Courtesy of the artist.

Contents

FIGURE 0.3. Tourists see bison (*Bison bison*) up close in the Lamar River Valley (2008). Photograph © Janet L. Pritchard, from her book, *More than Scenery: Yellowstone, an American Love Story* (George F. Thompson Publishing, 2022), 33. Courtesy of the artist.

Preface

YELLOWSTONE NATIONAL PARK remains a magical place more than 150 years after its creation. For many, the national park idea is among America's greatest gifts to the world, and in Yellowstone we have a place that is revered by locals as well as visitors from throughout the region, nation, and world. This book brings together a remarkable collection of geographers and historians who share a love for the park and a fascination for how its cultural landscapes as well as its natural wonders make it the special place that it is. Happily, with this book we fill in important gaps in what we know about Yellowstone, for *Designs upon Nature* is the first history of how and why those cultural landscapes—the built environment—have evolved since March 1, 1872, when Yellowstone became the world's first national park. This means roads, lodges, campsites, boardwalks, parking areas, waysides, and all the human artifacts that are part of the greater Yellowstone landscape and its ecosystems.

The story of Yellowstone's changing cultural landscape begins with the editors' introduction to the idea of a national park and the essential contributions that the built environment makes to the Yellowstone experience.

https://doi.org/10.5876/9781646427697.c000

Langdon Smith then focuses on the park's initial years. Smith, a cultural and historical geographer (now retired) at Slippery Rock University, reminds us that Yellowstone's landscape features and their larger cultural significance were inevitably wedded to the evolving idea of what a national park was supposed to be. As the first large-scale park, Yellowstone proved to be an amazing laboratory, an experiment that was shaped by a variety of local and national influences. Smith argues that residents living close to the park, especially in Montana, played an important role in defining the early agenda of park activities and development. Local travelers and entrepreneurs knew the park well and were key participants in early road-building activities and tourism ventures. Smith also assesses the "custodial" role of initial park superintendents, who were, in effect, "field-testing" the national park idea. Early park officials were soon challenged with balancing the same values of preservation and development that complicate park management to this day. Finally, Smith examines the experiences of early visitors in the park and ponders how they influenced the evolution of Yellowstone's cultural landscape.

Lee Whittlesey, in his chapter on the Mammoth Hot Springs area near the park's northern border, offers a detailed, meticulously researched portrait of one of the park's oldest developed areas. As a long-time Yellowstone archivist and historian, Whittlesey has had unique access to park records and has spent many years literally witnessing cultural landscape change in the Mammoth area (which serves as Yellowstone National Park's headquarters). Whittlesey reconstructs Mammoth's chaotic origins as a variety of private interests jockeyed for position and influence at the park's key northern entryway. He also traces the defining impact of the US Army upon the Mammoth landscape. When the Army took control of the park in 1886, it invested a great deal in Fort Yellowstone and watched over the evolution of tourist facilities in the area. Once the National Park Service (NPS) was established in 1916 and automobile use in the park increased, the Mammoth area saw tremendous growth in tourist facilities. Throughout his essay, Whittlesey relates a myriad of local changes at Mammoth to the larger evolution of American tourism and changing NPS policies. He concludes his Mammoth portrait in the early twenty-first century, noting how the local cultural landscape continues to evolve actively (as do the Mammoth Hot Springs themselves) and how they reflect the changing needs of the park's visitors and the evolving mandates of park managers.

Karl Byrand, a cultural and historical geographer (now retired) at the University of Wisconsin–Sheboygan, next explores Yellowstone's famed Upper Geyser Basin, home to Old Faithful Geyser and a complex accumulation of cultural landscape features. As one of the park's most visited localities, the Upper Geyser Basin became what Byrand calls "an urban island in an ocean of relative wilderness." Byrand's narrative begins with the birth of the park, when the area's remarkable thermal features were threatened with vandalism. An early encampment of soldiers helped maintain control over the basin, and a growing number of intrepid tourists were treated to a remarkable display of bubbling hot springs, multihued pools, and erupting geysers. An initial "shack hotel" and modest camping facilities were upstaged in 1904 with the grand opening of the spectacular Old Faithful Inn. To this day, the huge and sprawling inn epitomizes the "rustic luxury" of many national park hotels around the United States and remains an immensely important park destination on its own. Based on his research from the park archives, Byrand also reveals how changes at the Upper Geyser Basin development area track larger shifts in the visitor experience of park tourists. He notes the waxing and waning of bear-feeding grounds and swimming pools, all replaced in more recent years by a policy that has selectively removed some human landscape elements while formally preserving the legacy of others. The result is an amazingly complex accumulation of landscape elements that reflect multiple park management strategies, visitor preferences, and concessionaire initiatives, producing a cultural landscape that is as pluralistic and diverse as the agents who created it.

From the Upper Geyser Basin, a short journey to the east brings the reader to Yellowstone Lake and Yolonda Youngs's chapter on how that huge alpine body of water (one of the largest in the United States) has long served as another focal point for tourism development within the park. Youngs, a geographer at California State University–San Bernardino, also benefits from her many years of boating and guiding on the lake as well as from extensive overland journeys to the park archives. Her remarkable narrative uncovers a long story of human activity along Yellowstone Lake's shoreline, from archaeological sites more than nine thousand years old to recent controversies over the speed of motorboats on the lake. She begins her story with early narrative descriptions of the lake and then reconstructs how the lake became integrated into a larger "Grand Tour" of the park's attractions. Development areas at West Thumb, Lake (on the north shore), and Fishing Bridge catered to the varied needs of visitors. In addition, boat concessionaires and fishing supply stores enabled visitors to enjoy time on the water. Even though the imposing Lake Hotel remains today (along with Grant Village on the south shore), Youngs describes how shifting concessionaire services and park management policies (encouraging a reduction in human activities in ecologically sensitive zones) have actually reduced the human presence along the lake and in subtle ways made the lake a less prominent part of the contemporary visitor experience in the park.

Diane Papineau's reconnaissance of the Grand Canyon of the Yellowstone River is the next stop on our "Grand Loop tour" of the park's developed areas (and parallels the typical early tourist experience, which often culminated at the viewpoint of the Lower Falls). As with Youngs, Papineau's experience as a scholar in the park archives has been supplemented by additional time spent in the park as a seasonal employee. Papineau recounts how Native American oral traditions and the tales of fur trappers were gradually supplemented by scientific reports and by grand canvases of the Lower Falls that were used to promote the creation of the park in 1872. As with the Upper Geyser Basin, the Canyon area quickly became a must-see destination within the park. It became the site for a growing array of visitor cabins, lodges, campgrounds, and hotel services. Papineau reconstructs how each of these facilities shaped Canyon's cultural landscape and changing settlement pattern. She tells the story of Canyon's conversion to auto tourism and how older rustic-style visitor services were replaced by the modern, convenient "suburban sprawl" of Mission 66–era motel facilities. Indeed, Papineau discusses how Canyon's post–World War II evolution toward a more decentralized development pattern paralleled broader trends in urban America and how it offered a national park template reproduced in many other recreational settings around the nation.

Nearby Roosevelt Lodge in the northern portion of the park is our next stop on our journey through Yellowstone. Tamsen Hert, a distinguished historian of the American West and the retired head of the Emmett D. Chisum Special Collections at the University of Wyoming Libraries, is an ideal guide to this enduring developed area. Compared to other developed areas discussed in the book, Roosevelt Lodge was a comparatively later and smaller addition to the park's cultural landscape. Roosevelt Lodge's significance, however, lies not in its scale but rather its purpose. Compared to the larger and more grandiose hotels that were being developed elsewhere in the park during the early twentieth century, Roosevelt Lodge was designed to cater to a clientele who were of more modest financial means and who sought to visit the park at a different pace. Although the rustic facility had its roots in the camp companies that were sprouting up in the park during the late nineteenth century, the development of Roosevelt Lodge proper shortly followed the introduction of the automobile to Yellowstone's cultural landscape. The lodge served as a facility that catered to budget-minded visitors who wanted a taste of the Old West and who no longer wished to be confined to the bonds of the Northern Pacific Railroad and the timetables of the park's transportation company. In essence, Roosevelt Lodge reflects the increasing democratization of Yellowstone and the national parks in general, when the parks began catering to a wider swath of the visiting public.

Finally, Timothy Davis, a leading historian with the National Park Service, reminds us that Yellowstone's road system is an integral element of the park's cultural landscape. Davis provides a wide-ranging narrative that reconstructs the long, sometimes tortuous story of how Yellowstone's elaborate Grand Loop Road took shape. We follow the tale from the pioneer era of Yellowstone's primitive stage roads to how the National Park Service carefully managed and modernized highways and bridges to fit the changing needs of the twentieth-century traveler. Davis reminds us—in the tradition of J. B. Jackson—that roads belong in the landscape and are important parts of the built environment, along with all of the lodges, tent camps, and hotels they helped connect. Davis also demonstrates how their evolution has shaped the way in which millions of visitors have experienced Yellowstone's various features. Overall, his chapter helps knit together the various stories of the park's individual development areas, and he shows how its road system literally carved a path from one set of park attractions to the next.

The chapters in this book not only tell the story of the development of Yellowstone's dynamic cultural landscape but also reveal a deeper story of the changing wants and needs of the American public, their notion of what a national park experience should be, and the efforts of park overseers, concessionaires, and other agents of change to cater to those who would venture into Yellowstone's magnificent landscape. It is here, within America's and the world's first national park, that the national park experience has been defined, developed, and displayed.

FIGURE 0.4. Painting en plein-air along the Gardner River in Gardner Canyon, with Eagle Nest Rock in the top right (2010). Photograph © Janet L. Pritchard, from her book, *More than Scenery: Yellowstone, an American Love Story* (George F. Thompson Publishing, 2022), 41. Courtesy of the artist.

FIGURE 0.5. The Boardwalk at Mound Terrace, Mammoth Hot Springs (2006). Photograph © Janet L. Pritchard, from her book, *More than Scenery: Yellowstone, an American Love Story* (George F. Thompson Publishing, 2022), 65. Courtesy of the artist.

DESIGNS UPON NATURE

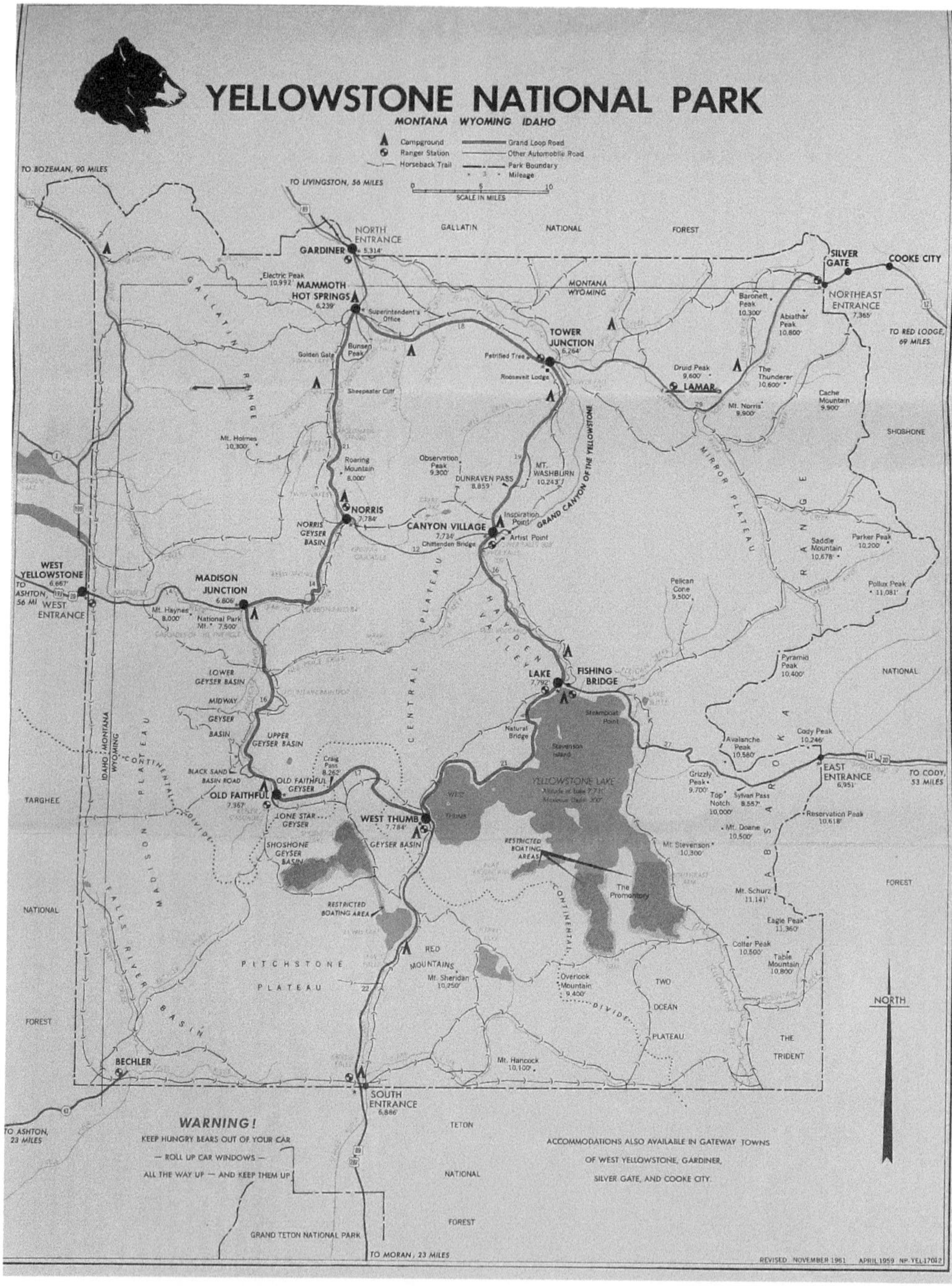

FIGURE 1.1. Map of Yellowstone National Park, 1961. Yellowstone National Park's many developed areas and roads are displayed in this simple map that was handed to visitors when they entered the park during the early 1960s. Source: National Park Service.

1

The Idea of a National Park

William K. Wyckoff and Karl Byrand

THIS COLLECTION of original, commissioned essays explores the evolution of the cultural landscapes and changing built environments of Yellowstone National Park since 1872. When most of us think about Yellowstone, we focus on its spectacular natural wonders, with its unique collection of geysers, wildlife, lakes, river, canyons, and backcountry that is duplicated nowhere else on Earth. Inevitably, many of us see Yellowstone primarily as a wilderness preserve, and our perceptions of landscapes of wilderness shape the way we see and experience the park. But there is also another Yellowstone landscape, the human landscape that is woven into the fabric of the park from Roosevelt Arch at the North Entrance to the trail system that winds its way through the Upper Geyser Basin. This human imprint—what geographers call a cultural landscape—has also become an essential part of America's first national park. Each essay in this book assesses the interplay between Yellowstone's natural and cultural worlds and examines how these dual landscapes unfold in key localities within the park (figure 1.1).

Yellowstone's cultural landscape is a product of three key agents of landscape change that include park administrators, concessionaires, and visitors.

https://doi.org/10.5876/9781646427697.c001

Throughout the park's history, these three groups transformed Yellowstone's cultural landscape in ways that reflected their respective visions of the park and its purpose. Further complicating the story is the fact that these visions of the park changed over time, were often in conflict with one another, and were always producing unanticipated responses from Yellowstone's natural setting. In addition, their expression within Yellowstone was inevitably tied to the larger cultural, political, economic, and technological transformations that were affecting all of the United States and the world beyond.[1] These changes have cumulatively created a built environment that reflects the diverse expectations and demands of visitors to the park, the uneven ability of concessionaires to cater to those needs, and the shifting priorities of park managers to both promote and preserve Yellowstone's unique natural environment. What remains today is a complex accumulation of buildings and landscape features that reflect these varied influences and continue to shape the way visitors enjoy the park and experience nature within its boundaries.

Yellowstone's story is particularly important given its status as America's and the world's first national park and its continuing role as one of the flagship parks within the national park system. Indeed, Yellowstone's record of cultural landscape change parallels larger trends that are evident in many other national parks. Thus, while certainly not representative of all national parks in every way, what we see in Yellowstone has often reflected and even guided changes in many other settings within the system. Since its inception, Yellowstone has always been a kind of laboratory regarding the national park idea.

LEARNING FROM LANDSCAPE

Think about Yellowstone's cultural landscape and what it entails. We emphasize three perspectives in our definition of a cultural landscape. First, we embrace the idea that a cultural landscape is a fascinating *built environment* within the natural landscape, a dynamic material artifact that, in Yellowstone, includes a combination of roads, hotels, lodges, visitor centers, campgrounds, trails, boardwalks, and myriad other features that have changed over time to fit the needs of travelers.[2] As the park evolved, simple bridle paths, tent camps, and rough-sided log hotels were replaced by paved highways, sprawling park lodges, and elaborate visitor amenities. Some of the early visual legacies have survived while others have not. All of these cumulative visual signatures offer important clues to how Yellowstone reflected

FIGURE 1.2. Framing nature at Handkerchief Pool. This vintage Frank Jay Haynes postcard (ca. 1920) displays how carefully managed walkways and well-established cultural traditions framed nature in Yellowstone's Upper Geyser Basin early in the twentieth century. Visitors enjoyed throwing a handkerchief into the pool and seeing it emerge sparkling clean a few minutes later. Source: private collection of William K. Wyckoff.

larger national cultural, political, and economic imperatives as well as how the National Park System itself changed through time.

Second, we recognize how cultural landscapes have helped to define the park's *identity as a place*, the way we experience Yellowstone as individual travelers or how we collectively as a nation represent and find meaning in the park.[3] What visitors recall about Yellowstone is shaped by these landscapes—by views of Yellowstone Lake captured from our tour boat, the special experience we have watching bison and elk from a hotel veranda, or a ranger's memorable evening campfire talk about wolves. The stories we tell ourselves about the park are inevitably wedded to both its natural and human elements, and these meanings become essential components of the cultural landscape. As the nation's first national park, Yellowstone has become a singular cultural landscape of symbolic importance that has contributed to the country's national identity.[4]

Finally, in an even more subtle way, the cultural landscape can be seen as *a normative framing of the natural world*.[5] Or, put more generally, the cultural landscape can be seen as how Yellowstone's human signatures shape the way people experience nature in the park (figure 1.2). We encounter a canyon vista from a built viewpoint. We see the lake from a shoreline highway (or a quite different view from the tour boat). Our appreciation of Old Faithful extends beyond our understanding of how a geyser works and is framed by the human elements: in the foreground, by the crowds we have to peer over to see Old Faithful, and, in the background, by the magnificent and famed Old Faithful Inn that overlooks this natural wonder and whose rooms are booked a year or more in advance. Here, the cultural harmonizes with the natural. These experiences of nature and their associated built environments (viewpoints, trails, highways, lake tours, hotels, campgrounds, visitor centers, &c.) are dynamic and have changed over time. In this book, we explain how and why that happens.

This perspective acknowledges that even the notion of "wilderness" is a human idea and that the concept of "nature" in the park is often contested and reworked through conflicting ideas and representations of park features. This approach suggests that the cultural landscape and the ways it changed over time offer a method for seeing the natural world through a set of conventions and expectations that are a function of changing aesthetics, tourist practices, and broader social and political relationships.[6] Thus, we need to look at how cultural landscapes become essential elements in the way people encounter nature in the park as well as how park features are remembered and preserved. The human geography of roads, the technology of the automobile, and the production of park guidebooks, for example, shaped which parts of the park people visited and how they experienced nature along the highway—the type of experience one historian of national parks has termed "windshield wilderness."[7] Each of our contributors ponders the importance of the cultural landscape's role in framing the varied wonders of the natural world that can be encountered in different portions of the park.

In the broadest sense, this collection of essays also demonstrates *why* it is important to preserve and more fully interpret the cultural resources of our national parks. With its long, rich, and varied history as a popular park, Yellowstone's story is an essential part of this larger national narrative of cultural landscape preservation.[8] Part of that story has focused on the preservation of key *historic sites* within Yellowstone and other park units. More recently, there has also been growing interest in preserving larger narratives of *cultural landscape evolution* in the parks. Perhaps, as historian Melody Webb noted more than thirty-five years ago, "with practice, the management of cultural landscapes will reach parity with the philosophical and theoretical framework of cultural landscapes. As managers gain knowledge and understanding, cultural landscapes will acquire greater significance, enhancing their value and the motivation for their own preservation."[9] Despite Webb's optimism, the notion of preserving entire cultural landscapes has been slow to blossom and bear fruit in many areas of the park, because the park's managers remain unclear on precisely what constitutes a "cultural landscape" or why its preservation and interpretation matters.[10]

What is the story of historic landscape preservation within the larger western parks? While the National Park Service has a long record of managing historic sites in the East (colonial legacy, Civil War battlefield sites, &c.) and in the Southwest (Native American, archaeological sites, &c.), the agency has placed less emphasis on such efforts in its western crown jewels, as the raison d'être for the founding of many of the western parks was their spectacular and unusual physical landscape features.[11] Indeed, many managers in the western units have traditionally seen the role of NPS interpretation in these parks as focused mainly on natural features, while historical interpretation is the focus at eastern military and battlefield parks.[12] But separating the two has not really worked, because historic-site parks have natural features, and natural parks have human history and cultural features.

The preservation of selected historic sites in some western settings gained attention after the passage of the Antiquities Act of 1906.[13] This legislation arose amid growing concerns about artifacts being removed from public lands, especially from historic archaeological sites in the Southwest. The act also facilitated the creation of dozens of national monuments (most administered by the National Park Service) by direct presidential proclamation. Later in the century, in 1933, President Roosevelt signed two executive orders that formally recognized the role of the National Park Service in preserving existing and future historic sites. This was followed by the Historic Sites Act in 1935, which prompted inventories of nationally significant sites within existing and proposed park units, but different parks each produced their own responses to the initiative.

The landmark passage of the National Historic Preservation Act (NHPA) in 1966 created the National Register of Historic Places (actually administered by the National Park Service) and also generated increased demand for new inventories and interpretation of historic structures (of both local and national significance) within park boundaries.[14] Still, a lack of staffing and low budgets often slowed the process of carefully identifying, evaluating, and preserving these historical resources.[15] In addition, for parks created before 1966 (such as Yellowstone), there were no mandates or guidelines for managing cultural resources within the park's authorizing legislation. There was also resistance to the idea within the NPS: Some personnel saw the task of maintaining old, rundown structures and other derelict cultural features in the parks as a drain on budgets. Others noted the conflict in maintaining "cultural resources" in areas that had been designated as "wilderness." For these managers, the notion of "preserving landscapes" meant restoring an area to its "natural state" rather than maintaining the historical structures and park infrastructure in "wild" areas.[16] Combining the two concepts was not considered in the National Park Service until more recent years, when the conflicts could no longer be ignored.

In the case of Yellowstone, before 1965 many concession-related structures were routinely removed without any regard to their historic value. Some experts have also speculated that the looming passage of the NHPA may, ironically, have promoted a flurry of building removals during the 1960s to prevent these structures from being considered as "historical resources," and a subsequent clean-up of the park may have contributed to similar removals just before the celebration of Yellowstone's highly publicized hundred-year anniversary in 1972.[17] At the very least, it is fair to say that in the years immediately following the passage of the NHPA, park managers adopted a variety of strategies that enabled them to continue removing buildings that were deemed safety hazards or within the limits of "acceptable loss" of potentially historic properties.[18] In addition, later removals of historic structures were approved to restore more natural ecological settings in some of Yellowstone's locations. For example, many older structures near Fishing Bridge were torn down during the 1980s to make way for prime grizzly bear habitat.

Gradually, however, new federal mandates and Park Service policies have codified and institutionalized historic preservation efforts within all of the parks, including the largely natural western units.[19] In 1970, the General Authorities Act codified a unified mission for the National Park Service, one that recognized the role of cultural resources and their preservation in every park unit. The previous year, the new US National Environmental Policy Act of 1969 (NEPA) also mandated that any proposed developments on federal lands be assessed for their potential environmental impacts and that public input be allowed and included in the decision-making process. As NEPA was implemented in later years (and formally amended in 1971 under Executive Order 11593), potential impacts on significant cultural resources became integral parts of these environmental assessments. In fact, Executive Order 11593 provided a clearer mandate for identifying and cataloging historic features in park units, and later, in 1980, that mandate was included in amendments to the NHPA. Meanwhile, prehistoric park features also received special attention with the passage in 1979 of the Archaeological Resources Protection Act (ARPA). Superseding the Antiquities Act of 1906, ARPA stiffened penalties for destruction and removal of federal archaeological resources and encouraged their documentation and protection within all park units.

But it wasn't until the 1990s that the preservation of cultural resources (including a greater focus on cultural landscapes) throughout the parks was given real visibility and definition within the system. The so-called Vail Agenda, published in 1992, was the result of a major conference held on the seventy-fifth anniversary of the National Park Service.[20] The Vail Agenda outlined the key challenges and goals facing the system in the twenty-first century, including the preservation of significant historical resources in the parks. Thereafter, a growing collection of NPS documents and guidelines clarified for park managers the procedures and definitions for recognizing historically significant sites and landscapes. For example, the NPS produced a detailed technical paper in 1993 (later published by Johns Hopkins University Press) entitled *Presenting Nature: The Historic Landscape Design of the National Park Service, 1916 to 1942*.[21] The report made it easier for park managers to identify historic architectural elements and to nominate park features for the National Register of Historic Places. The NPS also produced Preservation Brief 36, entitled "Protecting Cultural Landscapes: Planning, Treatment and Management of Historic Landscapes," which provided detailed definitions of the cultural landscape concept and guidelines for writing Cultural Landscape Reports, necessary for documenting the historical significance of park features, especially those in danger of being changed or erased.[22]

In 1995, new cultural resource management guidelines appeared in a policy designated NPS-28, and they represented the results of a comprehensive new agreement reached between the National Park Service, the Advisory Council on Historic Preservation (focused on implementing the NHPA), and the National Conference of State Historic Preservation Officers.[23] Essentially, NPS-28 mandated more specific procedures for incorporating historic resource preservation into various park management plans and for evaluating how changing park policies might impact those resources in the future.

Park superintendents were given primary responsibilities for implementing NPS-28 in each of their respective units. Under NPS-28, each park created a "Section 106 coordinator" (named after a provision in the NHPA), who facilitates the details of cultural resource and historic preservation in the unit.

Several of the essays included in this book explore how Yellowstone's park managers have increasingly responded to these evolving federal mandates and agency imperatives, and how selected historic sites within the park have certainly received increased recognition and interpretation. Not surprisingly, signature structures such as the Old Faithful Inn, the Lake Hotel, select historical ranger stations and museums, and historic park administrative buildings in the Mammoth headquarters area have been the focus of historic preservation efforts. The implementation of ARPA has also made the park's Native American legacy and its archaeological resources more visible to both visitors and park managers.[24]

Still, Yellowstone's historic preservation efforts have often been contentious. Consider the complex and shifting historical relationships between park managers and concessionaires. The preservation or destruction of historic resources has frequently hinged on mutual decisions reached by both of these parties. The story behind the complete redesign of the West Thumb area (essentially erasing a long cultural imprint) illustrates the process. Yellowstone's historic preservation efforts also reflect how some park managers remain skeptical about the value of preserving something diffusely defined as a "cultural landscape," even though these features have, since the 1990s, been recognized as worthy of preservation.[25]

CHANGING VISITOR EXPERIENCES

Exploring the changing nature of the visitor experience in Yellowstone helps to illustrate the important role played by the park's cultural landscape and why its preservation is important. Consider the details of three different visits to the park. Let's begin in 1885 and saddle up with George Wingate, who traveled through the park on horseback with his wife, his teenage daughter, and an outfitting party of various acquaintances and fellow visitors.[26] Their journey, once they left the comfort of the railroad at Bozeman, Montana, took several weeks and spanned more than four hundred miles. Their horseback view of the park was intimate: they traced a dusty route along primitive park roads from Mammoth Hot Springs to Old Faithful, over to the Grand Can-

FIGURE 1.3. Camping in Yellowstone, 1886. The simple rustic pleasures of roughing it in the early years of the park are illustrated in George W. Wingate's book, *Through the Yellowstone Park on Horseback* (New York: O. Judd Co., 1886), 47.

yon, and then out through the west side of the park along the Madison River; they tossed clothes and saddle blankets into geyser pools to do their laundry; and they took their meals under the stars except for an occasional steak purchased at one of the dining halls already built within the park (figure 1.3). While Wingate noted that each of the park's main attractions (Mammoth, the Firehole Geyser Basins, Yellowstone Lake, and Canyon) already had some form of accommodations (such as tent camps, cabins, or early hotels), he found it easy to avoid the crowds (which were then considerably smaller than they are today) and experience the world's only national park from the quiet prospect of his mount.

Four decades later, Yellowstone's landscape and the way visitors experienced the park had been dramatically transformed. During the late 1920s, both the Union Pacific and the Burlington Northern Pacific railroads promoted similar and highly standardized "four-and-a-half-day tours" of Yellowstone from their respective railheads on the western and northern boundaries of the park.[27] Depending on one's pocketbook, travelers could either pay up for "hotel" accommodations that featured overnight stays at large, often elaborate facilities or opt for more budget-conscious alternatives at park "lodges," which were usually collections of simpler cabin camps and dining halls.

FIGURE 1.4. Lake Hotel, ca. 1920. More elaborate lodging in the park soon augmented casual tent camping and shack hotels. The front of the Lake Hotel featured a grand approach and spectacular Greek-style columns. Source: private collection of William K. Wyckoff.

On the arranged tours, travelers using the North Entrance, for example, would arrive midmorning at Gardiner and take a short auto stage up to Mammoth Hot Springs. Visitors were encouraged to tour the museum at park headquarters, walk the trails among the travertine terraces, and spend the night nearby. The next morning, a touring car picked them up at 8:25 a.m. and deposited them at Old Faithful in time for lunch. The Upper Geyser Basin offered an elaborate trail system, a plunge for an afternoon swim in the geyser-fed bathhouse, and an evening orchestra at the Old Faithful Inn. After enjoying the following morning at Old Faithful, visitors crossed the Continental Divide and ventured to the shores of Lake Yellowstone, where they spent the night either at the elegant, colonial-style Lake Hotel or at the more rustic Lake Lodge (figure 1.4). Scenic boat trips and fishing excursions on the lake offered alternatives for those interested in more time on the water. Finally, the tour took visitors a short distance north to the Grand Canyon and Falls of the Yellowstone River, where either they spent a quick afternoon gazing at the white water and spectacular canyon walls before exiting the park (and returning to Mammoth) or they stayed overnight at Canyon and then headed north to catch a morning train back home. Thousands of travelers during this era simply drove through the park by themselves in their own automobiles, but even then, they typically experienced a similar, well-planned itinerary of park settings.

Fast-forward another century and ponder the park's cultural landscape in the early twenty-first century. Some of the grand hotels have vanished and been replaced by newer facilities elsewhere in the park and a growing number of accommodations in nearby gateway communities. These changes reflect evolving managerial and environmental initiatives within the National Park Service, as well as the increasingly diverse demands of park visitors. The reintroduction of wolves into the park during the 1990s, a carefully orchestrated, richly symbolic cultural and political act, has been popular with many visitors because sighting a wolf offers a powerful and immediate connection with the natural world, and a touchstone to Yellowstone's wilderness past. In addition, more restrictions on the use of boats on the lake, a greater all-season use of the park (including the much-contested use of snowmobiles in the winter), and a new set of interpretive guidelines for park rangers and visitor center personnel (which are used to explain issues such as the ecological consequences of the 1988 fires) continue to refashion both the landscape and the park experience for recent visitors. For many, an average stay at the park may be counted in hours rather than days or weeks. A quick swing through the park along portions of the Grand Loop Road may suffice and would include brief, but obligatory, stops at the Lower Falls of the Yellowstone River and at Old Faithful. At the same time, a changing clientele of visitors puts a greater number of cyclists along park highways and more hikers and canoeists into the backcountry. Each of these visitor experiences is a product of its time, reflecting changing perceptions of the natural world as well as the evolving infrastructure of available roads, facilities, and activities within the park.

NATIONAL PARKS AS CULTURAL LANDSCAPES

The historical, cultural, political, and institutional evolution of national parks has attracted growing popular attention and academic interest. A well-reviewed and widely watched PBS television series on the national parks, produced by Ken Burns, along with a companion book coauthored with Dayton Duncan, appeared in 2009.[28] The series emphasized the human stories behind the parks, calling the national parks system "the nation's best idea." The popular series built on a growing body of scholarship on national parks, including work focused on their distinctive cultural landscapes.

Several studies highlight the changing nature of the built environment found within national parks. Linda McClelland's *Building the National Parks: Historic Landscape Design and Construction* (1998) carefully documents the evolving architectural influences that have shaped park structures and landscapes. Her book had its genesis as an internal NPS document designed to help park managers understand and preserve the cultural settings found within park boundaries.[29] More recent park landscapes are the focus of *Mission 66: Modernism and the National Park Dilemma* (2007) by Ethan Carr.[30] His sweeping narrative explores the post–World War II initiative by the Park Service to upgrade park infrastructure. Often using modern, even futuristic architecture, the Mission 66 program indelibly transformed many park settings, including places such as the Canyon development area within Yellowstone.

Important work by Richard Sellars, Roderick Nash, and Thomas Vale has focused on how park landscapes have played into larger questions of nature management and preservation.[31] Other scholars have focused more centrally on changing priorities of park management and policymaking and how park landscapes are the products of particular political and institutional imperatives and the changing ways we think about nature and culture.[32] A growing interest in the history of tourism also has encouraged more work on the changing effects that railroads and automobiles have had on national park landscapes.[33]

As the nation's oldest and most-studied national park, Yellowstone has attracted particular attention for its own cultural landscape. Some have focused on the role of American Indians within the park, reminding us that the area was hardly a pristine, unpeopled wilderness before opening to Euro-American development.[34] Focusing on the park's early evolution, Judith Meyer's *The Spirit of Yellowstone: The Cultural Evolution of a National Park* (2003) reminds us that much of the park's modern identity is rooted in the early guidebooks, images, and descriptions of the region that became an enduring part of the park's character and personality.[35] Geographer Gareth John has explored related themes in his analysis of how visual representations of park landscapes reflected dominant practices of Gilded Age exploration and thus influenced later generations of park visitors and managers.[36] In addition, park historian Lee Whittlesey examines the enduring role of early park interpreters and travelers in his *Storytelling in Yellowstone: Horse and Buggy Tour Guides* (2007) and in *Ho! For Wonderland: Travelers' Accounts of Yellowstone, 1872–1914* (2009).[37]

Several valuable studies have synthesized the story of Yellowstone's evolution as both a natural and cultural landscape. Alfred Runte's *National Parks: The American Experience* (1984) suggests how the creation of Yellowstone and representations of its landscape satisfied larger late-nineteenth-century demands for national identity.[38] More detailed histories of park creation and management include the two-volume *The Yellowstone Story*, authored by Aubrey Haines in the 1970s.[39] The following decade, western historian Richard Bartlett added his *Yellowstone: A Wilderness Besieged* (1985), which included a general narrative summarizing the evolution of park administration, concessions development, and tourism.[40] Paul Schullery's *Searching for Yellowstone: Ecology and Wonder in the Last Wilderness* (1997), Hunt Jamin and Nicole Sheehan's *Yellowstone: The History, Ecology and Future of America's First National Park* (2021), and Randall K. Wilson's *A Place Called Yellowstone: The Epic History of the World's First National Park* (2024) offer more nuanced explorations of key past, present, and future management issues within the park and how they are shaped by larger-scale forces as well as by the unique character of the park itself.[41]

Other scholarship on Yellowstone focuses on narrower interpretive frameworks but often includes an assessment of its cultural landscape. Both Mark Barringer and Chris Magoc, for example, detail the park's commercial development, arguing that its elaborate, often inefficient system of concession-driven facilities exhibited some of the less attractive qualities of capitalism in the American West.[42] Similarly, Alston Chase offers a polemical view of how the NPS mismanaged the park's environment in his *Playing God in Yellowstone: The Destruction of America's First National Park* (1986).[43] Others have focused on particular policy issues within the park that have shaped its cultural landscape, whether actually or potentially. These studies have included the historical debate over railroad construction in the park, the changing regulations and mandates affecting boating on Yellowstone Lake, evolving park management priorities in the ecologically fragile Fishing Bridge area, and ongoing controversies surrounding the wintertime use of snowmobiles inside the park.[44]

Beyond Yellowstone itself, the literature on the cultural landscapes of other specific park settings suggests the growing importance of such an approach. A representative sampling among eastern parks would certainly include Lary Dilsaver's *Cumberland Island National Seashore: A History of Conservation Conflict* (2004), in which the author tells the complex story of what happens when multiple economic and environmental interests converge in a diverse coastal Georgia setting to produce a cultural landscape that includes a many-layered signature of human impacts as well as the largest surviving stands of maritime oak forest in the United States.[45] Similarly fascinating is the story told by Terence Young about Great Smoky Mountains National Park, where the challenges of historic preservation, ecological management, and promoting tourism have often come into conflict in one of the nation's most-visited national parks.[46]

In the West, the history of managing Arizona's Grand Canyon National Park has received considerable attention, with studies examining the creation of the park, the role played by railroads in developing park infrastructure, and how park promoters and managers have used the cultural landscape to shape visitor experiences within the park.[47] California's national parks have also drawn the interest of scholars; their narratives typically explore the impact of park managers, developers, and tourists in settings such as the Yosemite, Sequoia, the Mojave, Joshua Tree, and Channel Islands.[48] In the Rockies, the changing cultural landscapes of Glacier, Grand Teton, Mesa Verde, and Rocky Mountain National Parks, as well as those of Dinosaur National Monument, have also produced a growing shelf of significant work, much of it focused either on the genesis of these units within the system or on how tourism and park planning initiatives transformed their landscapes in later years.[49]

YELLOWSTONE AND THE NATIONAL PARK SYSTEM

Yellowstone's creation and maturation has been well narrated elsewhere.[50] Even so, it is useful to consider the park's origin and its evolution in the light of broader trends, including the development of the National Park Service. The larger narrative is valuable because it sets a context for tracking changes in the cultural landscape that unfold through time at particular localities within the park.

Early Years

The genesis of Yellowstone's cultural landscape is traceable to a long record of influence by Native Americans, but their signatures across the park are often difficult to read.[51] The Yellowstone Plateau first attracted Native hunters more than ten thousand years ago as the area's high-altitude environment slowly emerged from the Ice Age. In later years, the region became a cultural crossroads for a variety of Native peoples, including the Blackfeet and Crow (mostly to the north and east) as well as the Bannock and Shoshone (to the south and west). In addition, Sheep Eater Indians (a Shoshonean people) probably became more permanent residents in the park area, beginning perhaps as long as two thousand years ago. What remains of this enduring Native presence on the park's cultural landscape? That legacy includes a long record of subtle ecological manipulation, meaning the selective gathering and hunting of particular plants and animals, and the possible burning of natural vegetation (less likely in the lodgepole pine forests, more likely in the grasslands of the park's northern range). It also includes the development of important obsidian mining sites (which affected hunting practices over a huge area of North America), the construction of trails and camps (some of which became sites for later Euro-American development), and a varied array of tipi rings, animal driveways, and bison kill sites. But for most park visitors, these important human signatures remain muted and have been largely overwhelmed by a Euro-American cultural landscape fashioned in more recent times.

Yellowstone's Euro-American cultural landscape first took shape in the imaginations of those who explored it through small-scale expeditions in 1869 (the Cook-Folsom expedition) and 1870 (the Washburn expedition).[52] Led by Montanans, these early forays set the stage for the famed Hayden reconnaissance in 1871. That government-sponsored survey carefully documented the region's wonders; its reports included photographs, sketches, and paintings that highlighted its unique character. Fortunately, the call to preserve Yellowstone grew during the spring of 1872. If the park had not been created in March of that year, the region's cultural landscape might have evolved *very* differently. There were already requests to homestead the land around the Upper Geyser Basin, and two gentlemen from Deer Lodge, Montana, were busily cutting poles to fence the area off from the public. Elsewhere, other Montanans were constructing a primitive private hotel and bathhouses near Mammoth Hot Springs. Imagine how a privatized and commercialized Yellowstone Plateau might have evolved.

Even with the formal creation of the park, Yellowstone's early years were filled with uncertainty. There was neither sufficient federal funding nor an overall plan for park preservation and development.[53] Between 1872 and 1886, the park's managers depended largely on the abilities and authority of individuals, particularly those appointed by the Department of the Interior to serve as park superintendents. But even skilled park managers were underfunded and understaffed. Poaching, vandalism, and littering were common in the park, and early concessionaires seemed more powerful than the official overseers. Philetus Norris, park superintendent between 1877 and 1882, proved particularly effective in addressing some of these initial challenges. Norris launched a massive public relations campaign to protect and support the park, worked tirelessly to preserve the park's features, and implemented a variety of construction projects. Most importantly, by creating the park's first real road and trail system, Norris linked together Yellowstone's principal points of interest. In the process, he shaped how later travelers experienced the wonders of the park and where major points of development would be located.[54]

The US Army took direct control of park management between 1886 and 1916. The Army's major contribution to managing the park was to impose order in a time when many park regulations were still being ignored. The Army successfully cracked down on vandals, prosecuted poachers, and fostered a greater sense of regimentation and standardization of the park's affairs. Soldier stations were established at various points in the park and the headquarters area at Mammoth featured a new array of administrative and residential structures. Overall, however, many of the most substantive investments in the park's cultural landscape during the Army era came from private concessionaires who built a number of grand hotels, including the Old Faithful Inn. Concessionaires were also responding to the growing number of park visitors who were arriving by rail. Convenient spur lines brought thousands of new tourists to Yellowstone as connections were completed to the park's north (1883) and west (1908) entrances.

Creation of the National Park Service in 1916

During the early twentieth century, Yellowstone's larger identity and role as a national park remained unclear. After 1890, additional national parks had been created, but these units also struggled to find their place in the larger American system of public lands. What precisely was their value to the American public? Indeed, the utilitarian movement, which arose in the late nineteenth century, argued that public lands needed to be used, not simply preserved. Led by forester Gifford Pinchot, the utilitarian movement advocated a careful, planned harvesting of natural resources from the nation's storehouse of public lands. Such a philosophy posed a threat to the national parks because the utilitarians' "'gospel of efficiency,' as [Samuel] Hays calls it, subordinated aesthetic values and discounted any persons who were concerned with nature preservation."[55]

Preservationists who opposed such a movement saw advantages in creating a single federal agency that would be exclusively dedicated to maintaining the integrity of the national parks. The idea also gained support from private interests standing to benefit from a system of parks that would attract the traveling public. In particular, the preservationists and the railroads created what Alfred Runte terms a "pragmatic alliance."[56] The preservationists backed the railroads' development near parks, and in turn, the railroads elevated support for parks through promotional literature, magazines, and the construction of improved facilities. As a result, railroad capital profoundly shaped the cultural landscapes of many national parks, including Yellowstone. In addition, the preservationists gained support from many Progressive Era reformers who promoted the educational potential of the parks and also argued that the parks could serve as sanctuaries of wilderness and beauty amid an increasingly industrialized America.[57]

Born out of this philosophy was the National Park Service. The NPS was established in August 1916, and its creation was supported by the railroads, the media, and determined charismatic individuals such as Stephen Tyng Mather. A highly successful industrialist and a tireless booster for park development, Mather became the first director of the Park Service. His program for promoting the parks was so successful that his influence upon the system endures to the present day. Mather played a central role in implementing several key initiatives that profoundly shaped NPS policies as well as the cultural landscapes of the parks, including those of Yellowstone.

First, Mather upgraded and professionalized the role of park rangers. No longer were rangers simply park police. Mather's vision defined a new interpretive and educational mission for NPS rangers: they lectured, aided in informational services and museum development, and guided tours.[58]

Yellowstone's superintendent, Horace Albright, who served in that capacity between 1919 and 1929, enthusiastically embraced the Mather initiative. Indeed, both Mather and Albright saw the shift as part of a greater plan to educate visitors on the importance of the parks and, in turn, gain further popular support for the system.

Second, Mather adopted a new policy toward concessionaires that would not only provide visitors with higher-quality services but also protect the companies themselves from too much competition. Essentially, Mather believed in the merits of a controlled monopoly and thus made it mandatory that many park concessionaires consolidate their operations. As a result, by 1940, there were only three corporations serving visitors in Yellowstone. In addition, Mather directed that all concessionaire construction within the parks be reviewed by the landscape engineering division of the Park Service, thus ensuring that developments were somewhat in harmony with the parks' natural landscapes. For Yellowstone, this meant that a greater degree of central authority shaped the form and function of park services and concessionaire landscape features.

Third, Mather promoted an aggressive and highly visible campaign to promote the parks. During World War I, the NPS implemented the See America First program. This campaign took advantage of the war by promoting America's scenic lands as alternatives to those in Europe. The effort also received a boost from railroads and many local and state organizations that saw the effort as a way to spur tourism nationally. Touring the parks became an exercise in patriotism and helped promote the parks as a defining part of America's national identity.[59] Yellowstone benefited greatly from this promotional effort. It bolstered visitation to the park during and after the war years and made a trip to Yellowstone part of doing one's duty as a loyal American.[60]

Fourth, both Mather and Albright correctly anticipated the critical role of the automobile in promoting the parks, in transforming their cultural landscapes, and in shaping the very way that the parks would be experienced by generations of visitors (figures 1.5 and 1.6). Both men also saw how the automobile could be used to increase access to the parks for many middle-class Americans, thus ensuring the popularity and success of the system.[61] While railroads certainly played a key role in promoting many early parks and in shaping elements of their cultural landscape, it was the automobile that most fundamentally stamped the parks with their characteristic assemblage of scenic (often crowded) highways, viewpoints, pullouts, parking lots, automobile campgrounds, and other auto-oriented tourist facilities (figure 1.7). Indeed, automobiles (officially permitted on Yellowstone's roads in 1915) became such an integral feature of the cultural landscape that their arrival shaped a great deal of subsequent investment in park facilities and infrastructure. Automobiles also influenced how parks would be experienced. A visit to the parks—once subject to train and stage schedules, organized tours, and the costs of expensive hotels—now became a cheaper and more convenient adventure. Auto tourists, with camping gear stowed in their trunks, could sightsee at their own pace, which proved immensely popular with many middle-class Americans. In particular, Yellowstone's large size and the widely scattered nature of its chief attractions meant the park was ideally suited to automobile exploration. Thus, Albright and subsequent superintendents put a great deal of effort into improving the park's highways and seeing that its facilities answered to the growing needs of the car-traveling public.

The Great Depression, World War II, and the Automobile

Yellowstone's cultural landscape was profoundly shaped by other national and global events in addition to the arrival of the automobile. The Great Depression brought a coordinated federal response aimed at promoting the use of the national parks. The New Deal was designed to stimulate national consumption, and the government realized that increasing visitation to the parks would benefit both the park concessionaires and businesses in bordering towns. This was also a period of system expansion for the Park Service, and, as a result, overall park tourism greatly increased during the New Deal era. In 1933, almost 3,500,000 tourists visited national parks and monuments. By the end of the decade, the number had more than quadrupled to well over 16,700,000.[62] Yellowstone participated in the growing popularity of the parks: it witnessed significant increases in visitation, more than tripling from about 160,000 visitors in 1933 to nearly 582,000 visitors in 1941.[63]

The New Deal era also brought increased federal investment in national park infrastructure, mainly through efforts of the Civilian Conservation Corps (CCC) and other public works initiatives. These New Deal programs gave work to thousands of Americans and, in turn, provided the parks with much-needed improvements. Hundreds of young men, many from the eastern United States, arrived in Yellowstone beginning in 1933.[64] After some initial problems related to organization and discipline, the CCC in Yellowstone tackled dozens of jobs that enduringly upgraded park infrastructure and transformed its cultural landscape. For example, CCC work went into replanting bare ground in park campgrounds; building trails, telephone lines, and boat docks; improving park roads; and removing trash dumps

FIGURE 1.5. Automobiling through Roosevelt Arch, ca. 1920. The impressive Roosevelt Arch, named after President Theodore Roosevelt and traditionally attributed to architect Robert Reamer, who designed Old Faithful Inn, began welcoming visitors to the park's North Entrance in Gardiner, Montana, after it was dedicated on August 15, 1903. The distinctive columnar basalt was quarried nearby, and the arch rises fifty feet above the road. Just twelve years later, automobiles began replacing horse-drawn stagecoaches as the most common way to experience the park. Source: private collection of William K. Wyckoff.

and dilapidated buildings. More skilled CCC workers helped catalog photographs and plant and animal specimens for the park's archives and museums.

World War II, however, brought dramatic declines in visitation across the entire national park system. For Yellowstone, visitation plunged from more than 500,000 in 1941 to fewer than 65,000 just two years later.[65] Many hotels and park services, both in Yellowstone and elsewhere, simply closed due to the lack of demand. In addition, many park laborers left to join the war effort. Budgets were also squeezed as the nation mobilized for war. The result was a period of stagnation in which few improvements were made to park infrastructure, and comprehensive plans for park improvements and expansion were put on hold. Instead, buildings went unpainted, leaky roofs multiplied, and potholes increasingly peppered park highways.

FIGURE 1.6. Japanese tourists at Roosevelt Arch in Gardiner, Montana (2016). Photograph © Janet L. Pritchard, from her book, *More than Scenery: Yellowstone, an American Love Story* (George F. Thompson Publishing, 2022), 74. Courtesy of the artist.

Postwar Expansion and Mission 66

By the end of World War II, Park Service and concessionaire facilities were in shambles. At the same time, thanks to a healthy postwar economy, millions of Americans headed out on the road to visit the national parks—twice as many as compared to before the war. After the war, the American middle class had, in addition to greatly increased mobility, more leisure time and money, which many chose to spend in the national parks. Annual visitation to Yellowstone skyrocketed from 85,347 in 1944 to more than 1 million in 1948.[66] By the mid-1950s, the larger national park system played host to more than 50 million visitors each year, but with a level of funding, staffing, and infrastructure that was little changed from prewar years.[67] This postwar deluge of visitors hurt the parks because facilities "throughout the system, designed to accommodate prewar levels of demand, were degraded and destroyed by a combination of overuse and neglect."[68]

During the mid-1950s, Congress and the Park Service implemented a solution to this problem. In order to bring the parks back up to par and deal with increased visitation, they created Mission 66, a ten-year project

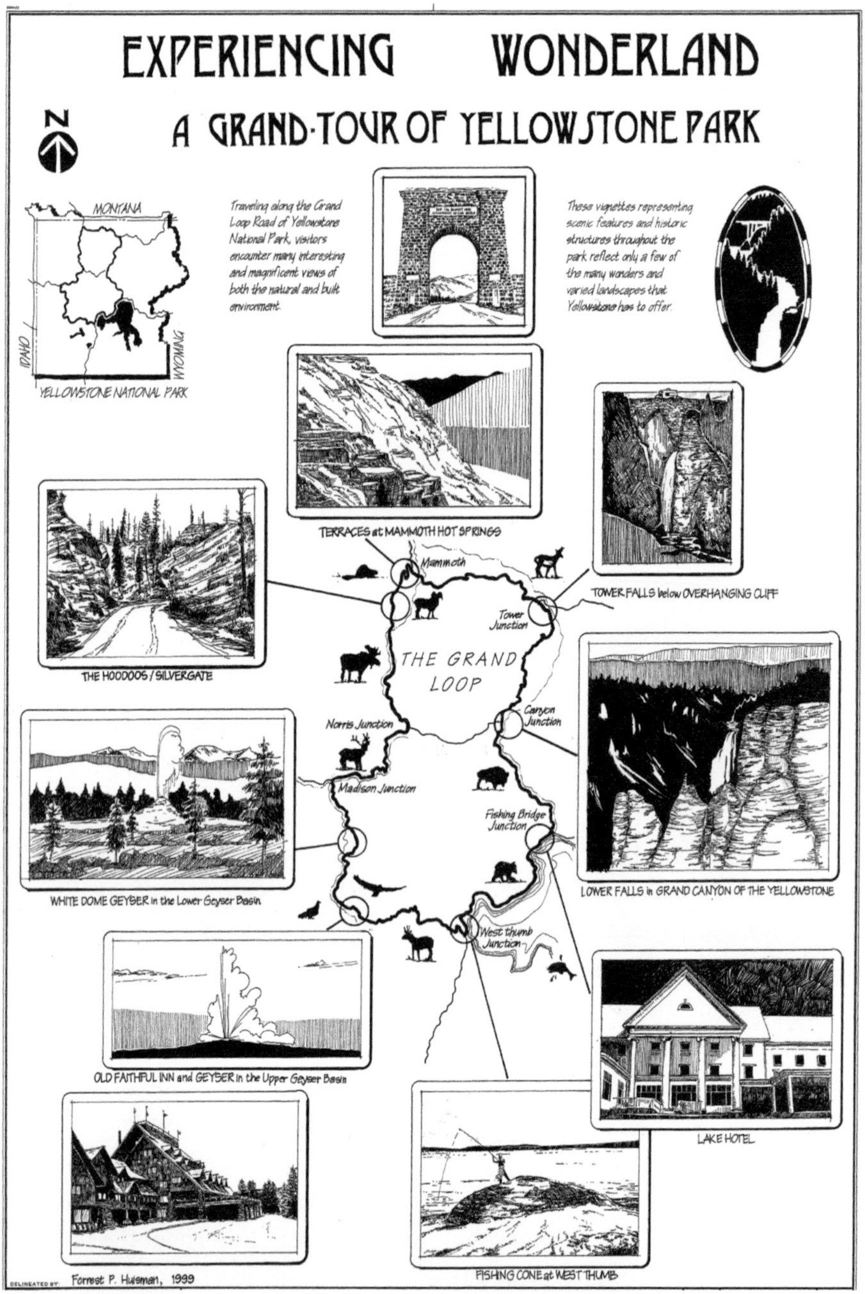

FIGURE 1.7. Experiencing Wonderland. Yellowstone's Grand Loop Road has long provided the primary means of experiencing the park's natural and cultural features. Source: Forrest Huisman, "Experiencing Wonderland, Addendum to Yellowstone National Park Roads and Bridges, HAER No. WY-34-2," 1999, Library of Congress, Washington, DC.

designed to "expand . . . the carrying capacity of the parks by reconstructing roads, adding visitor centers, and increasing overnight accommodations."[69] In the case of Yellowstone, Mission 66 focused primarily on development based on the needs of those who visited by automobile, who by 1956 made up 98.7 percent of all park visitors.[70]

The Park Service, newly flush with funds, met the challenge of Mission 66 with varied strategies, all of which transformed the cultural landscape of every park unit within the system.[71] Most fundamentally, the Park Service allocated new funds for training professional staff. The effort allowed the Park Service to reinstate and create new interpretive programs, as well as keep a closer eye on natural features. The Park Service established two training centers: one at Harpers Ferry, West Virginia, and the other at the Grand Canyon in Arizona.[72] The initiative produced a common educational experience for all staff who attended, and the training succeeded in energizing the interpretive mission of the Park Service.

In addition, the NPS used the Mission 66 program to take a fresh look at the location, impact, and seasonal availability of visitor services within the parks. Clearly, in many settings, the Park Service needed to expand visitor services to cope with the rising popularity of the parks. Often, this involved identifying new areas for development. But elsewhere, the Park Service was also committed to eliminating and downsizing facilities in heavily used areas of the parks. For example, it tried to downscale overnight facilities in high-impact areas such as Yosemite Valley and on the east side of Rocky Mountain National Park, shifting these visitor services to less used areas of the parks. In addition, the Park Service lengthened the visitation seasons of some parks and promoted winter use in others, including Yellowstone. With these modifications, Mission 66 also affected the concessions landscape as concessionaires tried to keep up with Park Service modifications. Concessionaires constructed more eating facilities, filling stations, and stores in newly identified centers of activity. Their most ambitious plans, however, involved increasing sleeping accommodations for visitors. For example, in Yellowstone, many of the concessionaires replaced older cabin quarters with modern motel-type units, aiming to increase accommodations from 8,500 to 14,500 persons.[73]

The basic infrastructure of roads, trails, campgrounds, visitor centers, and employee housing also received a great deal of attention in Mission 66. Specifically, the parks benefited directly from increased federal spending on roads. Legislation such as the 1956 Federal Aid Highway Act helped to build or upgrade some two thousand miles of roads in the parks, including improvements in Yellowstone's own Grand Loop Road, as part of the Mission 66 program.[74] These new and improved roads, including one-way avenues and bypasses, provided easier and quicker access for visitors throughout the parks. While these changes may have lessened traffic jams, the associated cloverleaf intersections and off-ramps did give some of the parks' landscapes the look of an interstate highway. Trail and campground improvements also blossomed under Mission 66. The Park Service improved or built hundreds of miles of hiking trails and added or upgraded more than ten thousand campsites under the program.[75]

More than 110 new visitor centers were added to the national park system under Mission 66.[76] The new structures often differed markedly from traditional rustic-style museums of the past:

> the new visitor centers were ambitious modern structures that housed information and interpretive facilities, exhibits, rest areas, and administrative offices. In larger parks they might also include souvenir stands, cafeterias, large audio displays, and even auditoriums.[77]

This new type of interpretive facility concentrated visitor activities, providing a specific place in a scenic area where everyone could obtain guidance and information. As splendid as these new visitor centers seemed, they were not without their early critics. Some visitors complained that new visitor facilities urbanized the national parks. In 1961, Weldon Heald commented in *National Parks Magazine* that "an overlay of our restless twentieth-century civilization is being imprinted upon the original wilderness with incongruous and disturbing results."[78] He believed that some of the new centers suffered from the sameness of many other modern structures found on the American landscape, possessing all the charm of airport terminals and post offices. In Yellowstone, for example, the new Canyon Visitor Center, opened in 1958, was sometimes criticized for its contemporary blandness, which seemed out of harmony with its wilderness surroundings.[79]

The residential landscapes of the parks' employees were also upgraded during Mission 66. As Park Service staffs grew larger, new lodging needed to be built for both permanent and seasonal employees. Some came in the form of modern trailer-court facilities, while elsewhere, basic ranch-style houses multiplied on the landscapes of national parks. In all, Mission 66's ten-year period saw the building of two thousand new houses for park employees.[80] These facilities provided badly needed housing, but in many of the parks, suburban-style residential neighborhoods and mobile-home parks reflected much of the bland uniformity found in other postwar American suburbs.

The NPS also made it a high priority to purchase private lands contained within the parks. These inholdings typically pre-dated the creation of the park and often complicated land management and administration of park units. During Mission 66's "first seven years, more money was made available to acquire private properties within the parks ('inholdings') than in all the preceding years."[81] The Park Service's goal was to buy, by the end of Mission 66, about 700,000 acres of once-private holdings within the boundaries of national parks.[82]

While some critics have argued that Mission 66 catered too much to the comforts of automobile visitors, the program also sought to preserve the parks' natural landscapes and wildlife. In many settings, overnight camping facilities in high impact areas were eliminated to help decrease erosion and promote revegetation. In some parks, such as Yellowstone, Mission 66 initiatives also promoted "use of the backcountry and thus take some pressure off the narrow strip of terrain adjacent to the roads."[83] Such an approach offered a more balanced use of park resources. New management strategies and educational programs were also implemented to protect the integrity of park wildlife. For example, in Yellowstone, bear-feeding was actively discouraged, garbage was disposed of more carefully, and "problem" animals were removed from popular areas of the park. These changes dispersed bears away from visitor facilities toward less-used areas of the park.

The Rise of Environmental Values and the Parks Today

As successful as Mission 66 may have been in expanding visitation to the parks, the program was not without its critics. During the 1960s, there was a growing belief among environmentalists that park development and preservation were incompatible goals. For the critics, the Mission 66 initiative epitomized the prodevelopment philosophy. As a result, a split occurred in which "environmental groups adopted increasingly strict preservation norms while the Park Service embarked on Mission 66."[84] Because this development program was in direct contrast to the new environmental philosophy, the parks lost the support of their traditional and most valued allies.

As the preservation movement became more pervasive during the 1970s, its chief supporters exerted growing political influence on Park Service policies and management philosophy.[85] This alignment against park development found support within the Ford and Carter administrations. Specifically, both Nathaniel Reed and Robert Herbst, assistant secretaries of the Department of the Interior under Presidents Ford and Carter, respectively, were environmentalists who strongly favored more preservation and less park development. While these men were in office, environmental groups had the ear of the Department of the Interior and, thus, more of a say in park development. This power from above, as well as from outside, forced NPS Director William Whalen to reevaluate the role of the Park Service and the role of the parks themselves. Whalen believed that the NPS was in a period of stagnation, and his goal would be "to bring the agency in line with modern times, socially, economically, and environmentally."[86] Financial constraints also limited development opportunities: with the establishment of the Office of Management and Budget under the Nixon administration, the Park Service no longer controlled budgets. This led to a significant reduction in funding for many development projects.

The combined influence of new environmental values and reduced funding has profoundly shaped the cultural landscape of the national parks since 1980. The Park Service has sought to limit development of new visitor services, and park managers are mandated to carefully consider the environmental impact of any new investment in park infrastructure. There has also been a continued effort on the part of the NPS to approve architectural designs that are in harmony with the surrounding physical landscape and with the existing architectural infrastructure already in place. In Yellowstone, for example, the revamped visitor center at Canyon, opened in 2006, features a neotraditional, Craftsman-style building that houses state-of-the-art interactive exhibits highlighting the role of volcanism and global plate tectonics within the park.

Overall, the NPS has enhanced its educational and interpretive mission to reflect the lessons of the environmental movement and to promote humanity's role in protecting and preserving natural ecological settings within park boundaries (figure 1.8). Such a land ethic is reflected in park interpretive exhibits, on ranger-led walks, and in promotional and educational material distributed at park entrances and visitor centers. There is

also increased awareness within the NPS of how climate change may alter park environments in the future and how that may affect park policies and management practices.[87] Recently, park managers have also worked with tribal peoples throughout the region to increase the visibility of the area's rich Native American heritage. These initiatives have resulted in the park's new Yellowstone Tribal Heritage Center (Old Faithful area), in multiple celebrations of Native history at varied park entrances, and in a growing number of interpretive exhibits throughout the park.[88] The overall effect of these policy shifts has been to produce a cultural landscape and a visitor experience that are significantly different from what one would have experienced only thirty years ago. As a result, as contemporary visitors wander along the various trails and boardwalks within Yellowstone, they are ushered into a physical landscape in a considerably different fashion than were their mid-twentieth-century predecessors. Today, as in many national parks, Yellowstone's contemporary cultural landscape frames the natural world in a

FIGURE 1.8. Looking for wildlife along the Madison River, Madison Information Station (2015). Photograph © Janet L. Pritchard, from her book, *More than Scenery: Yellowstone, an American Love Story* (George F. Thompson Publishing, 2022), 186. Courtesy of the artist.

way that promotes a powerful set of ecological lessons and an environmental ethic that aptly reflects larger changes in the science community and in the Park Service since 1980. Earlier settings in the park for outdoor recreation and visitor activity, such as swimming pools and bear-feeding grounds, have been quietly replaced with more backcountry trails, visitor exhibits promoting ecological education, and opportunities for the quiet contemplation of the natural world. The park's twenty-first-century cultural landscape offers a powerful visual and material medium through which that shift is both reflected and promoted.

NOTES

1. The various agents of landscape change and their links to a larger world are assessed in Richard A. Bartlett, *Yellowstone: A Wilderness Besieged* (Tucson: University of Arizona Press, 1985). For an attractive overview of Yellowstone geography and history, see W. Andrew Marcus, et al., *Atlas of Yellowstone*, 2nd ed. (Oakland: University of California Press, 2022).
2. Various ways to explore the cultural landscape are described in D. W. Meinig, ed., *The Interpretation of Ordinary Landscapes: Geographical Essays* (New York: Oxford University Press, 1979), 1–48. For the national parks, a valuable guide for assessing the built landscape is Linda Flint McClelland, *Building the National Parks: Historic Landscape Design and Construction* (Baltimore, MD: Johns Hopkins University Press, in association with the Center for American Places, 1998).
3. The role of landscape in Yellowstone's place identity is thoughtfully explored in Judith L. Meyer, *The Spirit of Yellowstone: The Cultural Evolution of a National Park* (Lanham, MD: Roberts Rinehart Publishers, 2003); Paul Schullery, *Searching for Yellowstone: Ecology and Wonder in the Last Wilderness* (Boston, MA: Houghton Mifflin, 1997); and Lee Whittlesey and Elizabeth A. Watry, eds., *Ho! For Wonderland: Travelers' Accounts of Yellowstone, 1872–1914* (Albuquerque: University of New Mexico Press, 2009).
4. Yellowstone's larger meaning as wilderness is assessed in Schullery, *Searching for Yellowstone*; Alfred Runte, *National Parks: The American Experience* (Lincoln: University of Nebraska Press, 1984), 33–47; and Roderick Nash, *Wilderness and the American Mind* (New Haven, CT: Yale University Press, 1982), 108–21.
5. The concept of the normative landscape as applied to American notions of race is defined in Richard H. Schein, ed., *Landscape and Race in the United States* (New York: Routledge, 2006), 1–21.
6. The idea of landscape convention is explored in Denis E. Cosgrove, *Social Formation and Symbolic Landscape* (Madison: University of Wisconsin Press, 1984); and in William Cronon, "The Trouble with Wilderness; or, Getting Back to the Wrong Nature," in William Cronon, ed., *Uncommon Ground: Rethinking the Human Place in Nature* (New York: W. W. Norton, 1995), 69–90. The idea of landscape convention in national park settings is also detailed in Yves Figueiredo, "Inventing Yosemite Valley: National Parks and the Language of Preservation," *Historical Geography* 35, no. 1 (2007): 12–35, and in Gareth E. John,

"Yellowstone as 'Landscape Idea': Thomas Moran and the Pictorial Practices of Gilded-Age Western Exploration," *Journal of Cultural Geography* 24, no. 2 (Summer 2007): 1–29.

7. David Louter, *Windshield Wilderness: Cars, Roads, and Nature in Washington's National Parks* (Seattle: University of Washington Press, 2006).
8. A thoughtful essay that reflects on the changing values of historic preservation and how these have shaped the National Park Service is Richard Sellars, "The National Park System and the Historic American Past: A Brief Overview and Reflection," *George Wright Forum* 24, no. 1 (2007): 8–22.
9. Melody Webb, "Cultural Landscapes in the National Park Service," *Public Historian* 9, no. 2 (1987): 89.
10. Personal communication by Lee Whittlesey to William Wyckoff, December 8, 2011.
11. Michael G. Schene, "The National Park Service and Historic Preservation: An Introduction," *Public Historian* 9, no. 2 (1987): 8.
12. Barry Mackintosh, "The National Park Service Moves into Historical Interpretation," *Public Historian* 9, no. 2 (1987): 52.
13. Both the Antiquities Act of 1906 and the Preservation of Historic Sites Act of 1935 are reprinted in Lary M. Dilsaver, ed., *America's National Park System: The Critical Documents* (Lanham, MD: Rowman and Littlefield, 2016): 29–30, 115–18. The fascinating story of the Antiquities Act is detailed by Richard West Sellars in "A Very Large Array: Early Federal Historic Preservation—The Antiquities Act, Mesa Verde, and the National Park Service Act," *George Wright Forum* 25, no. 1 (2008): 65–120. FDR's executive orders (1933) are reviewed in Richard West Sellars, "National Park System," 8–11. Background on the Historic Sites Act can be found in Edwin C. Bearss, "The National Park Service and Its History Program: 1864–1986," *Public Historian* 9, no. 2 (1987): 13–14; and Mackintosh, "National Park Service," 53–54.
14. The NHPA is reprinted in Dilsaver, *America's National Park System*, 268–73.
15. Stephanie S. Toothman, "Cultural Resource Management in Natural Areas of the National Park System," *Public Historian* 9, no. 2 (1987): 64–76.
16. Webb, "Cultural Landscapes," 81–82.
17. Personal communications by Lee Whittlesey to William Wyckoff (December 8, 2011, and December 12, 2011).
18. Webb, "Cultural Landscapes," 82.
19. The key policies and documents for this period are reprinted in Dilsaver, *America's National Park System*, 336–404.
20. The Vail Agenda is discussed in Janet A. McDonnell, "Reassessing the National Park Service and the National Park System," *George Wright Forum* 25, no. 2 (2008): 6–14.
21. The original report is National Park Service, *Presenting Nature: The Historic Landscape Design of the National Park Service, 1916 to 1942* (Washington, DC: Government Printing Office, 1993). It was later published as McClelland, *Building the National Parks*.
22. *National Park Service, Preservation Briefs 36, Protecting Cultural Landscapes: Planning, Treatment and Management of Historic Landscapes* (Washington, DC: National Park Service, Technical Preservation Services, 1994). Web version: http://www.nps.gov/hps/tps/briefs/brief36.htm.
23. National Park Service, NPS-28: *Cultural Resource Management Guideline, Appendix P* (Washington, DC: National Park Service, Office of Policy, 1995). Web version: https://www.nps.gov/parkhistory/online_books/nps28/28appenp.htm.

24. Particularly since 2010, park managers within Yellowstone have encouraged initiatives that highlight the importance of Native American history within the park. See https://www.nps.gov/yell/planyourvisit/attend-indigenous-cultural-events.htm.
25. Personal communication by Lee Whittlesey to William Wyckoff (December 8, 2011).
26. George W. Wingate, *Through the Yellowstone Park on Horseback* (New York: O. Judd Co., 1886).
27. Representative rail tours of the time are offered in Northern Pacific–Burlington Railroad, *Magic Yellowstone* (St. Paul, MN: Northern Pacific–Burlington Railroad, 1928); and in Union Pacific System, *Geyserland: Yellowstone National Park* (Omaha, NE: Union Pacific System, 1928).
28. Dayton Duncan and Ken Burns, *The National Parks: America's Best Idea* (New York: Alfred A. Knopf, 2009).
29. McClelland, *Building the National Parks*.
30. Ethan Carr, *Mission 66: Modernism and the National Park Dilemma* (Amherst: University of Massachusetts Press, 2007).
31. Nash, *Wilderness and the American Mind*; Richard West Sellars, *Preserving Nature in the National Parks* (New Haven, CT: Yale University Press, 1997); Sellars, "National Park System," 8–22; Sellars, "Very Large Array," 65–120; and Thomas R. Vale, *The American Wilderness: Reflections on Nature Protection in the United States* (Charlottesville: University of Virginia Press, in association with the Center for American Places, 2005).
32. An excellent collection of critical policy documents for the park system is Dilsaver's *America's National Park System*. Two general interpretations of park system policies are Ronald A. Foresta, *America's National Parks and Their Keepers* (Washington, DC: Resources for the Future, 1984); and Lary M. Dilsaver and William Wyckoff, "The Political Geography of National Parks," *Pacific Historical Review* 74, no. 2 (2005): 237–66. For an excellent discussion of research themes in doing national park historical geography, see Lary M. Dilsaver, "Research Perspectives on National Parks," *Geographical Review* 99, no. 2 (April 2009): 268–78. For varied case studies on the complexity of preserving both natural and cultural features, see Richard Longstreth, ed., *Cultural Landscapes: Balancing Nature and Heritage in Preservation Practice* (Minneapolis: University of Minnesota Press, 2008).
33. A sampling of studies examining the range and significance of tourist activities in the national parks and larger American West would include Louter, *Windshield Wilderness*; J. F. Sears, *Sacred Places: American Tourist Attractions in the Nineteenth Century* (New York: Oxford University Press, 1989); Hal K. Rothman, *Devil's Bargains: Tourism in the Twentieth-Century American West* (Lawrence: University Press of Kansas, 1998); Peter Blodgett, "Defining Uncle Sam's Playgrounds: Railroad Advertising and the National Parks, 1917–1941," *Historical Geography*, no. 35 (2007): 80–113; and Carlos Schwantes and James P. Ronda, *The West the Railroads Made* (Seattle: University of Washington Press, 2008).
34. See Peter Nabokov and Lawrence Loendorf, *American Indians and Yellowstone National Park: A Documentary Overview* (Yellowstone National Park: National Park Service, 2002); and Douglas H. McDonald, *Before Yellowstone: Native American Archaeology in the National Park* (Seattle: University of Washington Press, 2018).
35. Meyer, *Spirit of Yellowstone*.
36. John, "Yellowstone as 'Landscape Idea.'"
37. Whittlesey and Watry, *Ho! For Wonderland*; and Lee H. Whittlesey, *Storytelling in Yellowstone: Horse and Buggy Tour Guides* (Albuquerque: University of New Mexico Press, 2007).

38. Runte, *National Parks*, 33–47.

39. Aubrey L. Haines, *The Yellowstone Story*, vols. 1 and 2 (Yellowstone National Park: Yellowstone Library and Museum Association, 1977).

40. Bartlett, *Yellowstone*.

41. See Schullery, *Searching for Yellowstone*; Hunt Jamin and Nicole Sheehan, *Yellowstone: The History, Ecology and Future of America's First National Park* (Jefferson, NC: McFarland and Company, 2021); and Randall K. Wilson, *A Place Called Yellowstone: The Epic History of the World's First National Park* (New York: Counterpoint, 2024).

42. Chris J. Magoc, *Yellowstone: The Creation and Selling of an American Landscape, 1870–1903* (Albuquerque: University of New Mexico Press, 1999); and Mark Daniel Barringer, *Selling Yellowstone: Capitalism and the Construction of Nature* (Lawrence: University Press of Kansas, 2002).

43. Alston Chase, *Playing God in Yellowstone: The Destruction of America's First National Park* (Boston, MA: Atlantic Monthly Press, 1986).

44. For example, see Langdon Smith, "The Contested Landscape of Early Yellowstone," *Journal of Cultural Geography* 22, no. 1 (2004): 3–26; Michael J. Yochim, "A Water Wilderness: Battles over Values and Motorboats on Yellowstone Lake," *Historical Geography*, no. 35 (2007): 185–213; Michael J. Yochim, *Yellowstone and the Snowmobile: Locking Horns over National Park Use* (Lawrence: University Press of Kansas, 2009); and Paul Schullery, *Nature and Culture at Fishing Bridge: A History of the Fishing Bridge Development in Yellowstone National Park* (Yellowstone National Park: National Park Service, 2010).

45. Lary M. Dilsaver, *Cumberland Island National Seashore: A History of Conservation Conflict* (Charlottesville: University of Virginia Press, in association with the Center for American Places, 2004).

46. Terence Young, "False, Cheap and Degraded: When History, Economy and Environment Collided at Cades Cove, Great Smoky Mountains National Park," *Journal of Historical Geography* 32, no. 1 (January 2006): 169–89.

47. Barbara J. Morehouse, *A Place Called Grand Canyon: Contested Geographies* (Tucson: University of Arizona Press, 1996); Stephen J. Pyne, *How the Canyon Became Grand: A Short History* (New York: Penguin Books, 1998); and Yolonda Youngs, *Framing Nature: The Creation of an American Icon at the Grand Canyon* (Lincoln: University of Nebraska Press, 2024).

48. For background on a number of California park units, see Figueiredo, "Inventing Yosemite Valley"; William C. Tweed and Lary M. Dilsaver, *Challenge of the Big Trees: A Resource History of Sequoia and Kings Canyon National Parks* (Staunton, VA: George F. Thompson Publishing, 2016); Lary M. Dilsaver, *Preserving the Desert: A History of Joshua Tree National Park* (Staunton, VA: George F. Thompson Publishing, 2017); Lary M. Dilsaver and Timothy J. Babalis, *Restoring Nature: The Evolution of Channel Islands National Park* (Lincoln: University of Nebraska Press, 2023); Stanford E. Demars, *The Tourist in Yosemite: 1855–1985* (Salt Lake City: University of Utah Press, 1991); Elizabeth M. Hamin, *Mojave Lands: Interpretive Planning and the National Preserve* (Baltimore, MD: Johns Hopkins University Press, in association with the Center for American Places, 2003); Craig E. Colten and Lary M. Dilsaver, "The Hidden Landscape of Yosemite National Park," *Journal of Cultural Geography* 22, no. 2 (2004): 27–50; and Robert W. Righter, *The Battle over Hetch Hetchy: America's Most Controversial Dam and the Birth of Modern Environmentalism* (New York: Oxford University Press, 2005).

49. Some of the historical studies of park units within the Mountain West would include Robert W. Righter, *Crucible for Conservation: The Creation of Grand Teton National Park* (Boulder:

Colorado Associated University Press, 1982); C. W. Buchholtz, *Rocky Mountain National Park: A History* (Boulder: Colorado Associated University Press, 1983); Duane A. Smith, *Mesa Verde National Park: Shadows of the Centuries* (Lawrence: University Press of Kansas, 1988); M. G. Schene, "The Crown of the Continent: Private Enterprise and Public Interest in the Early Development of Glacier National Park, 1910–1917," *Forest and Conservation History* 34, no. 2 (1990): 69–75; William Wyckoff and Lary M. Dilsaver, "Promotional Imagery of Glacier National Park," *Geographical Review* 87, no. 1 (January 1997): 1–26; Lary M. Dilsaver and William Wyckoff, "Agency Culture, Cumulative Causation and Development in Glacier National Park, Montana," *Journal of Historical Geography*, no. 25 (1999): 75–92; Mark Harvey, *A Symbol for Wilderness: Echo Park and the American Conservation Movement* (Seattle: University of Washington Press, 2000); and Lary M. Dilsaver and William Wyckoff, "Failed National Parks in the Last Best Place," *Montana: The Magazine of Western History* 59, no. 3 (Autumn 2009): 3–24.

50. For useful interpretations and assessments of Yellowstone's early years, see Haines, *Yellowstone Story*; Meyer, *Spirit of Yellowstone*; Schullery, *Searching for Yellowstone*; Langdon Smith and William Wyckoff, "Creating Yellowstone: Montanans in the Early Park Years," *Historical Geography*, no. 29 (2001): 93–115; and Bruce T. Gourley, *Historic Yellowstone National Park: The Stories Behind the World's First National Park* (Guilford, CT: Lyons Press, 2022).
51. See Mark David Spence, *Dispossessing the Wilderness: Indian Removal and the Making of the National Parks* (New York: Oxford University Press, 2000); Schullery, *Searching for Yellowstone*, 17–30; Nabokov and Loendorf, *American Indians and Yellowstone National Park*; and McDonald, *Before Yellowstone*.
52. Dilsaver and Wyckoff, "Political Geography of National Parks," 241–48.
53. Dilsaver and Wyckoff, "Political Geography of National Parks," 241–48; Smith and Wyckoff, "Creating Yellowstone."
54. Bartlett, *Yellowstone*, 222–27.
55. B. W. Twight, *Organizational Values and Political Power: The Forest Service Versus the Olympic National Park* (University Park, PA: Penn State University Press, 1983), 6.
56. Runte, *National Parks*, 44–45, 83.
57. Susan R. Schrepfer, *A Conservation Reform: Saving the Redwoods, 1917 to 1940* (PhD diss., University of California–Riverside, 1971).
58. Haines, *Yellowstone Story*, vol. 2, 279–318.
59. Marguerite S. Shaffer, *See America First: Tourism and National Identity, 1880–1940* (Washington, DC: Smithsonian Press, 2001).
60. Prewar visitor numbers to the park averaged 20,000–30,000 annually. By the mid-1920s, with the help of the dedicated auto tourist, those tallies grew to more than 150,000 visitors annually. See Haines, *Yellowstone Story*, vol. 2, 478–79.
61. Anne F. Hyde, "From Stagecoach to Packard Twin Six: Yosemite and the Changing Face of Tourism, 1880–1930," *California History* 69, no. 2 (Summer 1990): 162.
62. Donald C. Swain, "The National Park Service and the New Deal, 1933–1940," *Pacific Historical Review* 41, no. 3 (August 1972): 312–32.
63. Haines, *Yellowstone Story*, vol. 2, 478–79.
64. Bartlett, *Yellowstone*, 295–302.
65. Bartlett, *Yellowstone*, 102.
66. Haines, *Yellowstone Story*, vol. 2, 478–79.

67. William C. Everhart, *The National Park Service* (New York: Praeger, 1972), 35.
68. Foresta, *America's National Parks*, 50.
69. Runte, *National Parks*, 173.
70. Haines, *Yellowstone Story*, vol. 2, 375.
71. Carr, *Mission 66*.
72. Carr, *Mission 66*, 290; Everhart, *National Park Service*.
73. Haines, *Yellowstone Story*, vol. 2, 375.
74. Carr, *Mission 66*, 287.
75. Carr, *Mission 66*, 292–93.
76. Carr, *Mission 66*, 357–58.
77. Foresta, *America's National Parks*, 54.
78. Weldon F. Heald, "Urbanization of the National Parks," *National Parks Magazine* 35, no. 160 (January 1961): 7–9.
79. Carr, *Mission 66*, 239.
80. Everhart, *National Park Service*, 37.
81. Michael Frome, *Regreening the National Parks* (Tucson: University of Arizona Press, 1992), 64.
82. John Ise, *Our National Park Policy: A Critical History* (Baltimore, MD: Johns Hopkins University Press, 1961), 548.
83. Haines, *Yellowstone Story*, vol. 2, 382.
84. Foresta, *America's National Parks*, 89.
85. Foresta, *America's National Parks*, 73.
86. Foresta, *America's National Parks*, 91.
87. An NPS overview titled "Climate Change and Your National Parks" is accessible at https://www.nps.gov/subjects/climatechange/index.htm. Also, see Jamin and Sheehan, *Yellowstone*.
88. For more on these Native American initiatives, see https://www.nps.gov/yell/planyourvisit/attend-indigenous-cultural-events.htmandhttps://www.nps.gov/places/000/yellowstone-tribal-heritage-center.htm.

FIGURE 2.1. This 1887 F. Jay Haynes glass-plate negative of Red Rock Point (Negative H-1893 from the Montana Historical Society in Helena) captures the sight of a visitor at Yellowstone's Grand Canyon more than a century ago. Photograph (2011) © Janet L. Pritchard, from her book, *More than Scenery: Yellowstone, an American Love Story* (George F. Thompson Publishing, 2022), 81. Courtesy of the artist.

2

Yellowstone and the Evolving National Park Idea

Langdon Smith

YELLOWSTONE NATIONAL PARK is the historic birthplace of the national park idea, which spawned hundreds of national parks around the globe. Some have gone so far as to say it was the best idea Americans ever had. Over time, the Yellowstone landscape has become a cultural icon, producing near-religious fervor in those who support the protection of wildlands and revel in the idea of public lands set aside for future generations. This makes it all the more ironic that, in 1872, the federal government had no real plan for Yellowstone beyond drawing boundaries on a vague map of this mostly unexplored region.

There were no visionary blueprints for what a national park was to be or how such an idea would be expressed across the landscape, and there was no funding or staffing provided by the US Congress until six years after the establishment of Yellowstone. Some in Washington, DC, believed that leases from hotels could pay for operating the young park, but the only access was by horseback; a railroad would not reach Yellowstone for another decade. With little or no guidance from Congress or the Department of the Interior, the park's future could have followed several different paths, including being

https://doi.org/10.5876/9781646427697.c002

crisscrossed by railroad tracks, opened to settlement, or auctioned off to the highest bidder.

Many Americans eager to learn the history of Yellowstone are often amazed to learn of such a rocky beginning for the nation's "best idea." They expected more initial planning and involvement by federal officials for such a significant event. But Yellowstone truly was an experiment—a place where the national park idea was field-tested for eighteen years. At the end of this period, in 1890, national parks began to spread across the United States. By then, the Yellowstone example demonstrated how national parks would inevitably be cultural landscapes actively shaped by many different actors and institutions.

During this critical time of experimentation, three key groups of people in Yellowstone helped shape the national park idea and, in so doing, also helped create the underpinnings of the cultural landscape we see in Yellowstone today. First, while the federal government ignored the park, nearby residents of the Montana and Idaho Territories explored Yellowstone's interior and began building roads and primitive hotels within. The footprint of this early geography remains virtually the same today, with much of the park remaining roadless. These hardy local explorers and entrepreneurs defined many of the spatial contours of Yellowstone's human geography through the selection of areas deemed worthy of visitation.

The second key group consisted of the early park managers and federal scientists charged with administering the new reservation. They were the first to be challenged with what would later become the "dual mandate" of the National Park Service—how to preserve Yellowstone for future generations while also opening the park to a growing number of tourists. These custodians defined the initial balance between development and preservation, which shaped the cultural landscape of Yellowstone for more than a century.

The third key group was the visitors themselves. They came in increasing numbers from throughout the United States and beyond, and they learned what to do in a national park—and also what not to do. To some extent, these early visitors dictated appropriate behavior within the parks. The increasing number of visitors was also a litmus test for Yellowstone, demonstrating that it had become a truly "national" park.

The story of Yellowstone's formative years is significant for several reasons. As the world's first national park, Yellowstone set the stage for later parks, both in the United States and beyond. For example, Yellowstone's arrangement for leasing land for tourism development, and the clustered village-style settlement of Mammoth Hot Springs, became the norm for future parks. Likewise, Yellowstone's initial primitive road system also marked the first broad-scale approach to park planning. Other parks soon followed the example and, in 1910, the Department of the Interior called for comprehensive plans for all national parks.[1] Ultimately, many of these management practices, as well as the cultural landscape features of Yellowstone, encouraged the establishment of national parks in almost one hundred countries. It has been suggested that the national park model developed in Yellowstone ranks among the few "thoroughly American contributions to world culture."[2]

INITIAL EXPLORATIONS

Montanans were curious about the mysterious lands to the south, especially after hearing the stories of spectacular geysers and mud volcanoes told by Jim Bridger and other mountain men. The first organized party to explore Yellowstone was the Folsom Expedition of 1869, comprised of David Folsom, Charles Cook, and William Peterson, all from Helena, Montana. A larger expedition was planned, but after learning that a military escort was not available from nearby Fort Ellis, all but three of the party refused to go. Although they lacked modern surveying and mapping equipment, the amateur members of the Folsom expedition were careful observers and were diligent in their responsibilities. They created the first relatively accurate map of Yellowstone and even measured the upper and lower falls of the Yellowstone River with a ball of twine and stick. Their estimate of the upper falls (115 feet) came remarkably close to the accepted measurement of 109 feet.[3]

The three explorers returned to Montana only to find that the spectacular landscape they described sounded too far-fetched for most people to accept. Folsom and Cook's written report of the trip was not immediately believed. Their account was rejected as "unreliable" by *The New York Tribune*, *Scribner's*, and *Harper's Monthly*. One magazine, *The Western Monthly Magazine* of Chicago, finally published it in July 1870.[4] Although their story was not widely distributed or believed, the Folsom party was successful in getting the attention of Henry D. Washburn, the newly appointed surveyor general of Montana Territory. Washburn led another expedition the following year and was accompanied by Nathaniel Langford, the former acting governor of the territory. Despite their credentials in Montana, and a much better-organized and -equipped expedition, the second round of explorers also raised doubts among members of the eastern press. Langford wrote about the expedition but was branded by one reviewer as the "champion liar of the Northwest."[5]

It was the credibility of Ferdinand Hayden, leader of the US Geological Survey, and his expedition of 1871 with artist Thomas Moran and photographer William Henry Jackson that finally substantiated the claims of previous expeditions. Hayden's official report of his expedition, combined with Moran's paintings and Jackson's photographs, helped convince Congress to pass the Yellowstone National Park Protection Act, establishing Yellowstone as a national park in 1872.

Although they were eclipsed by Hayden, the initial explorations by Montanans were still important because they shaped early written and visual images of the region during a time when most Americans had no access to it. They began the important process of producing Yellowstone's cultural landscape by identifying the area's key features through their speech, literature, and artistic endeavors, thus creating places where none had previously existed.[6] As geographer Judith Meyer has noted, simply by naming and describing the things and places they found, these local explorers provided the seeds from which the park's sense of place grew (figure 2.1).[7]

An example of the power of such place-setting language is evident in the naming of features by members of the Washburn expedition of 1870. By naming sites such as Hell Broth Springs, Hell's Half Acre, and Devil's Den, these explorers established Yellowstone's "hellish" reputation. Tourists seemed to respond well to the symbolism, which gave them a way to dare the gates of a "sinfully tempting and terrifying underworld" and live to joke about it.[8] These first images were critical in forming national opinions and policies concerning Yellowstone's future as a national park. The reports and descriptions brought back from the first expeditions were often copied directly into early guidebooks, serving as a template for the evolution of the public's perception of place in Yellowstone.[9]

PATTERNS OF CIRCULATION

Local residents were eager to experience firsthand the new national park established in their backyard and, as such, were the first tourists. A typical trip by locals to Yellowstone during the early 1870s meant spending weeks on horseback and facing the inherent risks of wilderness travel in mountainous terrain. Between Bozeman and the northern boundary of Yellowstone, the only human inhabitants were the Bottler brothers, who built a ranch in 1868 near Emigrant Gulch north of present-day Gardiner, Montana. The wilderness adventures of local tourists in early Yellowstone made trips by later visitors to the park more titillating. As historian John Sears has noted, a trip to the park gave tourists the feeling of being in Buffalo Bill's Wild West, without actually being in danger.[10] Many early travel accounts detailed the inherent dangers: people were thrown from their horses, stranded and isolated from companions, or caught in vicious storms. Local newspapers contained many such narratives:

> Major Manginnis, being *horse du combat*, the animal having bucked the Major off while going through the Grand Canyon, and the last seen of him (the horse) he was bucking over the range trying to free himself from the saddle. Two days search had failed to discover him.[11]

Almost any trip to Yellowstone in the first few years was worthy of newspaper attention, especially if the writer claimed a first, as was the case with an article in the Bozeman *Avant Courier* on September 5, 1872: "Mrs. Stone of Bozeman was the first lady that ever saw the geysers. Rah for Bozeman! She is the pioneer lady of the Upper Yellowstone."

Although risky, an early trip to Yellowstone was also an adventure to be savored. Camping out under the stars was a way to escape from the city and the conventions of society, or as one local traveler described it, to "hie away to some sequestered spot in the mountains, where separated from the busy world and your wife and mother-in-law, you put in a week or so shooting at marks and fighting mosquitoes . . . and admiring nature unadorned, in the shape of rugged peaks, rotten pine trees and gurgling streams."[12]

Once within the park, local travelers took note of existing trails made by Native Americans, but these pathways were influenced strongly by natural terrain and vegetation and reflected Native American needs rather than those of the tourist.[13] Without any government road-building during the first five years, local visitors for the most part had to cut their own trails to the major points of interest within Yellowstone, and the paths they chose indicate that they were drawn to the geysers and hot springs. The locals were familiar with the vast wild country surrounding Yellowstone's geyser basins; however, it was the thermal features that drew them to the park. This was no wonder, for Yellowstone contains roughly 60 percent of the world's geysers, and the Upper Geyser Basin has the greatest concentration of geysers in the world.[14] So the first trails connected the various geyser basins, where locals would sometimes camp for weeks, enjoying the bathing opportunities or waiting for geysers to erupt. As N. A. Switzer noted in his diary about reaching Old Faithful, the first tourists etched their names in the Yellowstone landscape: "We find the names of perhaps one hundred written on the krust [*sic*] and on pebbles. A great many of persons we knew."[15]

From Mammoth Hot Springs, Old Faithful, and the geyser basins, the early tourist trails then led to Yellowstone Lake and the Grand Canyon and Falls of the Yellowstone River. This route was established within a very short period of time and was called the "Grand Rounds" by locals as early as 1874.[16] Once emblazoned across the Yellowstone landscape, the trail network became a template that has changed little through time. With the exception of a road segment over Dunraven Pass connecting Madison Junction to Mammoth, these first trails approximate all of today's figure-eight-shaped Grand Loop Road, used by millions of tourists (figure 2.2).

Upgrading trails to wagon roads was the next logical step in developing Yellowstone for tourism. Local entrepreneurs understood that before they could reap the profits of tourism, visitors had to be able to arrive comfortably and in greater numbers. With Congress refusing to provide funding for park development, the burden of building safe wagon roads was initially left to private interests. Some of Montana's business owners in Bozeman and Virginia City raised money to build the first roads, and by 1873 the Bozeman Toll Road was completed from Bozeman to Mammoth Hot Springs. Later that same year, entrepreneurs in Virginia City raised $2,000 and built a road from Virginia City to the Lower Geyser Basin via Henry's Lake and the Madison River.[17]

When government funding for road building finally came during the late 1870s, construction crews followed the path of the tourist trails and primitive wagon roads, reinforcing the early patterns of use within the park. Philetus Norris, the second superintendent of Yellowstone, was the first to receive funding for road building, and he began a flurry of roadwork. In less than a month, without adequate exploration of the route, Norris and his crew built sixty miles of rough road during the summer of 1878, stretching from Mammoth to the Lower Geyser Basin near Nez Perce Creek.[18] When Norris left five years later, more than two-thirds (104 miles) of the Grand Loop Road had been completed in generally the same location as today.

The fact that Norris and other road builders did follow the early tourist trails so faithfully led to criticism by those who preferred a more scientific method of construction. Hiram M. Chittenden, an engineer assigned to design roads in Yellowstone in 1883, reported that earlier road crews followed the original trails, with all their "irregularities and excesses of gradients, regardless of what improvements could be made by something of a survey."[19] Norris's roads were infamous for jarring wagon rides. "The roads are outrageous," a writer complained in the *Avant Courier* newspaper. "A man cannot ride his horse up some of them. There is not a mule-driver or bull-whacker who could and would [not] make better roads over the mountains and through the Park than our old fossiliferous friend Norris has made."[20]

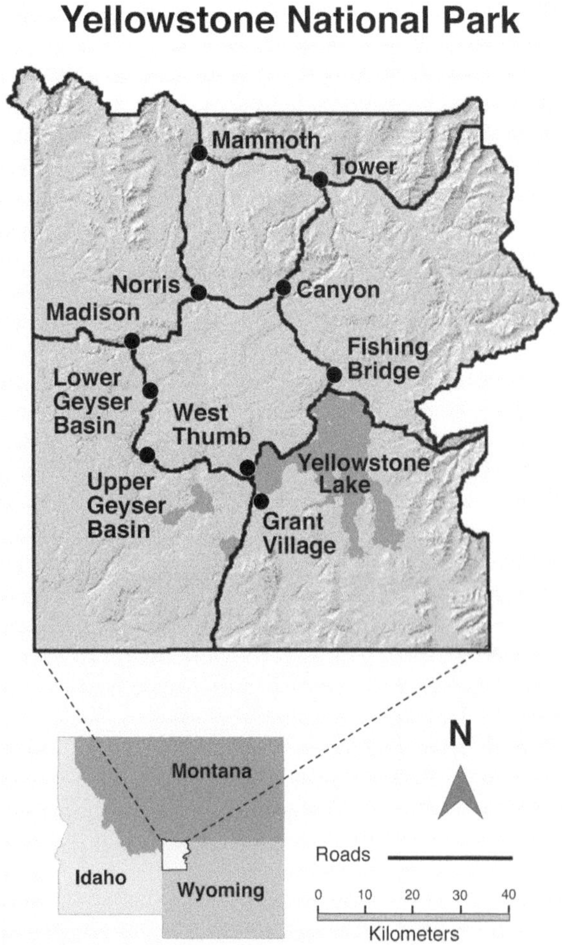

FIGURE 2.2. Grand Loop Road. Yellowstone National Park and its figure-eight-shaped Grand Loop Road is used by millions of tourists. Map by Langdon Smith.

Improving roads within Yellowstone became a priority of all the early park managers, which had two significant impacts. First, the focus on road building demonstrated the pressure that local entrepreneurs and tourists were applying to the park superintendents and the Department of the Interior to make the park accessible. This illustrated Yellowstone's evolving role as a destination point for tourists. Second, and perhaps even more important to the evolution of Yellowstone's cultural landscape, were those areas ignored by early tourists and engineers. By omission, the road builders had unwittingly determined which areas of the park would remain wilderness. The vast areas surrounding Yellowstone's original road network remain mostly roadless today, and they are seen by only a small percentage of the park's visitors.

Montanans were quick to come up with schemes to make money from tourists, and this meant building an infrastructure to support visitation. Several years before the government became involved in mapping Yellowstone's future, locals had already built the first hotel and restaurant, and several local entrepreneurs provided tourists with a variety of services. Before federal officials had even considered the long-term ramifications of a string of roads and hotels within the park, locals had already established an indelible pattern of tourism development across the Yellowstone landscape. Over time, these efforts would have important consequences for American national parks.

Allowing tourists to stay overnight in national parks necessitated the inevitable development of restaurants, garbage dumps, and eventually even sewer and electrical plants and other support facilities. The construction of hotels, roads, and other infrastructure brought even more people, which in turn required more development. This pattern of cumulative causation would repeat itself in parks established after Yellowstone, including Glacier National Park in Montana. In this process each infrastructural improvement encouraged more use, which then demanded more infrastructure.[21] This culture of development also promoted an entrepreneurial style to managing parks that carried well into the next century. Historian Richard West Sellars argues that such development fostered a capitalistic, business-oriented approach to national parks that focused on the miles of roads and trails, the number of visitors each year, and the need for continued tourism development. The end result would be natural resource management to serve tourism purposes.[22]

When Ferdinand Hayden, leader of the US Geological Survey, arrived in Yellowstone with his exploration party in the summer of 1871, two men were already hard at work cutting poles to fence off the geyser basins along the Firehole River.[23] Also that summer, Montanans Harry Horr and James McCartney built the first overnight accommodations at Mammoth Hot Springs (figure 2.3). Horr and McCartney's Hotel was a one-story log building with an earth-covered slab roof. The business partners boasted a fine restaurant, bathhouses managed by one of the "best physicians in the West," supplies for pleasure-seekers, and pack trains into the park.[24] Adventurer and author Thomas Windham (the Earl of Dunraven) called the hotel the last outpost of civilization—that being the last place where whiskey was sold. Horr and McCartney may have exaggerated the quality of their lodgings. Windham described the small hotel as an "inverse ratio to the gorgeous description contained in the advertisements."[25]

FIGURE 2.3. Early Hotel, Mammoth Hot Springs, ca. 1885. Horr and McCartney's Hotel at Mammoth Hot Springs was the only place to stay within Yellowstone during the first several years. Photograph by F. J. Haynes. Source: Yellowstone National Park Archives, YELL 9357 (courtesy of National Park Service, Yellowstone National Park; hereafter NPS-YNP).

Once wagon roads had been constructed, Bozeman entrepreneurs were quick to take advantage. "Ho! Ho! Ho! For the Mammoth Hot Springs," read an advertisement by John Werks of Bozeman during the first official tourist season in 1872. "I am now prepared to carry INVALIDS and PLEASURE PARTIES from Bozeman to the celebrated Hot Springs of Horr & McCartney."[26] Zack Root's Express advertised four-horse coaches to Mammoth Hot Springs in 1875, making connections with pack trains to "all parts of the Park." Root also offered mail service with stops in Hayden, Emigrant, Chico, Henderson, and Bear Gulch.[27] In 1883, Bozeman residents George W. Wakefield and Charles W. Hoffman began hauling passengers through the park; their stagecoach company charged twelve cents per mile. They also carried mail and, after visitor numbers increased, had five stagecoaches operating in different areas of Yellowstone. Wakefield and Hoffman were also given permission to cut wild hay within the park to feed their horses.[28]

Tourists were charged for a variety of services, despite the challenges of such a remote location. For example, sailboat rides were offered to tourists on Yellowstone Lake. In 1874, Eugene S. Topping and Frank Williams received permission to operate boats on Yellowstone Lake, and they took early horseback visitors sailing during the summers of 1874, 1875, and 1876. Topping advertised that the first woman to come to the lake would have the privilege of naming his boat. It became the *Sallie* (figure 2.4).[29] In 1880, another pair of boatbuilders advertised they had "just built, and launched[,] a strong and safe sail-boat on the Yellowstone lake. A competent man is in charge,

FIGURE 2.4. The *Sallie*, ca. 1874. Local entrepreneurs built the *Sallie* to give tourists boat rides on Yellowstone Lake during the summers of 1874 and 1875. The business was unprofitable and was abandoned in 1876. Photographer unknown. Source: Yellowstone National Park Archives, YELL 9188 (courtesy of NPS-YNP).

who will, at all proper times, be ready to accommodate all who desire to take pleasure excursions on this far-famed and beautiful sheet of water."[30]

Practically no idea was too far-fetched if it might lead to further attention and development of the park. A Montana newspaper correspondent came up with the idea of building an old soldiers' home in Yellowstone, where the government has "everything of its own—the finest medical springs in the world, grounds to any extent required—and all under government control." The veterans were to be used as park rangers, thus freeing them from the "bane of old soldiers—liquor."[31] Although a soldiers' home was never seriously considered for Yellowstone, it is another example of how locals became involved in imagining and shaping the cultural landscape of the park. Montanans obviously felt they had a stake in creating Yellowstone's future, and their actions suggest that, when it came to the overall plan for the nation's first national park, the slate was blank.

Montanans believed that if Yellowstone could be made accessible, safe, and comfortable, tourists would come by the thousands and that this success could enrich nearby communities. Early visitors from Montana who wrote about their recent trip through Yellowstone often anticipated that many more would follow in their footsteps. "The world will journey to this spot more and more," one writer predicted. "The mighty pilgrimage has but just begun."[32] By the mid-1880s, local business owners were also aware that tourists could provide substantial income. "No class of people leave so much money in a country as tourists," the *Avant Courier* proclaimed. "There are towns and cities in Switzerland that owe nearly their entire existence to tourists. . . . And the day is not far off when it will become a substantial source of revenue to Montanians [*sic*] living in its immediate neighborhood."[33]

THE CUSTODIANS

The custodians of early Yellowstone—the first superintendents, and later US Cavalry officers and federal scientists—had the job of field-testing the national park idea. At first the task was more akin to the role of settler, as the first superintendents had to cut trails, build shelter, and avoid conflicts with Bannock and Nez Perce Indians. As funding began to trickle in from Congress, the number of tourists increased, and park officials began to understand what the public demanded in a national park. The custodians began building a road network and crude "ranger" stations throughout Yellowstone, as well as dictating the location of hotels sprouting at the points of interest within the park. As demand grew for developing Yellowstone, the custodians eventually had to say no to several of the most outlandish proposals. These early judgments established an initial balance between development and preservation that both helped define the cultural landscape of the park and set a precedent for future national parks.

Philetus Norris was the first full-time custodian and the first to begin building park infrastructure. His actions were shaped by his fears of conflict with the Nez Perce Indians, who had traveled through Yellowstone the summer before Norris arrived, capturing several tourists and killing two.[34] In his annual reports, Norris often mentioned the threat of Indian attack, and when he built his headquarters building at Mammoth during 1879, it was designed more as a fort than as a park headquarters we might envision today (figure 2.5). As Norris noted, "I selected it as the site for our blockhouse headquarters, where it fully commands the entire mound, valley and terrace, within range of rifle or field artillery, and a fair view of the entire balance of the valley and its approaches."[35] The two-story log building featured an octagonal gun turret that was loopholed for rifles. As a further protective measure, the following year, Norris drafted regulations prohibiting all Native Americans from entering the park.[36]

Norris and his assistants were more settlers than managers, and their descriptions of life in Yellowstone were much like the reports of pioneers. They hunted game to feed themselves, built corrals for their horses and other stock, and experimented with a half-acre vegetable garden near the Mammoth headquarters. In 1880 Norris suggested a plan to pipe hot water from the nearby hot springs into his log fort.[37]

With their headquarters established, Norris and company began building smaller cabins throughout the park for shelter during their explorations

FIGURE 2.5. Blockhouse Fort, Mammoth Hot Springs, ca. 1881. Philetus Norris, Yellowstone's second superintendent, was worried about armed conflict with Nez Perce and Bannock Indian nations, so he built this blockhouse fort as his administration building on Capitol Hill at Mammoth Hot Springs in 1879. Photograph by H. B. Calfee. Source: Yellowstone National Park Archives, YELL-200 (courtesy of NPS-YNP).

and road-building operations. The first was a small cabin in a grove of trees between Castle and Beehive Geysers in the Upper Firehole Basin, followed by a cabin for Harry Yount, the park's first gamekeeper, at the mouth of Soda Butte Creek in the northeast corner of Yellowstone. Yount was the first employee of the park to spend the winter (1880–81) in Yellowstone and described the experience in the 1881 superintendent's report: "I there remained . . . during the entire winter, the early part of which was so severe that there were no mountain hunters. The snowfall was usually great, and remained very deep in the mountains." Although his thermometer broke and he could not record daily temperatures, Yount reported snow falling on sixty-six out of ninety days.[38]

IMPROVING NATURE

Yellowstone's early custodians came to the job with their own perceptions about natural resources, and each had his own ideas about "improving" nature. Wanting to improve nature was not unusual during the 1870s and the decades that followed. In New York's Catskill Mountains, proprietors at scenic Kaaterskill Falls routinely manipulated nature by damming the stream above the falls and then releasing the water for tourists to witness how the falls looked during spring thaw.[39] Another example of improving nature was the killing of predators in Yellowstone and elsewhere. These predators were considered "bad" animals, and they were killed to protect deer, elk, and bison, which were considered "good" animals.[40]

Norris, who received heavy criticism from the press for wanting to turn Yellowstone into his private ranch, probably had the strongest opinions about manipulating nature. In several of his annual reports, Norris suggested domesticating Yellowstone's wildlife for the sale of their "flesh, pelts, and furs."[41] Another pet project of Norris's was Liberty Cap at Mammoth, which he feared would topple without his help (figure 2.6). For several years he struggled with methods to support Liberty Cap, including building wooden scaffolding around it during 1878. Terrace deposits eventually destroyed the wooden scaffolding, but two years later Norris came up with a scheme to pipe hot springs water into the "ancient supply-pipe of the cone," or close enough to recoat the cone with a jet of terrace water. The following year, Norris received permission to try his experiment but had mixed success. Using the double barrels of a shotgun as a test pipe, he discovered that the mineral water would clog the barrels within a week, which effectively killed his plan of finding Liberty Cap's supply pipe. However, he was able to build troughs from nearby Devil's Thumb to transport the mineral water, and Liberty Cap was "covered and enlarged by a coating of beautiful white geyserite."[42]

FIGURE 2.6. Liberty Cap, 1871. Philetus Norris feared Liberty Cap would topple without his help and struggled for years with methods to support the structure, including wooden scaffoldings. Liberty Cap remains standing today at Mammoth Hot Springs. Photograph by William Henry Jackson. Source: Yellowstone National Park digital archives, photograph #03122 (courtesy of NPS-YNP).

Stocking fish in Yellowstone streams was another popular method of improving upon nature. F. A. Boutelle, a captain with the US Army's First Cavalry, served as Yellowstone's acting superintendent from June 1889 to February 1891. One of his first requests was for the US Fish Commission to begin stocking fish within the park. The following year, 7,000 trout were planted in the west and middle forks of the Gardner River above the falls, in the Gibbon River above Virginia Cascade, and in the Firehole

River above Keppler's Cascade. Another 150,000 fish were on order for the following year. The cavalry officer also suggested creating a water storage system to irrigate dry areas of the park to prevent forest fires. Fire was one aspect of wild nature that was fought equally enthusiastically by all of Yellowstone's early superintendents.[43]

FINDING THE LIMITS OF DEVELOPMENT

Yellowstone's early managers all welcomed the development of lodges and recreational activities within the park; however, there were limitations to what was acceptable. With the example of the highly commercialized Niagara Falls, Americans had some idea of what was too much development. Prior to European knowledge about Yellowstone and the Yosemite Valley, Niagara was widely recognized during the early 1800s as America's most significant natural feature, but by the 1830s, hucksters and private developers had acquired the best overlooks of the falls and created a carnival-like atmosphere by hawking cheap trinkets. European visitors condemned the commercialization of Niagara, and it eventually became a national embarrassment.[44] Yellowstone's custodians were not about to repeat that mistake in the first national park of the United States.

It was evident very early that Yellowstone should be adorned with numerous hotels near all the points of interest—and that these hotels should be comfortable and compare well with the hotels of Europe. But the great distances involved, bad roads into and within the park, and a lack of private investment prevented such favorable comparisons for many years. In 1888, Moses Harris, acting superintendent of Yellowstone, reported that Yellowstone's hotels were "temporary in character, of cheap and poor construction and a shame and discredit to the National park."[45] Boutelle also reported on the overcrowding and poor conditions of Yellowstone's hotels, being mostly concerned with the safety of visitors and the lack of adequate fire escapes at the Mammoth Hot Springs and Canyon hotels. The hotel at Norris burned to the ground during 1887, and Boutelle predicted a similar occurrence at either Mammoth or Canyon would lead to fatalities.[46]

One of the more interesting proposals for Yellowstone was to build an elevator to assist tourists at the Grand Canyon of the Yellowstone River. A man by the name of D. B. May, of Billings, Montana, was granted a lease to build an elevator at the lower falls of the Grand Canyon. When Boutelle heard about the plan, he urged the Department of the Interior to cancel or at least radically alter the lease: "It was a mistake to approve any elevator to reach the bottom of the canon [*sic*] without its coming into full sight and destroying the view from the head of the great falls. This is one of the grandest views on earth and double grand that the hand of man is nowhere visible."[47] Historian Duane Hampton suggests that Boutelle's stubborn stand against the elevator helped set a national park policy against such overt commercialization.[48]

A RAILROAD THROUGH YELLOWSTONE

While an elevator would no doubt have desecrated the Grand Canyon, a much greater battle soon loomed for the park's officials—and the outcome had huge implications for Yellowstone's cultural landscape and for the national parks that followed. During an eleven-year period beginning in 1883, officials of the Northern Pacific Railroad began a spirited campaign to breach Yellowstone with a rail line. The proposed spur line would have cut across the northeast corner of Yellowstone, snaking its way fifty-five miles from Montana along the Lamar River to reach the small mining community of Cooke City, just outside the park. Various proposals for the railroad would have also given the Northern Pacific control of as much as a mile-wide corridor along the proposed route.

Transporting ore and equipment to and from the Cooke City mines was the stated purpose of the spur. Opponents of the rail line, however, discovered that its construction was merely a way to get a commercial foot in the door, and that the company had surveyed the interior of the park for an additional track to carry tourists to all the major attractions within the park. The Northern Pacific already controlled the chain of hotels at key attractions within the park, so it made perfect sense for them to support those investments. The new spur would set a precedent, opponents argued, and once approved, there was no telling what might follow.[49]

Nearby residents of Yellowstone, especially the business owners and entrepreneurs, were naturally in favor of the proposed spur line. They were typical of many Americans of the time, who believed industrialization and nature were compatible. Many believed that the railroads, in opening the West, would bring forth a new version of Jefferson's pastoral vision for America. The idea that park managers could both protect and develop Yellowstone was evident in many letters to the editors of newspapers in

Montana. Often within the same letter or article, a local business owner would decry the slaughter of Yellowstone's wildlife or damage being done to geothermal features but then predict huge profits if areas within the park were opened to coal mining or some other form of resource extraction.

The debate over the railroad also illustrated that locals had a narrow view of the types of landscapes that were worthy of protection within a national park. These included the spectacular geysers, hot springs, mud volcanoes, and other geothermal features. The stunning Grand Canyon of the Yellowstone and massive Yellowstone Lake were also prized by locals. However, there was no shortage of wilderness in the northern Rockies at this time, and the landscape outside the geyser basins and the heavily traveled Grand Loop looked similar to areas just outside the park boundary. Local supporters of the proposed spur voiced this feeling. In the words of G. C. Swallow, the outspoken Montana mining inspector, "All well know there is not a single natural feature north of the Yellowstone and Soda Butte creek that is mentioned in the guide book as worthy of the tourists' attention."[50] In fact, when federal scientists later argued that the railroad would damage critical watersheds, timber, and wildlife habitat, it was the first time the northeast corner of the park had been publicly assigned any value.

There were two strong voices opposing the railroad development. The first came from those opposing the Northern Pacific Railroad's monopolization of hotel leases within the park. Northern Pacific created a unit to develop the needed tourist services, called the Yellowstone Park Improvement Company. In September of 1882, Acting Secretary of the Interior Merritt L. Joslyn granted this company exclusive rights to hotels, stages, and telegraph service within the park. Under the lease agreement, the Improvement Company would pay only two dollars per acre for 640-acre sections surrounding all of the park's most desirable sites. The lessees also were to have the right to cut timber for construction and fuel, and to farm some areas of the park.[51] The company cut timber in the park and contracted with local hunters to supply meat for its work crews. They built sawmills and erected the 250-room National Hotel at Mammoth Hot Springs (figure 2.7). This hotel was 414 feet long and 54 feet wide. It reached four stories in height at some places and consumed 1,600,000 board feet of park timber.[52]

The Improvement Company's heavy-handed progress in Yellowstone quickly came under attack, and local support for the Northern Pacific began to slip. After company officials were accused of killing game within the park

FIGURE 2.7. National Hotel, 1884. The National Hotel at Mammoth, designed in the Queen Anne style by L. F. Buffington and built in 1883, was the first luxurious hotel in Yellowstone. Within a few years, it became known as the Mammoth Hot Springs Hotel. Photograph by F. J. Haynes. Source: Yellowstone National Park Archives (courtesy of NPS-YNP).

to feed their workers, for example, the Bozeman *Avant Courier* published the following editorial against the "Despoliation Company":

> What a glorious place for a slaughterhouse! Here we [the Improvement Co.] can secure all the meat necessary to feed the men in our employ, without the difficulty attendant upon taking care for cattle or the expense consequent upon a purchase from a butcher. Such doings are infamous. Let it be known that there is no law to protect game, and no one will argue that it will not become extinct.[53]

In regard to this issue, a more powerful voice against the leases and the killing of wildlife came from George Bird Grinnell, editor of *Forest and Stream* magazine. A noted explorer and sportsman, Grinnell was later largely responsible for the establishment of Glacier National Park in 1910. His contribution to the Yellowstone leasing controversy consisted of publishing at least twenty-six articles on the subject within four months, beginning in December of 1882. In one article, entitled "The Park Grab," he reported that the plot to monopolize the "people's Pleasuring Ground" was flourishing.[54] When the Improvement Company began construction of its first hotel in Yellowstone before a lease was finalized, an incensed Grinnell wrote the following editorial:

> With a boldness that is astonishing, they have absolutely gone on and begun to build their hotels[,] thus virtually taking possession of a government reservation, using timber which is not theirs, and killing the government game and fish to feed their employees. They have seized a portion of the public territory and declare that the revenue to be derived from it shall flow into their own pockets.[55]

The second strong voice of opposition came from a group of federal scientists, Army officers, and bureaucrats who argued for protection of Yellowstone's timber, watersheds, and other natural features. This group included Arnold Hague, a scientist with the US Geological Survey; W. Hallett Phillips, a special investigator for the Department of the Interior; Lieutenant Dan Kingman of the US Army Engineers; and several army officers working as acting superintendents of Yellowstone. These men had become the "experts" on Yellowstone, and their views were often quoted by the national press and included in congressional committee hearing reports.

Hague was a professionally trained geologist and had been assigned to Yellowstone by John Wesley Powell after he became director of the US Geological Survey in 1883.[56] Hague's primary concern for Yellowstone was protecting its timber, which he argued would maintain healthy watersheds, and he was also concerned about the railroad's impact on wildlife.[57] Phillips, an attorney who came from a well-known family in Washington, DC, was appointed by the Secretary of the Interior to investigate the management of Yellowstone. Phillips spent the summer of 1885 in the park and returned with a thorough report detailing problems and threats. Most importantly, he summarized what he thought were the key caretaking responsibilities: protecting wildlife, "preserving the park as much as possible in a state of nature," and maintaining "the natural forests in a region where so many great rivers of the continent find their source."[58] Needless to say, Phillips was critical of railroads entering Yellowstone, and he predicted ruinous forest fires caused by locomotive sparks. Kingman was assigned to Yellowstone in 1883 by the US Army Engineers to bring professionalism to the design of interior roads. While completing this work, he joined other Army officers managing Yellowstone who spoke out against any railroads. "I have given this subject the most careful thought and study," he said, "and I should regard their introduction as the most serious injury that could be inflicted upon the park . . . and the construction . . . would be especially deplorable because it seems so unnecessary."[59]

The scientific arguments made by Hague, Phillips, and Kingman, combined with the charges against the Northern Pacific of monopoly and poor stewardship, turned the tide of public opinion against the proposed spur line. The victory of Yellowstone's supporters over the Northern Pacific signaled a shift in the way many Americans viewed the region. The battle waged by the park's supporters elevated the preservation and aesthetic values of wildlands to new heights and infused the idea of a national park with relatively new concerns about watershed sanctity and habitat protection. Yellowstone had become a contested landscape. It was known to have a vast potential for tourism development, possibilities for settlement, and nearby mineral resources, yet these traditional values were subordinated as Americans became aware of the natural values being protected.

THE VISITOR'S EXPERIENCE

The final element that helped to forge the national park idea and the cultural landscape was the growing number of visitors experiencing Yellowstone firsthand. After the Northern Pacific Railroad reached the northern entrance to the park in 1883, the majority of Yellowstone's visitors were Americans who lived outside the region. These national tourists played an important role by spreading the word about the new national park and by discovering how to behave in and experience this new type of "pleasuring ground." The growing number of visitors were also a test of Yellowstone's staying power—whether a visit lived up to the park's reputation, or if Yellowstone would fade to the role of a regional attraction on the scale of New York's Catskills or the Wisconsin Dells.[60]

Yellowstone did live up to its reputation, and visitation numbers climbed with each stage of transportation improvements. When wagon roads made the journey through the park an easier adventure in 1877, annual tourist numbers doubled, from five hundred to one thousand. When the Northern Pacific Railroad arrived in 1883, annual visitor numbers increased fivefold, from one thousand to five thousand. The arrival of the railroad not only opened the floodgates of tourists but also changed both the type of tourist and the nature of the visitor experience. In her study of the early western landscape, historian Anne Hyde found that the most noticeable changes in tourism followed the tracks of the transcontinental railroad breaching the country in 1869. Initially, only the very wealthy could afford to travel to the "Far West" on a train, with a packaged deal costing roughly $1,200 from a major city in the East.[61] But as railroad fares fell and American urban areas grew, "clerks, bureaucrats and others of modest means" were able to go on excursions.[62]

Travel accounts written before and after the Northern Pacific Railroad's arrival paint quite different pictures of what a visit to the park meant. A pre-coach trip meant having an adventure on horseback and roughing it along the trail. It gave the opportunity for tourists to be pioneers without having to face the hardships of actual settlement, to follow in the footsteps of the hunter and the trapper by stepping into the "half fictional world of the Wild West."[63] In stark contrast, a coach trip could mean sightseeing with a guide and a stop each night for a hot bath and a meal at a comfortable hotel.

While climbing visitor numbers influenced Congress and the Department of the Interior to take the national park more seriously, the visitors themselves were shaping the national park idea through their own behavior. Some of their activities were harmful to the park and would be judged harshly today. But standards had not yet emerged for appropriate behavior in national park settings. The national park idea was literally being field-tested during these early years, and Yellowstone's officials responded by developing rules and policy to protect both the park's features and the visitors. A good example of how visitor behavior shaped the cultural landscape was the development of policies to reduce the risk of forest fires. Believing that the majority of forest fires within Yellowstone could be traced to careless campers, Captain Boutelle received permission in 1890 to establish designated campgrounds. He reported that campers were not willfully careless, but many had no experience in camping and left their camps believing that all precautions to prevent fire had been taken.[64] The newly designated campgrounds signaled that park managers were anxious to educate visitors on the dangers of fire in the park. In this case, the visitors' behavior demanded a new park policy, and that policy in turn shaped the visitors' behavior.

The geysers' basins were another area where early tourists often encountered trouble. Without the walkways and protective railings and fences of modern Yellowstone, these areas were sometimes dangerous. One of the most intriguing stories came from four men from Butte, Montana, who thought they had lost one of their party to a geyser in 1882. Walter Watson had volunteered to descend a short way into the mouth of a large geyser to obtain a few mementos; then the crust gave way, tossing him in. His three companions lowered a light into the geyser, but could see nothing of Watson.

Eventually giving up hope, the dejected party returned to their camp, thinking Watson dead. The next morning a group of newcomers walked into camp with a shaken Watson in hand, who told the following story:

> After what seemed to me ages, the shouts ceased and I realized that my friends had given me up for lost . . . I suppose it was nearly five o'clock when I heard what sounded like distant thunder. The noise grew more and more distinct and the water surrounding me began to be troubled. I then realized that I was in the crater of an active geyser. Suddenly I discovered that the water was rising. . . . The water continued to rise more rapidly, and I at last found myself at the point from which I had fallen . . . When I recovered I was being cared for by the strangers, the men who conducted me to my comrades.[65]

Such misadventures led Yellowstone's officials to build the first plank walkways in the geyser basins. After leading terrified visitors gingerly over a thin "silicon crust" to see the Dancing Dunes in Porcelain Basin in 1887, Assistant Park Superintendent George L. Henderson promised a safer trip in the future: "The government will in due time construct plank pathways when individuals may safely reach this and other objects of interest."[66]

Pouring soap into the geysers to make them erupt was a popular activity until it was outlawed, as was breaking off samples of the geothermal features and taking home other mementos from a visit. To be fair, early tourists were encouraged to collect samples, in the pages of the first guidebooks published by Northern Pacific. Describing the area around West Thumb Bay on Yellowstone Lake as a "museum of all the varieties of hot springs," guidebooks published during 1883 and 1884 stated, "If one carefully collects specimens at this place of the different kinds which are visible, he will secure a perfect exhibit of every formation."[67] The park's protectors were at odds with such influences and when it came to park protection, they had their work cut out for them.

A FUNCTIONING NATIONAL PARK

The first eighteen years of the Yellowstone experience saw a transformation from a vague, ill-defined idea to a functioning national park that became a template for future parks across America and around the world. As such, Yellowstone was truly an experiment. The federal government had no experience managing such a huge tract of wildlands for recreational use and, in fact, let the young park languish. Yellowstone could just as easily have become an anomaly rather than a trendsetter in public land policy. Yet the combination of local involvement during the important early years, subsequent management of the park by the US Army, and the experiences of the American public created a unique kind of public land use in the West that set the stage for the protection of other scenic and valuable public lands.

The startling images and descriptions provided by Yellowstone's exploration parties galvanized a budget-conscious and war-weary Congress and ensured the creation of the first national park. The explorations also sparked the imagination of the American public, which began making pilgrimages to Yellowstone. The park's custodians, through trial and error, established a form of management that met the needs of the public while also preserving Yellowstone in an acceptable state of nature. It was during these critical years that park managers first fought off monopolistic economic interests and grappled with finding the balance between development and preservation, a debate that has dogged park managers and the public ever since. Through its experiences visiting the park, the American public would also help define the "character" of Yellowstone and the national park concept itself.

It took thousands of Americans experiencing Yellowstone before the park could make the leap in public perception from public-lands experiment to national icon. Annual reports from the Department of the Interior, and other documents, reflected this change, especially when Yellowstone was threatened by a lack of regulations and laws. In 1885, Wyoming's territorial governor requested laws to help protect Yellowstone because the park had assumed a "national importance."[68] That same year, Investigator Phillips argued that the increasing number of visitors justified Congress's original wisdom of setting aside its lands: "The Park has now assumed such national importance as to imperatively call upon Congress to provide some system of justice by which the Park and the public visiting it can be protected."[69]

The fact that the "best idea Americans ever had" experienced such a rocky start in Yellowstone should not detract from the end result—the birth of the national park idea. Following closely behind the Yellowstone experiment came some of the other most cherished American national parks, including Yosemite (1890), Mount Rainier (1899), Crater Lake (1902), Glacier (1910), Rocky Mountain (1915), Grand Canyon (1919), Zion (1919), Big Bend (1935), and Olympic (1938). The idea could not be contained within the boundaries of the United States, and quickly spread around the world. As a template for both preserving natural areas and making them available to large numbers of the public, the example of Yellowstone transformed many different and distant landscapes. Yellowstone's story also contributes to our understanding of America's western landscapes in general and perceptions that have had an important impact on American culture. When asked today what natural treasures they value most, Americans invariably include the scenery of Yellowstone, the Grand Canyon, Yosemite, and other western landscapes. As historian Anne Hyde notes, this wild, western landscape "clearly plays an important role in the maintenance of a national culture."[70]

NOTES

1. Richard West Sellars, *Preserving Nature in the National Parks: A History* (New Haven, CT: Yale University Press, 1997).
2. Dyan Zaslowsky and T. H. Watkins, *These American Lands: Parks, Wilderness, and the Public Lands* (Covelo, CA: Island Press, 1994).
3. Aubrey L. Haines, *The Yellowstone Story: A History of Our First National Park*, vol. 1 (Niwot: University Press of Colorado, 1996).
4. Haines, *Yellowstone Story*, vol. 1, 98.
5. Duane H. Hampton, *How the U.S. Cavalry Saved Our National Parks* (Bloomington: Indiana University Press, 1971), 21; and Freeman Tilden, *The National Parks* (New York: Alfred A. Knopf, 1968), 92.
6. Yi-Fu Tuan, *Topophilia: A Study of Environmental Perception, Attitudes, and Values* (New York: Columbia University Press, 1974).
7. Judith Meyer, *The Spirit of Yellowstone: The Cultural Evolution of a National Park* (Lanham, MD: Roberts Rinehart Publishers, 2003).
8. Chris J. Magoc, *Yellowstone: The Creation and Selling of an American Landscape, 1870–1903* (Albuquerque: University of New Mexico Press, 1999), 80.
9. Meyer, *Spirit of Yellowstone*.
10. John F. Sears, *Sacred Places: American Tourist Attractions in the Nineteenth Century* (New York: Oxford University Press, 1989).
11. *Avant Courier*, September 11, 1874.
12. *Avant Courier*, April 10, 1884.
13. Bob Randolph O'Brien, *The Yellowstone National Park Road System: Past, Present and Future* (PhD diss., University of Washington, 1965).
14. Karl John Byrand, "The Evolution of the Cultural Landscape in Yellowstone National Park's Upper Geyser Basin and the Changing Visitor Experience" (MS thesis, Montana State University, 1995).
15. Switzer, N. A., "Trip to the Geysers," written as a diary in an unpublished book, 1876. Collection 356, Montana State University Library Special Collections.
16. *Avant Courier*, September 18, 1874.
17. Haines, *Yellowstone Story*, vol. 1; O'Brien, *Yellowstone National Park Road System*.

18. Haines, *Yellowstone Story*, vol. 1.
19. Haines, *Yellowstone Story*, vol. 1.
20. *Avant Courier*, September 9, 1880.
21. Lary M. Dilsaver and William Wyckoff, "Agency Culture, Cumulative Causation and Development in Glacier National Park, Montana," *Journal of Historical Geography* 25, no. 1 (1999):75–92.
22. Sellars, *Preserving Nature in the National Parks*.
23. Alfred Runte, *National Parks: The American Experience*, 3rd ed. (Lincoln: University of Nebraska Press, 1987), 44.
24. *Avant Courier*, August 14, 1874.
25. Thomas Windham, *The Great Divide: Travels in the Upper Yellowstone in the Summer of 1874* (London: Chatto and Windus, 1876).
26. *Avant Courier*, August 22, 1872.
27. *Avant Courier*, October 29, 1875.
28. Haines, *Yellowstone Story*, vol. 1.
29. Yellowstone Foundation, A *Yellowstone Album: A Photographic Celebration of the First National Park* (Boulder, CO: Roberts Rinehart, 1997).
30. *Avant Courier*, August 26, 1880.
31. *Livingston Enterprise*, January 2, 1886.
32. *Livingston Enterprise*, September 30, 1880.
33. *Avant Courier*, June 7, 1886.
34. Haines, *Yellowstone Story*, vol. 1.
35. P. W. Norris, *Report upon the Yellowstone National Park to the Secretary of the Interior for the Year 1880* (Washington, DC: Government Printing Office).
36. Magoc, *Yellowstone*, 5.
37. Norris, *Report upon the Yellowstone National Park . . . 1880*, 4; Norris, *Report upon the Yellowstone National Park . . . 1881*, 25.
38. Norris, *Report upon the Yellowstone National Park . . . 1881*.
39. Sears, *Sacred Places*, 47.
40. Patricia Nelson Limerick, *The Legacy of Conquest: The Unbroken Past of the American West* (New York: Norton, 1987), 311.
41. Norris, *Report upon the Yellowstone National Park . . . 1877*.
42. Norris, *Report upon the National Yellowstone Park . . . 1881*, 843.
43. F. A. Boutelle, *Report of the Superintendent of Yellowstone National Park to the Secretary of the Interior, 1890* (Washington, DC: Government Printing Office); F. A. Boutelle, *Supplemental Report of the Superintendent of Yellowstone National Park*, attached to Boutelle, *Report of the Superintendent . . . 1889*, 7–8, 23.
44. Runte, *National Parks*, 5.
45. Moses Harris, *Report of the Superintendent of the National Park to the Secretary of the Interior, 1888* (Washington, DC: Government Printing Office), 11.
46. Boutelle, *Report of the Superintendent . . . 1890*, 10.
47. Boutelle, *Report of the Superintendent . . . 1890*, 11.
48. Hampton, *How the U.S. Cavalry Saved Our National Parks*, 99.
49. Congressional Record, *52nd Congress*, 1st session (10 May 1892); George Grinnell, "Railroad in Yellowstone Park," *Forest and Stream*, February 18, 1886; Magoc, *Yellowstone*.

50. G. C. Swallow, "Railroad to Cooke City," *Livingston Enterprise*, February 2, 1890.
51. George Grinnell, "The Park Grab," *Forest and Stream*, January 4, 1883.
52. Richard A. Bartlett, *Yellowstone: A Wilderness Besieged* (Tucson: University of Arizona Press, 1985).
53. *Avant Courier*, February 15, 1883.
54. Grinnell, "Park Grab."
55. George Grinnell, "Park Monopolists Checked," *Forest and Stream*, January 11, 1886.
56. Sarah Ellen Broadbent, "Sportsmen and the Evolution of the Conservation Idea in Yellowstone: 1882–1894" (MA thesis, Montana State University, 1997); John F. Reiger, *American Sportsmen and the Origins of Conservation* (New York: Winchester Press, 1975).
57. Arnold Hague, "Forest Conditions of the Rocky Mountains," in *Department of Agriculture, Forestry Division, Bulletin No. 2* (Washington, DC: Government Printing Office, 1889).
58. W. Hallet Phillips, Letter to Hon. L. Q. C. Lamar, Secretary of the Interior (Record Group 48, Microfilm 62, Roll 3, National Archives, Washington, DC, September 12, 1885).
59. US House, Committee on Public Lands, Rept. no. 1386. 53rd Congress, 2nd session (August 7, 1894).
60. Paul Schullery, *Searching for Yellowstone: Ecology and Wonder in the Last Wilderness* (Boston, MA: Houghton Mifflin Company, 1997).
61. Anne Hyde, *An American Vision: Far Western Landscape and National Culture* (New York: New York University Press, 1990), 108.
62. Sears, *Sacred Places*, 10.
63. Sears, *Sacred Places*, 158.
64. Boutelle, *Report of the Superintendent* . . . 1890, 5.
65. *Avant Courier*, September 7, 1882.
66. *Livingston Enterprise*, July 16, 1887.
67. Northern Pacific Railroad, *The Yellowstone National Park* (Chicago, IL: Rand McNally, 1883), 24.
68. Francis E. Warren, Letter to Hon. L. Q. C. Lamar, Secretary of the Interior (Record Group 48, Microfilm 62, Roll 3, National Archives, Washington, DC, 13 October 1885).
69. Phillips, Letter to Hon. L. Q. C. Lamar, Secretary of the Interior.
70. Hyde, *An American Vision*, 6.

FIGURE 3.1. Hymen Terrace, 1871. The bathhouses of James McCartney and Harry Horr are shown here on Hymen Terrace at Mammoth Hot Springs on July 21, 1871. The two men standing in the center of the photograph are probably McCartney and Horr. Photograph by William Henry Jackson. Source: Library of Congress, image 2s01150.

3

Mammoth Hot Springs

Lee H. Whittlesey

These [cabins and tents] are all for the shelter of the invalids, who come out to this modern Saratoga of the wilderness in search of that health which the use of these waters is said in the most marvelous manner to bring.[1]
—MAJOR-GENERAL JOHN GIBBON, 1872, AT MAMMOTH HOT SPRINGS

WITH THAT quote, military man John Gibbon summed up the hopes of the earliest residents of the village of Mammoth Hot Springs in the new Yellowstone National Park, Wyoming Territory, that the place would in time become a healthful and fashionable bathing resort. That would never happen; instead, Mammoth was to become much more—a place where both natural resources and cultural resources were preserved for future generations.

Like all of Yellowstone National Park's developed hamlets, Mammoth Hot Springs village has a colorful and complicated history. Geophysically, the area is a product of the deposition by hot spring waters of a massive white hillside of calcium carbonate along with complex geological forces (volcanism, glaciation, and ongoing erosion) that formed the valley in which the springs reside. Culturally the Mammoth area has the longest Euro-American history of any developed area within the park, because it was used early for hot-spring bathing and tourism and because P. W. Norris designated it park headquarters in 1878, for the reasons he then listed. Mammoth received its first known buildings in 1871.

https://doi.org/10.5876/9781646427697.c003

Although fur trappers of the period 1822–1840 and gold prospectors of the period 1863–1869 visited the Yellowstone area, formal discovery by Euro-Americans did not occur until 1870. Remoteness, mountain geography, extended winters, the Civil War, and a lack of information received about the region from Indians protected the area for many years against chance discovery by most wanderers and settlers. Thus, Yellowstone was among the last places in the American West to be discovered, explored, and occupied by non-Indians. Marveled about and fawned over by its Euro-American discoverers, who sometimes called it "Wonderland," the place was declared the world's first national park by Congress on March 1, 1872.[2] By that time, the village of Mammoth Hot Springs was eight months old.

THE EARLY VILLAGE OF MAMMOTH HOT SPRINGS, 1871–1882

Settlement at Mammoth, if one can call it that, began in 1871, and it was centered on the spectacular stair-stepping "basins or bathing pools" that were referred to as "almost fairy like in beauty" and available in "every variety of temperature." Three squatters named James McCartney, Harry Horr, and Matthew McGuirk decided to settle there that summer with an eye toward selling hot-spring baths, lodging, food, and supplies to travelers, whom they knew would soon flock to the new park in large numbers to see the natural attractions that were already known as "the wonders of the Yellowstone." They and others saw Mammoth as a new resort that could be modeled after New York's Saratoga Springs and Arkansas's Hot Springs Reservation. The settlement of Mammoth Hot Springs remained small through the 1870s, for there was no real way to reach it except by traveling for many miles overland on horseback from the north. Due to mountain ranges and the complete absence of nearby towns in Wyoming and Idaho Territories, reaching the new park was not yet practical from the east or south, so legitimate travel occurred initially only from Montana to the park's north and west entrances. The first road into Mammoth came over the eastern foothills of Sepulcher Mountain and dropped into the village using the route of today's electric plant road. That route proved too steep, so P. W. Norris built today's "old Gardiner road" in 1879. Army engineer Dan Kingman supplemented it in 1884 by building the first road through Gardner Canyon to connect with the town of Gardiner, Montana, a road that does not exist today.[3]

A wag lavished praise on the Mammoth Hot Springs in 1875 in this poetical tribute, published in Bozeman, Montana, seventy-five miles to the northwest:

> The Mammoth Springs, I now behold,
> With their wonders manifold,
> Seething, hissing, steaming, bubbling,
> Ever restless, ever troubling,
> Their yawning caverns of smoke and fire,
> Arrest the traveler in his wild desire.
> —*H. O'Donovan, 1875*[4]

This poem reflected a primitive consciousness that regional travelers were then gathering into their heads about the newly discovered scenic Wonderland located just to the south of them. Bozeman residents did not know much about it, but nearly everyone was hearing about it, and for that reason local residents were making horseback trips to see the new park for themselves. Early descriptions were lavish in their praise. "It is a veritable fairyland," proclaimed a writer in 1885, "over which nature has placed a guard of granite monsters, and the contemplation of either is sufficient for the deepest inspiration of poet, painter or musician."[5]

McCartney, Horr, and McGuirk claimed the Mammoth Hot Springs together but split their efforts into two proximate locales. McCartney and Horr set up bathhouses and a primitive cabin for a hotel at Hymen Terrace in Clematis Gulch, while McGuirk, farther east and lower down on the hill, claimed the several hot springs that then existed just above the big warm creek near Gardner River that would eventually become known as Boiling River.

Mathew McGuirk registered his claim, but he did it a few days too late—on March 9, 1872. Because the park had been established on March 1, Superintendent N. P. Langford could evict him, and made a special trip to the park to do so in 1874.[6] Thence, for about fifteen years, the park used his buildings for housing. But then Captain Moses Harris of the US Army took it upon himself in 1889 to tear down all of McGuirk's buildings and the fence that surrounded the garden, carrying off the doors and windows and scattering everything else.[7] Like that of Horr and McCartney, McGuirk's "vain enterprise" lasted only a couple of years, and he spent years trying to get reimbursed by the government, finally obtaining $1,000 in remuneration in 1899.[8]

McCartney and Horr remained longer. The two men ran their ramshackle business through the 1870s, always as technical trespassers and always on a "wing and a prayer." Harry Horr gave up by 1879, selling out to McCartney and moving north to establish the town of Horr, Montana, but McCartney continued running his hotel and bathing establishment for a few more years. It consisted of six buildings, which included his main hotel, a saloon and restaurant, and a small store (figure 3.1). One of these (or perhaps it was a seventh) was a northerly building that he rented to Assistant Superintendent G. L. Henderson for a post office. Superintendent P. W. Norris ejected McCartney from Mammoth in 1879 for selling whiskey, so McCartney wandered five miles north to establish the town of Gardiner, Montana. But he soon returned to Mammoth too, spending his time in both places. Supported by numerous friends and people who wanted whiskey, he ran his business at Mammoth until 1881, when Superintendent P. W. Norris tore down four of his buildings and let other people take the rest of them over. From Gardiner, McCartney pressed the government for compensation until he finally got $3,000 in 1899, probably giving some of it to Harry Horr.

During the 1870s, the tiny village of Mammoth was sustained by ragtag frontiersmen, all trying to make a living from the usual hunting and meat sales, freighting, farming, mining, dairying, and selling whiskey, but also from the newly discovered industry of tourism—commercial guiding of tourists, sales of animal parts as souvenirs, and sales of coated specimens as souvenirs.

P. W. Norris, who was one of the most important of all Yellowstone superintendents, declared Mammoth Hot Springs to be park headquarters in 1878 and erected its first administration building. Norris chose Mammoth because it was the closest park location to Bozeman and Fort Ellis ("the nearest permanent settlements of whites and a military post"); because of its "good pasturage, water, and timber"; and probably because it was warmer and more snow-free than points to the south. He built the first park headquarters—a fort-like wooden "blockhouse"—at Mammoth on top of Capitol Hill in 1879, which was cold, drafty, and far from water. Referring to the park as the "matchless wonderland," Norris, while headquartered at Mammoth, explored it extensively, wrote long reports about it, sent dozens of its specimens to the Smithsonian Institution, and built roads and trails to many destinations, at times even using his own money to pay his laborers.[9]

The years 1882 to 1886 brought chaos, difficulty, and drama to the village of Mammoth. Superintendent Norris left the park in early 1882 and Patrick

Conger replaced him. Conger was a difficult personality who got along with almost no one and who made everyone around him angry—his superiors, the new hotel company, and his employees. During his twenty-eight months as superintendent, Conger managed to upgrade Norris's headquarters building, make repairs to roads, construct a couple of buildings at Lower Geyser Basin, and build a dwelling at Mammoth for his assistants. He also added other ramshackle buildings to the Mammoth village: a blacksmith shop, storehouse, carpenter shop, large corral, wagon shed, and harness house. But mostly he spent his time arguing with hotel company officials and his own subordinates and writing annoying letters to his superiors at the Department of the Interior. Eventually they fired him. His successor, Robert Carpenter, was even worse, being an out-and-out crook who believed in using the park for his own personal gain and who cared little for its protection at a time when it greatly needed protection. Thus it was a toss-up as to who caused more trouble during these years: these two superintendents or the new hotel syndicate known as the Yellowstone National Park Improvement Company. Carpenter's successor was David Wear, an honest man who made great strides in stopping the abuses of his predecessors and setting the park on a proper path. But Wear arrived too late to undo the damage of Conger and Carpenter and thus to prevent Congress from opening the door to army administration.[10]

The simultaneous story of the Yellowstone National Park Improvement Company is longer and more complicated than that of the three mentioned superintendents. Between 1882 and 1886, the new Yellowstone National Park had misfortunes with corrupt and incompetent civilian officials and with other difficulties such as poaching, vandalism, souvenir collecting, tree cutting, road building, and forest fire setting. But those troubles paled when compared to the ones created by a park concessionaire known as the Yellowstone National Park Improvement Company (YNPIC). The activities of this company—in the form of structures and events—were to influence Yellowstone National Park for nearly one hundred years, and those influences arguably continue today in the location of the Mammoth Hot Springs Hotel. Although the company survived for only a little more than three years (1882–86), the YNPIC was a major player in launching the village of Mammoth beyond its earlier existence as a collection of a few log cabins and tents.[11]

With tracklayers for the Northern Pacific Railroad pushing west through Montana Territory in 1881 and 1882, anticipation about tourists finally being able to reach the much-vaunted Yellowstone was bubbling in eastern cities. Tapping into this emerging mania were entrepreneurs "Uncle" Rufus Hatch, Carroll T. Hobart, and a politically powerful cadre of their friends. Presenting their new company (YNPIC) to the Department of the Interior as financially endowed and morally respectable—neither of which would prove to be true—these men wrangled the first concessions contract in any national park and did it in the manner of a grasping octopus feeding on the carcass of a whale.[12]

Historians have applied the term *Gilded Age* to the post–Civil War period in American history, especially the period 1870–96, when explosions in the country's population occurred simultaneously with extravagant displays of wealth and excess in America's upper class. This upper-class group—consisting of financially elite investors and managers—began at that time through the creation of a modern industrial economy. Businesspeople made the corporation into the dominant form of commercial organization in the US, and these men also worked with the government to simultaneously create a national transportation and communication network that made businesses even wealthier and thus stronger and more influential. Abuses in this unregulated system were to be expected, and they happened.

Unfortunately for Yellowstone National Park, the YNPIC exemplified the pattern of abuse. The corporation was funded by one of the nation's most powerful transportation companies—the Northern Pacific Railroad (NPRR)—and it became the central commercial entity in Yellowstone, which itself was then seen as a potential focus for the nascent business of western tourism. Also during the Gilded Age, American observers revived the term *robber baron* to refer to businessmen and bankers who dominated their respective industries and who typically got rich as a result of pursuing anticompetitive or unfair business practices. Railroad executives, such as Jay Cooke of the Northern Pacific Railroad, and others often associated with railroads, such as Collis Huntington and Charles Crocker, have been touted as examples of robber barons.[13] Although historians have not so singled him out, Rufus Hatch—president of the YNPIC—was essentially a robber baron, and Secretary Henry Teller thus picked a bad candidate to give a hotel monopoly in Yellowstone National Park.

But that is what happened. Hatch looked good on paper and had influential partners. They included Carroll T. Hobart—who had worked as a section superintendent on the NPRR—and former merchant Henry F. Douglas, both from present North Dakota. Also involved was a board of directors of twenty-five persons, including US Senator Roscoe Conkling, lawyers, bankers, merchants, and even a US Supreme Court justice.[14] With influence like this, it is small wonder that Secretary Teller approved the agreement. Eventually, as many as six descendant companies of this corporation (YNPIC–Yellowstone Park Association [YPA]) would operate hotels, tent camps, restaurants, stagecoaches, buses, and smaller enterprises involving boats, fuel, ice, and souvenirs at all points in Yellowstone until the year 1936.

Park Superintendent Patrick Conger received hints of the agreement in August of 1882, but that was mere formality. When he read the application for contract, he saw it as a steal. "They ask to cover to[o] much ground," he declared, and for too many privileges. Conger objected but was effectively bypassed, because Acting Secretary M. L. Joslyn signed the contract before the objection could even reach Washington. The agreement called for the government to grant huge land leases—4,400 acres to the company at seven unsurveyed sites in the park—for an average of nearly 630 acres per site. These gargantuan land grants could be shaped as the company saw fit. Article II gave the company as much timber and coal from the park as it wished. Tracts were given for the company to raise fruits and vegetables. Park waters were given for hotels' power, cooking, and bathing. The company was allowed to construct any buildings that it needed for stages, telegraph lines, and delivery services, and on park lakes YNPIC could place "yachts and other sailboats and rowboats." For all these privileges, the company was to pay the tiny sum of two dollars per acre per year.[15] Although the governor of Montana lambasted Hatch as "an unscrupulous monopolist" who had found "a virgin field for plunder," and although Senator George Graham Vest of Missouri began looking into the scheme as a steal on December 7, such efforts were to no avail—at least at first.[16] Much like the Borg of 1990s *Star Trek* television episodes—the evil collective that insatiably assimilated everything around it—YNPIC and the railroad could initially brag that "resistance is futile." Fortunately, Senator Vest was able to convince others in Congress to scale back YNPIC's unreasonable privileges. Even so, the company was effectively ensconced in Yellowstone.[17]

Hatch and Hobart immediately began erecting the first Mammoth Hot Springs Hotel, and this more than any previous construction started the village of Mammoth. It was a three- and four-story, Queen Anne–style building that was 414 feet long and 54 feet wide with 151 rooms, and it cost $140,000

FIGURE 3.2. National Hotel, 1884. This stunning 1884 photograph by Carleton Watkins shows the newly completed National Hotel (Mammoth Hot Springs Hotel) with Superintendent Norris's blockhouse on Capitol Hill (center left). The "old Gardiner Road," the main road at that time (bottom), drops into the hotel. G. L. Henderson's complex (right center) appears along with one bathhouse on Hymen Terrace. The hotel's first company store (lower left) was later used as a commissary. Enlarging the photograph reveals that carpenters erected a temporary wall at the bottom left of the hotel and supported it with a metal pole, where they intended to add a separate wing that was never built. Rufus Hatch noted that "the architect's plans provide for two wings, each 250 feet long, to be built when the public necessity requires enlargement." Source: Carroll Hobart Collection, Yale University (courtesy of Beinecke Library).

(figure 3.2). Designed by Minneapolis architect Leroy S. Buffington to house eight hundred guests, the National Hotel never held more than three hundred, although "crowding tactics" could increase that number by up to two hundred more. Buffington, because of his location near St. Paul, was handy to railroad officials, and his proposals to use metal skeleton frames in tall buildings led to his referring to himself as the "father of the American skyscraper."[18] Hatch designed the building to accommodate a couple of additional wings, but they were never built, as many photographs through 1912 have made clear. He provided water by "damming a brook and leading the water into the hotel, nearly one-third of a mile, through iron pipes buried in the earth."[19] Hatch ordered Hobart to find a stagecoach company, so Hobart hired George Wakefield and Charles Hoffman in July in a verbal contract that eight years later would cause much trouble for liveryman Wakefield.[20] YNPIC also erected a bathhouse near the hotel that used hot water from

Hymen Terrace and a year later erected another one nearby. Meanwhile, as the Northern Pacific Railroad pushed its way west from St. Paul, it seemed that almost everyone wanted a piece of the tourism money that seemed to promise fortunes—or at least prosperity—down the tracks at Livingston, Montana, and the soon-to-be-reachable Yellowstone National Park.[21]

Hatch and Hobart were in a hurry to get their hotel built during the spring of 1883, for not only was the park's opening fast approaching—June 15 during most years in order that snow could "melt out"—but also the Northern Pacific Railroad's tracks were expected to be completed to near the park's North Entrance sometime that summer. The driving of the last spike of the railroad, it was thought, would occur late in the summer about the same time that the hotel was completed and when President Chester Arthur's large horse party with all of its military VIPs was to arrive in Yellowstone.[22] Also figuring into the chaos were Rufus Hatch's VIP party of more than seventy people to promote his hotel, and NPRR President Henry Villard's party of around one hundred to celebrate completion of the railroad to the west coast. Hatch and Hobart had many questions in their minds. Would all of these parties arrive at Mammoth at once? How could an unfinished hotel handle so many important people? Could the railroad get everyone in and out efficiently? Where would the NPRR's constantly moving terminus be located at that time? Questions abounded in the minds of every observer at the Mammoth Hot Springs Hotel. Hatch's party arrived first, reaching Mammoth on the evening of August 23. President Arthur was second on August 31, and Villard's party (without Villard) was third, trickling into Mammoth after the September 10 spike-driving ceremony at Gold Creek, Montana. The arrival of all three of these parties within two weeks of each other, along with the completion of the railroad to nearby Cinnabar, Montana, on September 1 and the accompanying anticipation and preparations for each, made it certain that a circus-like atmosphere would prevail for at least a month in the new park.[23] The year 1883 thus ushered in Mammoth's and Yellowstone National Park's "grand opening."

The presidential trip was a success, but both the Hatch and the Villard celebrations cost their leaders dearly. Villard soon lost the railroad presidency because of his zeal to get the railroad finished so quickly and because of the amount of money that he spent on celebrating it. Hatch fared even worse. He spent $35,000 in cash on his guests and lost another $425,000 in the stock market while absent. "I had railroad passes for every mother's son of my company," he lamented, "yet that picnic cost me $35,000 in cash. I didn't ask the boys to spend a penny, and you can gamble that none of 'em pressed me to allow them to. Besides, while I was gone, I got on the wrong side of the market, and went hopelessly lame before I got back. I lost $450,000 on that trip." Despite its high prices and a capacity house, the National Hotel lost money that first year. Looming larger were Hatch's other financial losses. They would continue to resound in Yellowstone for nearly three more years, as Hatch went bankrupt and Carroll Hobart was abandoned by Hatch and the railroad.[24]

Hobart hung on in the park for a couple more years, but in 1886 Charles Gibson and a syndicate from St. Louis, Missouri, purchased the YNPIC and renamed it the Yellowstone Park Association. On the heels of that, Congress—fed up with the many problems in Yellowstone—angrily cut off funds to pay the park superintendents and assistants, and that gave the Secretary of the Interior no choice but to ask the Department of War for army troops to manage the park.

THE COATED SPECIMEN BUSINESS AT MAMMOTH

In addition to hot spring bathing, an early use of park resources that is no longer allowed today was the coating of various items in Mammoth Hot Springs thermal waters so that they could be sold by businessmen as souvenirs to park tourists. The practice began as early as 1872. Traveler E. J. Stanley recorded that "beautiful specimens are . . . obtained by placing little baskets, frames, and other objec . . . in the water, where in a short time they become incased in a snow-white crust of rare beauty."[25] Many persons sold these specimens at Mammoth over a period of more than forty years, but the park's most long-term player in the enterprise was Ole Anderson (1857–1915), who arrived at Mammoth in 1883 to engage in the "magnesia crystallization business"—his term for coating specimens. He operated his business from a tent until 1896 but that year got a permanent lease and erected a building at Mammoth that he called the "Specimen House." He sold that business and its building in 1908 to sisters Anna K. Pryor and Elizabeth Trischman, who continued to sell coated specimens from there. Although the coated specimen business died gradually in the teens, and the sisters sold their business in 1953, their building remained next to the present US Commissioner's house at Mammoth until it was torn down in 1984.

CONCESSIONAIRES HAYNES, CLARK, AND THE HENDERSONS EXPAND THE MAMMOTH VILLAGE

During the years 1884 and 1885, enterprising businessmen F. Jay Haynes, James A. Clark, and G. L. Henderson added more buildings to the Mammoth village (figure 3.3). By 1885, the village was sporting forty-three buildings. Haynes was official photographer for the Northern Pacific Railroad. Falling in love with Yellowstone, he decided to spend the rest of his life there and got permission to build a combination house, studio, and salesroom in front of Mammoth Hot Springs Hotel in early 1885. Haynes saw a profitable Yellowstone future for himself in selling "views of Wonderland" to the public, and many visitors encountered him through the years at his sales stand in the hotel. Haynes later would branch into selling postcards and picture books at all park locations and still later into his own stagecoach and bus company.[26] By early 1894, he had added a studio-and-sales shop immediately to the west that was attached to the main house. By 1902, he had attached a corral to his barn and removed several of the outbuildings.[27] He built or at least planned for another addition in 1910.[28]

FIGURE 3.3. Mammoth Hot Springs Hotel, ca. 1885. In this cropped and lightened F. Jay Haynes photograph, probably from 1885, we can see the first Mammoth Hot Springs Hotel (center left) and the transportation company's wagon shed (center rear). The three James A. Clark white buildings (center) are just above and a little left of Liberty Cap. Clark's bathhouse is the closest white building, while his dwelling is in the trees at center, and his outhouse is the small white building at right. Photographer F. Jay Haynes's house is at center, above Liberty Cap. In the foreground, Palette Spring has been tapped with a pipe for its hot water. Also note both hotel bathhouses in place. Source: Montana Historical Society Research Center, Helena, MT (hereafter MHS), Haynes Collection, Photograph H-1599 (courtesy of Montana Historical Society).

Haynes initially occupied his buildings only during the summer, returning to his base in St. Paul, Minnesota, in winter. The Haynes House on the parade ground at Mammoth was a standard part of the scene at Mammoth until it was moved to the north base of Capitol Hill (just southwest of the village) in late 1902. Throughout its life, it was a gathering place for many important people both socially and commercially.[29]

The Haynes House remained on the site between today's Haynes salesroom and today's Wakefield-Huntley-Nichols house until 1928. Several sources state that it was razed that year following the construction of the Haynes Picture Shop (factory) by Jack E. Haynes (son of F. Jay Haynes).[30]

James Clark, originally a US Marshall at Mammoth, wanted to be a liveryman. He was present at Mammoth during the years 1883 to 1887, and during that time, he built a large stable, blacksmith shop, a bathhouse, and at least one if not two or three small dwellings. His large stable, taken over by the Yellowstone Park Transportation Company in 1887, remained at the foot of Capitol Hill until 1902, while his dwellings on lower Clematis Creek were razed earlier. His blacksmith shop was probably also razed earlier, but it may have remained on the site to become Marion Baronett's post office, Jack Baronett's residence, or both.

In the midst of the park's many problems with its hotel concessionaire and its civilian superintendents in 1884 and 1885, one bright spot emerged at Mammoth with the erection of another park hotel. Problems with YNPIC probably caused the Department of the Interior to grant a lease of land to Walter J. and Helen L. Henderson, the son and daughter of one of Mammoth's most important early residents—Assistant Park Superintendent G. L. Henderson (1827–1905). Ostensibly, the lease was granted to offer lower-cost lodging, and certainly Henderson believed that both the government and YNPIC had done an incompetent job of providing lodging for park visitors. His reason for building the Cottage Hotel, he said, was because "the first lease-holders under the Arthur administration had utterly failed to provide suitable accommodations for visitors and at times none at all."[31]

Whatever the reasons for it, the lease was timely, for in June of 1885, G. L. Henderson was losing his government job as assistant park superintendent. Realizing that a brighter future for him lay in ministering to the needs of tourists, he published his *Yellowstone Park Manual and Guide*, a four-page newspaper and guidebook to the park, which included advertisements for what he was calling the "Cottage Hotel, H. L. and W. J. Henderson, Proprietors" as well as for other Mammoth businesses. His family was politically well connected, for G. L. Henderson's brother, David Bremner Henderson, was a US congressman from Iowa who later became Speaker of the US House of Representatives. Obtaining money from his brother, G. L. and family began construction of their Cottage Hotel in August of 1885.

The Henderson family hired carpenters, plasterers, shorers, and painters to help them erect their Cottage Hotel and were able to report by November 7 that the hotel was three stories high and "built of round, peeled logs . . . very finely furnished . . . an imposing as well as unique structure." An afterthought was an addition two and a half stories high and 30 × 85 feet in size, and the family completed the building in December of 1885.[32] They celebrated it by opening for business on Christmas day, an unseasonably warm day. The family's initial five guests registered and then took a nude bath in Bath Lake at an air temperature of seventy-five degrees above zero—amazing in frigid, high-elevation Yellowstone in December! In February, the family welcomed Mammoth area friends with a masquerade ball at the new hotel. In April, they asked the Department of the Interior for price approvals on items they were selling there—coated specimens from Ole Anderson, beer, wine, tobacco, photographic views, horses, wagons, blacksmithing, and hot baths for their customers.[33]

This was the beginning of an enterprise that was to last a little more than three years. G. L. was excited because the new building allowed him to operate his own tour company with his own stable of horses and "fine Quincy" carriages. Cottage Hotel quickly became a center for parties and other social activities at Mammoth. Soldiers from the newly established Camp Sheridan and other Mammoth residents gathered there from 1885 through 1888 for songfests, poetry recitations, dinners, and dancing. In November of 1885, Henderson christened the rising building with "a splendid dance . . . forty couples . . . to welcome hoary old winter." In January of 1886, the Hendersons held a New Year's ball, and at Thanksgiving they held a grand dinner with "feasting and praise."[34] When the Army arrived in Yellowstone, the soldiers brought their musical instruments; at a January 1887 party, Uncle John Yancey was honored by enlisted men who sang and played zither, violin, and wind instruments.

Local adventurer Billy Hofer entertained everyone with tales of his recent skiing expedition, where "hungry wolves gyrated round and round, whose serenading made his sleep profound." G. L. and his clan hosted

Acting Superintendent Moses Harris and family in June of 1887, and the Hendersons held another masquerade ball at the hotel in February of 1888.[35] During these years, Henderson dazzled Mammoth and the park as a tour guide and a newspaper correspondent. He proclaimed loudly that Yellowstone was the world's greatest "Fairyland," declaring that even tourists on their second or third visits thought it a place for a lifetime of study. He called the park "the only field for amusement, recreation and study that can never be exhausted" and gushed that it was "the cosmopolitan Park of parks, wonder of wonders, [and] a world in itself that surpasses the wildest dreams of poet and philosopher."[36]

The year 1888 was successful for the Hendersons and their Cottage Hotel—the last such season. The family hosted 1,162 guests from May to October.[37] One satisfied patron gushed: "I made my home in the Cottage Hotel and found it in every respect a home. I found no better place between Mammoth Hot Springs and Chicago. The meals were better than in any dining room car, and everything was clean, comfortable and attractive."[38]

With all of its successes, G. L. Henderson's hotel could not compete with the railroad-owned Mammoth Hot Springs Hotel, whose employees did everything they could to drive him from business. In the spring of 1889, Henderson sold the Cottage Hotel to his old foes the Yellowstone Park Association and joined them. In return for selling the hotel for $30,000 instead of $40,000, Henderson accepted work from them as a "tourist agent" for $150 per month. In his new job, he was to go to Washington, DC, as a lobbyist for the Yellowstone Park Association (YPA), and when in Yellowstone to work as a park interpreter by giving evening programs, speeches, and walking tours for tourists. Thus, his new job was effectively the first paid interpretive job in any national park.[39]

THE US ARMY TAKES OVER THE PARK AND BUILDS CAMP SHERIDAN AT MAMMOTH

US Army Captain Moses Harris marched from Fort Custer, Montana, into Mammoth on August 17, 1886, with the fifty soldiers of Company M, First US Cavalry, and found the place deserted. Most, if not all, of the assistant superintendents had abandoned their posts, knowing that Congress had cut off park funding, including salaries. Harris assumed command on August 20 and set about the task of making "order out of chaos." He ordered his men to erect what were supposed to be temporary buildings and began issuing "Orders of the Day" as his operational decrees. Harris made a tour of the park and stationed small groups of men at the same locations that assistant superintendents had formerly occupied: Norris, Lower and Upper Basins, Riverside on Madison River, Grand Canyon, and Soda Butte. By mid-September, a visitor could write, "The park is now in the hands of the military and is getting along all the better for it."[40]

Many observers assumed that the US Army's duty in Yellowstone would not last long, but the army ended up staying for thirty-two years. Congress never made permanent by legislation the military's tour of duty in Yellowstone. Instead, army occupation was continued year after year due to Congress not providing the funds necessary for a reversion to civil administration. After years, the military system became entrenched. Historian Hiram Chittenden noted in 1910 that "it is not probable that public opinion will ever sanction a return to the old order. The administrative machinery has completely adjusted itself to the present system . . . and it is not likely to be disturbed."[41]

Disturbed it would be, and only six years later, but in 1886, pursuant to Special Orders Number 79, Harris and his men were establishing Camp Sheridan at Mammoth Hot Springs. They erected five large buildings before the end of December. The first five buildings were a T-shaped barracks, a storehouse or warehouse, a guardhouse, a cavalry stable, and a quartermaster stable.[42] Harris placed these directly in front of Marble, Pulpit, and Jupiter terraces, probably because he perceived that the army's main protection duty at this location was the Mammoth Hot Springs themselves. In 1886, there was no awareness that the very presence of buildings and human activity near natural resources could impair them. Given the rampant vandalism that had already occurred in Yellowstone, Harris was most concerned about guarding the springs and terraces. Although geologist Arnold Hague warned the Department of the Interior that the army's new buildings should not be placed on Hotel Terrace or "on the Hot Spring formation," Captain Harris disregarded that advice, believing that placing his buildings immediately below the terraces was acceptable, probably because he believed that the mere presence of soldiers would be a deterrent to vandalism and other law breaking.[43]

More buildings followed. By August 1887, Harris had added an officers' quarters, a post hospital, and a headquarters office. A flagpole and a "gun," apparently cannon, nearly completed his primitive but adequate post.[44]

Later the army added at least four more buildings, listed as a "commanding officer's stable," an "enlisted men's quarters," a "magazine" for storage of explosives and gunpowder, and an "ice house."[45]

After 1909, the army used all of these Camp Sheridan buildings as the headquarters for the post's pack train until most of them were razed in 1915.[46]

THE US ARMY BUILDS FORT YELLOWSTONE, 1891–1913

Authority for the construction of Fort Yellowstone was dated May 11, 1891, and was "Special Orders No. 45." This construction of a military post forever changed the face of Mammoth village and gave the settlement its distinct cultural identity, which the National Park Service still preserves today as a "cultural landscape." Construction at the "new post," as many soldiers called it, lasted for nearly twenty-two years.[47]

Acting Superintendent George Anderson's workmen built the fort from south to north because, at that time, the road from Gardiner, Montana, entered the Mammoth village at today's most southerly front-row residence—a point just north of today's chapel. The first row of buildings became known as "Officers' Row," and it fronted directly on what became the army's "parade ground." Workmen erected twelve buildings in 1891. These included a guardhouse, a headquarters, two duplex officers' quarters, a commissary, a quartermaster storehouse, a granary, a bakery, a troop barracks, a cavalry stable, and two noncommissioned officers' quarters.[48] The acting superintendent and his men occupied these initial buildings in November of 1891. As historian Aubrey Haines has noted, "For many officers and enlisted men, Fort Yellowstone provided the idyllic moment of a military career."[49] Captain Anderson saw his one-troop (sixty-man) fort completed in 1894 with the addition of more buildings, including a ten-bed hospital, a hay shed, and a hospital steward's (sergeant's) quarters (figure 3.4).

Water was supplied to the post from a point above McCartney's Hotel on Clematis Creek, and in 1899 the army built a covered hundred thousand–gallon reservoir there. A small sewerage system served the troop barracks, but many of the other buildings had "earth closets" (outhouses) behind them. In 1895, Anderson's men built nearly a mile of boardwalk in front of the buildings and elsewhere in Mammoth.[50]

In 1897, Superintendent Anderson's pleas for more money were heeded, and the army sent Major J. W. Pope from Bismarck, North Dakota, to oversee

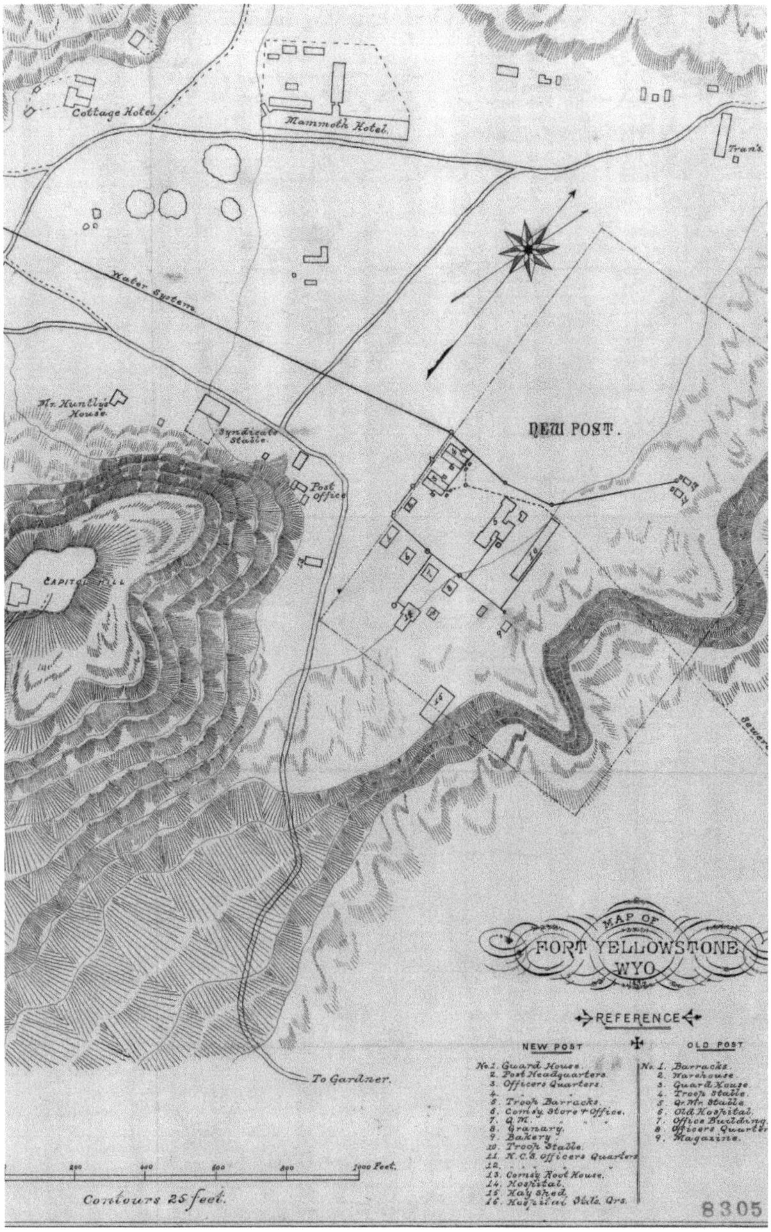

FIGURE 3.4. Fort Yellowstone, 1894. The 1894 Hade map shows what had been built at Fort Yellowstone by that year. Building 16 was the hospital sergeant's quarters before its number was changed, while building 14 was the hospital and building 15 a hay shed. The water and sewer systems to the fort are also shown here. Source: James Hade (Troop D, Sixth Cavalry), "Map of Fort Yellowstone, Wyo.," 1894, YELL 145676-M525, Yellowstone National Park Archives Maps collection (courtesy of National Park Service, Yellowstone National Park; hereafter NPS-YNP).

FIGURE 3.5. Fort Yellowstone, ca. 1910. This view shows structures built by the US Army after its arrival in the park during the 1880s. These include the row of officer's quarters (residences) on the far right and the large cavalry barracks (far left). Many of these buildings remain today. Source: Yellowstone National Park Museum, YELL 43552 (courtesy of NPS-YNP). (Original in color.)

construction of more buildings in order to boost the size of the fort to two troops.[51] The army built two more duplex officers' quarters, a second troop barracks, a second cavalry stable, and two more noncommissioned officers quarters on "Soapsuds Row." By 1904, the army added a quartermaster shop and plumbing shop, a large hay shed, a hospital annex, and a morgue. During the next nine years (1905–13), the army added numerous buildings. It was the stonework completed in 1909 that really gave the fort its present (characteristic) appearance. This work was performed by Scottish stonemasons using sandstone quarried from the bottom of the hillside between the Gardner River and the present Mammoth Campground.

Costs of the fort were recorded. The permanent buildings of the post came to about $552,000 with an additional $75,000 for utilities. Adding $75,000 for improvement of the parade ground, sidewalks, roads, and street lighting, and the grand total invested on Fort Yellowstone by the Department of War was about $700,000.[52]

After much arguing among Army officers between 1905 and 1909, Fort Yellowstone's official boundaries were finally established in that latter year. The fort's land was composed of 43.38 acres that included today's Pagoda and the rest of Hiram Chittenden's US Engineers' buildings but which did not include the post cemetery or the four military buildings (gone today) south of Capitol Hill. The Fort Yellowstone National Historic Landmark District was officially designated on July 31, 2003, and today consists of "over forty contributing resources."[53] These buildings remain today at Mammoth, used by the National Park Service for housing and offices and preserved by that agency as cultural landscape.

MAMMOTH EVOLVES AS A CENTER OF STAGECOACH TOURISM, 1894–1916

During the period 1894–1916, concessionaires and the government added many buildings to the Mammoth village (figures 3.4 and 3.5). As mentioned, Fort Yellowstone was expanded and completed to more than fifty structures: outbuildings including dormitories and storehouses were erected behind and near the Mammoth Hotel; individual concessioners built residences in numerous locations. Road engineer Hiram Chittenden revamped the park's water and irrigation system, planted the army parade ground into grass, and erected his own complex of buildings, including today's "Pagoda." Stagecoach tourism—spearheaded by four transportation companies and dozens of independents with their hundreds of gaily bedecked horses—evolved into a smoothly functioning adventure that guided thousands of visitors through Yellowstone and converted Mammoth from a frontier hardscrabble of log cabins into a picturesque, pastoral village that provided comfort in the midst of a wilderness, offered idyllic pleasure to the masses, and served as an inspirational and even patriotic park headquarters.

Built during this period were the following structures that are still standing today at Mammoth: the US Commissioner's stone house (1894); Jennie Henderson Ash's General Store and Post Office (1895); the mail carrier's cabin, known as "Love in the Rough" (1895); the Hiram Chittenden House (1902); the "Pagoda" office building (1903); the Huntley Child cottage (1903); the Harry Child Executive House (1908); and Juniper Dormitory (1913). Built during this period were the following structures that are no longer standing today: Ole Anderson's "Specimen House" (1896); the Monida and Yellowstone Stage Company complex (1898); a new Mammoth water supply, power plant, reservoir, irrigation fountain, aqueduct, and US Engineers' complex (1901–02); numerous other US Engineers' buildings (1902–16); the "Buffalo

House" at Mammoth Buffalo Corral (1902); Mammoth Hotel Commissary (1903); the US Weather Bureau station (1903); the YPT Company fancy headquarters building (1903); numerous other YPT buildings (1904–16); and the post commandant's house (1904 or 1905).

MAMMOTH HOT SPRINGS HOTEL

Because of its size, Mammoth Hot Springs Hotel became the central attraction and focus of the developing Mammoth village, and it retains that influence today (see figure 3.2). While subtleties in its color history have been lost, the general story is that the building went from olive green with a brick-red roof (1883) to (briefly) yellow (1889–90) to terra-cotta (1901) to brown and then light gray (1913) to light green (after 1936) and back to light gray (recent years). The Hotel's changing coloration also subtly influenced many other buildings in the vicinity.

In architecture, the hotel's Queen Anne style during the period between 1883 and 1913 influenced other Mammoth buildings in their styles. These structures included the F. Jay Haynes house, the Cottage Hotel, the Commandant's House, and the Huntley Child House. All of these buildings were a bit formal and gothic, and so they arguably fit with the village's developing—but loose—architectural scheme. However, at times designers went their own way, as the US Engineers' "Pagoda" building, the Hotel Commissary, and the Harry Child Executive House have demonstrated. The Wakefield-Huntley House seems not to have been influenced by the hotel until the teens, when it became the Nichols house and was gradually remodeled in line with the *second* Mammoth Hot Springs Hotel. But even Jack E. Haynes, when he built his salesroom in 1920, seems to have considered the village's gothic architectural touches in his building's design.

With Charles Gibson reorganizing YNPIC into the YPA in 1886, Mammoth Hot Springs Hotel was placed in better corporate hands. The structure—striking in its Queen Anne styling on the outside but poorly designed and drafty inside—was set to serve stagecoach-era visitors for twenty-seven more years. By the 1890s, officials at the Mammoth Hot Springs Hotel had learned how to treat their genteel guests in a manner that befitted that decade's moniker of "gay nineties." The term was a reference to merriment and frivolity, notwithstanding an economic depression and a railroad strike. The first Mammoth Hot Springs Hotel continued to serve stagecoach-era visitors through the summer of 1912. Cosmetically repaired in 1901, it was radically renovated in 1913 following years of fruitless planning for a completely new building.

FIGURE 3.6. Mammoth Hot Springs Hotel, 1913. The newly built wing of (the first) Mammoth Hot Springs Hotel is shown here (far right) in 1913, before the main part of the old hotel was remodeled into what was essentially a completely different building—the second Mammoth Hotel. This anonymous photograph—not present in the park photograph collection or scrapbooks—is a long-sought missing link in Yellowstone history. Source: Photograph 2006.044.1249, Yellowstone Gateway Museum, Livingston, Montana.

Unable to procure the full $300,000 required for renovations at the Hotel, company owner Harry Child trotted out a proposal for a "new wing" and settled on doing a wing for Old Faithful Inn as well. After asking the Department of the Interior for permission, Child was ready by March 1, 1913, to begin remodeling and adding on to the old Mammoth Hot Springs Hotel (figure 3.6).[54]

On February 18, 1913, the Livingston *Daily Enterprise* explained what was to happen:

> The wing will be added on the north end of the present Mammoth hotel. The present hotel is to be entirely rebuilt, and the construction of this wing is the first step toward that end. It will be of frame and besides the 150 [new] rooms will include about 50 bathrooms. It is expected the work of remodeling the present hotel will be finished in time for the season of 1915.[55]

Architect Robert Reamer—now well known because of his Old Faithful Inn—was involved. "You know from the work Mr. Reamer has done," stated company official Billie Nichols, "that he does much better to build as he goes along rather than to draw up a set of specifications and be tied down to them[;] consequently we have followed this procedure in the building of these two hotels."[56] President Child reported to his railroad loan-holders on May 19 that the renovations to Mammoth Hotel "will, of course, put up an entirely different appearance when the old building is removed and the front of this building completed."[57]

It was a "rush job," according to the *Enterprise*, and indeed workmen completed the wing by June 15, which was the official date of the park season's opening (figure 3.7). The wing contained 124 guest rooms, 28 private baths, and 8 public baths. The company repainted the hotel from terra-cotta (brown) to a light gray. Officials opened the park that summer with flags,

FIGURE 3.7. Mammoth Hot Springs Hotel, circa 1917. This photograph shows the (second) Mammoth Hot Springs Hotel around 1917 following the 1913 renovations. Photographer F. J. Haynes. Source: Library of Congress, image 1d08194.

a band, and fireworks. A few weeks later, the company exhibited the new wing with "the most magnificent ball that was ever given in the history of the Mammoth hotel." "It was estimated that between 950 and 1,000 people participated," said the *Enterprise*, "where soldiers and citizens generally joined with officials and employees and their families and gave a fitting finish to an evening that was filled with pleasurable events." With all this hoopla, it seemed strange that Park Superintendent Lloyd Brett hardly mentioned any of it in his annual report.[58]

When the wing was completed, Reamer's and Child's crews began a complete remodeling of the original hotel. Because the upper floors of the building were old and unstable, workmen removed the highest floors, except for a portion immediately west of the turret, and replaced the gable roof with a flat roof. They transformed the turret into bay windows on the second and third floors and added large oval-topped windows to the hotel's front. The new building thus resembled a hospital. Although its lovely Queen Anne styling was gone, it had newness and solidity at a much-reduced cost. These factors would allow it to stand for twenty-four more years.[59] As for the hotel's interior, a visitor who stayed there in 1924 wrote that "although this white, extended building is larger than the old Mammoth hotel, it did not seem [to me] to differ greatly from the hotel I remembered [in 1904]."[60] From this impression, it appears that the 1913 renovations left much of the interior intact.

THE YELLOWSTONE PARK TRANSPORTATION COMPANY

During the stagecoach era in Yellowstone (1878–1916), the primary livery (transportation) operation was the Yellowstone Park Transportation Company (YPT), although there were three others: the Monida and Yellowstone Stage Company, the Wylie Camping Company, and the Shaw and Powell Camping Company. Founded in 1883, the YPT Company was the oldest and largest of the four. Headquartered at Mammoth, it operated stagecoaches through 1916 and converted to buses beginning in 1917, and its descendant company continues today to employ tour guides and to offer bus tours, snow coach tours, and horseback rides in Yellowstone. This company's influence on the Mammoth village was huge because of the size of its complex on the site of present Aspen Dormitory (eventually twenty buildings) and the numbers of its drivers, horses, and vehicles.

TWENTIETH-CENTURY CHANGES SHAPE MAMMOTH, 1917–1929

Three important factors combined during the period 1915–17 to massively change conditions for visitors to Yellowstone—admission of automobiles, establishment of the National Park Service, and the United States' entry into World War I. As a result, Yellowstone and its headquarters at Mammoth Hot Springs experienced great upheaval until the early 1920s.

Congress's establishment of the National Park Service in 1916 changed all of the parks in the fledgling national park system. Although it took two years for the new NPS to complete the reorganization in Yellowstone, this period allowed park administrators to focus on the three original pillars of park management that had been set forth in the 1870s by Superintendent Norris, namely protection (today's Law Enforcement Division), improvement (today's Maintenance Division), and scientific and historical study and education (today's Yellowstone Center for Resources and the Division of Interpretation). A fourth division—Administration—had been small under the early civilian and army superintendents but was always, naturally, present. Historians of park administration during this period have stated that "much of the NPS's work toward improving the park for visitors was guided by the idea that the park was to become an 'all-summer resort.' "[61]

During the period 1916–18, acting superintendent Chester Lindsley found immediate difficulty at Mammoth in managing the park with the US Army still present. While the new NPS was in charge of concessionaires, automobiles, wild animals, water, electric, and telephones, the War Department oversaw all road and trail construction and general protection of the park. Lindsley feuded with the Army chief of engineers over these matters and housing at Mammoth.

Fortunately, the army's remaining time in the park was short. Army officials were "anxious to rid [themselves]" of the duty, and NPS Director Mather was simultaneously pushing to be rid of them. These events occurred at a time when the public was dissatisfied, because it saw troops as taking care of Yellowstone when they were needed to go to war. All of those factors combined to finally remove the army on October 31, 1918, as a result of the Sundry Civil Appropriations Act. Director Stephen Mather then declared the former US Engineer's Office, built by Hiram Chittenden in 1903 and eventually known as the "Pagoda," to be the official headquarters of the National Park Service in Yellowstone.[62]

Horace Marden Albright assumed Yellowstone's superintendency in 1919, and during his ten years, he oversaw massive projects and sweeping accomplishments. Soon after arriving, he stopped commercial fishing and woodcutting in the park, successfully fought proposed dams on Bechler River and Yellowstone Lake, and upgraded concession services. He ushered the park into the automobile age. Although automobiles had been allowed since 1915, park roads and facilities remained unimproved. Albright supervised the building and upgrading of both, and he refined the ranger force to deal with the increase of visitors and their mobility.[63]

Many of the changes Albright implemented occurred at Mammoth. By the mid-twenties, he had organized the new NPS into nine or ten departments, seven of which performed maintenance activities. Landscape engineers and landscape architects from the central NPS office in Washington, DC, began to play important roles in crafting the built landscape at Mammoth and all over the park, as the NPS gradually decided that protecting the park's wonders and educating the public were as important as maintaining its infrastructure. The NPS was also developing the philosophy that the built environment must "harmonize" with the landscape.[64]

During this period, Superintendent Albright and landscape architect Charles Punchard began working to conceal unsightliness and clean up messes in the buildings and structures that were long part of the cultural landscape in Yellowstone. Punchard developed philosophies for the NPS that remain in place today, influenced by "the naturalistic principles of nineteenth-century landscape gardening."[65] He recommended removing old employee dwellings between Liberty Cap and the new Mammoth Lodge, some of which were left over following the 1915 removal of old Camp Sheridan, and he suggested building new quarters near the "Non-com" dwellings and remodeling other fort buildings for housing in order to reduce new NPS construction. He policed and cleared debris at Angel Terrace, removed stumps and branches from the "old geyser craters" on the parade ground, cut dead branches from trees there, and began mowing the grass in front of and around Mammoth Hotel. Punchard and NPS personnel completed many of these initial improvements by 1920.[66]

Color schemes were next. In 1919, Punchard recommended that government log buildings should be painted brown and roofs of the ranger stations should be stained green, thus establishing a color scheme for the NPS that remains in place today. He recommended that sprinkling tanks near forests be painted a light green color and ones in open spaces should be painted a light gray. The newly built gas stations—such as the one at Mammoth erected in 1920—were attractively designed, said Punchard, and they were protected from competition so that garish advertising signs and bright-red gas pumps were not necessary. He wanted buildings at "Mammoth Village" (as he called it—perhaps the earliest use of this term) painted gray like Harry Child's house and Mammoth Hotel, and roofs painted green. Although he liked the idea of painting Fort Yellowstone's roofs green, he recognized potential criticism for changing the color of the historic red-tile roofs.[67]

But apparently Superintendent Horace Albright liked the idea, for in 1921, he oversaw a new color scheme for the fort. The stone buildings were given two coats of white paint and the window sashes were painted black, while the remaining quarters on Officers' Row were painted light gray with light-green roofs and the chimneys painted terra-cotta. This departure from historic colors would not last long.[68] In 1922, the YP Hotel Company repainted the Mammoth Hotel in colors approved by NPS landscape architect

Daniel Hull, apparently light gray.[69] And in 1936, the NPS painted all the Fort's roofs green.[70]

The 1920s also ushered in new ideas to the NPS in the realm of education. Superintendent Albright established the Educational Division, and the concept of park museums began to slowly take shape. In 1919, Albright hired the first park naturalist, Milton Skinner, to oversee this educational work, and in 1921, Albright pressed Fort Yellowstone's Bachelor Officers' Quarters into use as the park's main museum and information office. National writer Emerson Hough gave Albright the idea of adding exhibits to illustrate western history, especially transportation, including stagecoaches, bicycles, horses, and snowshoes (skis) from early park days. Albright hired Isabel Bassett Wasson (1919) as the park's first seasonal park ranger, whose function was to give educational lectures. These were presented in the evenings at Mammoth Hotel and Mammoth Lodge.[71]

After spending several years getting the trailside museums started in the park as a whole, Albright turned to Mammoth again in 1928. Initially he wanted a new building for a museum, but when others argued for a completely new plan for headquarters, Albright decided that he wanted to keep Fort Yellowstone. This was a change of direction for the superintendent, who earlier had wanted to tear down the military buildings. But now he argued in favor of keeping the fort: "The more I think about the proposition, the more I think it is of tremendous interest to the public to have here in the park an old army fort, and that we could do a lot worse than keep the old fort." Albright's support kept the army buildings in place but doomed the chance of getting a new museum building. Instead, the bachelor officer quarters (today's Albright Visitor Center) remained the site of Mammoth Museum, and park photographer Jack E. Haynes continued for some years to serve as its unpaid acting director.[72]

The period 1917–1929 brought additions and changes to the existing built environment at Mammoth Hot Springs.[73] Built during this period were the following structures that are still standing today at Mammoth: Mammoth Campground (1916, 1919, 1937), Mammoth Service Station (1920), Jack Haynes Sales Room (1920), Lodgepole Dormitory (1924), Haynes Warehouse (1927), and Haynes Picture Shop (1928). Built during this period were the following structures that are no longer standing at Mammoth: Mammoth Lodge (1917), Mammoth Horse Corral (probably 1917), Mammoth Swimming Pool (1920), and the Clematis Gulch Nature Trail (1928–32).

MAMMOTH DURING THE DEPRESSION YEARS, 1930–1940

Like the 1920s, the 1930s brought great changes to Mammoth and all of Yellowstone, notwithstanding the fact that a Great Depression was ravaging the nation. With the help of the Civilian Conservation Corps (CCC), the NPS demolished old buildings, obliterated old roads and barrow pits, greatly expanded the park's infrastructure (electricity, heating, sewer and water pipes, telephones, and radio communications), realigned the road into Mammoth from Gardiner, Montana, and added the first new buildings at Mammoth since US Army days.[74]

These changes began in 1929–30, when NPS landscape architect Thomas Vint invited Gilmore D. Clarke, another landscape architect, to spend ten days in Yellowstone developing a general plan for the Mammoth village and Mammoth area. Vint produced an important map of the Mammoth Hot Springs village and an assessment of conditions at Mammoth.[75] He and Clarke then moved on to a "master plan." Completed in 1931 and considered one of the first such large-scale development plans in the national parks, this "master plan" made it clear that Vint and Clarke saw the Mammoth village as "marked by a discordant array of structures and buildings and a system of congested roads, which contradicted the naturalistic principles that the national park designers sought to uphold." They wanted to tear down the Mammoth Hotel and much of Fort Yellowstone and replace them with more general government buildings and "curving streets around an elliptical lawn."[76] As usual, this was the idealism of landscape architects who were assuming they had unlimited money and no problems with obtaining ownership of the structures—and who were exhibiting no consideration for the area's cultural history. Their master plan would be modified in numerous ways over the succeeding few years, but it represented a start for NPS master plans.

When Vint and Clarke revealed their new plan, serious disagreements began. These disagreements—combined with a lack of money—prevented much of the plan from actually happening. Concessionaires complained bitterly about having their buildings and residences destroyed only to leave "unattractive" government buildings. For example, William "Billie" Nichols of the Yellowstone Park Hotel Company fumed that Clarke was unduly influenced by the fact that the government was his client. And he complained that the government's plan would move the hotel to a spot where guests could not see the terraces. Expressing his own opinion, he wrote, "I would more thoroughly enjoy a leisurely view of this beautiful sight from a comfortable chair on the porch of the hotel or lodge than to catch a fleeting glimpse from a motor bus or the back of a horse."[77] In this, Nichols had a point. The NPS seemed to be overlooking Mammoth's (and the park's) long history steeped in nineteenth-century grand hotels. Landscape architects must have seemed to Nichols to have been better with taking care of nature than with taking care of history. But of course, the concepts of cultural landscapes and cultural resources were not yet parts of NPS consciousness.

Nichols also wondered where the money would come from. Who would pay to raze the buildings and erect new ones and do all the landscaping? Unmentioned by NPS planners but undoubtedly on Nichols's mind was the money that the government would owe to all the concessionaires if their buildings were razed, because their buildings were privately owned. Even a legal "taking" through constitutionally sanctioned eminent domain would require "just compensation" to the owners, and that would require a fair amount of money—more than the NPS usually had.[78]

Vint and Clarke produced a 1933 Master Plan, which declared many roads and buildings at Mammoth obtrusive and obsolete and which suggested changing the park's entrance road from the north. But because of ongoing disagreements, a general lack of funds in the Depression, and no preferable alternative route for the north entrance road, much of the plan was never implemented. There also was general agreement that Mammoth as a location should not be bypassed, and this too prevented any bypass road from being constructed. However, by 1937 one of the NPS assistants could report that "the Master Plan for this [Mammoth] area is becoming fairly well tied down with the projects under construction and the proposed immediate construction."[79]

Both the 1931 and the 1933 master plans included the idea of a double boulevard running through the YPT Company area, which was in fact constructed during 1938 and which remains in place today at Mammoth.[80] This double boulevard and the buildings on both sides of it—initially called the "Mammoth Plaza"—is today known as the "Mammoth Esplanade."[81]

Another development that occurred during this period was a plan to increase topsoil around Mammoth headquarters buildings so that lawns could be improved. The first steps toward topsoil occurred in 1901, when geologist Arnold Hague oversaw the bringing of that material from the top of the hill behind the Mammoth Hot Springs Hotel and placing it on the army's Parade Ground. Then, following in the 1902–03 footsteps of Hiram Chittenden, park officials continued this plan in 1934 when "good top soil" was brought in and "placed 6–12 inches deep" over the lawns.[82] So massive was the construction at Mammoth during this decade that landscape architect Frank Mattson was confident enough to state that "this season [1935] will be the heaviest construction season in the history of the Park."[83]

In general, the period of the Great Depression (1930s) in Yellowstone was a time of change—park officials introduced master plans and standardized building designs, camping policies, and educational programs—but it was also a time of continuation and entrenchment. All of these activities were headquartered at Mammoth. The park remained a favorite spot for economically stressed visitors in search of rustic roots—a "refuge in rusticity"—and Mammoth continued as the place with the most buildings and deepest cultural history.[84]

Built during this period were the following structures that are still standing today at Mammoth: the YCC Area (CCC Camp, 1933), the NPS Tudor Apartment House (1935), Mammoth Utility Building/Garage (1935–37), Yellowstone National Park Post Office (1936–37), five elongated storage sheds (1937–39), a sign shop and "bake" shop (pre-1937), the third Mammoth Hot Springs Hotel (1936–38), Spruce Dormitory (1938), YPT Company Mess Hall (1938), and Mammoth Esplanade (double boulevard; 1938).

THE THIRD MAMMOTH HOT SPRINGS HOTEL: COMPLETELY REBUILT IN 1936–1938

The extensive renovations of the National Hotel in 1913, including the addition of its northern wing, extended the building's life for twenty-three years. But by the 1930s, the hotel was again suffering the effects of age. Company officials and the NPS together decided that another renovation—in this case, a completely new hotel except for the 1913 wing—was needed. Indeed, the NPS's evolving master-plan philosophy was soon to change the village of Mammoth dramatically. "The hotel, the largest part built in 1883, is ugly, a firetrap, and past the stage of satisfactory usefulness for the type of patronage it caters to," wrote NPS landscape architect Gilmore D. Clarke in 1930. "It should be replaced by an attractive, architecturally suitable, and appropriate fireproof structure."[85] In any event, the Great Depression closed the

Mammoth Hotel in 1933, 1934, and 1935.[86] By 1935, the NPS had progressed in the formation of its master plan for the Mammoth area, such that Frank Mattson could write, "The proposed plan contemplates cutting the existing hotel building in two, leaving the dining room as a one-story building on the west end . . . [and the] large east wing will remain at full height."[87]

In 1936, the NPS announced that renovations to the Mammoth Hotel would soon begin (figure 3.8). The announcement was coincident with the merging of several concessionaires into one company, newly named the "Yellowstone Park Company."[88] The company engaged its old architect, Robert Reamer, to do plans for the new building in what became known as the Colonial Revival and Art Moderne styles. Reamer proposed adding new cottages because he did not like the cabins at Mammoth Lodge (one mile to the south) and did not want them simply moved to the new location.[89]

Officials closed the Mammoth Hotel in August of 1936, and demolition of the entire building except for its 1913 wing began at that time (figure 3.9).[90] By September 2, the west half of the old building had been demolished, and by early November, workmen were erecting the present dining room as a separate building.[91] Builders placed the dining room on the far west end of the previous hotel's original location so that it stood on nearly, if not exactly, the same site as the west end of the original (1883) hotel. They placed the new, third Mammoth Hotel on the east side of the previous hotel's original location. And they left a paved street between the two sections of new hotel. All of these changes remain in place today in the present hotel, which architects refer to as designed in the "classical modern" style.[92]

Construction of the third (today's) Mammoth Hotel continued in 1937, and of course the hotel was not completely open to visitors.[93] By June 30, superintendent Edmund Rogers reported that the dining room was completed and the new lobby and lounge rooms (essentially today's main hotel building) were 90 percent completed. The new cabins—soon to be called "cottages"—behind the hotel's boiler room on the site of a previous swamp and of some government coach sheds—were 95 percent completed.[94] The NPS decided that the general color of this new hotel was to be light gray.[95]

In late 1937 and through June 1938, workmen completed the exterior project by adding the present Mammoth Recreation Hall. "In connection with the Mammoth Hotel," wrote the superintendent, "the Company built and completed the recreational building with dance hall, barber shop, beauty shop, cocktail lounge and curio shop, including plumbing, heating and

FIGURE 3.8. Mammoth Hot Springs Hotel, 1936. This anonymous photograph shows the second Mammoth Hot Springs Hotel on August 5, 1936, just prior to the beginning of its demolition. Source: *Monthly Report of Superintendent*, August 1936, Yellowstone National Park Archives (courtesy of NPS-YNP).

FIGURE 3.9. Mammoth Hotel area, 1936. This anonymous panoramic photograph was taken on September 2, 1936, after demolition of the second Mammoth Hotel had begun but before construction of the (present) dining room had begun. Debris from the hotel's demolition can be seen stacked in at least three places. The elongated wagon shed and main barn of the US Engineers are both partly demolished (rear left). The ramshackle dwelling with smoking chimney (center) would soon be demolished. At the smokestack is the hotel's boiler room, and behind it is the low roof of the Hotel Commissary. A second large YP Company dwelling can be seen just to the left of the smokestack, while at the rear of the photograph are the hotel's 1913 wing and the old US Engineers' buildings. In the foreground (bottom right) are Lodgepole Dormitory (right, closest) and Juniper Dormitory (left). Jack Haynes's complex of five buildings is at bottom left. Source: *Monthly Report of Superintendent*, August 1936, Yellowstone National Park Archives (courtesy of NPS-YNP).

wiring, and purchase of all material for same."[96] This latter, separate building located immediately west of the new hotel, was added—as a northern extension—onto the existing boiler room and existing structure that is today's Xanterra Accounting Office.

Work continued all during the summer of 1938, so that the superintendent could report:

> The Mammoth beautification project was completed during the summer of 1938 and resulted in a much improved appearance at park headquarters. The construction of 100 new cabins in the rear of the Mammoth Hotel added a new type of accommodation with running water and baths and should aid in again popularizing the Mammoth region.[97]

Still more work occurred in 1939, involving the interior of the new hotel, the new cabins, and additions to the new Recreation Hall.[98]

Today's Mammoth Hot Springs Hotel is the third hotel on this site, and it represents the most important building in the present Mammoth Hot Springs Historic District. According to the hotel's National Register Registration Form, this district has statewide (Wyoming) significance "as the administrative and concession headquarters of the largest national park in Wyoming. The district is significant under Criterion A for its historical association with the early history of the National Park Service, the development of Yellowstone National Park, and more specifically, with the development of administrative and concession policies in Yellowstone and the national park system." The district is also significant under Criterion C for its architecture. "Buildings erected after the military era in the administrative era of the district are significant for their representation of the work of architects of the National Park Service, and the landscape of the district reflects the influence of the agency's master plans and the efforts of its landscape architects" (figure 3.10).[99]

THE "MAMMOTH PLAZA" TODAY CALLED THE "ESPLANADE" (1938)

The headaches of southbound stagecoaches and automobiles having to circumvent the difficult hill on which Mammoth village was located—by traveling around it to the south and ascending it through the present lower Mammoth housing area, a less steep but decidedly longer route—finally resulted in the NPS's constructing the short, steep stretch of road in 1938 between today's campground and upper Mammoth village. Automobiles could easily negotiate that steepness, where the former stagecoaches could not. This double boulevard with the buildings along it in the Mammoth village is known today as the Mammoth Esplanade.[100] This short stretch of new road running past Cedar Terraces was opened to traffic on August 4, 1938.[101]

FIGURE 3.10. Mammoth Village, 1948. Mammoth Village is shown here in 1948 from near Minerva Terrace. A couple of the old US Engineers' buildings are still present just below the "old Gardiner road," and so are two of the elongated YPT coach sheds (rear center). Cottonwood trees on Officers' Row are well developed. Photograph by Jack E. Haynes. Source: MHS, Haynes Collection, H-48030 (courtesy of Montana Historical Society).

WORLD WAR II, MISSION 66, AND KEEPING THINGS NATURAL, 1942–1982

Historians Kiki Rydell and Marcy Culpin have summarized the history of Yellowstone National Park during World War II as follows:

> The war years were difficult ones for the nation and the park. Attendance figures plummeted from 581,761 visitors in 1941 to 64,144 in 1943, leading to a curtailment of services provided by both concessioners and the National Park Service (NPS). The number of NPS employees also dropped, as many rangers entered military service and recruitment of seasonal employees became all but impossible. Furthermore, Yellowstone's infrastructure suffered as the federal government diverted attention and money away from park maintenance and construction to the war effort. There were also threats to national park resources, as military officials sought ways to acquire timber, minerals, and rangeland to fuel the war machine. When attendance figures rebounded more quickly than anyone expected after the war, Yellowstone was poorly equipped to serve those visitors.[102]

Visitors who arrived in the park during the 1946–48 seasons found facilities inadequate and complained loudly. The park roads and all other facilities looked so deteriorated to many observers that historian Bernard DeVoto wrote the much-touted article "Let's Close the National Parks!" as a plaintive cry for protection of treasured areas such as Yellowstone, which the government and many Americans seemed not to want to protect.[103] The NPS's delayed response was to implement a service-wide modernization program known as Mission 66, a ten-year effort (1956–66) to bring buildings, structures, and services up-to-date in time for the seventy-fifth anniversary of the agency's founding. Most historians have not treated Mission 66 kindly, but it was arguably the best that could be accomplished at this time with the available money.[104] At the same time, the NPS continued what it had done in the 1920s and 1930s, razing old, undesirable structures and altering roads and infrastructure. The upshot of new buildings and new infrastructure was to create a new set of cultural items that needed to be protected, when these items had only been built to give the public a way to see the park's natural features. As Paul Schullery has noted, these features added "yet another significant, costly, and complicated element" to the missions of national parks, causing them to "become in effect museums for really big objects" such as visitor centers, bridges, and other less-than-beautiful structures.[105]

As usual, some of the 1950s proposals succeeded and others failed. Proposed alterations for Mammoth at this time included moving park headquarters to the North Entrance at Gardiner or moving the main offices to Lake. Neither plan came to fruition when both Superintendent Rogers and Director Conrad Wirth opposed the ideas.[106] But a walkways idea proved a good one. In 1946, the park's modern system of boardwalks in thermal areas began, when Superintendent Edmund Rogers accepted recommendations to utilize an idea called "duck walks." These portable, wooden sections of boardwalk preserved thermal areas from erosion caused by foot traffic (by stopping "aimless wandering about the thermal areas") and they could be moved when hot springs changed their activity or discharge. The boardwalks also encouraged visitors to remain on the trails for safety. Much superior to the 1930s-era blacktopped trails for both mobility and environmental protection, these new boardwalks were installed in the Mammoth Hot Springs and other park areas during the 1950s.[107]

With the Leopold Report's recommendations in 1963 for preserving "vignettes of primitive America" where "the maintenance of naturalness shall prevail," the park's management philosophy began to move slowly into the modern era. This change progressed from grudging acceptance of keeping things more natural, in the 1960s, to full acceptance, in the 1970s, under the new guiding principles of "ecological process management." The new philosophy would prove particularly challenging at Mammoth Hot Springs, where both natural resources and cultural resources existed together in close proximity and where it was not an easy matter to simply move the facilities away from the natural features.[108]

The National Historic Preservation Act, passed by Congress in 1966, moved the NPS into legislatively protecting historic buildings. But that was too late to save many old park buildings such as the Cottage Hotel, a vintage dormitory, the Yancey Hotel and Mail Station, and the US Weather Bureau office. Notwithstanding NPS recommendations to (again) tear down Fort Yellowstone, the buildings were once more saved through the intervention of ex-superintendent Horace Albright, then sixty-three years old, who still believed in keeping the old fort.[109]

During this period, the "Lower Mammoth" employee housing area was begun (1937–49) and then expanded (1958–60); the Mammoth School (1963), Mammoth Clinic (1965), and Aspen Dormitory (1978) were built; and numerous older structures were razed. The aging "Arnold Hague tree" located in the meadow north of the chapel was removed in 1950.[110] With the new keep-it-natural philosophy came the installation of "bear proof" garbage cans (1968–69) and the closure of open-pit garbage dumps (1968–70), where bears had fed for more than eighty years. Two "badly needed" parking areas at the base of the terraces (at Liberty Cap and Jupiter Terrace) were built in the summer of 1951, and radio repeaters were installed on mountaintops in 1957.[111] More work on parking areas at Mammoth occurred in 1965–66.[112]

Other substantive changes at Mammoth—many of them relevant to the entire park—that occurred during this period included the following: Mountain States Telephone taking over the park telephone system in 1958; the Montana Power Company becoming a park concessionaire on September 9, 1958;[113] NPS generation of electric power ceasing completely in 1966; a new fire policy allowing lightning fires to burn in 1972; a Central Communications Center in 1972; the AM radio interpretive system in 1972; over fifty trees and shrubs planted in the village in 1974; Youth Conservation Corps established in 1976; Golden Gate Bridge closed for repairs in 1976–77; discontinuation of Mammoth Incinerator in favor of land-filling garbage in

1977; Young Adult Conservation Corps founded in 1977; YP Company's contract terminated on October 31, 1979, all its assets purchased by NPS, and that concessionaire replaced by T.W.A. Services, Inc.; Mammoth Museum renamed Albright Visitor Center and formally dedicated in 1979; park-wide microwave radio system planned in 1979; park-wide microwave system for telephones in place 1981; Mammoth Hot Springs Hotel newly remodeled in 1982; and the park's first computer specialist, hired in 1982 for the NPS department, then known as "Administrative Data Processing."[114]

THE RESTORATION ERA, SINCE 1983

With Yellowstone National Park firmly on the road during the 1980s to accepting the management philosophy of ecological process management, the park moved into what Yellowstone Center for Resources Director Tom Olliff called the "Restoration Era." This was and is an era of restoring extinct (or near-extinct) native species to Yellowstone. Peregrine falcons were restored in 1985 and wolves in 1995.[115] Lynx, wolverine, and mountain lion are all being studied, but the skunk may not get its chance for restoration. Others such as raccoons and fishers have not yet been discussed or studied. Eradication and control of exotic plants began in the 1980s and continues today. No vascular plants are yet planned for restoration, nor have we reached the point of restoring amphibians, but those restorations could conceivably occur. The policy for natural fires was seriously tested by the "Fires of 1988" and reaffirmed during the 1990s.[116]

Park Superintendent Bob Barbee made the following arguably timeless statement about the park and its visitors when he arrived in 1982. It applies to Mammoth Hot Springs as well as to the rest of the park, and it remains relevant today:

> Yellowstone is a large, endangered, heavily[ ]visited natural system with worldwide significance and notoriety. In addition, it is a park encumbered by the inertia of tradition. While visitation continues throughout the year, most people visit the park from mid-May through mid-September. Visitor use is concentrated in several relatively small developed areas, or along narrow access corridors. Most visitors arrive with only superficial knowledge of the area, and with a mixture of anticipation and apprehension. Many of them have little free time and are intent on "seeing" Yellowstone in just a few hours enroute to another

> destination on a crowded itinerary. They often have common misconceptions about the nature of the Yellowstone system. It is a very different kind of country—at once spectacular, subtle, complex, and incompletely understood.[117]

Since 1980, Mammoth's cultural landscape has continued to evolve, reflecting the fluid character of visitors' needs and preferences as well as the changing priorities of the National Park Service.[118] In 1984, thirty-three NPS buildings at Mammoth were repainted in the historic colors of Fort Yellowstone, and other historic buildings in the village were rehabbed, repaired, and repainted later that decade. Year-round medical services (1987) were offered, the new Mammoth Garage added fueling stations (1995), and the new Yellowstone Justice Center was also completed (2007). Nearby trails, public restrooms, and parking lots were constructed along with the new North Entrance Station (1995). To serve the changing needs within the NPS, the park's Geographical Information Systems department was created at Mammoth in 1991, fire facilities and maintenance garages were enlarged, and a new duplex housing unit was built. Since 2019, a multimillion-dollar renovation at Mammoth Hotel has offered premium lodging services for the Park's growing visitor numbers, which consistently exceed 4 million per year. In addition, several dozen new modular homes for employees at Mammoth were completed in the early 2020s. The latest major alteration to the Mammoth landscape came in June 2022 when floods destroyed the old approach road to the area along the Gardner River and a new temporary route was built from the north, following an old stage road from Gardiner. This new approach road connected the North Entrance Station with the east end of the Esplanade. Time will tell whether this route into Mammoth will be improved further or whether it will be replaced by an entirely new alignment into this portion of the park.

With the completion of the Mammoth Esplanade in 1938 (figure 3.11), Mammoth Village reached its highest point of development and, arguably, the most that was needed to function as headquarters for Yellowstone National Park. Since then, buildings and roads have come and gone, but Mammoth Hot Springs remains as an iconic cultural landscape, the site of great natural resources and park headquarters for one of the world's greatest parks.

FIGURE 3.11. Mammoth Village Esplanade, 2022. The east end of Mammoth remains dominated by the Esplanade's grassy median. This view looks west and includes the Mammoth post office (left), a portion of the Mammoth Hotel (distant center right) and the Yellowstone Justice Center (far right). Photograph by William K. Wyckoff. (Original in color.)

NOTES

1. John Gibbon, "Rambles in the Rocky Mountains. I.," *American Catholic Quarterly Review*, April 1876, 320.
2. Lee H. Whittlesey, *Yellowstone Place Names* (Gardiner, MT: Wonderland Publishing Company, revised 2006), 265; and Whittlesey, "Yellowstone: From Last Place Discovered to International Fame," *Site Lines* (University of Virginia, Foundation for Landscape Studies) 5 (Fall, 2009): 8–10, available at www.foundationforlandscapestudies.org/pdf/sitelines_fall09.pdf.
3. All uncited paragraphs here are cited thoroughly in the author's much longer manuscript "'This Modern Saratoga of the Wilderness!': A History of Mammoth Hot Springs and the Mammoth Village in Yellowstone National Park," National Park Service internal draft (473 pages), July 2010.
4. H. O'Donovan, "Wonder Land," Bozeman *Avant Courier*, October 1, 1875, 1.

5. P. H. Cronin, "The Northern Wonderland," *Literary Life*, no. 3 (June 1885): 141.
6. Aubrey L. Haines, *The Yellowstone Story*, vol. 1 (Yellowstone National Park: Yellowstone Library and Museum Association, 1977), 212.
7. Statement from Aubrey L. Haines to Lee Whittlesey during personal tour of park, 1994, handwritten notes in author's blue notebook, and it is confirmed in Haines, "Research Notes," copy in Park Historian's office, 26.
8. Richard A. Bartlett, *Yellowstone A Wilderness Besieged* (Tucson: University of Arizona Press, 1985), 119; McGuirk, Archive Document 2702; McGuirk in US House of Representatives, "Report: [To accompany H.R. 6260]," 54th Cong., 1st Session, H.R. No. 1846, SN-3464 (May 15, 1896), 13; Aubrey L. Haines, "McGuirk's Medicinal Springs," *Yellowstone Nature Notes* 21, no. 2 (1947): 22–23; P. W. Norris, *Annual Report* . . . 1879, 4, made reference to Boiling River as "just below the surrendered McGuirk block and bathhouses upon the main Gardiner [River]."
9. Norris's annual reports, 1877–82, are the best sources of information on what he did as superintendent; but see also Lee H. Whittlesey, *Storytelling in Yellowstone: Horse and Buggy Tour Guides* (Albuquerque: University of New Mexico Press, 2007), 107–18; John S. Gray, "Trials of a Trailblazer," *Montana: The Magazine of Western History*, no. 22 (Summer 1972): 54–63; and Bartlett, *Yellowstone*, 217–29.
10. For Conger, Carpenter, and Wear, see Bartlett, *Yellowstone*, 233–51; Haines, *Yellowstone Story*, vol. 1, 261–326 passim; and Whittlesey, "This Modern Saratoga," 66–72, 147–53.
11. For YNPIC, see Haines, *Yellowstone Story*, vol. 2, 31–54; Richard A. Bartlett, "The Concessionaires of Yellowstone National Park: Genesis of a Policy," *Pacific Northwest Quarterly*, no. 74 (January 1983): 2–10; and Lee Whittlesey, "'Oh, Mammoth Structure!': Rufus Hatch, the National Hotel, and the Grand Opening of Yellowstone in 1883," *Annals of Wyoming* 83, no. 2 (2011): 2–21.
12. Whittlesey, "Oh, Mammoth Structure," 2.
13. A reputable study is Matthew Josephson, *The Robber Barons: The Great American Capitalists, 1861–1901* (New York: Harcourt, Brace, and Company, 1962).
14. Haines, *Yellowstone Story*, vol. 1, 264. The application letter is Carroll Hobart and Henry F. Douglas to H. M. Teller (July 28, 1882), in NA, RG 48, Microfilm No. 62, roll 1, YNP Library.
15. Bartlett, *Yellowstone*, 126; Conger to M. L. Joslyn (September 20, 1882), in NA, RG 48, No. 62, roll 1, YNP Library. See also a copy of this letter as Archive Document 96, YNP Archives. YNPIC's original lease along with Patrick Conger's original letter objecting to their proposal are both in "C. T. Hobart, Yell. Park Improv. Co.," box C-17, YNP Archives.
16. John Schuyler Crosby, "The Rufus Hatch Scheme," Helena *Daily Independent* (January 25, 1883). Crosby's letter is commented on in "The Yellowstone Park Lease," *New York Times*, February 8, 1883, 3; and in "The Yellowstone Park," *New York Tribune*, January 21, 1883, 6. See also Rufus Hatch, "Mr. Hatch and the Yellowstone Park," *New York Times*, January 4, 1883, 2; "Mr. Vest's Victory," *Forest and Stream*, March 8, 1883, 101; other articles in the issues of March 1, 13, and 22, 1883; Bartlett, *Yellowstone*, 126; and N. P. Langford to G. G. Vest (January 15, 1883; copied to H.M. Teller), calling the Hatch arrangement a "monopoly," in NA, RG 48, No. 62, roll 2, YNP Library.
17. Bozeman *Avant Courier*, March 22, 1883. The Northern Pacific Railroad's connection to YNPIC was as follows. For the first four years, the only connection was Carroll Hobart's

previous employment by the NPRR. But in 1887, the NPRR purchased 250 shares of YNPIC, and later that year, YNPIC gave the railroad stock in return for canceling outstanding bills. By 1891, the NPRR owned 3,088 shares of the park company, and by 1898, the railroad owned 5,213 shares—complete ownership of the Yellowstone company. In 1901, the NPRR sold all but a pittance of its stock to Huntley, Bach, and Child, thus essentially ending its formal ownership. However, because the railroad (later several railroads) continued to hold Harry Child's loans, there remained for many years a loose connection of railroads to the several park companies that would not completely end until 1955. But the initial deal by Rufus Hatch and Carroll Hobart was financially independent of the NPRR. In the Yellowstone Park Association papers at Minnesota Historical Society, there are numerous summaries of company history, which NPRR officials constantly updated through the years. For example, see J. H. P., "Memorandum Re Yellowstone Park Hotel Company and Yellowstone Park Transportation Company," September 12, 1918, in President's Subject File 209B, folder 9, YPA papers, Minnesota Historical Society, St. Paul. See also Bartlett, *Yellowstone*, 171–75, 189; and Haines, *Yellowstone Story*, vol. 2, 371.

18. Haines, *Yellowstone Story*, vol. 1, 272–73. The hotel was called the "National Hotel" for its first two summers but was simultaneously called "Mammoth Hot Springs Hotel" by 1883.
19. Hatch to Teller, December 1, 1883, in H. M. Teller, "Letter from the Secretary of the Interior," 48th Cong., 1st Session, Sen. Ex. Doc. No. 47, SN-2162, January 10, 1884.
20. R. Hatch to C. T. H, May 29 [1883], in Hobart papers, box 2, folder 3, Beinecke Library; "Local Layout," *Livingston Enterprise*, June 30, 1883, 3; "Montana," *Winona Daily Republican*, July 18, 1883, 2.
21. "The Northern Pacific. Its Profile, Trade, Scenery and Progress—The New Town of Livingston," *Winona Daily Republican*, January 13, 1883, 1.
22. "Extensive Preparations," *Winona Daily Republican*, July 2, 1883, 2.
23. Haines, *Yellowstone Story*, vol. 1, 290, says completion of the Park Branch was on September 3, but that was merely an official word. The last iron was laid on August 30, and the first regular train to Cinnabar left Livingston early on the morning of September 1. See the following: "The Presidential Party—Their Arrival in Livingston," *Livingston Enterprise*, September 3, 1883, 1; "Local Layout," *Livingston Enterprise*, September 3, 1883, 3; "Finale of Construction on the National Park Branch," *Livingston Enterprise*, September 3, 1883, 3; "The First Train on the Park Branch," *Livingston Enterprise*, September 4, 1883, 1; and the editorial "The National Park Branch," *Livingston Enterprise*, September 3, 1883, 2.
24. Hatch's quote is from "Cynic and Mocker—Some of the Peculiarities of 'Uncle Rufus Hatch,'" *Evening Gazette* (Cedar Rapids, Iowa), August 25, 1884, 7. This same quote later appeared in the *Livingston Enterprise*, September 5, 1885, using the figure $460,000, so by then, Hatch was either exaggerating his losses or else he had discovered that he lost $10,000 more than he originally thought. See also Haines, *Yellowstone Story*, vol. 1, 287 and 289; and "Uncle Rufus's Recent Pilgrimage," *Livingston Enterprise*, November 22, 1883, 4. The *Livingston Enterprise* for December 29, 1883, has the Villard misfortunes.
25. Edwin J. Stanley, *Rambles in Wonderland, or Up the Yellowstone, and Among the Geysers and Other Curiosities of the National Park* (New York: D. Appleton and Company, 1878), 60.
26. See generally Freeman Tilden, *Following the Frontier with F. Jay Haynes* (New York: Alfred A. Knopf, 1964).

27. Hand-drawn map, "Yellowstone National Park at Mammoth Hot Springs," no date [1884], in RG 48, roll 3, no. 62, folder 2 of 4, YNP Archives. There are actually two different hand-drawn maps in this folder, only one of which is titled, but both show F. Jay Haynes's new studio and house—begun in late 1884—as labeled "Building in Course of Erection at a cost of $3,000." Haynes's leases are in archive documents #5665–5666, YNP Archives. See also Moses Harris to Interior (May 25, 1888) in Letters Sent, vol. II, 250–251, YNP Archives.
28. These plans are in Item 45, file "54. Buildings and Building Sites, Haynes . . . ," YNP Archives.
29. Photo YELL 36643, reproduced in Lee Whittlesey, *A Yellowstone Album: A Photographic Celebration of the First National Park* (Boulder, CO: Roberts Rinehart, 1997), 43, shows such luminaries on the front porch as George Wakefield, E. C. Waters, and Haynes himself. *Gardiner Wonderland* (October 16, 1902) says that Haynes's house has been moved. See also archive documents 5132 (September 22, 1902); and 5221 (October 2, 1902), YNP Archives.
30. Jack E. Haynes, *Haynes Guide* (1939), 43; Chester A. Lindsley, "The Chronology of Yellowstone," bound typescript, YNP Library, 187; and Newell Joyner in National Park Service, *Ranger Naturalists' Manual* (Mammoth, WY: NPS mimeographed, 1929), 144, all state that the building was razed in 1928.
31. G. L. Henderson, "The Park Hotels," no date, probably 1889, in Ash Scrapbook, YNP Library.
32. The Hendersons recorded the names of laborers and construction costs in Bound Volume 141, YNP Archives. The *Livingston Enterprise* followed the hotel's construction in its September 26, October 10, November 7, November 21, and December 26, 1885, issues. Supplies were listed in Ledger 6290, George Ash Collection, YNP Library, 127–39.
33. Whittlesey, *Storytelling in Yellowstone*, 144–46; G. L. Henderson, "Yellowstone Park—The Great Winter Sanitarium," *Livingston Enterprise*, January 29, 1886, 4; H[enderson], "Masquerade Ball at Mammoth Springs," *Livingston Enterprise*, February 13, 1886, 3; Helen L. and Walter J. Henderson to L. Q. C. Lamar, April 14, 1885, in RG 48, roll 3, no. 62, folder 2 of 4, YNP Archives.
34. [G. L. Henderson], "From Mammoth Hot Springs," *Livingston Enterprise*, December 5, 1885, 3; H[enderson], "National Park Items," *Livingston Enterprise*, January 9, 1886, 3; G. L. Henderson, "Park Notes," *Livingston Enterprise*, December 4, 1886, 2.
35. G. L. Henderson, "Yellowstone Park Notes," *Livingston Enterprise*, January 1, 1887, 4; X. [G. L. Henderson], "Park Notes," *Livingston Enterprise*, May 28, 1887, 1; X. X. X. [G. L. Henderson], "Park Notes," *Livingston Enterprise*, June 18, 1887, 2; "Local Layout," *Livingston Enterprise*, February 14, 1888, 3.
36. X. [G. L. Henderson], "Park Notes," *Livingston Enterprise*, June 25, 1887, 1.
37. W. J. Henderson to Moses Harris (November 11, 1888), in Archive Document 1014, Yellowstone National Park Archives.
38. W. E. Hodges in G. L. Henderson, *Yellowstone Park Manual and Guide* (Livingston, MT: Livingston Enterprise, 1888), 4. At least one dinner menu from the Cottage Hotel has survived in the George Ash Collection, Yellowstone National Park Library, and it shows that the fare was extended and fancy. A photo of four women (who are probably the Henderson daughters), four men, and E. C. Culver on the porch of Cottage Hotel is in Whittlesey, *Yellowstone Album*, 39.

39. E. C. Waters to G. L. Henderson (hiring him) (May 21, 1889); Treasurer, Yellowstone Park Association (purchase of hotel) to G. L. Henderson (December 18, 1889); G. L. Henderson to C. S. Mellen (price of hotel) (February 20, 1900), all in George Ash Collection, Yellowstone National Park Library; Whittlesey, *Storytelling*, 153–54; and Lee H. Whittlesey, "The First National Park Interpreter: G. L. Henderson in Yellowstone, 1882–1902," *Montana: The Magazine of Western History*, no. 46 (Spring 1996): 26–41.
40. Haines, *Yellowstone Story*, vol. 2, 3–4; "Congress and the National Park," *Forest and Stream*, no. 27 (August 5, 1886): 22; "The National Park Police," *Forest and Stream*, no. 27 (August 12, 1886): 42; Moses Harris, "Report of Capt. Moses Harris . . . ," in Wear, *Report . . . 1886*, 6–7; J. M. T. Partello, "The National Park," *St. Paul* (MN) *Daily Globe*, September 19, 1886, 1. Letters to and from Interior announcing the army takeover are H. L. Muldrow to *Forest and Stream* (August 7, 1886); L. Q. C. Lamar to Secretary of War (August 6, 1886); H. L. Muldrow to D. W. Wear (August 14, 1886); and Moses Harris to H. L. Muldrow (September 1, 1886), all in Marcy Culpin files, Park Historian's Office, Yellowstone National Park.
41. Hiram M. Chittenden, *The Yellowstone National Park* (Cincinnati, OH: Robert Clarke Company, 1910), 115. This quote appeared in the 1910–14 editions of his book.
42. Haines, *Yellowstone Story*, vol. 2, 6; Moses Harris, *Report of the Superintendent of Yellowstone National Park to the Secretary of the Interior, 1887* (Washington, DC: Government Printing Office), 11–12.
43. Arnold Hague to H. L. Muldrow (September 21, 1886); and H. L. Muldrow to Captain Moses Harris (September 30, 1886), both in Marcy Culpin files, Park Historian's Office, Yellowstone National Park.
44. Harris to Secretary of Interior (January 12, 1887), in Letters Sent, vol. I, 71, Yellowstone National Park Archives; George Tutherly, map of Camp Sheridan, 1887–89, accompanying his manuscript "From the Writings of George Thutherly [*sic*]," no date [chronicling 1886–89], Yellowstone National Park Library.
45. Army Records, bound volume 167, Camp Sheridan building 9, near the end of the volume, Yellowstone National Park Archives.
46. Haines, *Yellowstone Story*, vol. 2, 169.
47. Haines, *Yellowstone Story*, vol. 2, 162.
48. Haines, *Yellowstone Story*, vol. 2, 162–63; George S. Anderson, *Annual Report of the Superintendent of Yellowstone National Park to the Secretary of the Interior, 1891* (Washington, DC: Government Printing Office), 5; "Early Pictures, Government Buildings, 1886 to 1912," an illustrated maintenance record, prepared by the Office of Quartermaster, Fort Yellowstone (March 13, 1909), Item 167, Yellowstone National Park Archives.
49. Anderson, *Report of the Acting Superintendent . . . 1892*, 5; Anderson, "Work of the Cavalry in Protecting the Yellowstone National Park," *Journal of the United States Cavalry Association*, no. 10 (March 1897): [3]–10; Haines, *Yellowstone Story*, vol. 2, 162.
50. Haines, *Yellowstone Story*, vol. 2, 162–63; History Card File, "Fort Yellowstone"; David Battle and Irwin Thompson, *Fort Yellowstone Historic Structures Report* (Denver, CO: National Park Service, 1972), 35, 37–38.
51. "To Fort Yellowstone," *Bismarck* (ND) *Daily Tribune*, July 2, 1897, 2.
52. Haines, *Yellowstone Story*, vol. 2, 169.
53. Montana Preservation Alliance, "Yellowstone National Park Cultural Resource Management and National Register Eligibility Recommendations," unpublished manuscript

(Helena, MT: Yellowstone Center for Resources, February 2010), 5; Battle and Thompson, *Fort Yellowstone Historic Structures Report*, 26.

54. Chester Lindsley to L. M. Brett (crew ready to work) (March 1, 1913); Major Brett to Huntley Child (approving work on new wing) (March 5, 1913); Lt. Col. [Brett], Acting Supt, to Secretary of Interior (Interior wants specifications on work) (April 21, 1914); both in Item 59, file "190—Leases and Contracts Yellowstone Park Hotel Company," Yellowstone National Park Archives.
55. "Put Addition on Mammoth," Livingston *Daily Enterprise*, February 18, 1913, 1. See also "Will Build New Yellowstone Park Hotel," *Atlanta* (GA) *Constitution*, April 27, 1913, 40 (copy in President's Subject File 210C, folder 1, Yellowstone Park Association papers, Minnesota Historical Society, St. Paul, Minnesota).
56. W. M. Nichols to L. M Brett (April 18, 1914), in Item 45 ("Buildings and Building Sites"), file "Yellowstone Park Hotel Company," Yellowstone National Park Archives, as quoted in Ruth Quinn, *Weaver of Dreams: The Life and Architecture of Robert C. Reamer* (Bozeman, MT: Leslie and Ruth Quinn, 2004), 94.
57. H. W. Child to "my dear Mr. [Howard] Elliott" (May 19, 1913), in President's Subject File 210C, Yellowstone Park Association papers, Minnesota Historical Society, St. Paul.
58. "Put Addition on Mammoth," Livingston *Daily Enterprise*, February 18, 1913, 1; "Park Season Is Opened with Ceremony," Livingston *Daily Enterprise*, June 19, 1913, 2; and "Yellowstone Park," Livingston *Daily Enterprise*, June 30, 1913, 2; Lloyd M. Brett, *Report of the Acting Superintendent . . . 1913* (Washington, DC: Government Printing Office), 5. See also "Expects 60,000 Tourists at Yellowstone Park," *Galveston* (TX) *Daily News*, October 20, 1913, 6. The exterior color of light gray is in James R. McDonald, "Historic Structures Report, Mammoth Hot Springs Hotel" (Missoula, MT: Historical Research Associates, November 1995), 8.
59. McDonald, "Historic Structures Report, Mammoth . . . ," 8, and photo, 93. See also Brett, *Report of the Acting Superintendent . . . 1914*, 7.
60. [A. B. Smith], "As It Was in the Beginning," unpublished manuscript for article from *Technology Review*, [post-1924], 5, in Yellowstone Park Association papers, President's Subject File 210B, folder 2, Minnesota Historical Society, St. Paul, Minnesota. Photos such as 23310 in the Jack Haynes collection at Montana Historical Society show the hotel's interior after the 1913 renovations.
61. Kiki Leigh Rydell and Mary Shivers Culpin, *Managing the Matchless Wonders: A History of Administrative Development in Yellowstone National Park, 1872–1965* (Mammoth, WY: National Park Service, 2003), 75.
62. Rydell and Culpin, *Managing the Matchless Wonders*, 77, quoting NPS Director's report, 1918, 39–40.
63. See generally Horace M. Albright, *Creating the National Park Service: the Missing Years* (Norman: University of Oklahoma Press, 1999); and Haines, *Yellowstone Story*, vol. 2, 279–318. Albright's annual reports of the superintendent of Yellowstone 1919–29 flesh out what he did. Many items relating to him, including some of his personal papers, are in the Yellowstone National Park Library and Archives.
64. Rydell and Culpin, *Managing the Matchless Wonders*, 78–79.
65. These principles are described in McClelland, *Building the National Parks*, 139.

66. Rydell and Culpin, *Managing the Matchless Wonders*, 80–81. The Punchard recommendations are Punchard to Superintendent, August 28, 1919, in box D-38, folder 1, Yellowstone National Park Archives.
67. Rydell and Culpin, *Managing the Matchless Wonders*, 82 and endnote 50.
68. Rydell and Culpin, *Managing the Matchless Wonders*, 90.
69. Albright to Hull, October 27, 1922, in "File 329, October 27, 1922," box L-56, Yellowstone National Park Archives.
70. "Final ECW Report . . . Summer, 1936," in "Final ECW Report for Yellowstone and Grand Teton National Parks by Gregg, Summer, 1936," box L-56, Yellowstone National Park Archives.
71. Rydell and Culpin, *Managing the Matchless Wonders*, 98–100.
72. Rydell and Culpin, *Managing the Matchless Wonders*, 103–4.
73. Landscape engineering reports, 1919–39, are in box D-38, Yellowstone National Park Archives.
74. These plans pervade the monthly and annual reports of the superintendent during the 1930s. For example, the CCC obliterated the Capitol Hill barrow pit in 1934–35. See the July report in "3 Emergency Conservation Work Reports [by Walter D.] Popham (E. C. W.) July 1934, August 1934, September 1934," box L-56, Yellowstone National Park Archives. NPS proposals (maps) for the Mammoth area in 1932, 1940, 1941, and 1950 can be found on the ETIC website (//etic.nps.gov), and these are NP-YEL-3124, NP-YEL-3277-D, NP-YEL-3124-J, and NP-YEL-3124-M, but much of what they depict was never built. Other important infrastructure materials for this decade are in box D-28, Yellowstone National Park Archives, where folders 4, 6, and 9 have water supply and power development materials.
75. Thomas C. Vint, "Preliminary Report on the Mammoth Hot Springs Plan," in "Folder 3, 1929" and the large map at rear of it in file 329. Vint's previous plans to modify the Mammoth area climaxed in 1928 with his attempts to build a new museum, a plan that could not find funding, although he remained hopeful.
76. McClelland, *Building the National Parks*, 300–301. This map is NP-YEL-3124 (January 11, 1932).
77. Nichols quoted in Rydell and Culpin, *Managing the Matchless Wonders*, 118.
78. Not until 1979–80, when Yellowstone Park Company was ousted from the park, did this company's buildings become owned by the government.
79. Howard W. Baker, Report for "June 5 to 22, 1937," in "Report to Chief Architect by Baker, June, 1937," box L-56, Yellowstone National Park Archives.
80. Rydell and Culpin, *Managing the Matchless Wonders*, 116–19. See also "MHS Area Developments," in the 1933 and 1939 Master Plans, Yellowstone National Park Archives.
81. The name "esplanade," as applied to this double boulevard and the buildings that front on it, should not be confused with the earlier natural feature known as the "Esplanade," which is a hill overlooking the village of Mammoth at the east end of Narrow Gauge Terrace. Whittlesey, *Yellowstone Place Names*, 99. This earlier Esplanade appeared on 1904 maps by geologist Arnold Hague.
82. "Mammoth Lawns" in "Report to Chief Architect . . . March 1–9, 1934," box L-56, Yellowstone National Park Archives.
83. Report of "May 5 to May 25" in "3 Reports to Chief Architect by [Frank] Mattson and [Robert G.] Hall, File No. 329, May 5–25, May 26–June 25, and June 26–July 30, 1935," box L-56, Yellowstone National Park Archives.

84. Rydell and Culpin, *Managing the Matchless Wonders*, 109.
85. Gilmore D. Clarke in "File 329, Report to Accompany Plan of Mammoth Hot Springs Area . . . June, 1930," Box L-56, Yellowstone National Park Archives.
86. These closures were reported in the superintendent's annual reports for those years.
87. Frank Mattson and Robert G. Hall, report for "June 26 to July 30," 1935, in "3 Reports to Chief Architect by Mattson and Hall, File No. 329, May 5–25, May 26–June 25, and June 26–July 30, 1935," box L-56, Yellowstone National Park Archives.
88. Edmund Rogers, "Annual Report for Yellowstone National Park, 1936" (Mammoth, WY: mimeographed), 32.
89. Quinn, *Weaver of Dreams*, 156–58.
90. Photos in Edmund B. Rogers, *Monthly Report of Superintendent*, August 1936; Rogers, "Annual Report . . . 1936," 32; and Rogers, "Annual Report . . . 1937," 41.
91. Photos in Rogers, *Monthly Report of Superintendent* (August and November 1936).
92. James R. McDonald, Architects, "Historic Structures Report: Mammoth Hot Springs Hotel, Yellowstone National Park," unpublished manuscript prepared for T. W. Recreational Services and National Park Service, November 1995, 2, Yellowstone National Park Library. Although NPS landscape architect Howard Baker wanted the fourth floor removed from the hotel's 1913 wing, this was not done. Baker, report for "June 5 to 22, 1937," in "Report to Chief Architect by Baker, June, 1937," box L-56, Yellowstone National Park Archives.
93. Mammoth Hot Springs Hotel did not open in 1933 (Roger Toll, "Annual Report for Yellowstone National Park, 1933," 2), or in 1934 (1933, 3); but in 1935, one wing was open (1935, 2, 22). One wing was also open in 1936 (1936, 32) and again in 1937 (1937, 3).
94. Rogers, "Annual Report . . . 1937," 41.
95. Sanford Hill, report for July, 1937, in "Monthly Narrative Report to Chief Architect by Hill and Gregg . . . June 28–July 30, 1937," box L-56, Yellowstone National Park Archives.
96. Rogers, "Annual Report . . . 1938," 33–34. A summary of the number of cabins completed to that time is in Howard Gregg, report for November 20–December 20, 1937, in "Monthly Narrative Report to the Chief Architect by Gregg, File No. 601, November 20–December 20, 1937," box L-56, Yellowstone National Park Archives.
97. Rogers, "Annual Report . . . 1939," 2.
98. Rogers, "Annual Report . . . 1939," 32.
99. CTA Architects Engineers [Lesley M. Gilmore], "Historic Structure Report, Nichols Residence, Mammoth, Wyoming," unpublished document with inserts and maps, August 5, 2008, Yellowstone National Park Library, 16, quoting from R. Laurie Simmons and Thomas H. Simmons, *Mammoth Hot Springs Historic District National Register Registration Form*, submitted September 28, 2001, and listed March 20, 2002, 48. For more history of the Mammoth Hotel and Mammoth village during the period 1948–61, see Fred T. Burke, "Tales of Yellowstone Park Company," Yellowstone National Park Library.
100. Rogers, "Annual Report . . . 1938," 27; Rogers, "Annual Report . . . 1939," 23.
101. Report of "July 18–August 4, 1938," in "Report to Chief Architect on Inspection Trip to YNP by Baker, file No. 601-15.1, July 18–August 4, 1938," box L-56, Yellowstone National Park Archives; and JEH photo 39025 of weather bureau, post office, and esplanade, Montana Historical Society.

102. Rydell and Culpin, *Managing the Matchless Wonders*, 137. Box H-2, file 101, 1944–51, Yellowstone National Park Archives contains a five-page document giving the park's general situation in 1945–46, including organization of NPS.

103. Bernard DeVoto, quoted and discussed in Paul Schullery, "The Development of Yellowstone: Myths, Realities, and Uneasy Prospects," *Annals of Wyoming* 69, no. 4 (Fall 1997): 21–29.

104. Mission 66 was the brainchild of NPS Director Conrad L. Wirth, and he has written about it in his book *Parks, Politics, and the People* (Norman: University of Oklahoma Press, 1980). See also McClelland, *Building the National Parks*.

105. Schullery, "Development of Yellowstone," *Annals of Wyoming* 69, no. 4 (Fall 1997): 27.

106. Rydell and Culpin, *Managing the Matchless Wonders*, 139.

107. Rogers, "Annual Report . . . 1948," 14–15; Rogers, "Annual Report . . . 1949," 12–13; Rydell and Culpin, *Managing the Matchless Wonders*, 141.

108. Rydell and Culpin, *Managing the Matchless Wonders*, 155–56. Secretary Stewart Udall's order to implement the Leopold Report is discussed in Kathy Mengak, *Reshaping Our National Parks and Their Guardians: The Legacy of George B. Hartzog, Jr.* (Albuquerque: University of New Mexico Press, 2012).

109. Rydell and Culpin, *Managing the Matchless Wonders*, 157–58.

110. Rogers, "Annual Report . . . 1950," 32. Early-days geologist Arnold Hague, who studied Yellowstone hot springs for thirty-two years (1883–1915), often camped under this tree, hence its name.

111. The author's first job in Yellowstone was to help install bear-proof garbage cans at West Thumb in 1969, where old-time maintenance staff were griping loudly about the new policy of keeping things natural. Parking areas and radio repeaters are in Rogers, "Annual Report . . . 1952," 22; and Lemuel Garrison, "Annual Report of Superintendent of Yellowstone National Park, 1957."

112. Robert McLaughlin, "Annual Report of Superintendent of Yellowstone National Park, 1966," 16.

113. Garrison, "Annual Report . . . 1958," 10ff; "1959," 23.

114. Match these events with their documentation simply by finding the year it occurred and using that year of the annual report of the superintendent from the following list. McLaughlin, "Annual Report . . . 1966," 20; Jack Anderson, "Annual Report . . . 1972," 8, 10, 13; Anderson, "Annual Report of Superintendent . . . 1974," 20; John Townsley, "Annual Report of Superintendent . . . 1976," 36; Townsley, "Annual Report . . . 1976," 31; 1977, 36; Townsley, "Annual Report . . . 1977," 35, 41; Townsley, "Annual Report of Superintendent . . . 1979," 4, 7; Townsley, "Annual Report of Superintendent . . . 1981," 79; Townsley, "Annual Report of Superintendent . . . 1982," 6; and Robert Barbee, "Annual Report of Superintendent . . . 1982," 74.

115. Barbee, "Superintendent's Annual Report . . . 1985," 23.

116. For discussions of these complex issues, see the various annual reports of the Yellowstone Center for Resources; the 1999 "State of the Park" report included with the annual report of the superintendent for that year; Paul Schullery, *Searching for Yellowstone: Ecology and Wonder in the Last Wilderness* (Helena: Montana Historical Society Press, 2004); and Paul Schullery and Tom Olliff, "Managing Yellowstone for Ecosystem Resilience in the Age of Human-Forced Climate Change," unpublished report, Yellowstone Center for

Resources, 2010. Literature on the wolf and its reintroduction in Yellowstone is massive, but see especially the works of Douglas W. Smith, Michael K. Phillips, L. David Mech, Norman Bishop, and Edward E. Bangs.

117. Barbee, "Annual Report of Superintendent . . . 1982," 9.
118. To find references on these events, simply use the listed year and relate it to the annual reports of the superintendent, per this list: Barbee, "1984 Annual Report of the Superintendent," 1, 12, 19; Barbee, "Superintendent's Annual Report 1985," 18, 2, 27; Barbee, "1986 Annual Report of the Superintendent," 10, 17, 18; Barbee, "1987 Annual Report of the Superintendent," 2, 4 (see also 1985, 4, and 1986, 5), 18; Barbee, "Superintendent's Annual Report 1988," 15; Barbee, "Annual Report of the Superintendent . . . 1989," 14, 33, 38; Barbee, "Annual Report of the Superintendent . . . 1990," 15, 21, 24; Barbee, "Superintendent's Annual Report 1992," 19, 28; Barbee, "Superintendent's Annual Report . . . 1993," 20, 25, 59, 31; Michael Finley, "Superintendent's Annual Report . . . 1994," 8, 29; Finley, "Superintendent's Annual Report . . . 1995," 7, 20, (50, 60), 24; Finley, "Superintendent's Annual Report . . . 1997," 33; Finley, "Superintendent's Annual Report 1998," 1.

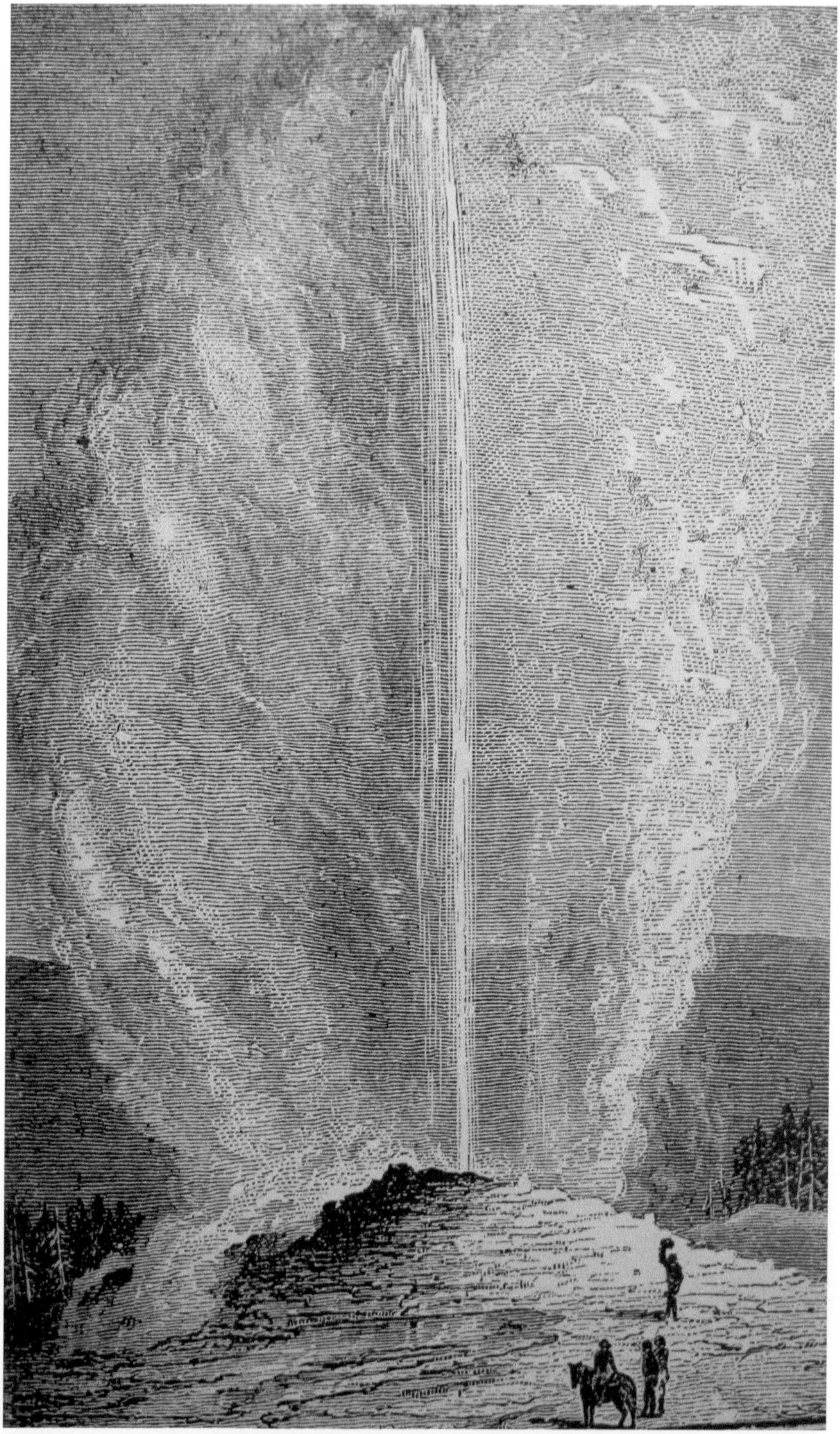

FIGURE 4.1. Old Faithful Geyser, Upper Geyser Basin, 1886. This view of visitors at Old Faithful reveals the casual nature of early tourism within the Upper Geyser Basin. Source: George W. Wingate, *Through the Yellowstone Park on Horseback* (New York: O. Judd Co., 1886), 105.

4

The Upper Geyser Basin

Karl Byrand

VISITORS TO Yellowstone have traditionally been drawn to the Upper Geyser Basin (UGB or Basin) in the vicinity of Old Faithful Geyser (figure 4.1.). As such, the area's many thermal features have become surrounded by hotels, shops, roads, bridges, boardwalks, and more. In turn, these large economic investments and infrastructural improvements help to make the UGB one of the most visited locations within Yellowstone. Of all the cultural signatures within the park, the developed area around Old Faithful contains the most visually evocative set of landscape features, suggesting a great deal about the cumulative forces at work there since the park was established in 1872. In this chapter, I reconstruct when and why these features appeared, explore how they were experienced by park visitors, and ponder how they reflect larger notions about American culture and the national park idea.

Located in the park's southwestern quadrant, the UGB is a forested river valley more than 7,300 feet above sea level. The Firehole River drains the relatively flat basin, flowing from the southeast to the northwest, through the center of the UGB. While offering prime fly-fishing and wildlife-viewing opportunities, the Basin's geothermal features are foremost on the minds of

https://doi.org/10.5876/9781646427697.c004

most visitors. Of the several groups of thermal features peppered throughout Yellowstone National Park, the Basin contains the Earth's greatest concentration of geysers, in an area of about one square mile. Its more than 150 geysers account for 25 percent of the total number of geysers in the world.[1]

The UGB's significance does not depend solely on the number of its geysers but also on their great size and strength. For instance, the intermittent geothermal fountains of Daisy, Giantess, and Beehive all spout to heights well over a hundred feet. The best-known geyser, however, is Old Faithful, which has become so iconic that most park visitors put it at the top of their must-see list.

More than four million people visit Yellowstone each year. This current level of popularity stands in sharp contrast to the time, more than 150 years ago, when reports of Yellowstone's wonders sparked disbelief. Once deemed preposterous, and then considered inaccessible to all but the most adventurous, Old Faithful Geyser and the other geothermal features surrounding it have now become the focal points of an ever-evolving cultural landscape.

From the time when the first crude wagon road reached this fuming setting, the UGB was on its way to becoming an urban island in an ocean of relative wilderness. It would eventually witness the construction of some one thousand structures, and each of these cultural features reflected an evolving array of larger influences that permanently reconfigured the visible scene. Moreover, as the UGB's cultural landscape changed, so did the way its agents promoted it: Different activities and selling points were emphasized at different times, creating a cumulative and synergistic, yet always-changing visitor experience. These changes can be seen in travel brochures, guidebooks, and visitor diaries, all of which help tell the story of how the UGB was promoted and experienced.

This chapter briefly highlights several different periods of development at the UGB that, in turn, shaped distinctive visitor experiences in the area. For each period, some of the larger cultural forces at work are identified, along with their particular impact on selective landscape features in the area. These changing visible signatures are then related to how park visitors have encountered and navigated their way through the UGB at different points in time.

EARLY CULTURAL DEVELOPMENT IN THE UPPER GEYSER BASIN, 1872–1904

From the initial investigation of the UGB by the Washburn expedition in 1870, the federal government understood the aesthetic value of the Basin's natural wonders and that many people would want to visit these spectacular geysers. Given the UGB's remote location, facilities for visitors would be necessary. As early as 1877, Yellowstone's second superintendent, Philetus Norris, stated in his annual report to the Secretary of the Interior that there should "be ten or twenty years' [*sic*] leases for hotel accommodations at each of the Fire Hole Basins."[2] The following year, Norris and his men inspected the UGB for areas where concessionaires could build. They concluded there were "several good building-sites, plenty of wood, fair water; and excellent water easily obtainable near the Castle and Old Faithful [Geysers]."[3]

The Basin's large-scale cultural landscape development began in 1879 when Norris ordered the construction of the first structure, a "loopedholed, earth-roofed log-house" to serve as an outpost for exploration to find the best route to Yellowstone Lake and to allow men to remain in the area during winter so they could collect information on the Basin's thermal features.[4] The construction project included a stable and corral as well as a ditch and a reservoir. The building itself measured sixteen by twenty feet, standing "in the little grove between the Castle and Beehive Geysers in the Upper Firehole basin."[5]

With the exception of the construction of a small house to shelter park employees, the cabin was probably the only development within the Basin until 1886, when the US Army moved into the park. Captain Moses Harris, the park's new acting superintendent, recognized that the thermal features were a constant target of vandalism, so he stationed a detachment of troops there to better protect the Basin's thermal features. Harris added a cluster of several small structures situated within the oxbow of the Firehole River, where Norris had built his cabin seven years earlier. Harris's men, and their horses, occupied this post from June 1 to November 1, wintering in Mammoth Hot Springs.[6]

The soldiers' efforts to protect the Basin's thermal features were needed given the overall nature of the visitor experience during this period. An examination of diaries and travel narratives written by visitors to the Basin reveals that they were in close contact with the UGB's natural features. The visitors' sensory experience was not only one of sights, sounds, and smells

FIGURE 4.2. The Upper Geyser Basin as a tactile landscape, ca. 1888. The curiosity of early visitors often led them to close encounters with the thermal features of the Upper Geyser Basin. Photograph by F. Jay Haynes. Source: Montana Historical Society Research Center, Helena, MT, Haynes Collection, H1500 (courtesy of Montana Historical Society).

but also one of touch—it was a tactile landscape. During the park's early years, visitors could venture to the thermal features and examine them close up (figure 4.2).

Diaries from this period contain numerous accounts describing not only seemingly benign acts, such as visitors peering directly into the craters of geysers, but even more damaging activities such as the throwing or stuffing objects such as towels, rocks, sticks, and soap into thermal features. Many visitors also wrote their names into the soft silicate formations of the geyser cones. For example, while touring the park on bicycle, one visitor, William Owen, stopped at Fountain Geyser and reported that he and his companions added their names "to the many autographs already inscribed here."[7] Likewise, Rudyard Kipling, who visited the park in 1889, commented that after Old Faithful's eruption, many tourists "betook themselves to writing their names in the bottom of shallow pools" with their hairpins.[8] Owen Wister, while in the UGB in 1887, also commented on the visitors' intimate contact with the Basin's features by remarking that in the shallow water-filled indentations around Old Faithful's cone, "the names of asses were to be seen, written in pencil."[9]

At this time, no formalized intervention occurred against such vandalism. The soldiers were in the park primarily to patrol, not to interpret, and the damaging effects of such actions by visitors were not yet well understood. The soldiers' mission was to thwart the efforts of poachers and squatters and to develop park infrastructure for visitors. Some interpretation was provided verbally through early park concessionaires, but most of it was in the form of nominal signage established to mark trails and notable features. Concessionaires such as Wylie and the hotel company hired interpretive guides to lead visitors on tours of the Basin. These guides primarily worked as porters or drivers, taking on the interpretive positions for tips; they found that interesting stories made for the best money, which led to less than accurate information.[10]

Park concessionaires evolved into a critical component of the visitor experience because visitors needed food, lodging, and other services. The history of concession structures at the UGB begins with the first monopoly in the park, the Yellowstone National Park Improvement Company (YNPIC). Its original lease gave it 640 acres of land, but that holding was soon reduced by the Senate. In March 1883, the YNPIC applied to the Department of the Interior for a new park lease and received a total of ten acres, one and a half of which was in the UGB. The YNPIC rushed to construct facilities as quickly as possible to accommodate summer visitors, erecting a Basin hotel camp that consisted of several small sleeping tents and a large dining tent. It was located in approximately the same area currently occupied by the oldest section of Old Faithful Inn (also simply known as "the Inn").

By the end of the year, the YNPIC was insolvent and placed in receivership, with Carroll T. Hobart becoming sole manager. In a January 1885 letter, Hobart submitted plans for a hotel in the UGB to the Secretary of the Interior. Hobart stated that the hotel would be completed by June 1st of that year at a cost of $20,000. He also included a line drawing that showed an elaborate layout of a two-story, T-shaped structure containing thirty-five guest rooms, a dining room, ladies' and gentlemen's parlors, and a large front porch. The actual building, however, was a far cry from the proposal. This first hotel in the Basin, a small building that replaced the YNPIC's tent camp, was pejoratively known as "the Shack" and apparently deserved that unflattering nickname. It could lodge around fifty persons, but many, including the hotel's carpenters and architects, considered this building an engineering disaster, as it was believed to be "unsafe and liable to fall down." Acting Superintendent Harris wanted it to be razed and replaced by a better facility (figure 4.3).[11]

Construction quality was not the only problem the Shack presented: its location within the Basin was the cause of much consternation. This was partly because F. Jay Haynes, the photography concessionaire, claimed

FIGURE 4.3.
Shack Hotel, 1889. This early view shows the front of the Shack Hotel, located within the Upper Geyser Basin. Photograph by George Eastman. Source: Yellowstone National Park Archives, YELL 10603 (courtesy of National Park Service, Yellowstone National Park; hereafter NPS-YNP).

to have a lease of his own on the site. Even more importantly, the hotel stood within one-quarter of a mile of Old Faithful Geyser—a direct violation of the Sundry Civil Bill of 1883. The first of these conflicts was eventually resolved when Haynes chose to build elsewhere in the Basin; the second problem, however, endured even as the hotel changed hands. Specifically, in 1886, when the YNPIC receivership ended, St. Louis–based lawyer Charles Gibson and his Yellowstone Park Association (YPA) took control of the park's hotel monopoly, including the problem-ridden Shack. The unsightly hotel fell into disrepair. By 1893, it was closed to overnight guests and used only as a lunch station. This change greatly inconvenienced visitors to the UGB, for "tourists ha[d] to return for the night to the Fountain [the hotel in the Lower Geyser Basin], and on the following morning make their third trip over this 10 miles [between Fountain and the Upper Basin]" in order to continue their journey to Yellowstone Lake.[12]

The YPA's siting dilemma was alleviated in 1894 with the passage of the Hayes Act, which increased the park's lease holdings from ten to twenty acres and reduced to one-eighth of a mile the distance that buildings could be placed from objects of interest. With this change in site policy, the Shack's location was no longer in violation of the Sundry Civil Bill, and a new overnight facility could take its place. Whether by coincidence or by design, in November 1894, shortly after Congress passed the bill, the dilapidated hotel burned to the ground. The YPA replaced it with a small, wood-frame building that served as a lunch station, and later the company added several stove-heated, wooden-floored tents to accommodate overnight guests. It would, however, be a decade until a new hotel was constructed in the Basin.

Meanwhile, William Wylie, a school teacher from Bozeman, Montana, petitioned for the rights to establish a camp company in the park in 1892. He wanted to cater to a different clientele than those served by the hotel company, specifically targeting the growing number of middle-class Americans.

Wylie, however, met some resistance from George Smith Anderson, the park's acting superintendent. Anderson was concerned about trash and unextinguished campfires and regarded these tent facilities as "unsightly, vermin-breeding shanties."[13] Nevertheless, in 1896, the Department of the Interior granted a license to Wylie. This lease gave him the privilege of conducting parties through the park as well as establishing four permanent camps where these parties could stay overnight. He was able to create these accommodations rapidly and cheaply because of their low overhead.

FIGURE 4.4. Wylie Upper Geyser Basin Camp, ca. 1916. This Haynes postcard view shows Wylie's casual tent camps that offered affordable lodging alternatives to many of Yellowstone's early visitors. Source: private collection of William Wyckoff.

Wylie's UGB camp was located on a timbered hill south of Daisy Geyser, near Cyclops Spring (figure 4.4). This put the camp close to the north end of the Basin and far from other facilities. Wylie used rows of wood-floored tents with red-and-white (sometimes blue-and-white) striped canvas tops. Each of the tent rows had clever "street" names, such as Rough Way, Pleasant Way, and No Way, reflecting the camp's emphasis on leisure and fun.[14] Along with the smaller sleeping tents, there were a few larger tents that served as a dance hall (dancing became a popular visitor experience during this period), a meeting hall, and a dining area. Marketing to middle-class visitors, the promoter sold the Yellowstone experience as the "Wylie Way," and he offered

FIGURE 4.5. Old Faithful Inn, ca. 1905. This Haynes postcard view from the Upper Geyser Basin shows the newly completed hotel to the south. Source: private collection of William Wyckoff. (Original in color.)

a seven-day tour for thirty-five dollars, while a six-day tour with the YPA cost fifty dollars.[15]

As Wylie's concession thrived, Gibson and the YPA fell into financial trouble. The Northern Pacific Railroad, one of YPA's major stockholders, bought out the rest of the company and then sold its shares to its subsidiary, the Northwest Improvement Company (NIC). Then, in 1901, amid concerns about its profits in the park, the NIC sold one-third of its YPA holdings to Harry Child, the vice president of the Yellowstone National Park Transportation Company. The Northern Pacific maintained its interest in the company through its Northwest Improvement Company until rumors emerged of its monopolizing businesses in Yellowstone. The Sherman Antitrust Act of 1904 quickly forced the Northern Pacific to sell all its YPA holdings to Child. The railroad, however, guaranteed its involvement in the park by periodically loaning Child sums of money.

Child's financial backing, however, contributed to what many consider the most notable architectural feature in Yellowstone National Park: Old Faithful Inn (figure 4.5). Construction of the Inn began in 1903, and it opened in time for the 1904 season, offering 140 rooms to accommodate 316 guests. After its completion, Acting Park Superintendent Pitcher wrote:

> "Old Faithful Inn" is a remarkably beautiful and comfortable establishment. It is constructed chiefly of stone and logs, and while rustic in appearance, it contains all of the modern conveniences which the traveler of to-day is accustomed to, such as electric lights and baths.

FIGURE 4.6. Old Faithful Inn Lobby, 1905. This postcard view of the lobby shows the huge stone fireplace and the elaborate interior woodwork. Source: private collection of William Wyckoff. (Original in color.)

In his description, Pitcher understated the monumental achievement of the Inn's chief architect, Robert C. Reamer. Originally from Ohio, Reamer trained in Chicago and then moved to San Diego to open his own firm. In San Diego, Reamer befriended Child, who wintered in California. Child, through the YPA, entrusted thirty-year-old Reamer with $200,000 to build the Inn, giving him complete freedom in design and supervision. The result was the "first 'rustic' hotel built in the national parks in a large-scale effort to harmonize construction with the natural surroundings."[16] Reamer tapped into Victorian and Adirondack design traditions by employing dormers and rustic materials to create what became a standard for resort hotels in the American West.

The crowning achievement of the Inn was its interior lobby (figure 4.6). From floor to ceiling, it measured eighty-five feet; surrounding it were balconies with gnarled, knotted wooden railings on each floor. The lobby featured a fourteen-square-foot chimney that served eight different fireplaces. A huge wrought-iron clock hung from one end of the chimney. All of the hotel's interior decorations—tables and chairs of heavy oak, Indian rugs, and electric lights that looked like candles—reflected the natural motif. Toward the rear of the lobby was a huge, half-octagonal dining room that measured sixty-two feet across. It contained a large fireplace and a series of plateglass windows, so diners could geyser-gaze.

The Inn also boasted enormous log walls, a capacious porte cochere, and a steeply slanted roof with dormers jutting out at various points. Topping it was a large observation platform that held a searchlight for nighttime illumination of the Old Faithful Geyser. Reamer oriented the entire structure so that visitors would not have the best view of Old Faithful Geyser from their room windows but, rather, could see it from the porte cochere as they pulled up in wagons. Overall, Reamer designed the Inn to give the visitor a sense of shelter within the Upper Basin's haunting, smoking landscape. The building, completed in 1904, continues to be the most spectacular and enduring structure on the Basin's landscape, if not in the entire park.

While not as grandiose as the Inn, F. Jay Haynes's UGB photo studio is also notable simply because of Haynes's influence on the Basin's cultural landscape and the visitor experience. Indeed, he and his heirs maintained a business in the park from 1881 to 1968. A photographer from Minnesota, Haynes contracted in 1875 with the Northern Pacific Railroad to photograph sights along its railway line. He discovered that Yellowstone presented many extraordinary opportunities for photography and for a lucrative business. In December 1881, he sent views of the park to the Secretary of the Interior along with a letter expressing an interest in leasing "a small tract of land in the Park [*sic*] upon which to erect a photographic studio."[17] He included his crude drawing of the desired site, a square ten-acre tract bordering the river across from the Beehive Geyser.

On March 20, 1884, Haynes acquired a ten-year lease for "eight acres of land in the Park [*sic*], at the UGB."[18] Focusing on his other business at Mammoth Hot Springs and on his disputes with the hotel company in the UGB, Haynes waited until 1897 to construct a log-cabin photography studio at the Basin. Haynes's studio was situated on the south side of the Firehole River, approximately 700 feet southwest of the Beehive Geyser (which lay on the opposite bank) and about 350 feet northwest of the current location of the front of Old Faithful Inn. The studio was regarded by many as an attractive and inviting cultural addition to the landscape, both for its external appearance and its offerings inside. When the studio opened, Acting Superintendent Young touted it as "the most beautiful and most appropriate in the park."[19]

Haynes's widely distributed images had an enduring impact on the way Americans perceived the Upper Geyser Basin. Moreover, in the annually published Haynes Guides, he subsequently offered suggestions on the best ways to photograph Old Faithful and thus influenced individuals in how they packaged their own personal memories of the park.

Shortly after Haynes constructed his studio, H. E. Klamer added a combined general store, curio shop, and post office to the UGB. Originally a mountain man and once a deputy sheriff of Uinta County, Wyoming, Klamer was the son-in-law of George L. Henderson (assistant superintendent of the park from 1882 to 1885 and builder of the Cottage Hotel at Mammoth Hot Springs). Klamer applied for a lease to build a store, and once his petition was accepted by the Department of the Interior and the NPS in 1898, he began construction of a two-story frame building measuring twenty by thirty feet and fronted by a small, planked porch (figure 4.7). He designed this structure as both a store and a dwelling for himself. In the shop, Klamer sold tourist supplies, Indian baskets, curios, and souvenirs, specializing in Indian blankets.

FIGURE 4.7. Klamer Store, ca. 1900. The Klamer Store offered visitors new opportunities to purchase souvenirs and supplies at the Upper Geyser Basin. Photographer unknown. Source: Yellowstone National Park Archives, YELL 777 (courtesy of NPS-YNP).

THE EMERGENCE OF A RECREATIONAL LANDSCAPE, 1904–1940

Following the completion of the Old Faithful Inn in 1904, the Upper Geyser Basin continued to attract visitors and increased development. More focused improvements and investments came with the creation of the National Park Service in 1916. With the departure of troops from the Firehole army post, the newly established NPS not only took over the former military structures for its own use but also added many new facilities. In the same year, it built structures that served interpretive purposes, added and improved trails and roads, and provided new campgrounds for automobile tourists keen to patronize camping facilities separate from those offered by the private camping companies. The park's automobile entrance fees funded the creation of these facilities.

The first automobile camp at the UGB was originally located just east of the Old Faithful Geyser, along the Firehole River and behind a permanent tent camp owned by Shaw and Powell Camping Company (SPCC), a competitor of the Wylie Camp that began development in the UGB in 1913. The automobile campground provided a wood-framed shed large enough to shelter a dozen vehicles beneath a corrugated steel roof. The campground also offered toilet facilities, cooking grates at each campsite, and free firewood. Across the park, such campgrounds became immensely popular for budget-minded tourists. By 1919, approximately two-thirds of the visitors to Yellowstone stayed overnight at these facilities.[20]

This popularity led to overcrowding, and the NPS responded in 1920 by creating a more expansive automobile camping facility on the other side of the road from Old Faithful Geyser. This facility's large size—with enough space for 350 automobiles—helped address the burgeoning demand for campsites in the park. The urban-like amenities, such as comfort stations and streetlights, also made these popular lodging options. For example, during the 1930 season, a total of 10,689 cars and 33,524 campers used it.[21] Throughout the 1930s, however, the facilities of the adjacent SPCC increasingly encroached on the auto camp. Given that the camping company's facilities were more permanent, the Park Service recognized that the only logical solution was to move the more mobile of the two, the auto camp, to yet another location.

As a result, the Civilian Conservation Corps (CCC) began work in 1939 on the Basin's third automobile campground, this one located southeast of the second. However, CCC staff completed only three sites before being called away to another project in the park. The completion of the third auto camp would have to wait until the end of World War II.

Earlier in the century, the interpretative facilities began to make their mark on the UGB's cultural landscape with the shift from the army to the NPS as overseers of Yellowstone. This shift in administration, in 1913, eventually resulted in the razing of the old army station located in the Firehole River oxbow and the construction of a ranger's office and living quarters closer to Old Faithful Geyser.

However, the new ranger station was strictly an administrative facility; it did not provide visitors with interpretation of the UGB's natural features.

Realizing the need to educate visitors and enhance their national park experience, the NPS slowly added interpretive features. During this early period in the NPS's history, however, ecological goals tended to be undermined by the promotion of recreational opportunities in an effort to increase park popularity. As such, interpretive landscape features sometimes took unusual forms.

For instance, visitors who came to the UGB during this period wanted to see bears as well as geysers. Recognizing this, the NPS built facilities to show off bears on a set schedule. While bear sightings are now a rarity, visitors during this earlier era simply attended one of the evening bear feedings. These events were an extension of the days when hotels discarded garbage nearby instead of hauling it to a dump. Visitors soon found they could watch bears congregate near garbage. Realizing the risks involved in this combination of fragrant garbage, hungry bears, and curious visitors, the NPS ordered the concessionaires to move their trash. However, the bears followed the garbage, and the visitors invariably followed the bears.

Finally, the NPS decided to construct more manageable bear-feeding grounds. In 1919, it established one in the UGB within walking distance of the automobile camp. Wooden benches allowed visitors to sit and listen to a ranger lecture while the bears ate nearby. They were separated from the bears only by a wire barricade strung between trees and posts alongside a shallow ditch so as "to keep people from going beyond the danger line." There was also an armed ranger in case things got out of hand.[22] There was a special feeding platform on which the bears could dine, and a sign claiming that this was a "LUNCH COUNTER FOR BEARS ONLY" (figures 4.8 and 4.9).

The number of bears and lectures made this feeding area, as well as others, "one of the most interesting features of the park to the majority of tourists," according to Superintendent Albright. Nonetheless, he advised that the facility be closely regulated because the garbage dumped there produced a "very bad odor" and the large number of bears the facility attracted constituted a potential danger to the Basin's visitors.[23]

Further concerns over safety arose. Assistant Superintendent Guy D. Edwards wrote that the UGB's bear-feeding grounds were in too close a proximity to the Basin's many campers (both those in the automobile campground and the permanent camp facilities) and that this situation was becoming "troublesome."[24] In 1934, a New Deal project proposed to build a better feeding facility a mile or more from the UGB. Before this new facility

FIGURES 4.8 AND 4.9. Top: Upper Geyser Basin bear-feeding grounds, ca. 1929. In this view, NPS staff oversee the daily feeding of Yellowstone bears at Upper Geyser Basin. Source: Yellowstone National Park Archives. Bottom: After the feast, ca. 1929. The daily visit to the "lunch counter" left behind plenty of trash and debris. Photographer unknown. Source: Yellowstone National Park Archives, YELL 44705 and YELL 27344-07 (courtesy of NPS-YNP).

could be started, though, the park discontinued all bear-feeding grounds in 1936, except at the Otter Creek pit near the Canyon area, since they were "entic[ing] grizzly bears into the crowded utility area, which condition was considered as hazardous because of the nature of this species of bear."[25] By 1940, the NPS had stopped bear feedings in the park altogether.

As artificial as bear feedings seemed, the NPS nonetheless used the activity to offer interpretive lectures, thus introducing important new elements to the visitor experience. Before 1916, interpretation came through the ad hoc, oral, and often inaccurate efforts of concession company employees and park soldiers. The UGB's landscape during this period clearly reveals that

FIGURE 4.10. Museum of Thermal Activity, 1939. This important interpretive facility just east of the Old Faithful Inn served as an architectural model for others in the park. Photographer unknown. Source: Yellowstone National Park Archives, YELL 38765 (courtesy of NPS-YNP).

the NPS was focused on creating a more structured interpretive program through signage, lectures, and other ranger-led activities.

In 1926, an inspection of the park's educational activities by Ansel F. Hall, Yellowstone's chief naturalist, found that there was "an acute educational problem at Upper Basin" because it had only two ranger naturalists on duty at any given time, thus reaching "less than twenty per cent" of the visitors at the Basin with the interpretive service.[26] Instead of requesting that more ranger naturalists be hired, Hall suggested several alternatives to the problem. Two of these were the creation of interpretive nature trails and the addition of a museum within the Basin. As a result of the first recommendation, the Formation Trail and the Black Sand Basin Trail were both established in the UGB during this period. These were fairly ambitious projects and included interpretive labeling of numerous features that lay along the trails. Work on the UGB trails continued through 1934 with additional New Deal funding. More hard-surfaced footpaths were added, along with a section of trail near Grand Geyser. The result of this effort was the expansion of the UGB's trail system to the northwest and the beginning of a self-guided interpretive landscape for Basin visitors.

Following Hall's second suggestion, the NPS constructed the Museum of Thermal Activity between 1928 and 1929, using part of an $118,000 grant from the Laura Spelman Rockefeller Foundation.[27] The UGB's museum was a primitive-looking, L-shaped building made of logs and stone, located about two hundred feet east of the Inn's east wing (figure 4.10). Its design became a standard for interpretive structures in the park. Herbert Maier, a

FIGURE 4.11. Museum Amphitheater, ca. 1933. This large outdoor amphitheater, designed by Herbert Maier, could seat eight hundred visitors. Opening in 1932, it offered evening campfire talks and slide shows. Photographer unknown. Source: Yellowstone National Park Archives, YELL 24186 (courtesy of NPS-YNP).

well-known architect who both designed and supervised the museum's construction, blended the structure into the surrounding physical landscape through the use of natural construction materials that were shaped with primitive tools. He also screened and situated buildings behind or within natural features, such as trees, rocks, and alcoves, and surrounded them with indigenous vegetation.

In addition to the museum, Maier also designed a nearby amphitheater, funded by the American Association of Museums, to "provide ample room for the large crowds that . . . taxed the capacity of the court almost since [the museum's] construction."[28] He located the semicircular, eight-hundred-person amphitheater behind the museum's courtyard and planted trees as natural screening. The seats themselves were long benches, made from rough-hewn logs. A low, log stage with a large projection screen stood front and center (figure 4.11).

The park dedicated this facility on August 27, 1932, and used it "each evening during the season for campfire talks on natural history and other Yellowstone subjects."[29] The usual format included community singing, announcements of upcoming activities, and illustrated lectures (with subjects ranging from natural history to park history).

While the amphitheater served as one medium to deliver lectures to visitors, rangers also gave cone talks at thermal features such as Old Faithful and led visitors on interpretive walks to destinations such as the Old Faithful Overlooks above the Basin. Then, in 1931, the NPS, recognizing the dominant nature of automobile tourism within the park, initiated a series of daily auto caravan lectures known as the "Chasing Geysers" program. Visitors would meet at the museum in the UGB and convoy, with a ranger vehicle in the lead, to areas such as Black Sand and Biscuit Basins. Although this was a popular activity, the NPS nonetheless discontinued it in 1939 because of the traffic congestion and parking difficulties it generated.

The evolution of concessions in the UGB after 1916 reflected new regulations of the NPS and its desire to preserve the natural integrity of the park as well as enhance the experiences of the park's visitors. The Yellowstone Park Company attempted to work within these guidelines as it built several employee dormitories, maintenance and laundry facilities, and a plethora of other accommodations designed to cater to the Basin's increasing popularity. Most of these structures were blended into the landscape and set back fairly well so that they remained relatively unobtrusive to the visitors' eyes.

The Old Faithful Inn was one focus of proposed changes. After a modest early expansion in the form of a wing in 1914, the company soon proposed another. While the Inn's first wing went up without complications, the second one did not. Superintendent Albright expressed concerns about the plan. In a letter to the company's president, Harry Child, Albright argued that the new wing's design was "so totally different from the old building" that he thought it was "bound to be commented on adversely," so much so that Robert Reamer, who designed the Inn and its additions, would "have his reputation considerably impaired."[30] Albright did not believe that the wing's proposed French "Mansard" style fit in well with the Inn's original log cabin motif. The proposed placement of the wing at the west end of the Inn exacerbated the problem, given that it would "be the first part of the building that the incoming tourists" saw when entering the UGB.[31] Reamer argued that there was no alternative location. Thermal features and other buildings restricted available land to a narrow corridor northwest of the Inn.

The NPS asked Reamer to redesign the wing to make its appearance conform more with the Inn. Reamer's second design was essentially identical as the one he had originally planned, except that the dormers on the third floor were flat instead of slanted. Although his revised plan was initially rejected as still incongruous with the inn, the NPS eventually accepted the design because the construction contract had been let and work begun on the new 150-room, 95-bath wing. During construction, the wing received further criticism. On a visit during the summer of 1927, P. H. Elwood, a professor of landscape architecture at Iowa State College, called it a "very serious architectural blunder" and noted that the park's landscape engineer must not have been consulted.[32] The NPS's landscape architect, Thomas Vint, had in fact been consulted; he initially objected to the design but later changed his mind. He said that the more he saw it, the better he liked it.[33] Likewise, Superintendent Albright also changed his opinion, believing that it grew "more harmonious with the surroundings" every time he went to Old Faithful; he further felt that when completed, it would not "be considered obnoxious at all."[34] Whether this wing truly grew on them or whether they were just accepting something they could not change, the wing was there to stay and it still hosts visitors to this day.

If visitors did not like the appearance of the new wing, they still had other lodging options aside from automobile camping. During this period, the Wylie Permanent Camping Company was consolidated with the Shaw and Powell Camping Company. The SPCC placed its first permanent camping facility in the UGB in 1913. The SPCC was actually older than Wylie's concession, having been created in 1892 when Amos Shaw, a Great Lakes ship captain (who moved to Livingston, Montana, in 1890) partnered with J. D. Powell. They ran camping trips together in the park for twenty-one years but did not construct any permanent facilities until 1913. The new holdings included sites at Canyon, Bridge Bay, Willow Park (just south of Mammoth Hot Springs), and the UGB. The UGB camp stood in a small grove just east of Old Faithful Geyser (in the same area where the Old Faithful Lodge stands today).

Along with the standard array of wooden-floored canvas tents, SPCC also constructed a 672-square-foot kitchen facility. Several months later, it applied to the Department of the Interior for permission to construct a dining room and office facility at the same site. The request was granted, and the structure was completed in 1915, with the combined dining room and office encompassing 3,200 square feet.

Wanting to consolidate concession facilities, the NPS forced the merger of Wylie's concession with the SPCC in 1917, forming the Yellowstone Park Camps Company. It closed the Wylie site, while keeping the original Shaw and Powell camp open, as the latter was closer to the UGB's other facilities.

The camp witnessed further expansion in 1919 with the completion of a new dining room and kitchen.

During construction, however, the managers of the merging campground companies were not getting along, and they terminated their alliance in 1920 by selling to Howard Hays. Hays continued the business for four more years under the name Yellowstone Park Camps Company and built a new recreation pavilion at the UGB camp in 1921. He then sold the company, in 1924, to Vernon Goodwin, who changed its name to the Yellowstone Park Lodge and Camps Company. Four years later, however, Goodwin sold the company to Harry Child.[35]

FIGURE 4.12. Old Faithful Lodge, ca. 1926. Sitting just to the east of Old Faithful Geyser, Old Faithful Lodge offered affordable cabin accommodations to visitors. This view shows people and tour buses in front of the main Lodge building. Photographer unknown. Source: Yellowstone National Park Archives, YELL 9560 (courtesy of NPS-YNP).

Under Goodwin's direction, the company began constructing the Old Faithful Lodge in 1924 (figure 4.12). The initial development entailed building a large dining room, a veranda overlooking Old Faithful Geyser, a new kitchen, and a commissary. The company finally completed all work by 1926, except for a new lobby and recreation hall. That same year Superintendent Albright sent a letter to Goodwin entreating him to complete work on the Lodge. He suggested that Goodwin make a trip to Zion National Park to see its lodges for ideas. He also warned Goodwin that the Department of the Interior and the NPS were "going to insist that the Camps Company finish the Old Faithful Lodge" by the fall of 1926.[36]

With Goodwin having difficulty meeting the completion deadline, Albright contacted D. R. Hull, who had helped in designing the Lodge's kitchen and dining hall with a Mr. Underwood. Albright requested that Hull and Underwood help with the design and completion of the Lodge's lobby and recreation hall. Apparently, planning for the Lodge had been poor, and without a new recreation hall, the dining room and kitchen buildings resembled a "factory more than a resort."[37] Albright told Hull that the old amusement hall, the one that was part of the SPCC's facilities, had to be torn down and the new recreation hall built. Hull and Underwood obliged, adding a new recreation hall and a new lobby to the Lodge in 1928. Still standing today, just east of the Old Faithful Geyser, this building still serves the same function.

Scattered among the Lodge, dorms, and service facilities were the tourist cabins—the smallest, but most important structures on the Camps Company's landscape. These wooden buildings, which ultimately would replace the stove-heated red-and-white striped canvas tents of the previous generation, first appeared in the UGB during 1921. In that year, the Camps Company built fifty cabins; when completed, they increased the capacity of the camp by more than five hundred. In 1923, the company constructed sixty more as part of its transition to offering more permanent and comfortable facilities. While still not quite a hotel room, the cabins (also known as lodges) offered more privacy and protection from weather. These structures—built in single, double, and quad room sizes—are essentially the same shelters seen on the UGB's landscape today. Development of these structures advanced at a rapid rate during this period. Over the next six years, the Camps Company built approximately 200 cabins in the area, and by 1940, the number of these cabins more than doubled to 414.[38]

In part, this cabin development took place because Superintendent Albright wanted to improve lodge facilities throughout the park. His goal was to remove most tent facilities in favor of "more than one hundred cabins dispersed as needed at the various camps."[39] These buildings far surpassed his desired count of a hundred, and they were unattractive and not terribly well constructed—and they were also numerous enough to generate what is arguably a significant visual blight.

Complicating this impact on the UGB's built landscape was the development of more Camps Company camper facilities across the road, next to the auto camp. Development began in what became known as the "Housekeeping" area in 1920. The housekeeping cabins offered an alternative to the other lodges, in that visitors could "prepare their own meals, furnish their own bedding, if desired, and have their automobile adjacent to the cabin."[40] Many of these facilities were "tent-top" cabins that were essentially holdovers from the Wylie and SPCC days, in that visitors slept in canvas tents with wooden floors. They gave park visitors the convenience and economy of camping without the burden of packing a tent. The popular units multiplied rapidly and reflected the changing demands of tourists over time (figures 4.13 and 4.14). By 1930, there were 256 housekeeping units in the area, and a decade later the Camps Company had established more than 400 cabins in the UGB (figure 4.15). Over time, these cabins were also wired with electricity, so the occupants might feel less like they were camping and more like they were staying at a cheap hotel.

While many UGB facilities went up without conflict, one in particular endured controversy, mistakes, and red tape while under construction. In 1912, a Salt Lake City attorney, Henry P. Brothers, wrote to the Department of the Interior for information on how to "establish and conduct public baths at one of the hot springs in the Yellowstone National Park."[41] Acting Superintendent Lloyd Milton Brett denied the request, believing the concession was not economically viable. Brothers persisted and solicited the opinions of several acquaintances who were annual visitors to the park. He forwarded their positive responses to the Secretary of the Interior and requested a lease. He argued that a denial at such an early stage of the application process was unfair, especially as it was based solely on the opinion of the park's acting superintendent. Brothers requested permission to examine a parcel of land in the presence of the acting superintendent so that the selection he made "would not interfere in any way with the proper protection and administration of the park."[42]

Assistant Secretary of the Interior Lewis C. Laylin honored Brothers's

FIGURE 4.13. Camper Cabins, Upper Geyser Basin, no date. Camper cabins such as these multiplied across the Upper Geyser Basin after 1900 and supplied affordable lodging for many Yellowstone visitors. Photographer F. B. Johnston. Source: Library of Congress, image #3c00865.

FIGURE 4.14. Old Faithful Lodge cabins, 2022. Many of these simple cabins at Old Faithful Lodge were built decades ago and still offer visitors affordable accommodations in the park today. Photograph by William Wyckoff. (Original in color.)

FIGURE 4.15. Cabins in Upper Geyser Basin in 1940. Between 1915 and 1940, hundreds of "camper" and "housekeeping" cabins were constructed in the Upper Geyser Basin, giving its landscape the appearance of a small village in the wilderness. Map by Karl Byrand.

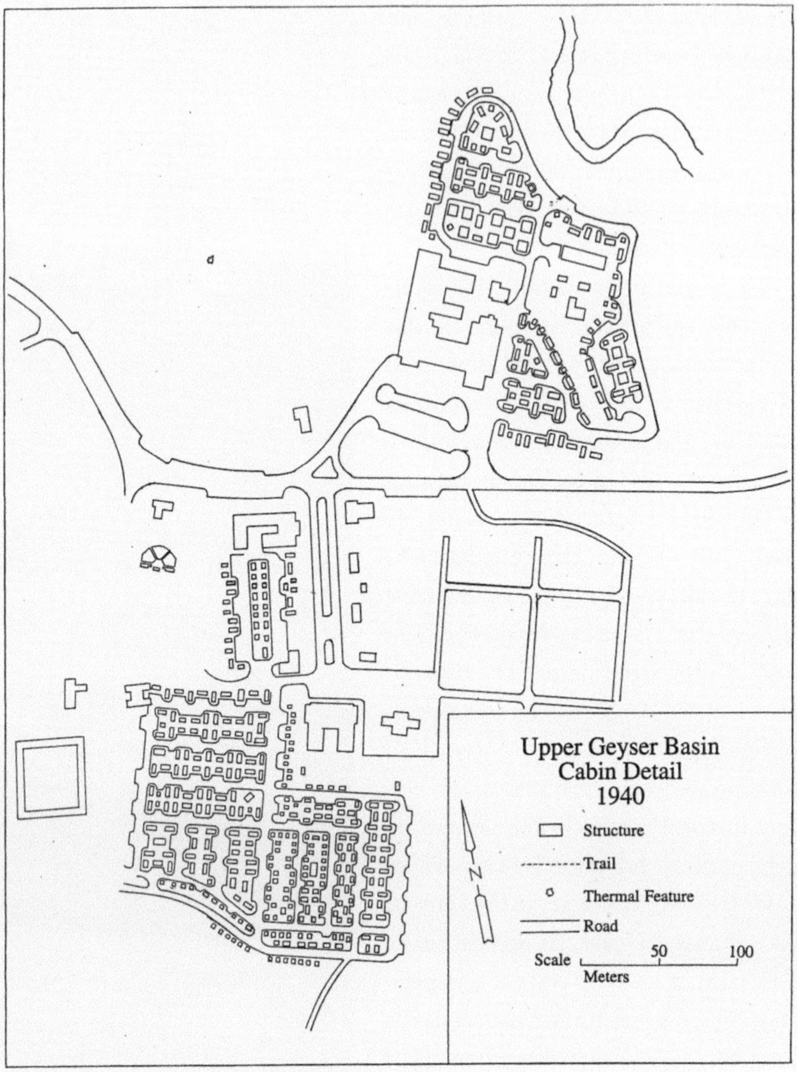

request but specified that the acting superintendent or another park official file a report on the selected sites. Brothers made arrangements to meet with Brett at Old Faithful Inn in June 1913. One can only speculate about what happened at their meeting, but one thing is certain: something was said or done that drastically changed Brett's opinion. Brothers selected a site on low ground near the Firehole River across the road from the first Haynes Studio. He proposed a log structure with a rustic appearance to fit in with the Inn's motif. He also planned a large plunge and several small baths that would use hot water from nearby springs and cold water from the river. The plunge apparently helped sell Brett on the idea: in his report, he said of the large plunge, "this method of bathing would appeal to the traveling public and would be enjoyed."[43]

After receiving Brett's endorsement, the Department of the Interior instructed R. B. Dole, a chemist for the US Geological Survey, to investigate the proposed facility's potential impact regarding water withdrawal and disposal. In his inspection, however, Dole looked at the wrong site, thinking Brothers wanted to develop a small marsh known as the Frog Pond, which stood between the Haynes Studio and the river; he was concerned that the site was "swampy and insanitary" and that the spring from which the water would be drawn would dry up every summer, leaving the bathhouse with an inadequate water supply, and likewise he was concerned that withdrawal from the only other viable water source, Chinaman Spring, would potentially affect "Old Faithful Geyser."[44]

Henry Brothers returned to the UGB in August of the same year and found Dole's locational error. Despite the discovery of this mistake and Brett's continued support, Brothers still faced a struggle. Specifically, Assistant Secretary Laylin raised the issue that the proposed plat violated the Hayes Act of 1894, given that it lay only "285 feet from Beehive Geyser."[45] Brothers argued that the Hayes Act only applied to hotels and their related structures. Brett concurred with Brothers's interpretation of the act and contended that the proposed structure would not inhibit views in the Basin, nor adversely impact thermal features.

Dole submitted another report, arguing that, while there were no possible health impacts, the bathhouse's potential effect on Old Faithful was unknown and therefore should not be built at the proposed site. Laylin contacted Brett and requested that he reconsider the site, but he also gave Brett the final say. Asserting there was no other suitable location and the facility's impact on the thermal features was purely speculative, Brett convinced the Department of the Interior to grant Brothers a ten-year concession.

In 1914, Brothers started construction across from Haynes Studio, creating both a five-thousand-square-foot plunge as well as five fifty-square-foot private pools (figure 4.16). Opening on July 1, 1915, the bathhouse proved "popular with travelers as well as with employees of the park," and throughout the next decade, it drew more than 11,000 bathers a year.[46]

After nearly two decades of operating his bathhouse concession, Brothers retired and, in 1933, sold his business to Charles Ashworth Hamilton.

FIGURE 4.16. Brothers Bathhouse, ca. 1915. The UGB's Geyser Baths facility near the Old Faithful Inn proved to be a popular attraction for thousands of park visitors. Photographer unknown. Source: Yellowstone National Park Archives, YELL 5575 (courtesy of NPS-YNP).

Hamilton came out to the park from St. Paul, Minnesota, shortly after the turn of the century and had worked several seasonal jobs, including office positions with YPA officials such as L. C. Wells (purchasing agent) and Harry Child (president). Hamilton thus became well acquainted with doing business in the park.

In 1915, Hamilton seized his own first business opportunity. For just over $20,500, he bought the UGB store from the widow of Henry Klamer, who had died in 1914. Hamilton paid Mrs. Klamer one-quarter of the price up front and Hamilton's friend Huntley Child, Sr., the son of Harry Child, backed him with another third. Hamilton maintained the Klamer tradition by selling general merchandise, curios, and souvenirs. He made improvements to the site, significantly increasing the square footage of the building through the addition of two wings and a second floor, making his UGB store "the largest and best operated in the national park system."[47]

Hamilton then sought to expand his UGB enterprise by constructing an even larger store near the Basin's automobile campground. In 1928, he appointed Rasmus Detlef Rasmussen, his employee since 1921, to manage this project. When completed, the large log building was a U-shaped structure with a 150-foot frontage and a second-floor dormitory that could sleep forty-eight people. Huge square stone pillars supported the store's three large gabled entrances. Upon entering, the visitor found a vaulted ceiling supported by stripped and varnished logs. At the store's rear stood an enormous stone fireplace and chimney. The store also had several counters for displaying goods. It opened during the spring of 1930 and remains a fixture on the UGB's landscape.[48]

Hamilton expanded his enterprise further by adding a curio shop in Old Faithful Lodge—bringing the number of his UGB stores to three—and, capitalizing on automobile tourism, he established two filling stations at either end of the Basin. He then further diversified by entering into the business of providing baths to the UGB's visitors by purchasing Henry Brothers's concession in 1933. The NPS allowed the transfer from Brothers to Hamilton but only under the condition that the bathhouse be "moved to another location" in a year's time, because it was generating a negative visual impact on the Basin's physical landscape.[49] This request was part of new NPS policies designed to remove what were seen as "artificial intrusions" on scenic landscapes. Given this new NPS perspective, it considered the bathhouse an intrusion because visitors who approached the UGB from the north got their first view of the eruption of Old Faithful from over its roof.[50]

In spite of the NPS's order, Hamilton did not move the bathhouse. In fact, he commenced improvements on it immediately. He cut trees from the nearby woods and, with Rasmussen's help, put up a new building around the plunge. He converted the bathhouse into an enormous log structure with a stone base. It contained an employee dorm, showers, and a public laundry facility. The structure's crowning achievement was its roof, with skylights made of two-inch-thick glass to allow the sunlight to shine on the bathers. There was also a twenty-five-foot lifeguard tower that had a rope swing attached for rescuing any drowning victims; even so, two youths did drown during this period (both in 1937) and another drowned in later years.[51]

FIGURE 4.17. Hamilton Upper Geyser Basin Bathhouse, ca. 1940. The expanded Bathhouse at Old Faithful was operated by Hamilton after 1933. Photographer unknown. Source: Yellowstone National Park Archives, YELL 31221-01 (courtesy of NPS-YNP).

Hamilton completed renovations during the spring of 1934 and used the remodeling as an excuse "for retaining the bathhouse/pool at its original location."[52] It proved to be "quite popular during the warm summer days," and afforded "comfortable bathing both day and night."[53] Its clientele may have appreciated it, but the NPS did not. It would survive this period, but not the next (figure 4.17).

A REASSESSMENT OF PARK VALUES, 1945–1972

As in other national parks, limited funding, few visitors, and a lack of employees marked Yellowstone's years during World War II. There was little new development at the UGB, with infrastructure and facilities falling into disrepair (figure 4.18). However, things changed after the end of the war. Dramatic increases in visitor numbers put even greater pressure on existing facilities. In addition, new concerns over appropriate levels and types of development shaped NPS policies because some existing facilities (including many at the UGB) were increasingly seen as intruding upon natural features within the area.

Mission 66 became a national NPS strategy designed to address all of these issues.[54] The system-wide development initiative, begun in the mid-1950s, undoubtedly had a lasting effect on the UGB, but most of the changes were slow in coming. The lag was attributed to a conflict over the direction that visitation would take within the Basin. Specifically, the NPS sought to eliminate and relocate many of the UGB's facilities. Its justification was outlined in the 1956 park master plan, which expressly stated that past development at Old Faithful, "including the roads, now encroaches seriously upon the thermal areas of the Upper Geyser Basin," and specified that all of the development "is programmed for removal and new facilities of comparable capacity are to be provided on a new site."[55]

The UGB was to become strictly a day-use area, with new parking areas, restrooms, and boardwalks with interpretive displays for self-guided tours. The plan proposed to build new overnight accommodations and restaurant facilities several miles to the north in the Lower Geyser Basin, to be dubbed Firehole Village. Park administrators believed such a plan would more efficiently handle future visitors as well as protect the environmental and scenic integrity of the UGB.

Documents within the park archives do not reveal any objections to the plans on the part of concessionaires. It may have been that they did not take the plan seriously, or that they did not think it would have a significant effect on their businesses. The Yellowstone Park Company (YPC) knew that Old

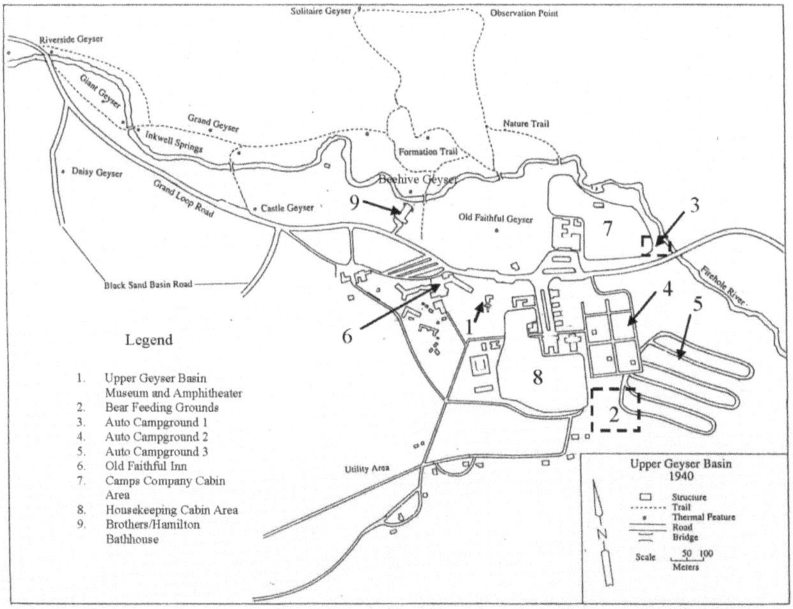

FIGURE 4.18. This map of the Upper Geyser Basin in 1940 shows the sprawling nature of development at the Upper Geyser Basin by 1940. Map by Karl Byrand.

Faithful Inn was a candidate for the National Register of Historic Places: the chances of this building being razed were slim. Moreover, the YPC was in debt and trying to complete its new development at Canyon Village. Targeted by Mission 66 for development, Canyon Village would supposedly replace any profits lost from closing other holdings within the Basin. The other main concessionaire, Hamilton Stores, Inc., did not object, because the plan allowed it to keep a store and service station in the UGB, as park planners believed they would "not intrude on the [UGB's] central activity."[56]

Ultimately, the more draconian plan, to close all overnight guest facilities at UGB, never materialized. However, some modest development, mostly involving upkeep of existing facilities, did take place in the area during the early years of Mission 66. The NPS believed that "during the interim years, it [the UGB] must function and some improvements are necessary."[57]

By 1966, the UGB had still not been converted to a day-use area, though plans continued to call for the removal of overnight facilities. Park managers also scrapped the plan to construct Firehole Village, and the UGB's new potential replacement at Grant Village, on Yellowstone Lake, was plagued with problems. With Yellowstone's centennial rapidly approaching, the NPS wanted its facilities—especially its crown jewel, the UGB—to be at their best.

Thus, although Mission 66 officially ended in 1966, it left in its wake a number of specific plans that would radically alter the UGB's landscape between 1970 and 1972.

Camping facilities in the UGB witnessed major changes after World War II. Lack of funding and personnel both during and immediately after World War II contributed to the revegetation of the UGB campground, and many of the facilities fell into disrepair. It wasn't until 1949 that the NPS began improving campgrounds at the older facility. It also resumed construction of the additional campground begun a decade earlier. This facility, taking the form of three long, parallel loop roads, increased camping accommodations by about 110 campsites.[58] Ironically, this new campground was short-lived because of the Park Service's UGB day-use conversion goals. In the end, both the Basin's second campground (the one begun in 1919) and its third campground (the one begun in 1939) were removed to make room for a bypass road and new parking facilities. Once the camps were eliminated in 1969, the Old Faithful Inn and Lodge remained as the only options to host overnight visitors in the UGB. The removal of all campgrounds represented a watershed event for visitors to the area: for the first time in several decades, no one could legally pitch a tent and camp within the confines of the Basin.

The creation of an elaborate boardwalk system was another cultural landscape change that dramatically altered the visitor experience. Historically the UGB trail system posed a problem by tempting many visitors to wander from established paths—thus causing potential harm to thermal features and to the visitors. In March 1947, the Park Engineers' Office sponsored a conference to discuss the "problem of the development of walkways for the protection of thermal areas."[59]

The park's engineers and landscape architect resolved to create a boardwalk system; therefore, during the summer of 1947, the park's staff built two thousand feet of boardwalk throughout Yellowstone, with nearly half of it being installed around the UGB's Castle Geyser and Morning Glory Pool. It was estimated that the installation of this prefabricated wooden trail system "reduced wear at [thermal] formations by some 90%."[60] By 1953, the Park Service had completed all of the boardwalks in the park's geyser basins.

The creation of this boardwalk system represented a significant shift in the visitor experience. Formerly able to feel and hear the crunch of the cinderous material beneath their feet and more readily approach thermal features (and violate long-established park policy), visitors were now more removed from the thermal landscape. The result was a safer but less tactile experience.

This distancing of the visitor from the physical landscape continued through the 1950s and 1960s. Although staffing and programming eventually returned to prewar levels, the years of Mission 66 radically altered the UGB's interpretive landscape. While there was a continued desire on the part of the NPS to interpret this landscape, increased postwar visitation necessitated new methods of interpretation. In the UGB, this delivery took the form of increasing the use of signs and pamphlets that would eventually replace most of the ranger-led geyser walks.

Thus, as the boardwalks reduced visitors' contact with the Basin's thermal features, the standardized pamphlets homogenized the process of how they experienced the landscape. Visitors could now pick up a pamphlet from a box next to the beginning of the boardwalk and walk around the geyser basin (usually in the same direction as everyone else), reading the same material and stopping at the same points. This literature for the self-guided tours, combined with the carefully constructed network of boardwalks, strongly limited and dictated what visitors encountered as they hiked through the UGB.

The goals of Mission 66 and its subsequent influence on the homogenization of the visitor experience would culminate in the UGB in 1972. In that year, both the Museum of Thermal Activity and the nearby amphitheater were razed, replaced by a new visitor center complex.

This large-scale addition seemed to contradict the mandate for downsizing evident in the Mission 66 guidelines, until one considers how the UGB was being designed as a very large day-use area once all overnight facilities and concessions were gone. Superintendent Anderson placed the visitor center on the "highest priority on planning for major interpretive developments" because "the Yellowstone Centennial [was] on the horizon and approaching as high speed freight."[61]

Although the new visitor center was originally designed in 1968, construction did not begin until 1971, but it was completed in time for the park's centennial. This set of buildings offered quite a change from the old museum, whose site it usurped (figure 4.19). In addition to all the necessary amenities, such as restrooms, the new complex contained three theaters, with staggered programs to alleviate visitor congestion as presentations ended, and an electronic geyser prediction board to reduce the time rangers would spend

FIGURE 4.19. Old Faithful Visitor Center, 2006. The updated visitor center featured this modernistic structure with angled roof and large windows. Photograph by Richard Collier. Source: Library of Congress, image # HABS WY-157-4.

answering the ever-popular question, "What time is [geyser name] scheduled to go off?"

Considerably more modern in appearance than its predecessor, the new visitor center did somewhat resemble the old museum in its architectural motif. The park's landscape architect, John A. Ronscavage, argued that the center's size and shape were not of concern; rather, for him, it was most important that it was built of wood and stone building materials and that brown was its predominant color. He believed that the employment of such materials and color palettes would allow the visitor center, as well as any other new buildings constructed in the UGB, to "blend fittingly with their forest background."[62]

As with the boardwalks and trail literature, the creation of the new visitor center complex served to further define and homogenize the visitor experience. Viewing the same films and reading information from the same prediction boards, most visitors would now obtain the same interpretive information from the same media. Although ranger talks and ranger-led hikes still occurred, the vast majority of UGB visitors did not seek them out.

Automobile travelers experienced a similar transformation. Undoubtedly the most radical alteration to the UGB's landscape during this period was the reorientation of the old road system that ran through the area. Although

FIGURE 4.20. Aerial view of Old Faithful Interchange, 1971. Although the new bypass handled visitor traffic to Old Faithful more efficiently than the old road, many observers criticized the freeway-like character of the interchange that delivered visitors to the Upper Geyser Basin. Photographer unknown. Source: Yellowstone National Park Archives, YELL 115100 (courtesy of NPS-YNP).

planned in the early 1960s, the bypass road was not completed until 1971 because of financial priorities in other areas, debates over potential location, and a dispute over whether the road was actually necessary.

Originally, park planners developed two potential sites for the roadway. The first bypassed the Basin by ascending the hill to the east; this would have led visitors behind Solitary Geyser and Observation Point, giving access to the Basin via a side road. The second followed the current road southeast of Biscuit Basin, then slanted south until well past the UGB. The road would then resume its earlier alignment, with access to the UGB gained by an interstate-style exit ramp and cloverleaf (figure 4.20).

Believing that the first option was considerably more visually intrusive, Frank E. Mattson, the park's landscape architect, supported the latter. However, while favoring the location in the valley, he nonetheless had reservations about establishing a bypass road system. In his report to the NPS, he noted that given that the UGB was such a popular visitor destination, very few visitors would choose to bypass it, and therefore road rerouting would provide little alleviation in traffic congestion.[63]

Despite Mattson's concerns, in 1971 the NPS finished the bypass—complete with overpass, cloverleaf, and one-way routing—giving the entrance to the UGB the character of an exit on the New Jersey Turnpike. Complementing the overpass and in keeping with the Mission 66 plans, the NPS installed two new parking areas for 1,500 automobiles. These lots—with improved lighting systems and planted trees—greatly altered the UGB's landscape by requiring the removal of not only the automobile campground but also some concessionaires' facilities.

Although the NPS construction of boardwalks, a visitor center complex, and a new road and parking system contributed to a greater appreciation for and preservation of the UGB's thermal landscape, the establishment of these cultural features also generated a more uniform visitor experience. Specifically, the same bypass road funneled visitors into the Basin, where they all left their vehicles in one of two consolidated parking lots and walked the same trail to the visitor center. Most would view the same interpretive film and read the same interpretive pamphlet.

The NPS's facilities were not the only ones affected by wartime neglect and Mission 66. Yellowstone's concessionaires also felt the impact of these events. Actually, for them, the neglect began even earlier. In the still economically depressed late 1930s, they balked at spending money on improvements, even though their businesses were busy. Then, during the war, "all construction, and nearly all planning, ceased." Because of the "reluctance to upgrade facilities in the late 1930s, [they] were totally unprepared for the tide of humanity expecting service and facilities in the immediate post–World War II years."[64]

The park's principal concessionaire, the YPC, lost approximately $750,000 during the 1940s. By the early 1950s, the YPC wanted out of the park concessions business, but the company did not find a buyer until 1966 when the Goldfield Corporation bought the company. Six months later, the General Baking Company (which later changed its name to General Host) purchased Goldfield's outstanding stock in the YPC.

The YPC made minimal improvements to its facilities. The most substantive changes were to the Old Faithful Lodge and Housekeeping areas when running water was added to all of the tourist cabins and lodges during the war. Then, in 1953, the YPC began construction on thirty cabin units in the lodge area as part of its plan "to either replace or rehabilitate every lodge and tourist cabin now operated, and to build additional cabin accommodations," and then four years later, rehabilitated and moved campers' cabins from Mammoth Hot Springs to West Thumb and the UGB.[65] The NPS's decision to move in older existing units to more popular spots, rather than build new

FIGURE 4.21. New Snow Lodge, 2000. The Snow Lodge greatly expanded opportunities for winter recreation in the Upper Geyser Basin. Photograph by Jim Peaco. Source: Yellowstone National Park digital archives, #16429 (courtesy of NPS-YNP). (Original in color.)

ones, suggests prudence in the face of the NPS's plan to downsize the UGB's overnight facilities.

The YPC also replaced its office and employee dormitory in the Housekeeping area. The old facilities burned in 1955. The YPC spent $160,000 toward erecting a new structure in another location. While the year of construction is unclear, the building went up sometime between 1955 and 1968. It was originally used as the new housekeeping cabin office and a cafeteria. The YPC placed it just west of Hamilton's Upper Store so that it would be farther from the UGB's thermal features. In 1972, the YPC converted this structure into the Snow Lodge, and a newer version of the Lodge was completed in 1999 (figure 4.21). Up until this time, there were no overnight facilities for those visiting the UGB in winter. While the Snow Lodge contradicted Mission 66's plan to scale down overnight activities, it reflected the goal to extend visitation into the winter season. Furthermore, it helped to attract more types of visitors, complying with another Mission 66 objective. In its first season of operation, the Snow Lodge was so popular it received 3,411 overnight guests; the following year many new cabins had to be added.[66]

Aside from the Snow Lodge, the greatest concession change made during this period was actually forced upon a concessionaire: the elimination of Hamilton's bathhouse. In 1944, Director Drury reminded C. A. Hamilton that he was in violation of his previous contract and that the bathhouse had to be removed. As noted earlier, Hamilton's acquisition of the bathhouse from Brothers was contingent upon his moving it to a less visible location. Up to this point in time, the structure had been allowed to remain on-site for so long because of improvements Hamilton made in the 1930s and because of the distraction caused by the war.

Hamilton lobbied through his political ties in Washington. With post-war national park funding still low, Hamilton was granted an extension until the end of the 1949 season, which allowed him to amortize his investment.[67] Moreover, Secretary of the Interior Julius A. Krug wanted the facility to remain until a replacement went up. Per the Secretary's request, Drury selected another site for the pool, a "centrally located site in the Old Faithful area."[68] The site was most likely the one indicated on the UGB's 1939 and 1940 master plans: a plot of land in the old auto camp, across the road from the Lodge cabins. Hamilton was told to remove the facility with the expiration of his contract in December 1949.

However, the end of December came, and the bathhouse still stood. The bathhouse remained dormant for the 1950 season because of health code violations. It was finally demolished in the summer of 1951 and Hamilton made no attempts to build a costly new bathing facility in the UGB.

CONCLUSION: A CONTINUATION OF VALUES

The removal of Hamilton's bathhouse served as an indicator of the National Park Service's attitude toward cultural development in the park. The NPS mindset seems ironic given that the 1970s marked a period of large-scale development within the Basin. However, while the addition of Park Service infrastructure and interpretive structures, such as a bypass road, vast parking lots, and a substantial visitor center complex, did represent the apex—or, depending on one's perspective, the nadir—of human alteration of this landscape, these late-term Mission 66 additions were developed with the specific goals of catering to increased visitation, educating visitors about the Basin's ecology, and simultaneously reducing visitor impact on the UGB's physical landscape.

This period of cultural landscape change in the UGB initiated a longer-term shift in the park's policies that has remained important in guiding development and visitor experiences in the area ever since. Since 1972, the NPS has continued to remove cultural landscape features that were considered incompatible with what was defined as an appropriate visitor experi-

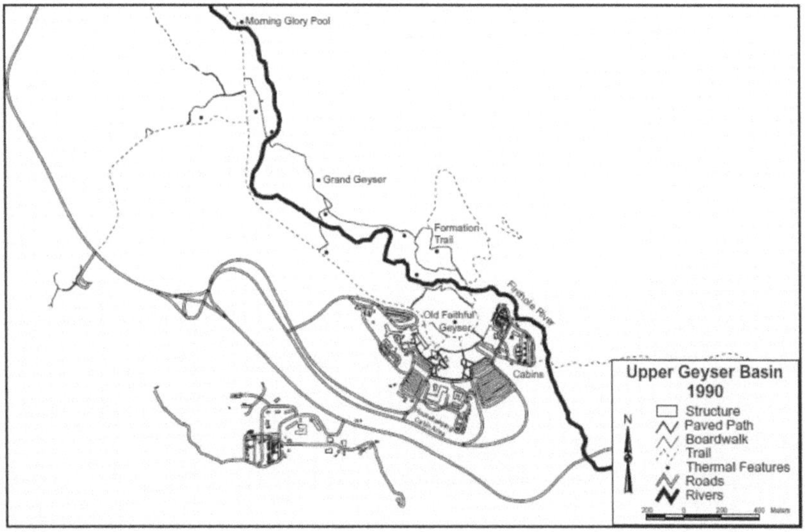

FIGURE 4.22. Upper Geyser Basin, 1990. By the late twentieth century, the Upper Geyser Basin remained one of the park's signature cultural landscapes. Map by Karl Byrand.

ence. For example, the NPS has reduced cultural landscape "visual noise" by placing certain structures (those necessary to the functioning of the UGB's infrastructure, but not requiring visitor access) well out of the visitors' view, and it has eliminated what could be considered redundant and unnecessary structures.

The above tactics were outlined in two separate NPS plans that were set in motion during the 1970s and the 1980s: the 1974 Master Plan for Yellowstone National Park and the 1984 Draft Development Concept Plan (DCP).[69] The first of these documents echoed Mission 66 by emphasizing eventual conversion to day-use only, and the latter focused on "protect[ing] and enhanc[ing] the thermal features of the Upper Geyser Basin, the Firehole River and other significant natural resources" and taking into consideration the Basin's cultural resources.[70] The 1984 plan specified that certain elements of the UGB's natural landscape, such as the thermal features, the Firehole River, and the winter wildlife habitat, were better off undisturbed by development. However, the plan also recognized the significance of some of the Basin's cultural landscape features and that they too have become an important part of Yellowstone's visual landscape and the overall visitor experience (figure 4.22). Specifically, the plan emphasized that all UGB buildings on the National Register of Historic Places (for example, Old Faithful Inn and the Lodge) deserved protection because of their unique architectural significance and because they reflected the early concession business in the park. Likewise, other buildings in the Basin were valued for being "representatives of visitor accommodations from the early period of automobile tourism and as examples of rustic architecture."[71]

The DCP called for preserving some UGB historic structures, but it designated others for demolition. First, the park planned to eliminate certain overnight facilities, specifically all the tourist cabins and most of the support buildings. All summer season lodging was supposed to occur in the Old Faithful Inn, and winter season lodging would be hosted in the Snow Lodge.

Likewise, the study reported visitor "services and support facilities were intermixed in an undesirable way."[72] To remedy this, the NPS placed infrastructure not directly utilized by visitors in the "utility area," a collection of maintenance buildings, employee housing, and sewage facilities that became concentrated in the southwest portion of the Basin on the opposite side of the Grand Loop Road.

Within the Basin proper, other human landscape removals continued. For example, the park's concession companies that oversaw the UGB's lodging removed more than 150 lodge cabins during the 1970s and 1980s. These structures were eliminated in order to fulfill a portion of the 1974 Park Master Plan and the DCP goals of removing overnight facilities at the UGB and converting it into a day-use area. Complementary to cabin removal was the elimination of the Basin's cafeteria by the YPC around 1975—not only as a way to comply with the NPS's goal of further ridding the Basin of facilities that were artificial intrusions but also because there were now several other alternative dining options for visitors.

The largest change involved the construction of a new Snow Lodge and the removal of the old facility. Dedicated in May 1999, and constructed out of rustic materials and employing a design that better complemented historic structures in the Basin, this facility was considerably more congruent with the physical landscape as compared to its rectangular brick predecessor. Likewise, the construction of this hundred-guestroom facility allowed for the old Snow Lodge cabins to be removed and the winter lodging within the Basin to be consolidated under one roof.

More recently the NPS has made significant alterations to the UGB's cultural landscape through the razing of the visitor center complex and the development of the Old Faithful Visitor Education Center. As with the Snow Lodge built in 1999, this education center also incorporated rustic materials and a design more congruent with the historic buildings within the Basin.

The architects sought to reveal Park Service values not only through the building's appearance but also through the use of "high performance, environmentally friendly 'green' materials."[73] Ground breaking began in May 2008 and the facility opened in August 2010. Located on the site of the former visitor center, this $27 million, two-story, 26,000-square-foot structure houses four main exhibit areas, an auditorium, a spacious lobby, a bookstore, and a multipurpose classroom. Conforming to the National Park Service's goals of catering to increased visitation and providing visitors accurate interpretation of the Basin's ecology, this facility was built to "serve 2.6 million on-site visitors every year" and "feature[s] new exhibits and host[s] new programs to help visitors understand and appreciate geysers, hot springs, and other hydrothermal features in Yellowstone" and the overall facility has "been designed to set new standards for accessibility and for the interpretation of complex scientific information to the public."[74]

In 2022, the addition of the Yellowstone Tribal Heritage Center, located between the Lodge and the Visitor Education Center, marked a heightened NPS commitment to recognizing the region's Native American history. The Center hosts exhibits, demonstrations, and visitor activities designed to make more legible Yellowstone's long Native American heritage. Set in one of the most visited parts of the UGB, the Center celebrates the region's enduring connections with more than two dozen tribes historically associated with Yellowstone National Park. It also marks a larger NPS effort to integrate Native American voices to future management of the park.[75]

These most recent additions to the UGB's cultural landscape continue a focus on ecology education, the area's Native American heritage, and on further reducing visitor impacts to the area. They reflect the NPS's current values, goals, and aspirations, just as previous landscapes reflected earlier park management priorities. In the late nineteenth century, the evolving cultural landscape revealed an early era in which visitors directly and intimately encountered an extraordinary thermal environment. Later, the UGB's cultural landscape was modified to more effectively preserve that thermal environment while at the same time adding recreational opportunities such as swimming in thermal baths and viewing bears after an evening meal at the hotel. But these fashions also passed out of popularity, replaced by an increasingly managed UGB landscape that offered a more uniform experience and an infrastructure that was able to cope with the growing numbers of automobile-oriented visitors. At the same time, there were growing attempts to reduce the human imprint in the area and to educate visitors on the fragile nature of Yellowstone's environment, but these goals were not always compatible with the challenges of managing large numbers of park visitors.

As incongruous and as mutually incompatible as many of these past values and their respective cultural landscape signatures may seem, they simply reflect the cumulative visual and historical record of evolving visitor expectations, changing park management philosophies, and shifting concessionaire strategies. Indeed, Yellowstone's UGB has become one of the richest repositories of that cultural memory within the park, and its mosaic of past and present cultural landscapes forms a visible scene just as fascinating as its steam-filled pools and erupting geysers.

NOTES

1. T. Scott Bryan, *The Geysers of Yellowstone* (Niwot: University Press of Colorado, 1991).
2. Philetus Norris, *Report of the Superintendent of Yellowstone National Park to the Secretary of the Interior, 1877* (Bound File, Yellowstone National Park Library), 841.
3. Norris, *Report of the Superintendent* . . . 1878, 986.
4. Norris, *Report of the Acting Superintendent* . . . 1879, 6.
5. Norris, *Report of the Acting Superintendent* . . . 1879, 9.
6. Moses Harris, *Report of the Acting Superintendent of Yellowstone National Park to the Secretary of the Interior, 1887* (Bound File, Yellowstone National Park Library), 1300.
7. William O. Owen, "Account of a Bicycle Trip to Yellowstone National Park, 1883," in *Old Yellowstone Days*, edited by Paul Schullery (Boulder: Colorado Associated University Press, 1979), 33.
8. Rudyard Kipling, "Account of a Trip to Yellowstone National Park, 1889," in Schullery, *Old Yellowstone Days*, 106.
9. Owen Wister, "Account of a Trip to Yellowstone National Park, 1887," in Schullery, *Old Yellowstone Days*, 74.
10. Aubrey L. Haines, *The Yellowstone Story*, vol. 2 (Yellowstone National Park: Yellowstone Library and Museum Association, 1977).
11. Harris, *Report of the Acting Superintendent* . . . 1888, 637.
12. George S. Anderson, *Report of the Acting Superintendent of Yellowstone National Park to the Secretary of the Interior, 1893* (Bound File, Yellowstone National Park Library), 4.
13. Anderson, *Report of the Acting Superintendent* . . . 1896, 4.
14. Richard A. Bartlett, *Yellowstone: A Wilderness Besieged* (Tucson: University of Arizona Press, 1985).
15. Haines, *Yellowstone Story*, vol. 2.
16. Linda F. McClelland, *Presenting Nature: The Historic Landscape Design of the National Park Service, 1916 to 1942* (Washington, DC: US Department of the Interior, 1993), 62.

17. Official correspondence, Haynes to Secretary of the Interior (December 30, 1881), Letter Box, no.1, Yellowstone National Park Archives.
18. Official correspondence, Joslyn to Superintendent of Yellowstone National Park Conger (March 20, 1884), Document no. 113, Letters Received, Yellowstone National Park Archives.
19. Samuel B. Young, *Report of the Acting Superintendent of Yellowstone National Park to the Secretary of the Interior, 1897* (Bound File, Yellowstone National Park Library).
20. Horace M. Albright, *Annual Report of the Superintendent of Yellowstone National Park to the Director of the National Park Service, 1919* (Bound File, Yellowstone National Park Library), 21–22.
21. Roger W. Toll, *Annual Report of the Superintendent of Yellowstone National Park to the Director of the National Park Service, 1930* (Bound File, Yellowstone National Park Library), 9.
22. Toll, *Annual Report of the Superintendent . . . 1930*, 60–61.
23. Toll, *Annual Report of the Superintendent . . . 1930*, 60–61.
24. Correspondence, "Justification for additional Public Works Projects," Edwards to Director of the National Park Service, 10 February 1934, Civilian Conservation Corps and PWA Files, Box A-12, Yellowstone National Park Archives.
25. Edmund B. Rogers, *Annual Report of the Superintendent of Yellowstone National Park to the Director of the National Park Service, 1936* (Bound File, Yellowstone National Park Library), 20.
26. Report, "Permanent Educational Improvements at Upper Basin, Yellowstone National Park, Wyoming, Made During the Season of 1926," Ansel F. Hall, 1926, p. 2, Interpretive Files, Box K-10, Yellowstone National Park Archives.
27. Albright, *Annual Report of the Superintendent . . . 1928*, 1–2.
28. Reports of the Naturalist Division, Yellowstone National Park, Volume I, 25 July 1931—31 July 1932 (Bound Files, Yellowstone National Park Archives), 6.
29. Reports of the Naturalist Division, Yellowstone National Park, Volume II, Summary Report, 1 July 1935–30 June 1936 (Bound Files, Yellowstone National Park Archives), 2.
30. Official correspondence, Albright to Child (June 1, 1927), Concessionaire Files, Box C-14, Yellowstone National Park Archives.
31. Official correspondence, Albright to Child (June 1, 1927).
32. Official correspondence, Albright to Nichols, Assistant to the President of the Yellowstone Park Hotel Company (September 17, 1927), Concessionaire Files, Box C-14, Yellowstone National Park Archives.
33. Official correspondence, Albright to Director of the National Park Service (September 17, 1927), Concessionaire Files, Box C-14, Yellowstone National Park Archives.
34. Official correspondence, Albright to Director of the National Park Service (September 17, 1927).
35. Haines, *Yellowstone Story*, vol. 2, 421n35.
36. Official correspondence, Albright to Goodwin (April 15, 1926), Concessionaire Files, Box C-14, Yellowstone National Park Archives.
37. Official correspondence, Albright to Hull (April 15, 1926), Concessionaire Files, Box C-14, Yellowstone National Park Archives.
38. Official correspondence, Toll to Director of the National Park Service (October 21, 1935), Concessionaire Files, Box C-1, Yellowstone National Park Archives.
39. Bartlett, *Yellowstone*, 96.

40. Official correspondence, Toll to Director of the National Park Service (October 21, 1935), Concessionaire Files, Box C-1, Yellowstone National Park Archives.
41. Official correspondence, Brothers to Acting Superintendent of Yellowstone National Park (October 14, 1912), Yellowstone National Park Archives.
42. Official correspondence, Brothers, to Secretary of the Interior (May 8, 1913), Yellowstone National Park Archives.
43. Official correspondence, Brett to Secretary of the Interior (June 25, 1913), Yellowstone National Park Archives.
44. Report, Dole to the Secretary of the Interior (September 23, 1913), p. 5, Yellowstone National Park Archives.
45. Official correspondence, Brett to Secretary of the Interior (October 18, 1913), Yellowstone National Park Archives.
46. Lloyd M. Brett, *Report of the Acting Superintendent of Yellowstone National Park to the Director of the National Park Service, 1915* (Bound File, Yellowstone National Park Library), 8.
47. Albright, *Annual Report of the Superintendent . . . 1924*, 29.
48. Gwen Petersen, *Yellowstone Pioneers: The Story of the Hamilton Stores and Yellowstone National Park* (Santa Barbara, CA: Sequoia Communications, 1985).
49. Bartlett, *Yellowstone*, 197.
50. Bartlett, *Yellowstone*, 197.
51. Lee H. Whittlesey, *Death in Yellowstone* (Boulder, CO: Roberts Rinehart Publishers, 1995).
52. Bartlett, *Yellowstone*, 198.
53. Toll, *Annual Report of the Superintendent . . . 1934*, 4, 22.
54. Ethan Carr, *Mission 66: Modernism and the National Park Dilemma* (Amherst, MA: University of Massachusetts Press, 2007).
55. Rough Draft Report on Yellowstone Mission 66 No. 1. 1956, p. 172, Development and Maintenance Files, Box D-20, Folder no. 3, Yellowstone National Park Library.
56. John A. Ronscavage, "Developed Area Narrative to Accompany Drawing No. NP-YEL-2264-E Old Faithful," September 1968, p. 3, Box A-11, Yellowstone National Park Archives.
57. Mission 66, The Development Program: A Part of the Project Construction Program. 1955, no page number. Archival Files, Box No. D-21, Folder No. 3, Yellowstone National Park Library.
58. Rogers, *Annual Report of the Superintendent . . . 1949*, 17–18.
59. Reports of the Naturalist Division, Yellowstone National Park, vol. 2, Annual Report for the Naturalist Department, March 1947, Yellowstone National Park Archives.
60. John A. Ronscavage, "Developed Area Narrative to Accompany Drawing No. NP-YEL-2264-E Old Faithful," September 1968, p. 4, Box A-11, Yellowstone National Park Archives.
61. Official memorandum, Anderson to Assistant Director (Operations), Division of Interpretation and Visitor Services, WASO, 23 July 1969, Interpretive Files, Box K-10. Yellowstone National Park Archives.
62. John A. Ronscavage, "Developed Area Narrative to Accompany Drawing No. NP-YEL-2264-E Old Faithful," September 1968, p. 4, Box A-11, Yellowstone National Park Archives.
63. F. E. Mattson, "Report on Bypass Roads for Old Faithful Geyser Basin," August 17, 1962, p. 5, Master Plan Studies and Mission 66, Box D-23, Yellowstone National Park Archives.
64. Bartlett, *Yellowstone*, 366.

65. "A Comprehensive Improvement Program: Now Under Way for the Ultimate Modernization or Replacement of All Lodge and Tourist Cabin Units," Yellowstone Park Company, ca. 1953, Concessionaire Files, Box C-1. Yellowstone National Park Archives.
66. J. K. Anderson, *Annual Report of the Superintendent of Yellowstone National Park to the Director of the National Park Service, 1972* (Bound File, Yellowstone National Park Library), Concessions Section.
67. Petersen, *Yellowstone Pioneers.*
68. Official memorandum, Rogers to the press, "Old Faithful Swimming Pool Concession Will Expire," June 15, no year, Concessionaire Files, Box C-1. Yellowstone National Park Archives.
69. *Draft Development Concept Plan: Old Faithful, Yellowstone National Park*, National Park Service, Denver Service Center, February, 1984.
70. *Draft Development Concept Plan*, 8
71. *Draft Development Concept Plan*, 13.
72. *Draft Development Concept Plan*, 1.
73. National Park Service, Old Faithful Virtual Visitor Center (http://mms.nps.gov/yell/ofvec/orientation/construction.htm).
74. National Park Service, Old Faithful Virtual Visitor Center.
75. For more, see https://www.nps.gov/places/000/yellowstone-tribal-heritage-center.htm.

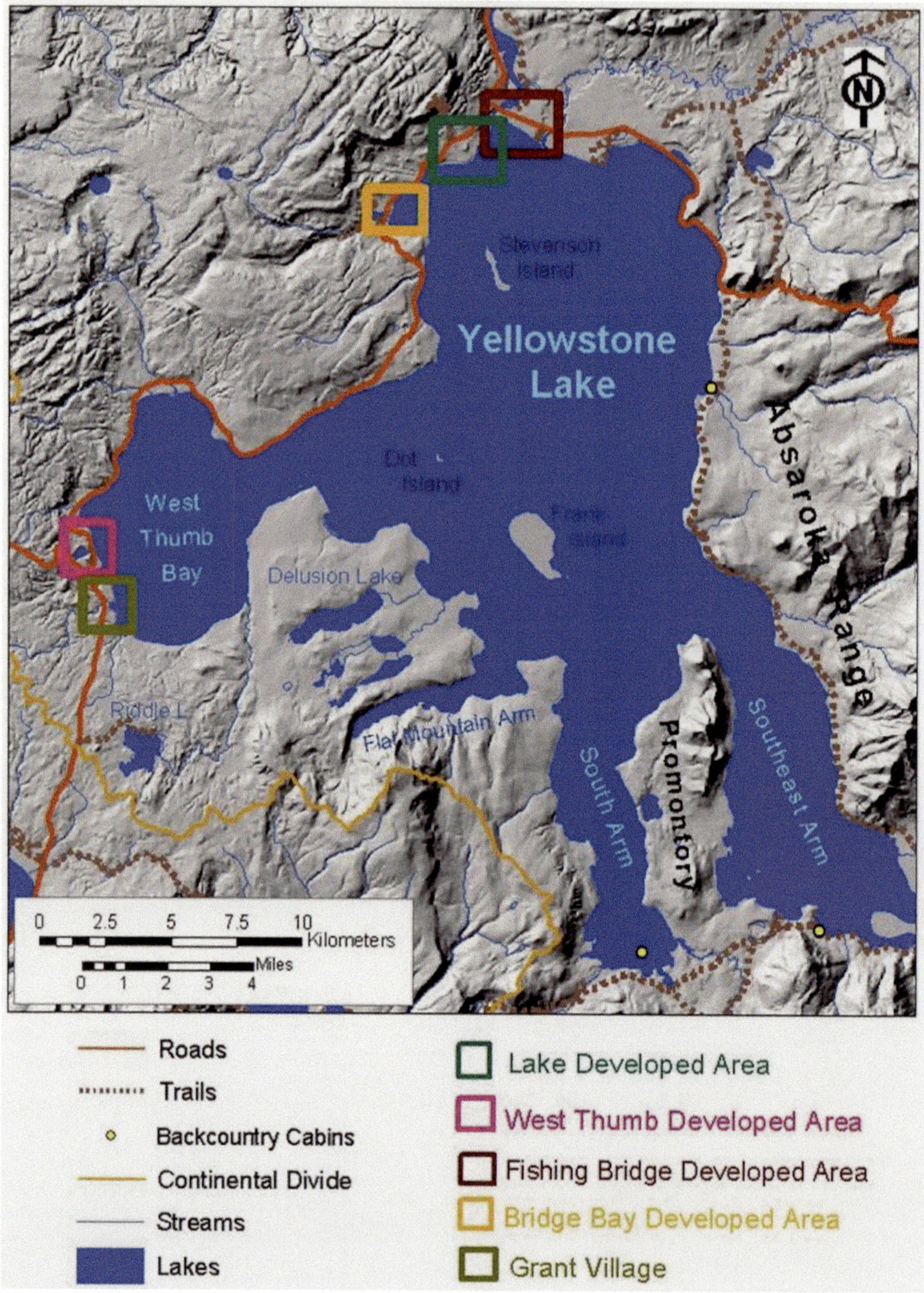

FIGURE 5.1. Map of Yellowstone Lake noting its physical layout and major developed areas. Most of the major developed areas around Yellowstone Lake are focused along its western and northern shoreline. Map by Yolonda Youngs.

5

Yellowstone Lake

Yolonda Youngs

DIVE BELOW the surface—of a lake, of history, of a landscape—and you will be amazed at what you find. I first became familiar with Yellowstone Lake in 1991. At that time, I was working as a commercial kayak guide and interpreter. I knew the lake then as an emotional and physical space, as a refuge for quiet paddling defined by water, wind, and rhyolite. My job entailed leading intrepid park visitors into the lake's more remote bays, setting up camp, preparing their meals, and entertaining them (or putting them to sleep) by the campfire reading from the journals of Ferdinand V. Hayden or Truman Everts, both nineteenth-century adventure-seekers at Yellowstone. One day, however, this cadence of life changed pace during a brief respite from the lake's daily tantrums of strong winds and incessant waves. As my boat glided along the southeastern shoreline, I slowed my pace and scanned the lake's sandy floor. I was abruptly caught off guard by a dark shape passing a few feet beneath me, dwarfing my seventeen-foot boat. As I slowed down to inspect this mystery, I could make out little more than wooden boards—lots of them. Indeed, I had paddled right over a dock. But why was a dock lurking beneath the water on an isolated shoreline of Yellowstone Lake? At the

https://doi.org/10.5876/9781646427697.c005

time, I had little information to guide my musings. Of the few interpretive signs posted around the lake, most were devoted to descriptions of the area's ecological and geological setting. The mysterious dock spurred my curiosity and I wondered what other stories of Yellowstone Lake were hidden from my view, submerged below the surface of the park's history.

THE HIDDEN CULTURAL LANDSCAPE OF YELLOWSTONE LAKE

Yellowstone Lake is a large, cold, high-elevation lake that sits centrally in Yellowstone National Park's "grand loop" tour of attractions (figure 5.1). At an altitude of 7,733 feet, it is a place of extremes: great natural beauty and striking contrasts. It is the largest lake in Yellowstone National Park and one of the world's most sizable natural freshwater lakes. Framed by the Absaroka Mountains to the east, Yellowstone Lake is jostled by gusty afternoon breezes in the summer and frozen solid for much of the rest of the year. Sprinkled all around the lake's shoreline and mountains are geothermal features—geysers, fumaroles, mud pots, and hot springs—indicative features of the lake's volcanic history and scenic attractions. But Yellowstone Lake is more than a sum of its physical environment, more than a scenic drive past forested shorelines and mountainous vistas. It is also a cultural landscape shaped by a deep history of powerful and sometimes conflicting social forces, an area reformulated and renegotiated as a national park and wilderness area, and a landscape designed and arranged as a selective representation of nature.

To understand better the history of Yellowstone Lake's cultural landscape, it is instructive to delve deeper into the stories of the people, the policies, the ideas, and the physical environment that shaped this setting over time. The location and placement of the built landscape, including roads, buildings, and boardwalks, are all part of a scene crafted to frame an objectified image of the physical landscape that is deemed "natural." The placement of boardwalks around geothermal features; the location, shape, and size of buildings; even the ordering of developed areas or visitor service complexes at the lake are not accidents. Evolving negotiations with, and resolutions between, multiple and often conflicting groups have reworked how the lake was experienced by visitors, what people expected when they visited the lake, and how these expectations translated into material landscape features. A deeper exploration of Yellowstone Lake's cultural landscape reveals a palimpsest of stories, a layered accumulation of different activities, designs, and management decisions that are still discernible with a closer reading of the lake's cultural and historical context.

In this chapter, I explore the evolution of Yellowstone Lake's cultural landscape as it informs our understanding of Yellowstone National Park and plays a vital, though often overlooked, role in its history and development. What would evolve into a constellation of villages, shops, cafeterias, boardwalks, and campgrounds at Yellowstone Lake started out as two small outposts along the shoreline. Over the course of most of the lake's cultural landscape history, Yellowstone Lake rarely swayed from this scheme of locating development near significant natural features and close to the shoreline. When park managers—under the influence of emerging ecological science, park system policies, and wilderness values—advocated for development away from historic lakeshore use areas and natural landmarks, the results marked the beginning of the end of an era for visitation of Yellowstone Lake. Diving deeper into the landscape history of Yellowstone Lake is more than a simple history lesson or roadside diversion along the grand tour of the park. It is an opportunity to connect contemporary scenes and experiences at the lake to the people, events, decisions, and ideas that shaped this lake's cultural landscape over time.

DESIGNING YELLOWSTONE LAKE: YELLOWSTONE LAKE PRIOR TO 1872

Yellowstone Lake has a long history of human use. The earliest archaeological sites in Yellowstone National Park may be found at Yellowstone Lake, with evidence of "tool stone procurement, tool manufacture, and repair activities" that are more than nine thousand years old.[1] Early inhabitants may have been attracted to the lake for its plant, animal, and stone resources but found that their use of this landscape was limited by changing lake levels and the availability of good camping locations.[2] Archaeological evidence suggests that most human land use at the lake was concentrated along the shoreline in the Southeast Arm, the western shoreline of West Thumb Bay, and the northern shoreline of the lake, particularly near the outlet of the Yellowstone River.[3]

When Euro-American fur trappers and exploration parties journeyed to Yellowstone Lake during the mid-1800s, they found abundant evidence of

Bannock, Crow, Sheep Eater, and Shoshone peoples. There is also ample proof that Euro-American trappers and explorers often sought out the knowledge and expertise of Native American groups familiar with the area, particularly in terms of their knowledge of the landscape and routes of travel. Osborne Russell—a fixture in Rocky Mountain trapper lore and legend—recorded a scene of geographic communication during an encounter with a Native American group he identified as the Tibuboes (People of the Sun):

> One of them drew a map of the country around us on a white Elk Skin with a piece of Charcoal after which he explained the direction of the different passes, streams etc[.] From them we discovered that it was about one day[']s travel in a SW direction to the outlet or northern extremity of the Yellow Stone [*sic*] Lake, but the route from his description being difficult. . . . Our Geographer also told us that this stream united with the Yellow Stone [*sic*] after leaving this Valley half a day[']s travel in a west direction.[4]

Russell's reference to Yellowstone Lake became a common practice evident in many written accounts and cartographic representations of the area that were created by nineteenth-century Euro-Americans who traveled through the region.[5]

Written accounts such as Russell's are representative of a geographic dialogue between Native Americans and Euro-American trappers that heavily influenced the routes and sites of visitation at Yellowstone Lake for subsequent exploratory groups.[6] Over time, this accumulated information about the lake and surrounding region appeared in more formalized maps and descriptions of the region.[7] These written descriptions and cartographic representations revealed (figure 5.2) the grandeur of Yellowstone Lake to a wider audience, and they played an important role in the creation of Yellowstone National Park in 1872.

EARLY YEARS OF PARK DEVELOPMENT, 1872–1891

After Yellowstone National Park was established in 1872, the Native American presence around the lake challenged the designs envisioned by park promoters who were charged with managing this landscape. Native Americans continued to use trails, access spiritual sites, and inhabit campsites around the lake well into the park's early years. Park officials were keen to erase and ignore these Native American signatures in Yellowstone, preferring

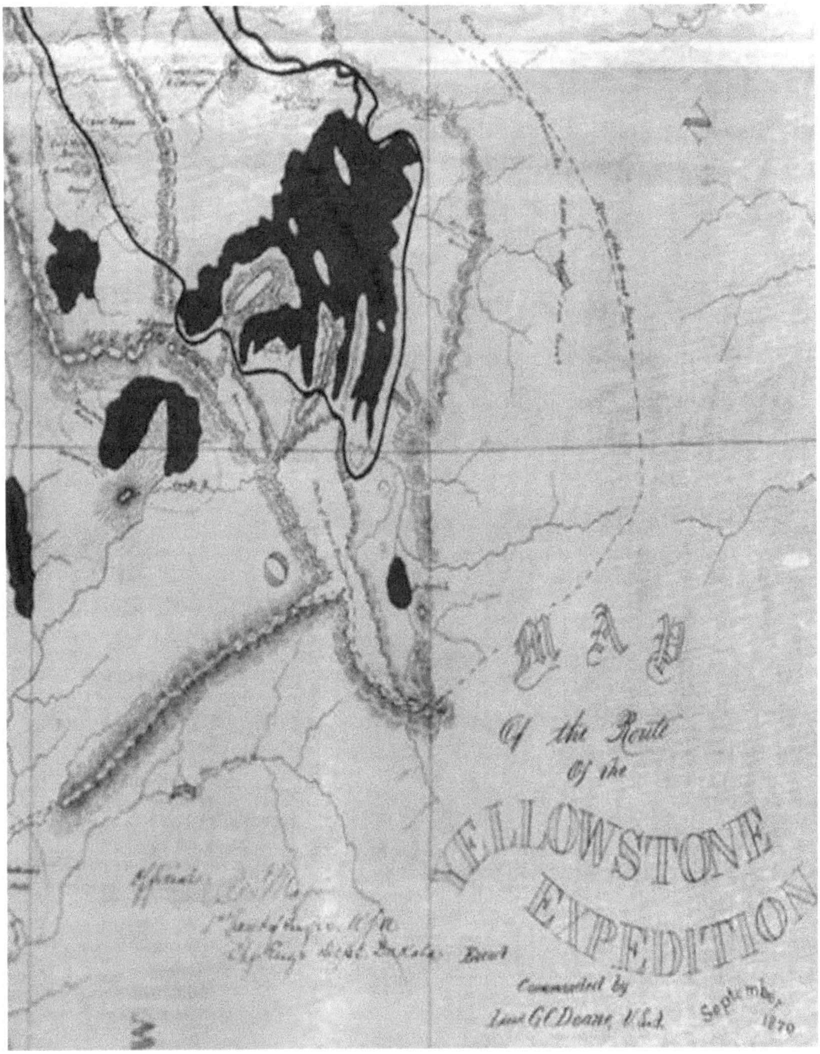

FIGURE 5.2. "Map of the Route of the Yellowstone Expedition, Escort Commanded by Lieut. G. C. Doane, U.S.A., September 1870," 1870. This map shows the cartographic emergence of Yellowstone Lake in the years immediately before the establishment of the national park. Source: Headquarters map file, Q 329-30, Records of the Office of the Chief of Engineers, Record Group 77, National Archives.

instead to promote the region as an example of wild, uninhabited wilderness.[8] Seasonal groups of Bannock, Shoshone, and Crow peoples challenged this image by traveling in and residing throughout the park well into the late nineteenth century.[9] As one of the oldest inhabited areas of Yellowstone, the lake's shoreline landscape had long been used for hunting and camping, creating in the process an enduring record of human occupancy in the region.[10] But confrontations between Native Americans and federally appointed park overseers percolated to the top of pressing policy and development issues as these groups clashed over park uses and activities soon after the establishment of Yellowstone. For example, in 1880, Superintendent Norris described "skin-covered lodges or circular upright brush heaps called wickeups, decaying evidences of which are abundant near . . . the shores of Yellowstone Lake."[11] Although Norris documented many such features around the lake, these descriptions were not reproduced or referred to in park guidebooks from this era. Subsequent park managers also discouraged traditional Native American uses of the land such as the gathering of plants for subsistence or the use of fire to clear hunting areas.[12]

Clearly, early park officials envisioned a different lakeside landscape, one that included roads, lodging concessions, and other tourist services, but not Native American features. After Yellowstone was created, one of the strongest guiding principles for the park was the preservation of natural features for the "benefit and enjoyment of the people."[13] Early park overseers and private developers interpreted this principle as a call to create a system of roadways and visitor services that would make the park more accessible to the traveling public. When considering the possible layout of the road network, Superintendent Langford—the first park superintendent and member of an 1870 expedition into the region—suggested that "these roads, when completed, would enable the visitor to reach all the great points of interest by carriage. . . . The opening of these roads would insure the early erection of large and commodious public houses at Mammoth Springs, Yellowstone Falls, Yellowstone Lake and the Upper and Lower Geyser Basins."[14]

Park Superintendent P. W. Norris played a crucial role in shaping early park design and development in the vicinity of Yellowstone Lake. Indeed, Norris took a strong lead in promoting Yellowstone Lake as one of the park's outstanding tourist attractions. In his 1878 superintendent's report, Norris suggests that a combination of hotel and steamboat service would be the best option for development at the lake. He notes that "with another season's improvement and construction of roads and bridle-paths, [and] the promised routes of access . . . I have all confidences of being able to effect leases to responsible parties for the construction of much-needed hotels, and also for a yacht or small steamer upon the mystic Yellowstone Lake."[15] Eager to encourage travel to the "matchless mountain lake," Norris also pushed for a network of established trails around the lake.[16] In 1879, he describes the opening of a trail around the western shore of Yellowstone Lake for "26 miles to its outlet" that connected the major features of the lake: "hot springs at west thumb, cliffs on lake, bridge creek bay, [and] foot of Yellowstone Lake."[17] By 1881, the bridle path for horse traffic was extended from the Upper and Lower Falls of the Yellowstone River (Grand Canyon Area) south to the outlet of the Yellowstone River. The trail roughly followed the north and west shorelines of the Yellowstone Lake between the lake outlet and the West Thumb geothermal basin.[18] Later park supervisors would extend Norris's vision of development at the lake, through planning and encouragement of concessionaire investment.

Overall, however, park trails offered limited accessibility. Norris believed that roads were even more important because road building "assures immediate coach connection with civilization, convenience for tourists and ultimate self sustaining [*sic*] character of the park."[19] But Yellowstone Lake roads were developed later than other portions of the park road network. During the earliest years of developing park transportation networks, travel to and along Yellowstone Lake remained restricted to bridle trails along the northern shore of the lake, which generally followed Native American foot trails. Most visitors traveling to the lake moved along the north shore. Although there were trails along the southern shoreline that were well used by Native American groups and Euro-American explorers and trappers, the southern region of the lake shifted to a more peripheral status as park development focused on routes closer to developing visitor services at Old Faithful and Canyon.

Compared to other sites in the park, the Yellowstone Lake area also initially lagged when it came to other visitor services.[20] Early concessionaire activity at the lake began with the modest outposts of a few trappers who realized that profits resided with tourists, not with pelts. One of the earliest lodging options along the lake was Eugene S. Topping's log cabin. Norris describes Topping's cabin as built at "the foot of Yellowstone Lake," a location probably along the northeast shoreline close to Yellowstone River outlet.[21] Most of Topping's business came from tourists, who traveled to the lake by horseback along park trails then ventured onto the lake for a ride aboard his boat. Norris recorded that Topping's boat was "a small sail-boat of green whipsawed timber built by Captain Topping at his cabin, near the foot of Yellowstone Lake, during the summer of 1875, and which, after perilous service during a small portion of the seasons 1875 and 1876, was dismantled, abandoned, and finally lost."[22] Topping's boat was important to Yellowstone Lake's early tourism infrastructure, as it provided one of the earliest recorded tourist boating trips on the lake and an attraction for tourists to travel to the then-remote eastern area of the lake.

Although the park's early overseers may have had grand visions for the lake's future, logistical issues curtailed their development schemes. Lean funding, uncoordinated management efforts, and the immense size of the newly christened park hampered early park overseers from extending beyond basic administrative tasks. After several years of personnel shortages and vague guidelines for park management, the United States Army stepped in as the primary park management agency in 1886.

Under the direction of the US Army and the US Army Corps of Engineers, major roads and trails were finally constructed in the park. Concessionaires used these routes of travel to transport tourists through the park and connect their burgeoning visitor service complexes. Park managers, developers, and businesses operating in the park coordinated on several levels, including the placement and design of infrastructure features. Park overseers and engineers constructed trails, roads, and tourist facilities based on their personal experience in the area, limitations presented by physical landscape features, and concessionaire demand for access. In the lake area, these transportation corridors generally followed established Indian paths and bridle trails along the north and west shoreline; these decisions about travel paths proved pivotal in dictating the longer-term evolution of travel corridors and development areas within the lake region.

By the end of 1891, developments at Yellowstone Lake offered new opportunities for visitors. Simply getting to the park was much easier than it had been a decade earlier. Many tourists made most of the trip via train, along lines operated either by the Northern Pacific or Union Pacific railroads. Most visitors arrived at the northern boundary of the park through Mammoth Hot Springs and then met a stagecoach tour that took them into the interior of the park.

The typical direction of travel for early stagecoach tours ran counterclockwise around the park from Mammoth Hot Springs to Old Faithful, then onwards to West Thumb at Yellowstone Lake. Travelers would then continue along the lakeshore toward the outlet of the Yellowstone River, and then north to the Grand Canyon of the Yellowstone, returning to Mammoth Hot Springs. In terms of Yellowstone Lake's attractions along this route, the West Thumb basin was an appealing stop. Its allure combined expansive views across the lake with the curiosities of a large basin filled with brilliantly colored geothermal pools and boiling mud pots. After a lunch stop at West Thumb, visitors could choose between continuing along in the stagecoaches or climbing aboard a steamboat operated by the colorful captain E. C. Waters for an afternoon cruise across the lake. This steamboat ferry service was a unique element in Yellowstone's transportation system, and park overseers encouraged its development. Even early park superintendents saw the benefits of a steamboat ferry service across the lake, while noting the considerable challenges to boating on the lake. In his 1881 annual report, Park Superintendent Philetus Norris recorded his opinion about the potential benefit of a lake transport service and ultimately the construction of a large hotel:

FIGURE 5.3. The first Lake Hotel, built in 1891, was financed by the Northern Pacific Railroad. Photographer unknown. Source: Yellowstone National Park Archives YELL 128122 (courtesy of National Park Service–Yellowstone National Park; hereafter NPS-YNP).

> On this account and because of narrow deep seas, rocky shores, and sparse anchorage, this lake, while one of the most beautiful and interesting is one of the most dangerous for sailing craft. I am confident, however, that with even a small steamer, well built and managed, there would be little danger attending regular trips around the fingers, thumb, and palm of the lake, and for at least seven miles down the river. . . . With a suitable steamer making regular excursions of, say, three hundred miles, it is safe to predict that a hotel on some one of the many charming terraces near the foot of the lake would ultimately prove a profitable investment in this region of wonders.[23]

As the steamer left the dock and traveled across the wave-studded lake, travelers marveled at the Absaroka Mountains to the east. The steamboat traveled east across the West Thumb Bay to the outlet of the Yellowstone River on the northeastern shore of the lake. The ferry passed near two islands—Dot Island and Stevenson Island—before arriving at a dock in front of the newly built Lake Hotel (figure 5.3).

The Lake Hotel was opened in 1891 and was financed by the Northern Pacific Railroad. Opening with eighty rooms, this simple lodging offered visitors an opportunity to enjoy lakeside diversions, and it initially received high praise from park managers. Park Superintendent Anderson describes the hotel in 1891:

> The Lake House has one wing completed, and this is all that will be needed until the tide of travel sets more in that direction. It is one of the pleasantest, best kept hotels in the Park, and deserves better patronage than it has yet received. I regard it as the most desirable place in the park for a prolonged stay.[24]

Concessionaires and federal agents developed a small outpost around the Lake Hotel that included a boat dock for the steamboat ferry and a US Army ranger station. While some visitors enjoyed only a brief overnight stay at the hotel, others chose longer stays that included walks along the shoreline, picking wildflowers around the hotel, or trying their hand at fishing for trout.

By 1891, Yellowstone Lake was a dynamic cultural landscape that had been cumulatively shaped by Native Americans, early park superintendents, the US Army, park concessionaires, and visitors. Both West Thumb and the Lake Hotel, the two primary areas of development at Yellowstone Lake, proved important in supporting future lakeside infrastructure, as they both offered essential tourist services. Superintendent Norris's glowing description of what later developed into a bustling visitor services complex around the Lake Hotel anticipated and encouraged the importance of the lake as a key landscape feature within the park:

> My favorite camp on the Yellowstone Lake (and it has evidently been a favorite one for the Indian) has ever been upon the grove-dotted bluff, elevated thirty or forty feet above the lake, directly fronting Indian Pond. . . . This cove, so landlocked as to be safe except during southern gales, and the bluffs at its head will doubtless remain a chosen haunt for the scientist and tourist.[25]

NEW SHORELINE EXPERIENCES, 1892–1932

Yellowstone Lake in 1932 was vastly changed from the cultural landscape that visitors experienced in 1891. These transformations reflected increasing levels of accessibility and movement within the park, new notions among visitors and concessionaires about how to experience and consume nature while there, and evolving ideas among park officials about how best to manage and promote Yellowstone. During this period, park engineers further developed a wagon and eventually an automobile road system of two large loops that connected with spur roads to the park entrances. Stagecoach tours offered by the Yellowstone Park Transportation Company and the Monida and Yellowstone Stage Company incorporated the lake in their extensive park itineraries. As automobile tourists arrived after 1915, they independently navigated around the park and continued to include the lake as part of their tour.

Concessionaires and park overseers played an influential role in shaping visitor experiences at Yellowstone Lake throughout this period. Stagecoach concessionaires crafted their tour routes by considering a variety of factors: the locations of visitor services such as lodging and dining, the position of scenic features in the park, and the pathways of accessible roads. These tours traveled between points that provided scenic attractions for visitors and that could be reached in a day's travel. In 1898, for example, the Monida and Yellowstone Stage Company provided service between the Fountain Hotel in the western part of the park and the West Thumb area of Yellowstone Lake, all within about five and a half hours of travel time. Concessionaires also offered lodging and eating facilities and worked in cooperative agreements with the stagecoach companies to develop guest services at these locations.

Road building around the western shoreline of Yellowstone Lake was a tedious and challenging task. Engineers faced the hurdles of thick lakeside forests, steep rocky slopes, or soft sandy beaches as they cut their new and improved roadbeds along the lake's edge. However, by the early 1890s, a passable wagon road to Yellowstone Lake was completed. By 1892, Acting Superintendent Anderson reported, "an excellent new road opened from the Canyon to the Upper Basin, via the lake. This [*sic*] 52 miles of road is destined to become one of the most popular, as it is one of the most beautiful, drives in the park."[26] This road connected a growing visitor services complex at Old Faithful with the West Thumb Bay at Yellowstone Lake, then continued from West Thumb northeast toward the Lake Hotel area, then left along the lake to proceed north to the Grand Canyon of the Yellowstone River.

US Army superintendents and road engineers used roads and trails to design and coordinate visitors' experiences at the lake. The routes and views along the way shaped what visitors would see and experience in the park and at the lake (figure 5.4). Park officials focused on a plan to create and maintain a road system that allowed visitors to travel—via a loop route—to key park features deemed scenic and significant to the Yellowstone experience. In 1900, Hiram M. Chittenden, chief engineer of the US Army Corps of Engineers, reported six "principal centers of interest in the park," including Yellowstone Lake.[27] Tour guidebook descriptions also reveal that park managers encouraged road-building projects as ways of providing easier access to selected locations at the lake—places that these agents promoted as aesthetically attractive. For example, a 1908 park guidebook referred to the completion of the east entrance road as the "construction of the road from the outlet of Yellowstone Lake to the eastern boundary of the Park," which "opened up a delightful portion of the Park scenery."[28]

FIGURE 5.4. Dirt road from Canyon to Yellowstone Lake (north shore, near present Lake Village), 1895. This early view looks south, with Yellowstone Lake in the background. Photographer unknown. Source: Yellowstone National Park Archives, YELL 128111 (courtesy of NPS-YNP).

By guiding the placement of transportation networks and visitor services, park overseers, engineers, and concessionaires choreographed the timing, order, and selection of sights that tourists visited, and the locations where they experienced the park.[29] These spatial practices added a distinctive geographic element to an escalating story of what people did in national parks and expected of the experience while there. A road in poor condition or a lack of road access to a feature in the park translated into low visitor contact and a marginalization of that feature in park advertising.

Guidebook descriptions reinforced efforts by park overseers, engineers, and concessionaires to shape visitor experiences. Guidebook authors encouraged visitors to travel along established roadways and ferry routes at Yellowstone Lake, often emphasizing sightseeing features found along these travel corridors.[30] A closer reading of guidebook descriptions reveals that scenic features beyond the reach of roads may have been mentioned in guidebooks, but travel was discouraged to these locations. For instance, an 1893 description of Yellowstone Lake discouraged visitor excursions to hot springs areas beyond the West Thumb thermal basin. The guidebook suggests that there are "no less than seven hot-spring areas surrounding Yellowstone Lake" but "those of the west arm or Thumb []bay . . . are by far the most interesting."[31] Yellowstone Lake does indeed have seven (if not more, by some counts) hot spring areas scattered around the shoreline of the lake and along the lake's floor. Many of these basins included colorful hot springs, active geysers. or fumaroles and offered views across the lake. However, not all of these areas could be easily accessed by roads, and most lacked concessionaire development. West Thumb, on the other hand, had all these amenities.

FIGURE 5.5. Fishing Bridge, outlet of Yellowstone Lake, ca. 1919. This early view of Fishing Bridge suggests its enduring popularity with anglers and tourists. Photographer unknown. Source: Yellowstone National Park Service Archives YELL 34676-2 (courtesy of NPS-YNP).

Fishing Bridge (figure 5.5) was another important addition to the cultural landscape of Yellowstone Lake. Built in 1902 on the lake's northern outlet, the Fishing Bridge provided safe crossing over the Yellowstone River's cold and deep waters and offered access to the lake's eastern shore. The bridge was rebuilt and realigned several times over the course of its life, but the early bridge had an arch at its center to accommodate rowboats passing underneath. Later, a floating boat-rental hut was built nearby. By 1914, this bridge acquired the moniker "Fishing Bridge" because of the many fishing enthusiasts who sought out this location to take advantage of the trout spawning grounds.[32]

Boating continued to be a significant form of tourist travel on the lake. After a respite at West Thumb from the arduous stagecoach journey to the lake, many visitors cruised across the lake on the *Zillah*, a steamboat operated by Captain E. C. Waters, owner and operator of the Yellowstone Lake Boat Company. US Army park managers approved of Waters's concessions and continued to support other tour-boat operations and even encouraged additional boating development around the lake:

> The boat [the *Zillah*] has been put in excellent condition, and it furnishes one of the most delightful bits of travel on the tour. The proposition to put a few small steam or naphtha launches on the lake has not been carried out, but I believe it would prove remunerative and certainly would be a great accommodation to tourists.[33]

Waters enlarged his operations along the north shore of the lake just down the hill from the Lake Hotel between 1895 and 1906, creating a cluster of wooden docks and structures, including his house, a boat rental and fishing supply store, and various buildings used for equipment and storage. He also offered tours of the lake:

> The steamer Zillah, running daily trips on Yellowstone Lake . . . has given full satisfaction to the public. I have made many trips on the boat, always found her in perfect condition, and thoroughly safe. The entire personnel of the boat are always attentive and polite to the passengers, doing everything for their pleasure and enjoyment. In addition to the regular tourist business, this steamer has had many excursions.[34]

The popularity of the boat trips rose steadily from 1897 to a peak in 1909; of the 10,825 visitors to Yellowstone National Park in 1897, no fewer than 2,589 traveled on the steamboat across the lake during their park tour.[35] By 1909, 7,959 of the 32,545 Yellowstone tourists boarded the wooden-planked boat to cross the lake.[36] Although these figures suggest the popularity of the boat tours, they do not indicate the storm brewing at Yellowstone Lake between park management, concessionaires, and visitor demands in the intervening years.

The steamboat ferry service permitted to and operated by E. C. Waters started in 1891 but soon expanded to offer a variety of boating related services. In 1895, this operation was renamed and given a new permit as the Yellowstone Lake Boating Company, which held exclusive rights to commercial boating on the lake until 1906; however, tensions began to escalate between park overseers and concessionaires. In 1902, John Pitcher, acting superintendent of the park, added his voice to the growing call for more diverse boating activities around the lake: "very little use is made of the lake at present beyond taking the trip from the Thumb to the Lake Hotel, but I believe that its beauties and attractions would be greatly enjoyed by many tourists if the boating facilities were better."[37] Pitcher continues his discussion of the "boating facilities" to suggest that there needed to be more competition for the boat company on the lake. This friction between the government authorities and the Yellowstone Lake Boat Company came to a climax in 1908 and resulted in a transfer of boating operations permits to the T. E. Hofer Boat Company.

The friction between tour-boat concessionaires and park management under the US Army was indicative of changes ahead for the larger concessionaire scheme at Yellowstone Lake and throughout Yellowstone National Park. Before 1916, there was a variety of concessionaires in the park that offered visitor services at Yellowstone Lake. Changes in park policies in 1917, however, altered concessionaire management schemes and the cultural landscape at Yellowstone Lake. In 1917, the newly created National Park Service (NPS) mandated a reorganization of concessionaires, concentrating all of the existing concessions into operations organized by the type of services offered to visitors.[38] Under this reorganization, four new companies emerged (see table 5.1): Yellowstone Park Transportation Company (park transportation); Yellowstone Park Hotel Company (park hotels); Yellowstone Park Camping Company—formerly Wylie and Shaw and Powell (camping facilities); and Yellowstone Park Boat Company (boating activities).

The effects of this concessionaire reorganization played out a bit differently at Yellowstone Lake than in other regions of the park. This was due, in part, to the varied geography of the lake—it was more of a region of development with multiple sites of visitor services than a single location. As visitation to the park increased through the 1910s, so too did visitors' demands for more diverse lake experiences at multiple locations. Park overseers echoed these sentiments by encouraging additional visitor services at the West Thumb, Lake, and Fishing Bridge areas.

For example, the establishment of the NPS in 1916 and the subsequent forced concessionaire consolidations in 1917 created new administrative pressures for the expansion and diversification of boating facilities at Yellowstone Lake. By 1919, Hamilton Stores operated a boat rental business under an agreement with the Yellowstone Park Boat Company. However, the park superintendent was not impressed, proposing that Hamilton Stores:

> should be required to purchase new equipment before the opening of the next season and be prepared to meet all demands for row-boat and launch service, as well as for longer trips to the upper arms of Yellowstone Lake. If it can not meet the requirements of the Service[,] some other individual or corporation should be found who will develop the recreational advantages of this beautiful Lake.[39]

As with earlier park superintendents, Horace Albright lodged complaints and suggestions about lake operations that demanded more from these concessionaires. Despite this friction, boating continued to be a prominent activity at Yellowstone Lake as steam-powered and hand-propelled boats

TABLE 5.1. Government Agencies and Concessionaires Operating at Yellowstone Lake, 1895–1919

Year	Agencies and Concessionaires
1895[a]	Yellowstone Park Association, Yellowstone Lake Boat Company
1897	Yellowstone Park Transportation Company
1898	Wylie Permanent Camping Company, Monida and Yellowstone Stage Company
1903	US Fish Commission
1906	US Bureau of Fisheries, Yellowstone Park Transportation Company name change to Yellowstone National Park Transportation Company
1908	T. E. Hofer Boat Company takes over operations of Yellowstone Lake Boat Company
1912	Yellowstone Park Boat Company, Holm Transportation Company, Yellowstone Park Hotel Company
1913	Shaw and Powell Camping Company
1914	Yellowstone Western Stage Company replaces Monida and Yellowstone Stage Company
1915	Yellowstone Western Stage Company
1916	National Park Service replaces United States Army, Cody-Sylvan Pass Motor Company
1917	Yellowstone Park Camping Company (formerly Wylie Permanent Camping Company and Shaw and Powell Camping Company), Yellowstone Park Transportation Company, Yellowstone Park Hotel Company, Yellowstone Park Boat Company
1919	1919 Hamilton Stores

SOURCE: Compiled from Annual Superintendent Reports for Yellowstone National Park (1895–1919).

a. Dates listed indicate the year that the agency or company started businesses at Yellowstone Lake or when agencies or companies changed names or ownership.

gave way to motorized boating options. Three boating centers—West Thumb, Lake (figure 5.6), and a rental hut at Fishing Bridge—fed the visitor demand for ways to access the lake's waters.

Another notable development centered on the park-wide influx of automobile traffic after the entrance of the first car in 1915. After this date, park tour operators discontinued their stagecoach operations and began offering group automobile trips in specially built cars. Yellowstone Lake concessionaires were not far behind in this shift: steamboat concessionaires shifted their operations toward motorized boating and group travel. A Northern Pacific Railway brochure notes that "a speed boat operating between the Thumb and Lake Hotel . . . meets the regular park-tour automobiles, offering visitors a pleasant diversion during the journey around the Park."[40]

Lodging and dining options at Yellowstone Lake also expanded in the early twentieth century. These once-modest facilities sprouted into larger complexes offering visitor services in a variety of shapes, sizes, and prices. The Lake Hotel grew into a full-service enterprise, complete with many amenities oriented around the lifestyles of its affluent visitors. By the late 1890s, the hotel offered services for tourists desiring an extended stay at the lake:

> This spacious and elegantly appointed hotel tends greatly toward making the Yellowstone Lake the resort, par excellence, of the Park. Here everything is so arranged that guests can spend the entire season, if they so desire, making short, easy trips of sightseeing or explorations to all points of the great reserve. . . . To visit any or all of the points circumjacent to this grand mountain lake, vehicles of all kinds, saddle and pack animals, guides, rowboats, and steamers are ever at command.[41]

FIGURE 5.6. Boat dock at Lake Village, ca. 1892. This early dock sat just below the newly built Lake Hotel. Photographer unknown. Source: Yellowstone National Park Service Archives, YELL 41283 (courtesy of NPS-YNP).

Beginning in 1904, the Lake Hotel expanded through extensive renovations. A park superintendent's report from this period noted that "the hotel at the lake outlet has been practically rebuilt and refurbished, and, like the Old Faithful Inn, it also has all of the modern conveniences. . . . It is now the largest hotel in the park. It has 210 rooms and can accommodate 466 guests. The Old Faithful Inn has 140 rooms and can accommodate 316 guests."[42] In later years, the Lake Hotel flourished as auto tourists made frequent use of its facilities. The hotel renovation brought more than new water pipes and a few extra rooms to the lake. The changes to the hotel transformed it into a grand building that was more in harmony with modern values and aesthetic tastes of upper-class consumers than was its rustic predecessor. Both the interior and exterior of the hotel were transformed. From the simple wooden exterior and undecorated facade, the Lake Hotel now boasted classical architectural features such as ionic columns in the front of the building (facing the lake) as well as newly installed, ornate window frames. The roof was extended in three places for large porches, and fifteen false balconies were added onto the front of the hotel.

The hotel's increasingly formal architectural elements stood in sharp contrast to the lake's otherwise undecorated shoreline, reflecting traditions of social power and class difference that had been transplanted from eastern resort settings. The interior spaces included a fine dining hall with prompt wait staff, a viewing deck with comfortable wicker chairs, and rooms that possessed all the modern conveniences. The hotel renovation repackaged nature at the lake to fit the expectations of affluent tourists, who also stood out in this landscape, particularly when they viewed grizzly bears at nearby feeding platforms. During a 1928 auto tour through the park, Mrs. N. E. Corthell remarked: "At the Lake Hotel I saw women in party silks and loaded with diamonds strutting out to the garbage glen to look at the bears."[43]

FIGURE 5.7. Wylie Tent Camp. Campers enjoy a Wylie Way tent camp in Yellowstone National Park. These camps offered affordable accommodations to many visitors with modest travel budgets. Photographer unknown. Source: Yellowstone National Park Service Archives, YELL 40326 (courtesy of NPS-YNP).

Less expensive and more informal overnight options were developed for budget travelers unable to afford the grand Lake Hotel. Permanent tent camps at West Thumb and Lake became very popular with travelers once park managers approved these accommodations (figure 5.7). Early park superintendents initially disapproved of these commercial camp complexes within the park. Although park managers realized the need for an intermediate form of lodging for those visitors on slim budgets but with ample camping supplies, they were hesitant to encourage camping concessionaires in the park. The early park superintendents struggled to deal with the aftermath of campers, who often left a wake of litter and uncontrolled fires near campsites after their visits.[44] Acting Superintendent Anderson discouraged permanent camping leases such as the one that the Wylie Camping Company sought in 1893, because he feared that such sites might lead to a "shanty" that would be a "desecration of the Park."[45]

The popularity of tent camps at Yellowstone Lake soon swayed the opinion of park managers. In 1896, park superintendents granted Wylie Permanent Camping Company an annual pass with the rights to establish permanent camps and to operate stagecoach tours around the park and between camps.[46] By 1898, the Wylie Permanent Camping Company set up shop at three locations around Yellowstone Lake—Lake, West Thumb, and Fishing Bridge.[47] These camps were attractive to hardy visitors, as well as to those on modest budgets. One historian commented that "sitting by the hour on a veranda or in a luxurious lobby had little attraction for people who spent most of their lives working long hours fifty weeks a year."[48] The camp complexes built by the Wylie Company included "tent cottages" with "wooden floors and sides four to six feet high; from there on up the sides and roof were of canvas, often livened with red and white or blue and white stripes."[49] In 1913, another company entered the camping scene at Yellowstone Lake. Park superintendents issued the Shaw and Powell Camping Company a license to operate transportation and permanent camping facilities at the "West Thumb of Lake."[50] Both the Wylie and the Shaw and Powell permanent tent camps became sprawling, bustling lakeshore complexes that included lodging tents for overnight guests, dining tents, barns, stables, and a variety of support service structures.

After 1917, however, the concessionaire consolidation mandated by the NPS dramatically shifted the organization and operations that supported the overnight camping companies in the park, both in terms of their administrative structure and in their spatial organization on the landscape. The required consolidation was precipitated by the growing popularity of automobile touring. Park managers took the opportunity of this transportation shift in the park to slim down the concessionaire organization. The various stagecoach and wagon tour operators (which also ran the permanent camps) were consolidated and replaced by one large private company to handle all transportation—the Yellowstone Park Transportation Company. In terms of lodging, the Yellowstone Park Hotel Company was directed to operate all hotels in the park. A consequence of the NPS-mandated consolidation was the removal and abandonment of the multitude of unplanned, dispersed, permanent tent camps throughout the park as campsites were eliminated or consolidated under the new system. The new camping system was condensed from multiple companies (Wylie Permanent Camping Company and the Shaw and Powell Camping Company) into one concessionaire that operated outposts at five points in the park (Mammoth, Old Faithful, Lake, Canyon, and Tower).[51]

Although the Wylie Permanent Camping Company name continued to be used for a brief time afterwards, the Wylie Company and the Shaw and Powell Company merged into one permanent camps enterprise. These companies sold off their holdings and equipment in exchange for tour buses and support for motor vehicles. The concessionaire consolidation had definitive consequences for the lake's environment as well. By forcing the concessionaires to consolidate and remove outdated structures and activities in the park, the NPS was inadvertently concentrating the human disturbance and limiting the wide footprint from the permanent camps.[52] Private tent camps at the West Thumb Developed Area, Fishing Bridge Developed Area, and Lake Developed Area were abandoned and dismantled during this process, and one permanent tent camp was established near the contemporary Lake Lodge area. As this transition occurred, a system of lodging developed around the lake that included wooden, hard-sided housekeeping cabins and hotels.[53] Indeed, the current Lake Lodge site is at the approximate location of the former Wylie Camp at the Lake Developed Area.[54]

On the other hand, the growing number of automobile tourists increased the demand for public campgrounds in the park. Both organized touring groups and independent travelers (known as sagebrushers) needed campgrounds designed for automobile travel. To fill the gap in camping options for lake visitors, the NPS developed three new public auto campgrounds at Yellowstone Lake: one at Fishing Bridge, a second campground at West Thumb, and a third near the Lake Hotel.

The Lake Lodge offered another form of support structure for overnight visitors that was designed and publicized to attract independent and budget-minded visitors. Superintendent Albright's annual report for 1919 included a description of an "exceedingly attractive log building of ample proportions" that was being built on the site of the old permanent Wylie Camp.[55] Indeed, his assessment of the new Lake Lodge included its use "as a dining room and lobby, and will be in most respects more interesting and attractive than any building in the park except Old Faithful Inn and the Canyon Hotel."[56] The new Lake Lodge provided a dining room and other visitor services for the nearby permanent camp guests.

By 1932, all three of the developed areas of the lake—West Thumb, Lake, and Fishing Bridge—included visitor service complexes (figure 5.8). These complexes offered visitors overnight accommodations, ranger stations, general stores, dining facilities, boat docks, automobile campgrounds, and automobile service stations. There were notable differences, however, between each developed area. West Thumb offered visitors a boardwalk trail around a colorful geothermal basin, cabins, an automobile campground, a general store, a cafeteria, and a boat dock. The Lake Developed Area, on the other hand, featured a hotel, a lodge, an automobile campground, boat docks, a US Fish Commission fish hatchery, and bear-feeding grounds. Finally, the

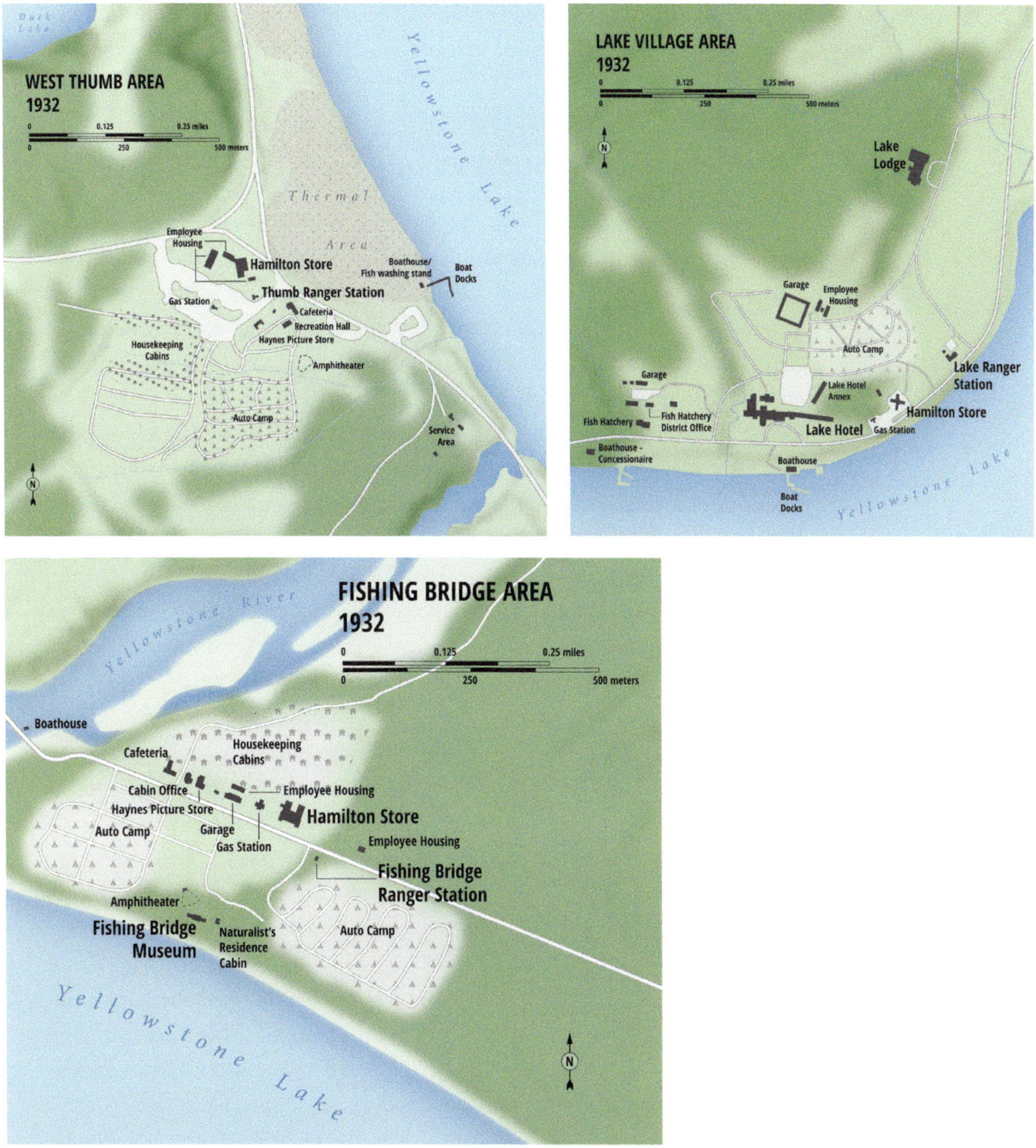

FIGURE 5.8. Developments at Lake, 1932. These maps show development footprints at West Thumb, Lake, and Fishing Bridge in 1932. Cartography by Robert M. Edsall. Map design by author. Source: NPS and USGS.

Fishing Bridge area offered another variation with fishing, museum tours, cabin and auto campground lodging, a general store, a gas station, and a repair shop for vehicles.

CREATING A WILDERNESS EXPERIENCE, 1933–1966

Although the major road system accessing Yellowstone Lake was in place by 1933, road projects on a smaller scale were conducted throughout this period. These projects augmented the route of the primary or Grand Loop road system. Three types of road projects between 1933 and 1966 included those that realigned existing roads to and around developed areas, those that maintained secondary roads to scenic attractions, and road-building and maintenance endeavors that extended the road system to newly developed sites. Private automobile tourists provided a strong customer base, and their numbers continued to increase during this period—with the notable exceptions of the years around the Great Depression and World War II. Automobile tourists throughout the postwar years found a growing number of overnight lodging facilities, dining areas, and interpretive stations at Yellowstone. However, even these facilities fell short of growing visitor demands. In response, the NPS proposed vast changes and additions to the park's infrastructure, culminating in the ambitious Mission 66 program.

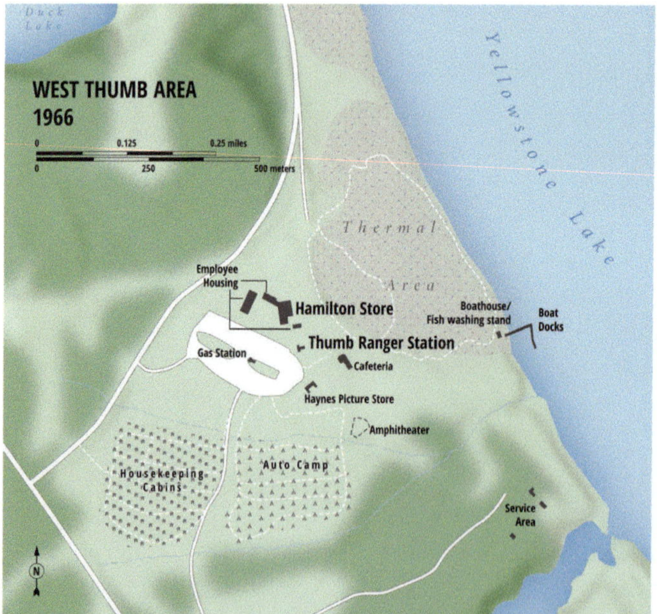

An increasing public demand (particularly after World War II) for additional recreational experiences and lodging opportunities spurred changes in Yellowstone Lake's cultural landscape between 1933 and 1966. By 1966, overnight accommodations, dining, and interpretive and recreational activities were located at five different developed areas: West Thumb, Lake, Fishing Bridge, Bridge Bay, and Grant Village (figure 5.9). With five boat

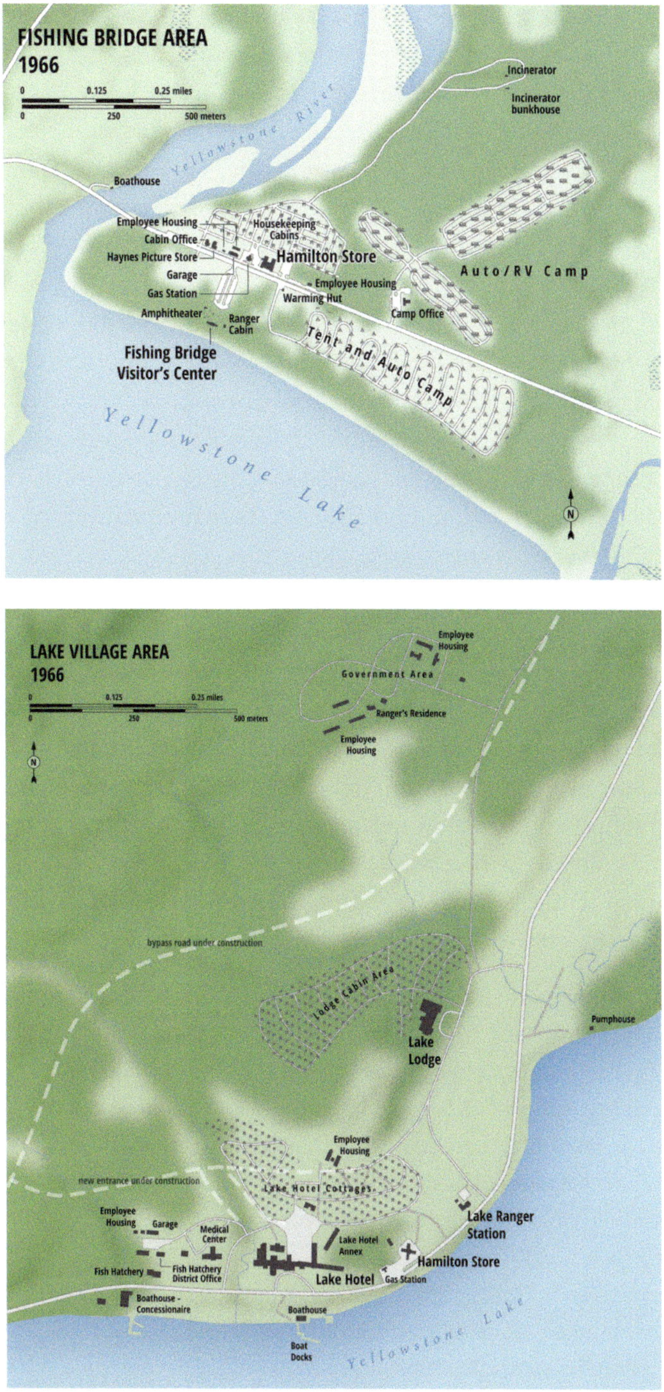

FIGURE 5.9. Developments at Lake, 1966. These maps show development footprints at West Thumb, Lake, and Fishing Bridge in 1966. Cartography by Robert M. Edsall. Map design by author. Source: NPS and USGS.

docks and over five thousand boaters on the lake each year, Yellowstone Lake continued to be a popular place to have a memorable fishing or boating holiday. Cabins were available at Fishing Bridge, Lake (including new units at the Lake Lodge complex), and West Thumb. Campground locations and sizes changed dramatically over this period. Camping options were removed from West Thumb, Lake, and Fishing Bridge (except for hard-shell camping) but were relocated to the newly developed Bridge Bay and Grant Village areas.

Between 1933 and 1966, concessionaires at Yellowstone Lake built and maintained overnight accommodations that included a hotel, a lodge and cabin area, housekeeping cabins, and cottages. Most of these facilities were closed from 1933 to 1935 during the economic disruptions of the Great Depression. However, after this period of inactivity, all of these overnight facilities were reopened. The NPS and concessionaires advertised their hotels, cabins, and lodges at Yellowstone Lake for those tourists seeking a "wilderness setting" but with cosmopolitan amenities. Yellowstone Lake's cultural landscape was designed and (re)arranged to appeal to private automobile tourists seeking a rugged yet convenient outdoor experience.

Changes to the Lake area are a good example of the complicated forces at work between the NPS, concessionaires, and tourists throughout the 1930s and 1940s. Park managers and concessionaires were reconsidering the Lake Hotel and Lake Lodge designs and layout in 1940. According to a 1940 letter from the Yellowstone Park Company president to the park superintendent, the concessionaire intended to eliminate the high-cost operations of the Lake Hotel completely from the cultural landscape of Yellowstone Lake and to extend the Lake Lodge onto the "present Lake Hotel site":

> This site has been chosen after very careful consideration of both the Lodge site and the Hotel site. The Hotel site offers the advantage of much better ground, level, and much more easily developed . . . It contemplates the gradual tearing down of the Lake Hotel. . . . The main object is to put cabins in the rear of the hotel and have them made presentable and comfortable. . . . The operation of the hotel as an hotel is out of the question on account of the expense involved and particularly in view of the fact that train Park tours, under the present schedule, do not call for a stop at the Lake. The patronage there will, therefore, be mainly private motorists who, in view of our experience of the last several years, have shown great partiality towards cabins rather than toward hotel rooms.[57]

Although the Lake Hotel was not razed, parts of the plan were eventually carried out; cabins were constructed behind the Lake Hotel and additional units placed near the Lake Lodge. By the end of World War II, the Yellowstone Park Company also constructed additional cabins around the Lake Lodge. In 1946, the concessionaire advertised "guest lodges" at the Lake Developed Area that catered to private automobile tourists. These small cabins were strategically located around the Lake Lodge, which served as a central location for a variety of guest services. The 1946 Yellowstone Park Company brochure described their lodges in the park as "huge rustic log and stone buildings, containing attractive dining rooms, lobbies, halls for entertainments and dancing, stores, soda fountains and rest rooms. Nearby are compact cottages for one, two, three, and four guests."[58] The company described the convenience of the cabins as places where "you can drive your car alongside your cottage, unpack and there you are" with nearby dining facilities in the lodges attended by "college girls to wait on you."[59]

Other concessionaire construction and relocation plans focused on the West Thumb Developed Area. The Yellowstone Park Company became involved with negotiations to temporarily move cabins and build new structures at West Thumb as part of a project designed to relocate the road through the West Thumb Developed Area. These plans, however, became muddled in concessionaire-park negotiations. During discussions about the proposed cabin development project, the president of Yellowstone Park Company wrote to the park superintendent in 1941: "Regarding the Thumb lay-out . . . It has never been our intention to build all cabins with bath in this particular area, as it was to be primarily a housekeeping site. Possible we had better let this whole matter go until we can get together in the Park and really have the plat interpreted to us."[60] Overall, communications hurdles, negotiations over design layouts, and shifting concessionaire business plans slowed progress on this project well into the next decade. However, rising demands for cabins at Yellowstone Lake's developed areas and park-wide development plans in the 1950s changed the terms of this discussion and resulted in the growth of cabin accommodations at West Thumb. Convoluted negotiations between these two parties marked this era of growth, readjustment, and contentious relations between park managers and concessionaires.

Profound alterations to the cultural landscape of Yellowstone Lake came with the Mission 66 initiative—a nationwide plan to modernize, refashion, and improve park infrastructure. Overall, the number and locations of some services around Yellowstone Lake—particularly at the Fishing Bridge, Lake, and West Thumb sites—were considerably reduced and relocated as a result of Mission 66. Evoking the long legacy of friction between managers and concessionaires at Yellowstone Lake, park superintendents during the 1950s increasingly found fault with outdated concessionaire operations and challenged their permits. These troubled relationships and unresolved contests came to the foreground as park managers implemented Mission 66 policies. In the process of this facelift, the lake lost several historical resources as many of its cultural landscape features were removed or relocated to other park areas.

Park improvements associated with the Mission 66 initiative also produced a varied array of new lakeside services by the 1960s. However, both park managers and the Yellowstone Park Company (the main park concessionaire) lacked a comprehensive plan for the lake area, resulting in an uneven mix of lakeshore developments. Grant Village and Bridge Bay were the latest additions to the landscape and featured only limited services. By 1966, Grant Village—a newly developed visitor site about a mile and a half to the southeast of West Thumb—offered an auto campground, a ranger station and visitor center, a small marina, and boat launch. However, new roads built by the NPS to proposed lodging and dining areas led to "vacant sites" where Yellowstone Park Company had not matched the federal investment at Grant Village and failed to construct facilities there. The concessionaire was hesitant to take on the enormous financial burden of relocating its profitable stores, boat docks, and overnight accommodations from the adjacent development at the West Thumb Developed Area to Grant Village. Although the NPS had completed initial visitor services, roads, and utilities at Grant Village, many visitors had a difficult time finding the development, which was hidden in trees.

Facilities at Bridge Bay, along the north shoreline slightly southwest of Lake Area, expanded after World War II. As with Grant Village, the Bridge Bay site received a sizable investment of NPS funds and construction compared to the few concessionaire services available at this development. Here, visitors could catch a scenic boat tour across the lake, visit the ranger station, buy fishing tackle and groceries at the general store, and stay the night at the vast automobile and RV campground.

The southern and eastern shoreline of Yellowstone Lake tells a very different story, one associated with the growing wilderness movement. Visitors sometimes traveled to the southern and eastern shorelines of the lake, but they did not typically stay there overnight. For example, popular commercial boat tours of the Molly Islands in the Southeast Arm of the lake throughout the early 1930s featured stops at the islands where visitors could view white pelicans and other avian species that used the island as an active rookery. These boating ventures were limited to day-long trips and access via a concessionaire dock on one of the islands. Development along the southern and eastern shoreline consisted of a few scattered NPS backcountry patrol cabins and support structures reached by boat traffic and foot trails instead of roadways.[61] Beginning in the late 1950s, however, the NPS shifted more of its attention to the southern arms of the lake in response to growing use and demands for recreational boating and hiking in this region of the park. Unlike the northern and western shoreline developments of the lake that were dominated by concessionaire development, the majority of the southern and eastern shoreline remained under the direct control of the NPS.

During the same period, wilderness enthusiasts persuaded more visitors to seek remote regions of the lake as they reimagined the lake's isolated southern bays as part of a Yellowstone "wilderness experience." This portion of the lake emerged as a hotbed of controversy as battles over zoning regulations ensued across the lake.[62] By 1961, park regulations called for reduced motorboat speeds in the South and Southeast Arms of the lake and (eventually) nonmotorized boating zones in the farthest southerly reaches of these arms.[63] The NPS also improved and maintained more extensive trails around the lake, particularly in the southern arms. Private and commercial boaters increasingly sought out the islands and shoreline of the South and Southeast Arms for fishing, camping, and sightseeing. The NPS built and maintained more backcountry cabins for ranger patrols of these areas and enforced speed zones and watercraft laws for the southern arms of the lake.

Yellowstone Lake's cultural landscape thus was bifurcated in development, visitor usage, and conflicting management imperatives between 1933 and 1966; the result was a curious juxtaposition of expansive development into undisturbed sites along the north and west shore, and the creation of a wilderness experience marked by less development and restricted access along the southern and eastern shores. On the one hand, Mission 66 encouraged the expansion of infrastructure along the lake's long-accessible northern and western shoreline: improved highways, expanded boat docks, and growing accommodations offered travelers diverse opportunities to enjoy lake amenities in this portion of the park. On the other hand, a growing hunger for backcountry experiences inspired renewed interest in the lake's remote South and Southeast Arms. This portion of the lake attracted visitors who were more interested in quietly enjoying the wilderness than they were in hotels and snack bars.

A PLEASURE GROUND FOR THE FUTURE? YELLOWSTONE LAKE SINCE 1966

While exploring Yellowstone Lake in 1889, Army Lieutenant Gustavus Doane found himself overwhelmed by the grandeur of the lake:

> The Yellowstone Lake is larger than that of Geneva or Constance. . . . It is an incomparable enchanted solitude, where winter's snow and summer's sunshine battle with each other. Here is the pleasure ground for the future. Here the overworked will come for rest, the feeble to build up their strength, the old to take a measure of renewed existence, the young and vigorous to enjoy. The studious will find here the book of nature opened at its brightest pages. The artistic and poetic will find here Inspiration, Genius, and expansion of ideas.[64]

Throughout much of its history, Yellowstone Lake met and surpassed the predictions of Lt. Doane as a "pleasure ground for the future." By 1966, the cultural landscape of Yellowstone Lake included five major boating areas. In the course of only a few summer months—the season of peak activity at this high-altitude lake environment—at least five thousand visitors were fishing, boating, and exploring the lake's shoreline. During these same months, thousands of park visitors were also spending the night at Yellowstone Lake. With large cabin and auto campground areas at Fishing Bridge, Lake, Bridge Bay, West Thumb, and Grant Village Developed Areas, there were thousands of beds and camping sites available each night for visitors. Change, however, was on the horizon for Yellowstone Lake.

At Yellowstone Lake, Mission 66 plans called for the expansion, development, and, in some cases, relocation of visitor facilities with the cooperation of park concessionaires. However, the main park concessionaire—the Yellowstone Park Company—did not always embrace NPS plans for all of the proposed new developments, and the company resisted relocating visitor services from the busy and profitable lakeshore; as a result, Yellowstone Lake became a showcase for conflicts between park policies and concessionaire responses. Indeed, as NPS superintendents and staff continued their push to enact Mission 66 plans in the park, they met with increasing resistance to these changes from concessionaires, local communities, and park visitors. This clash over policies and ideals coursed through Yellowstone Lake's cultural landscape as each of these agents sought to create the lake according to their own vision of what people do, and should expect to do, in a national park. Adding to the tensions was the growing political clout of the burgeoning wilderness movement as well as emerging concepts in ecological science that called into question many human activities in and around the lake area.

The power struggles between the NPS and the Yellowstone Park Company created uneven fits and starts of development around the lake for much of the 1970s and 1980s as some lakeshore development was relocated, other features were removed entirely, or new locations were developed. Striking examples of these landscape alterations may be found at the West Thumb, Fishing Bridge, and Lake Developed Areas. For example, most of the lodging, dining, and recreation facilities at the West Thumb Developed Area were removed or relocated to the Grant Village area. A NPS ranger cabin and bookstore, a parking lot, and a boardwalk around the geothermal pools are all that remains. In the not-too-distant past, this location buzzed with activity as park visitors stayed at the cabins or auto campground, rented a fishing boat at the docks, or launched their own personal boat along the shore. Visitors could also stop at a cafeteria for lunch, fill up their gas tanks at the service station, stop by the ranger station for park information, or buy souvenirs at the Hamilton Store.

Adding to the friction between the NPS managers and concessionaires, new concerns for the environmental integrity of the lake began to emerge as ecological theory suggested how earlier policies and activities actually played out in the lake area. At West Thumb, NPS concerns about nearby trout spawning grounds, the fragile thermal basins, and encounters between grizzly bears and humans culminated in increasing pressure to relocate visitor services away from this area. While Park managers required concessionaires to relocate their lodging and dining operations to Grant Village, they were slow to do so. The cabins and facilities at West Thumb had been hugely popular for many years. A Yellowstone Park Company brochure from 1966 testifies:

> The rugged West Thumb Camper Cabins are in keeping with the mood of their wilderness setting on the western shore of Yellowstone Lake, where steaming hot springs meet the cool lake waters. They offer shelter for hardy folk who, on a vacation lark, enjoy roughing it for a bit without any frills . . . The fishing and boating on Yellowstone Lake is an outstanding recreation.[65]

This concessionaire testimony describes the cabins—part of a sprawling complex of small structures near the large automobile campground—as "rugged" and in harmony with the "wilderness setting" of the lake. This description typifies the ideas about nature that shaped the material landscape during this period.

The cabins were a profitable venture for the Yellowstone Park Company, so the concessionaire was reluctant to remove these buildings from the landscape. Tensions increased with the NPS. The family that owned the Yellowstone Park Company could not see eye to eye with the Park Service and sold its permit (and name) to another operator (new management, same name). This battle of wills continued throughout the 1970s and 1980s as NPS personnel and the YPC's successors clashed over these proposed changes.[66] Ultimately, West Thumb village was not dismantled in one week or even one year. The YPC grudgingly removed or relocated these features in a piecemeal fashion.[67] The deteriorating relationship between the Park Service and the concessionaire at Yellowstone Lake led to the loss of permit for the concessionaire, the cessation of all business in the park for the concessionaire, and the eventual sale of the company in 1965 to another private corporation.[68]

The Fishing Bridge area suffered a similar fate. Under pressure from the NPS's Mission 66 plans as well as from environmental advocates concerned about bear–human encounters during trout spawning season, the concessionaire removed many features from the Fishing Bridge area. However, this process was filled with controversy that drew in regional as well as national voices.[69] Within this atmosphere, a variety of groups lodged objections to the removal of the Fishing Bridge developed area. For example, individuals and businesses in gateway communities such as Cody, Wyoming, near the east park entrance, grew apprehensive about decreasing tourism dollars. Scientists and policymakers voiced their concerns about the ecological sensitivity of the area and the complicated process of changing its character and facilities. In addition, historic preservationists were alarmed over the loss of culturally significant landscape features. The negotiations between

FIGURES 5.10 AND 5.11. Top: Aerial image of Fishing Bridge Village, ca. 1966. This photograph shows the extensive developments at Fishing Bridge that included camping areas, housekeeping cabins, and hospitality complex before these facilities were removed. Source: Yellowstone National Park Archives, YELL 27119 (courtesy of NPS-YNP). Bottom: Aerial image of Fishing Bridge Village, no date. This later image reveals the removal of cabins and a majority of the hospitality services for this area. Source: United States Geological Survey.

these groups and the Park Service resulted in the removal of the large auto campground near the lakeshore, the cabin complex behind the gas station (located just to the north of the east entrance road), and a boat dock and other visitor facilities near Fishing Bridge. The bridge was also closed as a fishing and recreational site (figures 5.10 and 5.11). Services now located at Fishing Bridge developed area include an RV-only campground, a service station, a general store, a natural history museum, and an amphitheater for evening interpretive programs.

Proponents of wilderness values continue to shape policies in the southern and eastern sections of the lake. Wilderness supporters lobbied for the restriction of motorized boats from Yellowstone Lake's South and Southeast Arms and challenged the location and development of new visitor service complexes along the lake's shoreline. As a result, there are no concentrated developed areas in the South Arm or Southeast Arm of the lake that come close to the level of activity along the northern and western shorelines of the lake. Instead, the southern bays of the lake are typified by backcountry campsites, a few NPS patrol cabins, and limited motorboat activity. Through the efforts of wilderness advocates and Park Service personnel who also lobbied for restricted motor activity on the lake, the South and Southeast arms of the lake are now zoned for boat type and speed.[70] Specifically, the South and Southeast arms of the lake allow motorized boats, but at a reduced speed (five-mile-per-hour zones), and the last two miles of the South, Southeast, and Flat Mountain arms of the lake are restricted to hand-propelled boats only. Today, the roadless wilderness of the southern arms of the lake cater to the backcountry hiker or hand-propelled boater, a contrast to the more developed northern and western shoreline of the lake where road networks, developed visitor service centers, and other services support scenic driving, day fishing, and light hiking opportunities.

Overall, boating activities have diminished on the lake since the 1960s because of the removal of boating support infrastructure, the decrease in lodging capacities, and growing environmental concerns. As early as 1958, one park superintendent saw the boat dock at Lake as an increasingly unattractive and unusable development:

> This site is most impractical both from the standpoint of present operations and/or future expansion. Unprotected waters force loss of boating business for as many as 25 afternoons in one month. . . . Steep slope at this site, lack of parking, poor approach and rough weather all combine to make this site unsuitable for further development.[71]

Indeed, many of the historic centers of boating activity and their supporting facilities along the lake have been eliminated or reduced since the 1960s. The docks at the Lake Developed Area—one of the oldest continuous boating sites at Yellowstone Lake—were downsized and then dismantled during the 1970s and 1980s. The boat rental hut near the Fishing Bridge also was dismantled, as was the marina and dock at West Thumb. Boating services—including scenic boat tours, fishing tours, boat rentals, and a marina—are now centralized at one location on the north shore of the lake. This north shore site is a NPS development located at Bridge Bay a little over a mile to the west of the Lake Hotel. Boating activities and facilities at Grant Village are limited to a few NPS patrol boats and hand-propelled craft because of lake erosion. In fact, park employees often refer to the now-defunct public marina at Grant Village as the "mistake on the lake." From five boat docks in 1966 to only one full-service marina at the lake (Bridge Bay), there are dramatically fewer options and attractions for fishing and boating enthusiasts today than in previous years. However, for nonmotorized boaters and those who seek more wilderness settings, the southern arms of the lake remain attractive. Canoeists and kayakers seek out these areas for multiple-day backcountry experiences fostered by zoning boundaries enforced by the NPS.

Yellowstone Lake seems to be a pleasure ground more for the past than the future. The NPS's planning and management tactics, stated through the Mission 66 program, aimed to increase visitor services throughout the national parks; yet these ideals came into conflict with burgeoning wilderness values and ecological science, creating a complicated mosaic of visitor use sites at the lake. Efforts to curb encounters between bears and humans at West Thumb and Fishing Bridge resulted in the relocation of hundreds of cabins, campground sites, and associated dining and maintenance structures. The Grant Village and Bridge Bay sites—the inheritors of what remained of the West Thumb and Lake and Fishing Bridge complexes, respectively—were created and sited at locations that lacked historical human use and occupancy but were in places considered (at the time) less ecologically sensitive. The lake currently hosts a lodge complex, a hotel (now the oldest hotel in Yellowstone National Park), and cabins at the Lake Developed Area, a lodge complex at Grant Village, and an RV-only campground at Fishing Bridge, all concessionaire-operated. In addition to these lodging options, the concessionaire also operates auto campgrounds at two sites at the lake: Bridge Bay and Grant Village. In the middle of July—the peak of the tourist season for Yellowstone—sites around the lake are often vacant, so it resembles more of a ghost town than a thriving visitor service area. One commentator of Grant Village described it as "a curious mixture of Cape Cod and Star Wars" and as a "wilderness ghetto" (figures 5.12 and 5.13).[72]

Yellowstone Lake's cultural landscape is a product of conflicts and negotiations between park managers, concessionaires, and visitors over time. As park managers, planners, and concessionaires selected areas for development,

FIGURES 5.12 AND 5.13. Top: Grant Village Restaurant, 2007. The Grant Village Restaurant offers meals to visitors in this newer development area located near Lake Yellowstone. Bottom: Grant Village Lodge, 2007. Grant Village Lodge offers an odd mixture of modern design and sharp angles tucked in the pines and set back from the lake's shoreline, adding a "wilderness ghetto" feel to this development. Photographs by Yolonda Youngs.

they not only made these areas attractive and more comfortable for visitors, they also guided the visitors to ways of seeing and experiencing the park. Yellowstone Lake, at the height of its recreational use and development, included five extensive villages that offered a range of visitor services, government offices, employee housing, and developed recreational opportunities. These five nodes of concentrated development, connected through a network of roads and trails, were the result of many years of site selection, designing, and development with multiple, sometimes conflicting ideas in mind. With 110 miles of shoreline, park managers and concessionaires had a vast selection of lakeside areas that could have been developed for visitor services. Park managers and concessionaires, however, decided to create nodes of visitation at five specific sites: West Thumb, Grant Village, Bridge Bay, Lake, and Fishing Bridge. Their selection of these locations was influenced by local and national events, the physical environment, individual and group decision-making, previous historic use, and park managers' and concessionaires' ideas about the meaning and value of nature and wilderness. Each of these locations was a selected representation of nature that the park overseers and concessionaires actively promoted. Visitors, in turn, would be drawn to locations with road or trail access, lodging and dining services, and recreational opportunities. Yellowstone Lake's cultural landscape is more than a mere architectural assemblage of buildings, roads, and trails. It is a window into past cultural contexts and processes that helped shape how this landscape is experienced today and how expectations of this lake inform visions for Yellowstone in the years yet to come.

While the contemporary Yellowstone Lake landscape includes five major developed areas, the current development scheme strips the lake of many material landscape features that connect it to its historic use and experiences. Indeed, a journey to the lake today reveals a vastly changed landscape from its earlier heyday. A modern visitor to Yellowstone Lake is more likely to be welcomed by the quiet lapping of the lake's waves on the shoreline and by empty parking lots than by the brisk activity that was once a hallmark of this area (figures 5.14 and 5.15). A contemporary visitor would also have few interpretive resources for learning more about the lake's deep human history. One resolution to this discrepancy and lack of information about the transition between contemporary and historic cultural landscapes at Yellowstone Lake would be the initiation of a cultural landscape interpretive program. Interpretive programs, brochures, signage along the shoreline trails and near

FIGURES 5.14 AND 5.15. West Thumb, then and now. The top view (no date) shows that early development at West Thumb Village included a boat dock such as the one pictured here, quite close to the delicate geothermal pools, which posed a hazard to visitors to cross and had thin crust for supporting the dock site. Photographer unknown. Source: Yellowstone National Park Archives, YELL 36073 (courtesy of NPS-YNP). The bottom view (2007) shows a more contemporary scene at this approximate site, revealing little of the former boat docks or the bustling activity that was a hallmark of this area during the height of its popularity. Photograph by Yolonda Youngs.

historic boating sites, and museum exhibits could increase visitor understanding and appreciation for the people, places, and events that shaped this landscape over time. For example, the boating history of the lake could be related through signage featuring images, maps, and historic descriptions of the West Thumb steamboat ferry dock or the sprawling Lake Hotel docks and support structures. The Fishing Bridge museum would be an excellent site to feature rotating exhibits with images, maps, and other archival materials emphasizing the human-environmental history of the area.

Gustavus Doane's vision of Yellowstone Lake as a "pleasure ground for the future" is not out of reach just yet. The present and future of this tale is still unfolding. Powerful and sometimes conflicting forces continue to shape this cultural landscape as the NPS, concessionaires, and park visitors reformulate and renegotiate the national park idea and concepts about nature and wilderness. Negotiations with, and resolutions between, multiple and often conflicting groups have revised how the lake is experienced by visitors, what people have expected when they visited the lake, and how these expectations have translated into material landscape features. Although national parks are often considered notable reserves of natural beauty, they are also rich sites of cultural history, social memory, and national heritage that may be explored to reveal the many hidden stories that lie just below the surface.

NOTES

1. Ann Johnson, "Archaeology Around Yellowstone Lake," in *Yellowstone Lake: Hotbed of Chaos or Reservoir of Resilience? Proceedings of the 6th Biennial Scientific Conference on the Greater Yellowstone Ecosystem*, edited by Roger Anderson and David Harmon, 82–87 (Yellowstone National Park, WY: National Park Service Yellowstone Center for Resources, 2002).
2. Johnson, "Archaeology Around Yellowstone Lake," 87; Paul Sanders, "Prehistoric Land-Use Patterns Within the Yellowstone Lake Basin and Hayden Valley Region, Yellowstone National Park, Wyoming," Anderson and Harmon, *Yellowstone Lake*, 218–28.
3. Sanders, "Prehistoric Land-Use Patterns," 218–28.
4. Osborne Russell, "Journal of a Trapper or Nine Years Residence Among the Rocky Mountains Between the Years of 1834 and 1843 . . . ," in *Osborne Russell's Journal of a Trapper*, edited by Aubrey Haines (Lincoln: University of Nebraska Press, 1965), 27.
5. For a more detailed discussion of Euro-American trappers and a geographic dialogue about Yellowstone Lake between these adventurers and Native American groups, see Yolonda Youngs, *Pleasure Ground for the Future: The Evolving Cultural Landscape of Yellowstone Lake, Yellowstone National Park 1870–1966* (MS thesis, Montana State University, 2004), 34–91.
6. For a more detailed accounting of routes and documentation created by the many scientific and exploratory groups that traveled through Yellowstone and documented their

trips in journal accounts, maps, and illustrations, see Aubrey Haines, *The Yellowstone Story: A History of Our First National Park*, vol. 1 (Yellowstone National Park: Yellowstone Library and Museum Association, 1977).

7. For more examples of early European-American cartographic representations and descriptions of the Yellowstone Lake region, see Nathaniel Langford, *The Discovery of Yellowstone Park: Journal of the Washburn Expedition to the Yellowstone and Firehole Rivers in the Year 1870* (Lincoln: University of Nebraska Press, 1905; repr. 1972); Ferdinand Hayden, *Preliminary Report of the United States Geological Survey of Montana and Portions of Adjacent Territories . . . Fifth Annual Report . . .* (Washington, DC: Government Printing Office, 1872); Ferdinand Hayden, *Sixth Annual Report of the United States Geological Survey of the Territories, Embracing Portions of Montana, Idaho, Wyoming, and Utah . . . 1872* (Washington, DC: Government Printing Office, 1873).
8. Nineteenth-century European American explorers and trappers reported frequent sightings of active Native American trails and camps at Yellowstone Lake in their journals and reports describing their expeditions around the lake. For a more detailed discussion of this point, see Mark Spence, *Dispossessing the Wilderness: Indian Removal and the Making of the National Parks* (Oxford: Oxford University Press, 1999), 42. For an example of historic descriptions of Native Americans crossing paths with European American explorers at Yellowstone Lake, see Nathaniel Langford, "The Wonders of Yellowstone," in *Scribner's Monthly: An Illustrated Magazine for the People* 2, no. 2 (1871): 69; compare to 7, 113–28.
9. Peter Nabokov and Lawrence Loendorf, *Amerindians and Yellowstone National Park: A Documentary Overview* (Yellowstone National Park: National Park Service Yellowstone Center for Resources, 2002).
10. Nabokov and Loendorf, *Amerindians and Yellowstone National Park.*
11. Philetus Norris, *Report of the Superintendent of Yellowstone National Park to the Secretary of the Interior for the Year 1879* (Washington, DC: Government Printing Office), 35.
12. Spence, *Dispossessing the Wilderness*, 41–70.
13. Lary Dilsaver, ed. *America's National Park System: The Critical Documents* (Lanham, MD: Rowman and Littlefield Publishers, 2016), 20.
14. Nathaniel Langford, *Annual Report of the Superintendent of Yellowstone National Park for the Year 1872* (42nd Cong., 3rd Session, S. Exec. Doc. No. 35), at 2–3 (1873).
15. Norris, *Report of the Superintendent . . .* 1878, 987.
16. Norris, *Fifth Annual Report of the Superintendent . . .* 1881, 18.
17. Norris, *Report upon the Yellowstone National Park*, 1879, 6-7; Norris, *Report of the Superintendent . . .* 1879, 59.
18. Norris, *Fifth Annual Report of the Superintendent . . .* 1881.
19. Norris, *Report upon the Yellowstone National Park, 1879*, 24.
20. For a more thorough analysis of early concessionaire development in Yellowstone National Park, see Haines, *Yellowstone Story*, vol. 1; Lee Whittlesey, *A Yellowstone Album: A Photographic Celebration of the First National Park* (Boulder, CO: Roberts Rinehart Publishers, 1997).
21. Norris, *Report of the Superintendent . . .* 1880, 37.
22. Norris, *Report of the Superintendent . . .* 1880, 37.
23. Norris, *Fifth Annual Report of the Superintendent . . .* 1881, 12–13.
24. George Anderson, *Report of the Acting Superintendent of Yellowstone National Park to the Secretary of the Interior, 1891* (Bound File, Yellowstone National Park Library), 6–7.

25. Norris, *Fifth Annual Report of the Superintendent* . . . 1881, 17.
26. Anderson, *Report of the Acting Superintendent* . . . 1892, 5.
27. Hiram Chittenden, Letter from the Chief Engineer, in George Goode, *Report of the Acting Superintendent of Yellowstone National Park to the Secretary of the Interior, 1900* (Washington, DC: Government Printing Office, 1900), 9 (appendix A).
28. Albert Guptill, *Haynes Guide to Yellowstone Park: A Practical Hand Book* (Saint Paul: Pioneer Press, 1908), 86.
29. For a more thorough analysis of National Park Service efforts in cultural landscape creation and choreography, see Terence Young "Virtue and Irony in a U.S. National Park," in *Theme Park Landscapes: Antecedents and Variations*, edited by Terence Young and Robert Riley (Washington, DC: Dumbarton Oaks Research Library and Collection, 2002), 157–81.
30. Judith Meyer, *The Spirit of Yellowstone: The Cultural Evolution of a National Park* (Lanham, MD: Roberts Rinehart Publishers, 2003).
31. Albert Guptill, *All About Yellowstone Park: A Practical Guide* (Saint Paul: F. J. Haynes, 1893), 73. Another specific reference to the geothermal features at Yellowstone Lake and tourism transportation patterns may be found in William Riley, *Official Guide to the Yellowstone National Park: A Manual for Tourists*, rev. ed. (St. Paul: Northern News Company, 1887), 100–101.
32. Whittlesey, *Yellowstone Album*, 80. An excellent overview of the Fishing Bridge site is Paul Schullery, *Nature and Culture at Fishing Bridge: A History of the Fishing Bridge Development in Yellowstone National Park* (Yellowstone National Park, Wyoming: National Park Service, 2010).
33. Anderson, *Report of the Acting Superintendent* . . . 1894.
34. James Erwin, *Report of the Acting Superintendent of Yellowstone National Park to the Secretary of the Interior, 1898* (Washington, DC: Government Printing Office), 7.
35. Samuel Young, *Report of the Acting Superintendent of Yellowstone National Park to the Secretary of the Interior, 1897* (Washington, DC: Government Printing Office).
36. Harry Benson, *Report of the Acting Superintendent of Yellowstone National Park to the Secretary of the Interior, 1909* (Washington, DC: Government Printing Office).
37. John Pitcher, *Report of the Acting Superintendent of Yellowstone National Park to the Secretary of the Interior, 1902* (Washington, DC: Government Printing Office), 12.
38. For a more detailed analysis of the concessionaire consolidation in Yellowstone National Park, see Mary Shivers Culpin, "For the Benefit and Enjoyment of the People": A History of Concession Development in Yellowstone National Park, 1872–1966 (National Park Service, Yellowstone Center for Resources, Yellowstone National Park, Wyoming, 2003, YCR-CR-2003-01). See also Haines, *Yellowstone Story*, vol. 1; Paul Schullery, *Searching for Yellowstone: Ecology and Wonder in the Last Wilderness* (Boston, MA: Houghton Mifflin, 1997).
39. Horace Albright, *Annual Report for Yellowstone National Park, 1919* (Bound File, Montana State University Library Special Collections, Bozeman, MT), 81.
40. Northern Pacific Railway and Burlington Route, *Magic Yellowstone* (St. Paul: Northern Pacific Railway, 1928), 19.
41. Guptill, *Haynes Guide*.
42. Pitcher, *Report of the Acting Superintendent* . . . 1904, 9.
43. Eleanor Corthell, *A Family Trek to the Yellowstone* (Laramie, WY: Laramie Printing Company, 1928), 42.

44. Anderson, *Report of the Acting Superintendent* . . . 1893, 10.
45. Anderson, *Report of the Acting Superintendent* . . . 1893, 10.
46. Anderson, *Report of the Acting Superintendent* . . . 1896, 4.
47. Richard Bartlett, *Yellowstone: A Wilderness Besieged* (Tucson: University of Arizona Press, 1985), 187; Erwin, *Report of the Acting Superintendent* . . . 1898, 6; Young, *Report of the Acting Superintendent* . . . 1907, 8.
48. Bartlett, *Yellowstone*, 188.
49. Bartlett, *Yellowstone*, 187.
50. L. Brett, *Report of the Acting Superintendent of Yellowstone National Park to the Secretary of the Interior, 1913* (Bound File, Yellowstone National Park Library), 4.
51. Haines, *Yellowstone Story*, vol. 2, 273–74; Schullery, *Searching for Yellowstone*, 134–38.
52. For a more detailed analysis of the ecological impacts of early camping concessionaire operations in Yellowstone National Park, see Schullery, *Searching for Yellowstone*, 181–82.
53. Haines, *Yellowstone Story*, vol. 2, 362.
54. *Map of Permanent Camp* No. 6 *at Wylie Camping Co at Yellowstone Lake*. Dated August 28, 1915. Found in "Miscellaneous Blueprints" folder. Drawer 32, Yellowstone National Park Archives.
55. Albright, *Annual Report for Yellowstone National Park, 1919*, 24–26.
56. Albright, *Annual Report for Yellowstone National Park, 1919*, 24–26.
57. W. Nichols, letter to Mr. Edmund B. Rogers, Superintendent (June 5, 1940). Box C-37. File "Buildings (Yellowstone Park Company) January 1940–December 1943." Yellowstone National Park Archives.
58. Yellowstone Park Company, *Yellowstone Park Season 1946, Folder B, Hotels-Lodges-Tourist Cabins*. Brochure. From the collection of William Wyckoff, 4.
59. Yellowstone Park Company, *Yellowstone Park Season 1946*, 4.
60. Yellowstone Park Company, *Yellowstone Park Season 1946*, 4, Nichols, 1940.
61. Toll, *Annual Report for Yellowstone National Park, 1934*, 20.
62. For a more detailed discussion of wilderness values and park policies at Yellowstone Lake, see Michael Yochim, "A Water Wilderness: Battles over Values and Motorboats on Yellowstone Lake," *Historical Geography*, no. 35 (2007): 185–213.
63. Haines, *Yellowstone Story*, vol. 2.
64. Gustavus Doane, *Memorandum*, 1889, Gustavus Doane Papers (Montana State University Special Collections, Bozeman, MT).
65. Yellowstone Park Company, *Visitor Services and Recreations, Scenic Bus Tour Schedules 1966*. Brochure. From the collection of William Wyckoff.
66. Goldfield Enterprises bought the Yellowstone Park Company in 1965, then resold it to General Hosts a few months later. For a discussion of the sale of the park's major concessionaire, see Haines, *Yellowstone Story*, vol. 2, 378, 423.
67. The complex and evolving negotiations between the National Park Service and the Yellowstone Park Company over West Thumb development continued well into the Mission 66 era for the park. The National Park Service encouraged the concessionaire to expand and change the location of the cabin units, but the concessionaire did not like the NPS plan. These two groups engaged in a push-pull dialogue that brought their different missions, budgets, and goals into high profile. When the National Park Service shifted the dialogue toward an entire relocation of West Thumb visitor services to Grant Village, the

concessionaire balked and pushed for continued use of West Thumb and expansion of this profitable site. These two groups continued this exchange well into the Mission 66 era. In 1958, a survey was completed that assessed the "personnel, equipment, operating methods, building layouts, sources of income, advertising and other phases of operations—together with recommendations of items for immediate action and items deserving further analysis and study for future action" by Orr Pickering and Associates, a Billings, Montana, architecture and engineering firm. This study—launched to assess facilities in the park in conjunction with the Mission 66 program—evaluated concessionaire operations at the Lake, Fishing Bridge, and West Thumb sites. The two hundred cabins at West Thumb and many of the structures at that site were deemed "old but in fair condition." Given these grim reviews, it is interesting that the survey found redeeming qualities in the West Thumb Developed Area, to the point of opposing the Mission 66 plans to eliminate all services from the site; the survey suggested that "eventual and complete abandonment of this area may not be appropriate." The story of this discussion and the breakdown of park manager-concessionaire relations over the West Thumb and Grant Village sites reveals many of the changing attitudes and values both in the concessionaire's development goals and the park service's management priorities. See Haines, *Yellowstone Story*, vol. 2; Orr Pickering and Associates, *Survey of Facilities and Operations for Yellowstone Park Company* . . . (June 1958), Box C-7, Concessions Files, Yellowstone National Park Archives.

68. For a more detailed review of the concessionaire operations and Mission 66 policies, see Haines, *Yellowstone Story*, vol. 2.
69. For more detailed discussion of the capricious and contested battles over Fishing Bridge, see Schullery, *Searching for Yellowstone*, 187–92.
70. Yochim, "Water Wildernes."
71. O. Pickering and Associates, *Survey*, 38.
72. Alston Chase, *Playing God in Yellowstone: The Destruction of America's First National Park* (New York: Harcourt Brace Jovanovich, 1987), 198.

FIGURE 6.1. Geologic features at Yellowstone's Grand Canyon. The image below is a satellite view of the entire Canyon area (1994). Source: Montana State Library. An aerial oblique image (right) also shows the Canyon area (1991). Source: Photograph by Larry Mayer, Billings, Montana (courtesy of Larry Mayer/Billings Gazette/Lee Enterprises). (Original in color.)

6

Grand Canyon of the Yellowstone

Diane Papineau

Today, when tourists turn off the Grand Loop Road to see the Upper Falls of the Yellowstone and begin their visit at the Grand Canyon of the Yellowstone, few realize they are traveling through multiple human geographies created at different points in time. On the way to Upper Falls, tourists travel on an old portion of the heavily traveled Grand Loop Road that was constructed at a time when settlement patterns were very different at Canyon. As the road curves toward the Upper Falls, drivers steer past an unmarked, treed-in, and somewhat buried historic road junction where an overgrown, abandoned roadway joins from the left. Farther along toward Upper Falls, they pass a curious, rectangular, tree-lined field on the left, containing two narrow openings, each suspiciously wide enough for an automobile. With a keen eye, the backseat passenger may wonder about an unsigned, southbound, uphill road farther ahead on the right. That asphalt looks old. Where does that road go? The geography that today's tourists navigate en route to the brink of Upper Falls terminates at a large modern parking lot with restrooms. While finding a place to park, the driver's attention is dominated by a paved lot and other tourists. This pavement also simultaneously

https://doi.org/10.5876/9781646427697.c006

obscures the old cultural landscape of a once-bustling yet quaint human place. In fact, today's Upper Falls parking lot occupies most of an old central business district at Canyon—its former "main street," where for decades tourists and park staff stopped for a soda or gasoline, mailed packages home, and shared stories about where they were going and where they had been.

Canyon, as a human place and settlement, has experienced radical change. Between 1940 and 1970, in an effort to protect park resources, the road junction and entire development were relocated to the north, away from the canyon's rim. When Canyon's earlier settlement was established, the cultural landscapes of national parks were only beginning to take shape. With initially weak government control in Yellowstone, a settlement developed close to the Grand Canyon's rim. Canyon's earlier overnight guests enjoyed and valued a rustic, western cultural landscape, and its proximity to the canyon enabled a sustained, intimate experience of the sublime in nature. But later, an increasingly empowered National Park Service (NPS), influenced by the nationwide acceptance of zoning and by a growing preservation ethic, mandated moving the settlement away from the canyon rim. In the 1950s, the earlier rustic-style buildings were replaced by a new built environment at Canyon Village, which emphasized modernity and convenience reflecting cultural shifts prevalent in postwar America.

The original settlement at Canyon developed for reasons similar to other visitor locations in Yellowstone (and many western national parks). The settlement was established because it was near a valued natural feature—the Grand Canyon of the Yellowstone—and it grew in response to visitor demands and available moneys. Most early development in Yellowstone was located near the great hydrothermal features and geyser basins, but the Grand Canyon of the Yellowstone was an enormous draw. In the early years, the Canyon's grand scenery served as the climax of a Yellowstone tour, ranking high on the list of park touring stops. Consequently, Canyon became one of the park's first four developed areas.

Visitors marveled at the Grand Canyon's colorful walls, two dramatic waterfalls, and hydrothermal features dotting its lower reaches (figure 6.1). Its classic V-shaped gorge is the result of river erosion, not glaciation, although ice thousands of feet thick buried the canyon during the last glacial period. The colorful, deep, wide part of today's canyon was cut by the Yellowstone River through a rhyolite lava flow that has been altered and weakened through time by hydrothermal fluids rising up through the Earth's crust—the same forces that fuel the park's geysers, hot springs, mud pots, and fumaroles. This hydrothermal alteration is also responsible for the warm colors seen on the canyon's walls. The hydrothermal activity and alteration in the canyon is ongoing, evident by geysers and hot springs visible today near the river's edge in the gorge.[1]

EMERGING PLACE AT CANYON THROUGH 1885

From a little-known geologic wonder hidden in the woods, a place of occasional visits and quiet contemplation, the Grand Canyon of the Yellowstone was transformed in human terms into a bustling tourist destination. The Grand Canyon attracted an increasing number of Euro-Americans, not just as part of Yellowstone National Park but because of its unusual geology and remarkable beauty.

The archaeological record of precontact people in Yellowstone suggests that subsistence use of the Canyon area was minimal.[2] The canyons of the Yellowstone River, including the Grand Canyon's North Rim and South Rim, contain few if any archaeological sites. Archaeologist Mack Shortt has hypothesized that the canyons were too difficult and dangerous to negotiate. Transient Native American people spent time here, but the difficulty of the terrain and access to water meant that their stays at Canyon were brief.[3] Nonetheless, their repeated travel through the area produced an enduring trail system that was elaborated upon by later visitors.

Anthropologists have recorded two oral Native American traditions related to the Grand Canyon and its falls. To the Mountain Crow in Montana, the natural forces and rugged terrain at Canyon, including topographic formations such as Artist Point, were tamed by a heroic Crow figure to make the area safe for the Crow. The Northern Shoshone-Bannock tribes in Idaho attribute the unintended creation of the canyon and falls to their legendary figure Coyote.[4] Beyond creation stories and through-trails, a cultural landscape of any substance and permanence at Canyon developed later because Euro-Americans had both the desire to create permanent structures and the financial and technological means to do so.

Early fur trappers visited the canyon area in search of pelts and adventure. Some left enduring markings on trees near the Upper Falls. These markings are the earliest known evidence of Euro-American travelers to the Yellowstone Plateau.[5] Many trappers passed along their knowledge of the area to

FIGURE 6.2. Thomas Moran, *The Grand Canyon of the Yellowstone*, 1872. This view, one of several painted by Moran, helped to popularize Yellowstone National Park in its early years. Source: US Department of the Interior Museum, Washington, DC, INTR 03001.

Montana Territory settlers, beginning a process of knowledge diffusion about the region that ultimately spread to senators and businesspeople in the nation's capital. Awareness and curiosity led to official expeditions to the Yellowstone Plateau between 1869 and 1871, each of which contributed to the process of establishing Yellowstone as the world's first national park in 1872. In addition, these expeditions initiated a process of Euro-American landscape change in the canyon area. At Canyon, these early visits produced inspired descriptions of vistas and camping sites; the creation of numerous place names, paintings, sketches, and maps; the recording of technical measurements such as the height of the falls and the canyon's width; and written botany, zoology, and mineralogy records (figure 6.2). While not visible on the landscape, these recordings set the foundation for human settlement and for the area's distinctive place identity to take shape.

Early horseback and wagon access to the Grand Canyon was primarily from the north because tourists and explorers traveled from populated areas mainly in Montana Territory. As the park's road system developed, visitors attracted to a full park tour ultimately arrived at Canyon from the south, after visiting the great geyser basins on the park's west side and Yellowstone Lake to the south. Upon arrival, tourists eagerly looked forward to experiencing the great canyon. Along with descriptions published in popular guidebooks, the dissected, complex topography at Canyon heightened anticipation of the forest-obscured scene ahead.[6] The manner in which the canyon and its two falls were revealed to tourists was distinctly different from the visitor's experience at features along the park's west side. Each of the geyser basins were, for the most part, wide open and visible from some distance away. Many individual geothermal features were encountered via relatively easy, albeit dangerous walks through the basin. By comparison, the Grand Canyon as a single feature was not completely comprehended until numerous viewpoints were seen through openings in the forest along the meandering canyon rims—all serving to coalesce in the mind and to create an impression of the canyon as a whole.

The task of reaching these vantage points was an adventure. It required more effort on foot or horseback, traveling through ravines along the canyon rim, and risking safety while peering over the canyon's vertiginous edge. Early tourists wanting to view the canyon from its South Rim had to ford the Yellowstone River above Upper Falls, adding to the excitement. The adventurous experience slowly revealed the canyon's features, bit by bit, with ever-changing views of the two dramatic waterfalls, and this measured revelation of the canyon's grandeur probably contributed to its status for some as the most interesting park feature.[7] That Canyon did not contain the pervasive (and, to some, offensive) hydrogen sulfide smell of a geyser basin likely contributed as well.

The basic, primitive trails scratched out at Canyon were eventually developed into bridle paths and later into roads. Bridging the area's dissected terrain along the West and North Rims was necessary before efficient and convenient access to canyon viewpoints was possible. Bridge designs and site selection reflected the technology and economic resources available at the time. These bridges, along with the initial log overlook railings, mark the first constructed and semipermanent structures on Canyon's cultural landscape (figure 6.3). Even with these early railings, only those who were fully confident of their abilities and footing traveled to some of the more dangerous canyon overlooks. After the turn of the century, overlook infrastructure was upgraded from rudimentary log and pole structures to government-designed overlooks made of milled lumber.[8] These changes ensured that everyone, including older and younger tourists, could have a similar national park experience while visiting the Grand Canyon of the Yellowstone.

Tourist overnight accommodations were the next addition to Canyon's cultural landscape. In 1883, an early park concessionaire with financial ties to the Northern Pacific Railroad established temporary "tent hotels" around Yellowstone. At Canyon, these accommodations were located along the

FIGURE 6.3. Primitive Bridge Across Cascade Creek, ca. 1881. Early park administrators built this simple log bridge across Cascade Creek in the Canyon area. Note the ladders (lower right) that led down to Grotto Pool below. Photographer unknown. Source: Yale University (courtesy of Beinecke Library).

canyon's West Rim, very likely at the point where the primary northbound road from Yellowstone Lake passed Upper Falls.[9] After traveling long distances over dismal roads, visitors staying at Canyon had about twenty-four hours to enjoy and explore the Grand Canyon of the Yellowstone. They retired for the evening in Canyon's new tent hotel and prepared for the

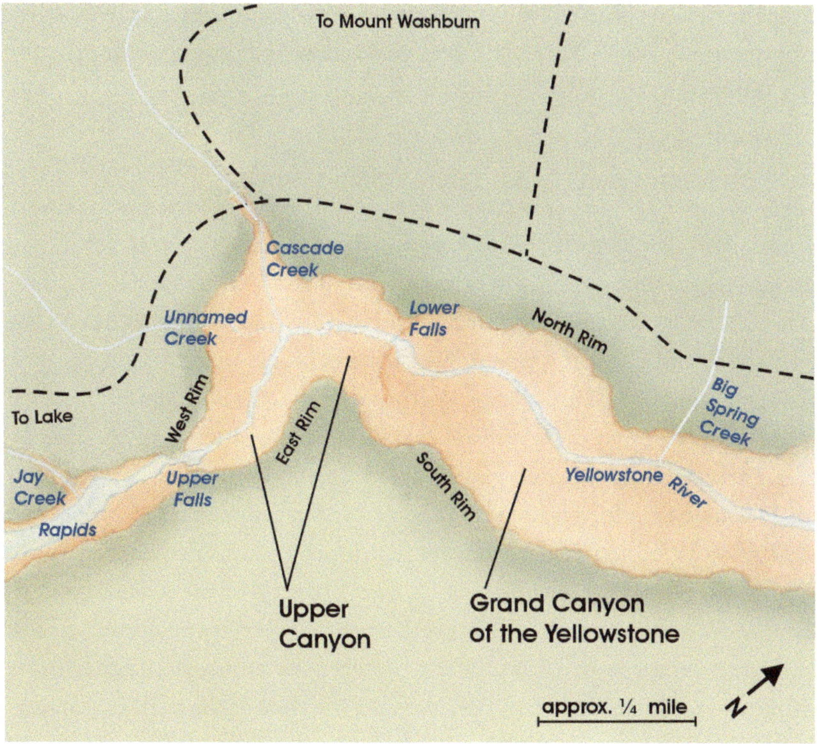

FIGURE 6.4. The Canyon Setting. This locational map of the canyon area (based on a 1933 Master Plan Map) shows the basic configuration of the Upper and Lower Falls along the Yellowstone River and the location of Cascade Creek. Map by Diane Papineau.

return trip. Canyon's tent hotel could accommodate approximately seventy-five guests. It consisted of large canvas sleeping tents with a large dining tent at the central point. Canyon's tent hotel was considered the most comfortable of the park's tent hotels; even so, the high-elevation setting meant that visitors were subjected to daytime storms, cooler weather at night, and snow in the fall, making these tent arrangements far less than ideal.[10]

More permanent settlement structures erected after this tent camp continued to be placed where the primary road from Yellowstone Lake met the canyon and Upper Falls. Placing visitor facilities near the canyon's rim, especially between the two falls, seemed an obvious choice for early entrepreneurs concerned with pleasing tourists. For these concessionaires, the canyon and falls were remarkable natural features to have in their backyard. Also, Canyon's settlement began when transportation methods were by hoof or foot. Services close to the rim and falls made for shorter trips to canyon features. If the canyon and falls served as a draw, however, then the Yellowstone River, canyon rim, and the dissected terrain also limited and defined settlement location and extent. It was not until the construction of a bridge over the Yellowstone River in 1903 that the canyon's East Rim witnessed visitor development—once again between the two falls and near the canyon's rim (figure 6.4).

BUILDING PLACE AT CANYON, 1886–1915

Throughout this period in Canyon's evolution as a place, the sound of freight wagons and teams, clacking hammers, whirring sawmills, and electric generators competed with the natural soundscape of nearby waterfalls and the tranquil Grand Canyon. During this period of increased visitation, the government constructed six bridges (many of them upgrades), miles of gravel roads, a government duty station, and numerous overlooks in the canyon area. Park concessionaires also built three hotels and two tourist camps, adding to Canyon's cultural landscape and to its identity as a place.

Human settlement in a national park differed from settlement on private land in that it developed under more direct control of the federal government. A federally managed visitor settlement, reviewed and permitted following government mandates, should protect park features and experiences while providing needed visitor services. At the time of the park's establishment in 1872, however, there were no rules. National parks demanded new rules for governing local land use. The only formal direction provided was in the Yellowstone National Park Protection Act, and the brief document did not address specific development topics such as where visitor settlements could be built in the new national park.[11]

Although the original act creating the park offered little guidance, Congress passed two additional acts that did. Eleven years after the park was established, the 1883 Sundry Civil Appropriations Act offered the first guidance regarding development location. This act prohibited concessionaires from constructing hotels within one-quarter mile of any geyser or Yellowstone Falls. The first tent hotel at Canyon violated this prohibition. Eleven years later, the Hayes Act of 1894 revised these specifications again, in some ways loosening them, stating that no hotel could be constructed within one-eighth mile of any geyser, Yellowstone Falls, the rims of the Grand Canyon, or the banks of the Yellowstone River.[12] This change permitted the inn at Old Faithful to remain close to its namesake geyser. But at Canyon, the new language made development near the canyon's rims and the Yellowstone River off-limits, as well as curtailing development near the great waterfalls.

At Canyon, the tent hotel location still remained in violation of the language within the Hayes Act. With the passing of the Hayes Act of 1894, any permanent development near Upper Falls and the canyon's rims would be questionable if government officials enforced these development specifications.

These two congressional acts influenced visitor lodging locations, but they were not applicable to the government's development of roads. The North Rim Road (also called "Inspiration Point Road") was the first canyon rim route developed for tourist enjoyment. For two decades before the turn of the century, work to upgrade the Canyon area bridal paths into a wagon road was done incrementally from the West Rim and Upper Falls to and along the North Rim Road, including access to Lookout Point and Inspiration Point. Between 1905 and 1907, the tourist overlooks at Upper Falls and along the North Rim Drive were also improved. Basic log and pole structures were incrementally upgraded to safer designs having sturdy stairs, roomier platforms, and seats made with milled lumber.[13]

Viewing the canyon from several different vantage points with these overlooks was an experiential product sold to tourists, which played a role in Canyon's developing cultural landscape. Supporting this touring approach were very well-known and dramatic paintings of Yellowstone's Grand Canyon by Thomas Moran (figure 6.2). Moran's artistic vision influenced tourist expectations and consequently the way guides and transportation companies planned park tour routes and tourist stops. Seeding these expectations were reproductions of Thomas Moran's *Grand Canyon of the Yellowstone*, 1872, which hung in nearly every American grade school. For generations of young people, these reproductions connected Canyon's magnificence to what it meant to be an American. Reinforcing this impression were tourism brochures and park advertisements with imagery of the canyon and its settlement. At the must-see viewpoints for the canyon, government-built overlooks increased tourist safety and protected the canyon at locations that grew steadily more popular.[14]

Consequently, the Grand Canyon of the Yellowstone was incorporated into a cultural landscape creation that was akin to an enormous museum exhibit. Since it was impossible to bring the canyon indoors for exhibition, the government constructed the exhibit infrastructure of roads, trails, and overlooks around the object of attention. This created a fairly predictable, homogenous tourist experience at the canyon's rims, day after day, summer after summer. The only substantial difference between tours probably involved the weather, especially its effect on illuminating the canyon walls and waterfalls.

After touring the Grand Canyon, visitors staying at Canyon slept, ate, and socialized in large tents near Upper Falls until a temporary wooden structure, the first Canyon Hotel, was erected in 1886 near the tent hotel. The first Canyon Hotel was a comfortable and well-kept accommodation, although its exterior was rather unattractive. Supporting these visitor services at Canyon were stables, corrals, and bunkhouses for the transportation companies. These were tucked into the woods south of the hotel. Also nearby was a duty station housing park rangers charged with protecting the area. None of these first structures endured.[15] While these structures influenced the visitor experience in the mid-1880s, they had little effect on the experience of later generations of visitors, with one exception. The chosen location for these structures near Upper Falls inside the "no development" area set a precedent for where much automobile tourist development would form near the canyon's rim after cars were permitted in the park in 1915.

FIGURE 6.5. The Second Canyon Hotel, ca. 1901. This image of the second and enlarged Canyon Hotel shows touring stagecoaches lining up and assisting park visitors in their guided excursions through the park. Photographer unknown. Source: Yellowstone National Park Archives (courtesy of National Park Service–Yellowstone National Park; hereafter NPS-YNP).

During the late 1880s, while stagecoach tourism was still the primary way of seeing Yellowstone, the concessionaire and park officials recognized the need for a permanent and larger hotel for Canyon. Honoring the intent of the 1883 Sundry Civil Appropriations Act, government officials chose a new hotel site well north of the canyon's rims. By 1891, the second Canyon Hotel opened (figure 6.5), permitting the abandonment of the first Canyon Hotel site, near the West Rim. Hotels built in the park during this period intentionally mimicked the style and function of hostelries in the East and in Europe. The second Canyon Hotel also resembled similar hotels built about the same time near Yellowstone Lake and the Lower Geyser Basin. Several of these ventures were financially backed by the railroads that delivered paying rail passengers to the hotel and stagecoach concessionaires.[16]

Until the late 1890s, the second Canyon Hotel was the only full-service, overnight tourist facility at Canyon. It was considered unattractive, its

FIGURE 6.6. The Grand Canyon Hotel, ca. 1911. This early postcard view of the new Canyon Hotel shows how the earlier hotel (back left) was incorporated into Reamer's design. Source: Collection of Diane Papineau. (Original in color.)

foundation was inadequate and built on unstable soil, but it functioned well nonetheless. The hotel was enlarged during 1901 with a back-wing addition. The dormer windows also added at this time made the hotel look more attractive.[17] Although the second Canyon Hotel provided a comfortable stay, the style of the building was heavily criticized in the local press and by park administrators. The park's primary concessionaire sought funding for a new hotel from the railroads. A trip to view the great hotels in Europe inspired concessionaire architect Robert Reamer to envision a new Grand Canyon Hotel. Reamer designed the new hotel in the Prairie Style—an architectural style in the Arts and Crafts tradition employing natural and organic principles. Between June 1910 and August 1911, the new Grand Canyon Hotel was constructed on the site of the second Canyon Hotel. In fact, the second Canyon Hotel was incorporated into this new sprawling lodging structure. The Grand Canyon Hotel was the largest structure ever built in Yellowstone National Park (figure 6.6).[18]

When the Grand Canyon Hotel opened in 1911, it boasted 375 guest rooms, each piped with hot and cold running water and steam heat. The foundation circumference was often cited as a full mile. Extending downslope from the front of the hotel was the massive lounge, the hotel's dominant feature—a social space where tourists planned their uniquely American vacation from a naturalistic built environment set close to the canyon's rim. An extravagant hostelry, the Grand Canyon Hotel continued serving wealthy, carriage-trade tourists of the day, along with dignitaries and high-profile visitors. Grand Canyon Hotel's visitors typically stayed there as part of a larger, well-planned itinerary that was coordinated between hotel concessionaires, stage operators, and railroads.

During the Grand Canyon Hotel's first summer, the hotel played host to a convention of concessionaires and national park superintendents, who debated when and how automobile tourists could be accommodated in Yellowstone.[19] Unlike the carriage trade tourist, automobile tourists were autonomous travelers who followed their own touring itinerary. They needed different services and at varying times of the day. Consequently, the new Grand Canyon Hotel was not the last concessionaire project to add materially to the cultural landscape near the Grand Canyon of the Yellowstone. Others oriented around automobile touring would soon follow.

FIGURE 6.7. Tourists Along Uncle Tom's Trail, ca. 1897. These adventurous folk are scrambling down the canyon walls on a series of ropes to gain better views of the Lower Falls. Photographer unknown. Source: Yellowstone National Park Archives (courtesy of NPS-YNP). (Original in color.)

While the majority of tourist sightseeing took place along the canyon's West and North Rims, some adventurous souls paid concessionaire Tom Richardson to ferry them across the Yellowstone River at a point about a mile above Upper Falls. There, Richardson guided tourists on a scramble to the base of Lower Falls in the colorful, wide part of the Grand Canyon. "Uncle Tom," as Richardson was affectionately known, constructed a rudimentary trail with ropes and ladders along the most accessible route to the bottom of the falls, permitting him to charge a fee for his ferry and guide service (figure 6.7).[20] Uncle Tom's Trail was redeveloped many times, made more and more substantial and safe through the years by Richardson and later by the federal government.

The Department of the Interior preferred that most features in Yellowstone be made accessible to as many tourists as possible without requiring a guide or a fee. This stance played a role in prompting the government to build a bridge over the Yellowstone River near Uncle Tom's ferry route and to build

FIGURE 6.8. Chittenden Bridge (after 1903). This Haynes postcard view shows Hiram Chittenden's remarkable steel-reinforced concrete arch bridge that graced the Yellowstone River and permitted easy access to the South Rim of the Canyon area. Source: Private collection of Diane Papineau. (Original in color.)

a wooden stairway over his trail, essentially putting Richardson out of business. The construction of this bridge across the Yellowstone River during 1903 coincided with the construction of many overlook upgrades at Canyon and a new South Rim Road (also called "Artist Point Road"), in keeping with the government's growing attention to meeting the needs of visitors. Chittenden Bridge over the Yellowstone River—a concrete bridge of Melan Arch design—not only made the South Rim access for touring easier but also facilitated the expansion of Canyon's tourist settlement to the east side of the Yellowstone River (figure 6.8).[21]

With easy access across the Yellowstone River provided by this new concrete bridge, anyone could enjoy views of the canyon from its South Rim. The view was particularly grand from a mile east of Lower Falls at Artist Point where the government constructed wooden stairs and an overlook platform. The trend toward concrete bridge construction continued when an older wooden bridge over Jay Creek along the West Rim was replaced by another designed of concrete, opening to the public in June 1915.[22] For decades to come, sturdy, sculptural concrete bridging of the complex topography near Upper Falls would greet tourists as they arrived at the canyon's West Rim, contributing to the feel of Canyon as an adventurous yet tamed place.

Late in the nineteenth century, the park also began permitting alternate touring opportunities provided by private camping companies. These concessionaires offered a less expensive and less elaborate visitor experience, challenging the exclusive hotel and stage transportation company offerings. Ultimately, these camping companies were permitted to build support structures such as kitchens and dining rooms at their sites to minimize the amount of equipment and supplies they needed to haul with each group. This began a process of establishing the park's later "Lodge" operations, albeit still with tent cabins for sleeping. These "permanent camps," as they were called, catered to the independent-minded tourist—and later tourists arriving in their own automobile. The first camping company to build structures at Canyon was the Wylie Camping Company.[23]

Wylie conducted his mobile tourist business, without a lease, to specific sites until 1893. That year, the Department of the Interior granted him a lease for permanent camps throughout the park, including one along the West Rim of the Grand Canyon near Cascade Creek. His camp was moved slightly south in 1903, still along the West Rim, to make way for a road realignment.[24]

Another camping company, the Shaw and Powell Camping Company, was also issued a permit for a permanent camp at Canyon on the east side of the Yellowstone River, made accessible by Chittenden Bridge.[25] The camp, with its main lodge and tent cabins, was nestled between the falls along the canyon's East and South Rims. Its lodge, kitchen, and support structures were constructed in the pioneer log tradition, much the same as most informal buildings throughout the mountainous American West. Thus, with both the Wylie and the Shaw and Powell camps near the canyon rims, park officials in effect reinitiated a process of development within areas that had been restricted by the Sundry Civil Appropriations Act of 1883 and by the Hayes Act of 1894.

This was a challenging period for park administrators. Park regulations underwent frequent revision. Tourist expectations of the time were seeded by the carnival-like tourist experiences at Niagara Falls, New York. At Canyon, several tourist rides and "appliances" were proposed along with the hotels, transportation services, and movable camps. One unsuccessful proposal included an elevator accessed from the North Rim to bring tourists to the base of Lower Falls. Another entrepreneur envisioned an aerial tramway to carry tourists from the North Rim near Lookout Point across the canyon to the southern side of the brink of Lower Falls.[26] Even an electric power-generating plant was proposed to harness the waterfalls in the canyon.[27] If these developments had been permitted, they would have dramatically changed how tourists experienced the Grand Canyon, then and now. Negotiating such a variety of proposals for tourist services illustrates the pressure placed on the federal government by tourists, concessionaires, and entrepreneurs as they sought to mold Canyon's initial tourist environment.

A MATURING SETTLEMENT, 1916–1945

During the first fourteen years of Yellowstone's existence, responsibility for protecting Yellowstone fell solely on the Department of the Interior until the US Army arrived to help in 1886. The Army remained the park's local law enforcement until the nation neared involvement in World War I. At that time, an ideological conflict involving public land management and conservation threatened the future of the national parks and monuments. Utilitarians in the United States proposed using the resources contained within parks and monuments to protect national interests; however, preservationists wanted these areas left undisturbed as originally planned.[28]

During this time of debate, national parks and monuments were not funded well, yet they were experiencing greater visitation. The threat to these reserves and their increasing popularity sparked the idea of establishing a distinct organization—the National Park Service—whose sole responsibility would be to protect and manage national parks and monuments. With the establishment of the NPS in 1916, the agency not only assumed responsibility for protecting these lands, but it also made two significant changes that influenced how Yellowstone would be managed and developed. First, the NPS diminished the number of Yellowstone concessionaires permitted to do business in Yellowstone. This made leasing lands and concessionaire management easier. Second, and more profoundly, the service began planning for how Yellowstone would accommodate and physically adapt to automobile touring, which had begun in August of 1915.[29] Admitting private automobiles to Yellowstone significantly changed land-use patterns, tourist development, and park planning from that point forward.

Leading up to the establishment of the NPS, Canyon's cultural landscape included one hotel on a hillside above the canyon; two "permanent" camps near Upper Falls, each with kitchen, lodge, and storage structures; one government duty station, also near Upper Falls; at least two stagecoach transportation complexes with stables, corrals, and bunkhouses; plus roads, trails, and overlook infrastructure. Once the NPS took over responsibility, park touring design and concessions leases shifted from accommodating just stagecoach travel and lodging to reworking the overall development to accommodate automobiles. Cafeterias and snack shops, expanded permanent camps, garages, and filling stations had to be permitted, planned, platted, and built. Parking lots near points of interest were significantly expanded and an auto camp (precursor to "campground") was built.

Yellowstone was changing in many ways. Visitation to the park blossomed during the 1920s, facilitated by increased automobile ownership and federally funded road building. NPS engineers responded by reworking the design of roads and infrastructure to create attractive viewsheds conveniently framed through the windshields of tourist automobiles.[30] Stephen Mather, the first director of the NPS wrote, "the automobile should revolutionize the park tour, just as it changed travel conditions everywhere and turned into memories cherished methods of seeing and doing things."[31] This focus on automobile tourism led to more visitor development in parks, often with unforeseen consequences. Overcrowding in the park and damage to the environment were the outgrowth of more development (more parking lots, widened trails, &c.), leading to an accumulation of unanticipated changes in the cultural landscape.[32] Consequently, the automobile set in motion decades of change in Canyon's cultural landscape.

With the consolidation of concessionaires required by the NPS, the functions of the two permanent camp operators at Canyon were merged onto the Shaw and Powell leased area even though it was questionably sited, within one-eighth mile of the canyon's East Rim. The new combined camp, called Canyon Camp, went through a series of expansions to its main lodge and nearby cabin capacity as it sought to accommodate increases in patronage. Facilities such as men's and women's bathhouses were also added, though each guest cabin remained equipped with water pitcher, wash basin, and a chamber pot. Montana architect Fred Willson contributed many designs for remodeling the lodge building through time, as well as designs for other new structures such as tourist and staff cabins. Each Willson design maintained the pioneer log tradition, some with decorative stone masonry—an architectural style still commonly associated with national park buildings today. The structures and the camp setting made for a unique park experience. Tourists were drawn to Canyon Camp in part by advertisements stating that the camp was within a few steps of the canyon's edge: "at Canyon Camp the falls and canyon walls are seen without leaving the camp grounds." By 1927, the

FIGURE 6.9. Canyon Lodge, 1928. This Haynes postcard view shows the Canyon Lodge after the completion of the west-end extension and the covered entrance. Source: private collection of Michael Francis, Billings, Montana. (Original in color.)

role that Canyon Camp played in popular Yellowstone tourism was firmly in place, and it was renamed Canyon Lodge (figure 6.9).[33]

Though Canyon Lodge evolved somewhat dramatically from a collection of rudimentary structures and tents to a charming, rustic facility with sturdy cabins, the Grand Canyon Hotel changed minimally through this period in terms of the visitor's experience. Tourists continued to enjoy the hotel's grand entryway, the enormous lounge, and traditional railroad-era dining, services, and formal entertainment. Other than changes in furnishings and interior design, continuity ruled. Different generations of tourists exchanging stories of their stay at the Grand Canyon Hotel would perhaps marvel at how similar their experiences were, though separated in time by decades. On the other hand, the concessionaire had a very different view of some significant change happening below the Grand Canyon Hotel's lovely hardwood floors. The soil around and under the hotel was subject to "creep," a slow, mass-wasting process that moved soil almost imperceptibly downhill toward the Grand Canyon. The hotel's foundation and utility fittings were warping and straining under the weight of a massive structure set on unstable, moving soil. Even with the known instability and foundation problems, the hotel was expanded during this period with a new four-story wing of guest rooms on its west side, new staff dormitories, and an enlarged parking lot.[34]

Along the West Rim, the pace of tourist service development mimicked that of Canyon Lodge (figures 6.10–6.12). Near the site of the abandoned

FIGURES 6.10 AND 6.11. Top: Whittaker General Store, ca. 1920s. George Whittaker, a former member of Yellowstone's Army detachment, opened a general store at Canyon, which catered to the growing needs of tourists visiting the West Rim's "Main Street" after World War I. Photographer unknown. Source: Yellowstone National Park Archives, YELL 36501-3 (courtesy of NPS-YNP). Bottom: Canyon Ranger Station and Community Center, ca. 1921. This attractive log building served as both a local NPS Ranger Station and a community center, where evening lectures on the region's natural history were held. Photograph by Merrill F. Daum. Source: Yellowstone National Park Archives, YELL 31641 (courtesy of NPS-YNP).

Wylie Camp, a new building that served as a ranger station and community center was constructed, replacing the earlier, rustic government duty station. The NPS also carved out and managed a larger, public auto camp at the West Rim. Nearby, independent concessionaires built the Haynes Photo Shop and a general store with a filling station. Adjacent to the government's public auto camp, the railroad-backed concessionaire established a separate rustic cabin camp with cafeteria. This operation accommodated tourist overflow from Canyon Lodge and provided basic shelter for auto campers during inclement weather. These additional cabin camps were common throughout Yellowstone and were referred to as "housekeeping cabins." At Canyon the operation was later officially named Canyon Tourist Cabins. This developing West Rim tourist center along the primary road through Canyon was becoming a kind of "Main Street" for Canyon.[35] With all this human activity along the West Rim, automobile and foot traffic was concentrated in a relatively small geographic area, all ironically within the off-limits one-eighth mile specification outlined in the Hayes Act. At the West Rim, overnight and day tourists parked their cars, bought supplies and services, and set out on the local trails to Upper Falls, Crystal Falls, and the brink of Lower Falls.

FIGURE 6.12. Haynes Photo Shop at Canyon, 1929. This log structure replaced an earlier, smaller shop located at the automobile campground. Source: Yellowstone National Park Archives, YELL 36512 (courtesy of NPS-YNP).

Canyon's establishment and evolution as a settlement to this point can be compared to the origin and growth of a city. Throughout the history of Western civilization, the establishment and evolution of cities can be classified broadly as either preconceived or organic. An organic city is said to be "established at a geographic point but left to evolve in physical pattern as functions and fates determine." Most settlements are established in a manner considered to be organic. The preconceived city is unusual and has been possible when "overall plans have required a degree of power and control." Ample financial resources must be available as well. The Roman Empire executed such control when establishing new places such as Milan. Similarly, Washington, DC, was envisioned by architect Pierre-Charles L'Enfant and executed under the control of the US federal government.[36]

Given the Grand Canyon's early fame, it inevitably became a focus of tourism and development in the park. The establishment and growth of Canyon's settlement occurred, predictably, at the intersection of the primary transportation route from Yellowstone Lake and the most accessible, remarkable natural feature at Canyon, the Upper Falls. This settlement developed and grew organically. With development, managers increasingly transformed the natural landscape into a cultural landscape that changed the local Canyon environment. Trees were cleared for roads, trails, and building sites. Construction of roads and trails (whether graveled or surfaced) required bridging or infilling over local streams and ravines. When employee housing and visitor lodging were constructed, this invited people to remain at Canyon for months at a time. Extended human presence warranted even more landscape alteration to meet survival and sanitation needs. Potable water–capture systems altered local stream flow, human waste was channeled into miles of pipe laid in the ground, power and telephone poles were installed, and settlement refuse was aggregated in numerous local dumps. For the safety of visitors, many trails, railings, staircases, overlooks, and signs were constructed along and down into the canyon—arguably sacrificing some of the setting's natural integrity in favor of the human experience. The early infrastructure and buildings first placed along the West Rim seeded Canyon's developing organic settlement—its economic core—where people were drawn to gather and where goods and services could be exchanged.

All of the structures on either side of the brink of the Upper Falls were built using pioneer log construction—representative of regional folk building styles. Indeed, many travelers to the West and to Yellowstone had seen old, often decaying log cabins across various portions of the American landscape. Log construction seemed synonymous with the challenging settlement conditions endured by hardy American pioneers not so long ago. The building styles at Canyon, both pioneer log and the Prairie style of the Grand Canyon Hotel, pre-dated the formal adoption of any architectural guidelines by the NPS. However, each was an example of a contributing style that used native materials (logs, rustic wood surfaces, and stone masonry). Architects and crews also preserved the contours of the existing natural landscape and harmonized the built environment with the natural, making these human-made structures an attractive contribution to tourists' visual experiences in national parks. These architectural and landscape priorities were employed consistently in the developing national park system beginning in the late 1920s. The style was later termed "Parkitecture."[37]

Older national park visitor settlements, including the settlement at Canyon, exuded a feeling of nature and leisure—a wild yet settled place in a western national park. Its sense of place was primarily constructed by local entrepreneurs backed by railroad capital. As cultural geographer Wilbur Zelinsky suggests in his "doctrine of first effective settlement," the initial cultural landscape that developed in a place often played a critical role in the social and cultural experience of subsequent visitors and residents.[38] Canyon's initial Euro-American cultural landscape created an important legacy at the canyon's rims that also influenced how the settlement grew through time.

Visitors to Canyon often remained for days in these rustic accommodations near the canyon and falls. The proximity of a settlement close to the canyon rim fostered a tourist experience of the sublime, arguably surpassing that at Niagara Falls—the natural feature against which the falls of the Yellowstone were often compared. Unlike Niagara, the development of a human settlement at Canyon was more successfully controlled and kept to a minimum, while meeting tourism needs in a national park. This is not to say that each concession facility did not grow and change within their leased site with additional structures and decorative touches—a process known as "landscape intensification."[39]

In this example, landscape intensification translated into a growing infrastructure of roads and utilities, an overall increase in the density of structures, and the heightened emphasis placed on architectural style and aesthetic ornamentation, all designed to cultivate a growing awareness of place identity. With the exception of the Great Depression years, Canyon experienced this intensification along the West and East Rims through the first half of the twentieth century, contributing to its feel as a well-established tourist settlement. Canyon's settlement intensification near the rims was not unusual. This process took place elsewhere in Yellowstone and at most national parks during this same period. What was different about Canyon was that a growing settlement took shape and intensified at a site previously abandoned because it had seemed to conflict with provisions of the Hayes Act.

During the Great Depression, Canyon's cultural landscape more slowly matured, evolved, and intensified with the help of New Deal laborers enlisted in the Civilian Conservation Corps (CCC). Congress established the CCC on March 31, 1933. The CCC was a popular program in President Franklin Roosevelt's New Deal relief package. It provided jobs for young American men whose families were suffering from unemployment and poverty. CCC men were stationed in rural camps across the nation for six months at a time. They provided a manual labor force for projects focused on conservation in rural areas and in federal, state, and local parks.[40]

Canyon's CCC camp was established in 1933 opposite the general store and adjacent to the campground at the West Rim. Hundreds of enrollees at Canyon's CCC camp assisted with this process of landscape intensification. They built trails, structures, amphitheater seats, sewer lines, and dams; painted existing buildings; and cleared trash and downed timber from the road corridors and nearby woods. CCC men also did a significant amount of cultural landscape obliteration. With the program such a success, the NPS launched a park-wide beautification program employing CCC enrollees. Much of this cleanup work focused on removing evidence of the park's stagecoach era. CCC workers razed old buildings, removed trash dumps behind hotels, and recontoured slopes to hide abandoned road scars.[41] At Canyon and elsewhere in Yellowstone, the CCC program had a strong influence on the cultural landscape beginning in 1933 and lasting through the summer of 1941.

More landscape intensification involved replacing turn-of-the-century wooden overlooks along the canyon's rims, with more naturalistic designed structures that blended in with the environment. Designs to replace the wooden structures at Artist Point, Lookout Point, Grand View, and Inspiration Point had been created in 1927 by the NPS's landscape architects; implementing these designs, however, depended upon receipt of private funding. Although these plans were not executed then, they were the first naturalistic, professional landscape architecture designs applied to Canyon's cultural landscape.[42] The first overlook to change to a more natural design was the overlook at Upper Falls, made urgent after a 1936 snowslide and washout damaged the existing platforms and stairs. The walkway and overlook were replaced for that touring season using curvilinear stonemasonry construction with help from emergency public works funds. The overlook was much stronger and it blended with the canyon walls, making it far less visibly intrusive.[43] In 1938, the Artist Point wooden overlook, which could be seen from across the canyon, was also reconstructed with native stone. Not only was the old overlook unstable, aesthetically it presented hard lines in an otherwise natural canyon view (figures 6.13 and 6.14).[44] Between 1938 and 1940, the tourist infrastructure near Lookout Point was also upgraded to meet landscape architecture standards. Lookout Point's wooden viewing platform was replaced with stonemasonry, and the trail to Red Rock Point and its terminal platform were also improved.[45] Reconstruction of the Grand View platform, using stonemasonry, was not completed until after World War II.

Through the first few decades of the twentieth century, the Canyon settlement reached its greatest extent and its most visible footprint on Yellowstone's landscape. Concessionaires and the federal government made significant investments in utility infrastructure (roads, power cables, telegraph lines, water and sewer systems, &c.) on both sides of the canyon near the government duty station along the West Rim and at Canyon Lodge on the

East Rim. The economies of scale gained by expanding existing facilities where they had originally been established helped leverage previous investments in Canyon's infrastructure. However, this continued development along both sides of the brink of the Upper Falls proved less than permanent.

When the NPS was established in 1916, it inherited the cultural landscape decisions made for Canyon by the Department of the Interior. Just before the Great Depression, the NPS's planners and landscape architects began to explore city planning tools such as zoning and master planning. The spread and enormous popularity of zoning

FIGURES 6.13 AND 6.14. Top: Artist Point Overlook of Lower Falls of the Yellowstone River, 1923. President Warren Harding (right) peruses the Lower Falls on an official visit in the early 1920s. Note the simple railing and the wooden overlook. Photographer unknown. Source: Yellowstone National Park Archives, YELL 142393-04 (courtesy of NPS-YNP). Bottom: Artist Point Overlook, ca. 1948. This Haynes postcard view shows the reconstructed overlook, using a more naturalistic design. Source: Yellowstone National Park Archives, YELL 206329 (courtesy of NPS-YNP). (Original in color.)

nationwide provided the precedent and tools needed for the NPS's planners and landscape architects to evaluate existing tourist developments, guide and control their growth, and protect particular park features and values.[46]

In Yellowstone, while producing master plans for each developed area, these planners questioned the location of Canyon's mature settlement near the rims. They returned to the Hayes Act and interpreted the development at Canyon as being in violation of the one-eighth mile "no development" area cited in the 1894 Act. Almost forty years later, at the height of the Great Depression, planners mapped the Hayes Act restriction onto Canyon's 1933 master plan and labeled the area within one-eighth mile of the canyon as the "Canyon Rim Sacred Area." The NPS's "sacred areas" were small zones around revered park features such as Old Faithful Geyser, Yosemite's Sentinel Rock, and the rims along the Grand Canyon of the Yellowstone. Establishing these zones protected that land from development or any other disturbance. In some circumstances, a sacred area designation also prohibited human access.[47]

A sacred area designation at Canyon presented one of the more difficult landscape architecture problems for the NPS. It wasn't possible to prevent development using a sacred area designation at Canyon. Canyon's tourist settlement had been in place near the rims for decades and it was still growing in step with increasing visitation (figures 6.15 and 6.16). When planners looked closely at the landscape, they could not ignore degraded vegetation caused by so many footsteps gradually altering the natural landscape for miles along—and even down inside—this cherished park feature. Planners at the NPS ultimately proposed that all of the tourist development at Canyon be moved. They used the master-planning process and zoning over the next few years to propose a resolution to this landscape architecture problem in Canyon's sacred area. On a relatively flat, forested area about one mile north of the canyon, park planners and landscape architects envisioned a new tourist settlement for Canyon. The so called "Canyon Village" eventually contained replacements for all the tourist facilities slated for removal from the sacred area, including the campground and stores as well as food and lodging operations. The Grand Canyon Hotel, however, was outside of the sacred area. Canyon's new master plan, therefore, called for keeping this fine railroad-era hotel in service as it had been for over twenty years. Government officials had sited it properly before the turn of the century—well outside the newly designated sacred area.[48]

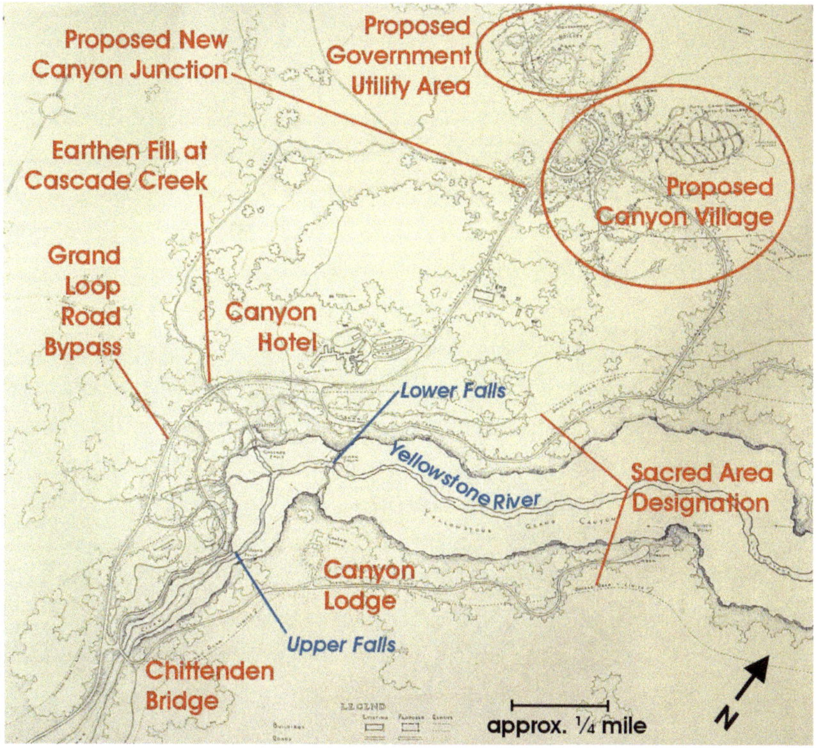

FIGURES 6.15 AND 6.16. Top: Aerial Photograph of the Canyon Area, ca. 1935. This image shows areas within the dashed lines that were being earmarked as "sacred" by the National Park Service after 1933. Photographer unknown. Source: Yellowstone National Park Archives (courtesy of NPS-YNP). Bottom: Proposed Canyon Village Development. This map, based on the park's 1941 Master Plan, shows the approximate location of the proposed Canyon Village Development, designed to move visitor activity away from the canyon rims. Map by Diane Papineau based on the Master Plan of Canyon area (1941). Source: Yellowstone National Park Archives (courtesy of NPS-YNP).

Negotiating the move with each of the park's concessionaires added yet another layer of difficulty. The NPS was asking them to both abandon investment in existing tourist facilities and to invest more money in new construction in the forest away from the Grand Canyon. In 1939, after a few years of negotiations, the last and largest concessionaire finally gave in. The Yellowstone Park Company agreed to move their tourist facilities to the new site in the coming years. The concessionaires employed Montana's Fred Willson as their architect. Willson proposed a rustic architectural design for a large new tourist structure capable of hosting the cabin lodging office and food services as well as the general store and photo shops that were also slated for the move. Each individual concessionaire operation would be accommodated in this one large structure with tourist views overlooking Cascade Meadows and tiny Dollar Lake, not the Grand Canyon of the Yellowstone, or its falls.[49]

Work to move the Canyon tourist development began in the mid-1930s with surveys and staking out the new settlement while the NPS was still negotiating with the concessionaires. To ease traffic and parking congestion near the canyon's rims, the NPS planned to move several miles of the eastern portion of the Norris road to the north and reroute a three-mile section of the Grand Loop Road near the West Rim. This new Grand Loop Road "bypass" would route through-traffic away from the canyon's sacred area and away from the West and North Rims, using a new, earthen-fill crossing of Cascade Creek. The existing road near the canyon's rim would be used as a scenic byway. The new road section from Norris would create a new Canyon Junction close to the site of the new village. While work began in earnest on the new Grand Loop Road bypass and Canyon Village, further progress was interrupted by American involvement in World War II.[50]

Visitation to Yellowstone plummeted during the war because of gas and tire rationing. The flow of federal money to Yellowstone slowed to a trickle. For three summers most of Yellowstone's concessionaire facilities were allowed to remain closed. Dismal visitation could not generate the revenue to keep them open. In addition, maintenance and upgrades of existing concessionaire facilities and government infrastructure did not occur. Tourist settlements, including Canyon's, deteriorated significantly during the war years in the high-elevation climate of the Yellowstone Plateau. The war also halted all work and planning for Canyon Village, so Willson's prewar architectural drawings for a new rustic-style development gathered dust.

TRANSFORMING PLACE AT CANYON, 1946 TO THE PRESENT

Once war rationing was discontinued in August 1945, there was an immediate increase in park visitation, although most overnight lodging remained closed. All three of Canyon's overnight accommodations reopened to tourists in the summer of 1946. Prior to the war, planning and basic surveys were completed for the new Canyon Village, along with portions of the water system. Changes to the settlement infrastructure at Canyon resumed almost immediately once the park reopened to tourists, including additional utility surveys in 1946–47. Dramatic changes in American life and culture outside of the parks also directly influenced planning initiatives within the parks. Three broad changes in postwar American society played a critical role in the evolution of Canyon's cultural landscape. These included the continual growth of automobile tourism, a shift toward more rapid suburbanization, and the growing popularity of mass-produced housing designed to satisfy the enormous need for postwar veteran and "baby boom" households.

Between 1945 and 1950, automobile ownership in the United States almost doubled, from 25 million to 40 million, reflecting a postwar increase in personal income and free time. With exploding rates of automobile ownership, new highways, and rearranged transportation networks, suburbia was fast becoming the dominant land-use pattern in America. Automobiles not only facilitated the development of suburbs, they also altered retail business configurations. New "shopping centers" emerged at interstate highway interchanges and became a large part of the new suburban retail paradigm. These suburban shopping centers blossomed all across the postwar American landscape.[51]

Residential development changed after the war as well. At the start of the postwar baby boom, the housing shortage was extreme. Large builder-developers such as Levitt and Sons (builder of "Levittown" and other enormous new housing subdivisions) realized large profits through buying in quantity as well as employing cheaper construction practices, including the use of slab foundations, unfinished attics, insufficient sewer systems, and inadequate insulation. The builder-developer passed these inevitable costs along to the buyers. By the late 1950s, two-thirds of new housing in the United States was produced by builder-developers such as Levitt and Sons.[52]

More free time and the means to travel at will meant that Americans were on the highways heading to the national parks in far greater numbers than before the war. On a single day in August 1954, Yellowstone's overnight accommodations were unable to lodge all 16,435 visitors. Six thousand tourists had to either leave the park or sleep in their cars. This large increase in visitation to the park, coupled with deteriorated and outdated facilities, put Yellowstone (and most other national parks) in a bind. Across the United States in the early to mid-1950s, national parks experienced an all-out recreation crisis. It was so evident and seemingly so hopeless that many articles appeared in the popular press at that time with titles such as "National Parks: Tomorrow's Slums?," "Twenty-Four Million Acres of Trouble," and Bernard DeVoto's famous piece titled "Let's Close the National Parks."[53]

Postwar federal funding to support parks was about the same in the mid-1950s as it had been at prewar levels, making park upgrades difficult. While the NPS continued the planning and infrastructure work for moving Canyon's settlement, they oversaw contributing projects such as the completion of the Grand Loop Road bypass near the West Rim and the rerouting of the eastern portion of the road from Norris away from the West Rim to meet the new village site.[54] The NPS also upgraded two tourist overlooks along the Grand Canyon's rim. During this period of Canyon's evolution, the style of landscape architecture employed for Canyon's overlooks entered a transition away from naturalistic designs, but not before a fourth and final rustic-style overlook was constructed at Grand View. Reconstruction of the Grand View overlook was in progress during 1950 using native stone and masonry, and the job was completed and available for tourists in 1952.[55]

Just two years later, hints at how the overall cultural landscape at Canyon would soon change became evident with new construction at Inspiration Point. There, the trail and overlook were located on a narrow promontory that jutted out into the canyon—known as a fairly vertiginous downhill jaunt since well before the turn of the century. To improve safety, Yellowstone's engineers drew plans for a long stairway and platform using tubular steel rails and concrete. Construction of the new modern stairway and overlook began in November 1954 and was completed in time for the 1955 touring season. This project marked the point in time when rustic overlook styles at Canyon gave way to more economical and modern construction. Reworking the overlook at Lower Falls using concrete and steel rails followed a couple of years later.[56]

While Yellowstone workers rebuilt overlooks, the NPS's planners once again contemplated a more radical shift in the decades-old cultural landscape

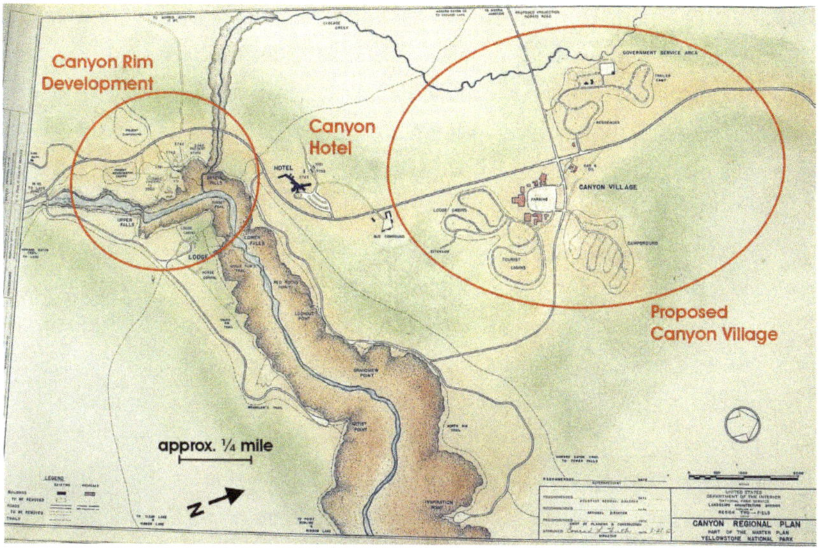

FIGURE 6.17. Canyon Village Plan. This 1952 postwar plan revisited the Canyon Village concept, setting the stage for the suburban-style development that followed. Map by Diane Papineau. Based on Canyon Master Plan (1952). Source: Yellowstone National Park Archives (courtesy of NPS-YNP).

at Canyon, altering the way people would experience the area in the future. The postwar recreation crisis underway made changes more urgent and plans more ambitious.

Postwar tourists demonstrated an unmistakable preference for traveling to parks in their own automobiles. Accordingly, during 1951 and 1952, the NPS's planners modified Canyon's master plan from the prewar layout (figure 6.17). Planners rearranged the layout of the village to resemble a shopping mall—the retail development form that was spreading fast throughout the country.[57] This choice complemented the NPS's existing Depression-era plans to, in essence, "decentralize" Canyon's development, similar to so many suburban business and residential developments built away from traditional urban economic cores. Outside of parks, this economic "core" was associated with the central business district of urban areas. Within the parks, these economic cores were wherever unique and significant features were present.

Shopping malls aggregated services in one high-density, easily accessible area. Mimicking this, a central aspect of the new Canyon Village layout was a commercial area for business, complete with a large parking lot. Making it effortless for tourists to transition from their cars into concessionaire businesses at Canyon would help ensure good patronage for these seasonal operators. Each summer, these private businesses had to earn a year's worth of revenue in ninety to one hundred days in order to stay viable. At Canyon, the concessionaires had the added burden of significant new construction and the loss of their existing investment near the canyon's rim. Planners also changed the orientation of the village, placing access along a secondary road. The new arrangement preserved a portion of the forest along the Grand Loop Road, making the new Canyon development less noticeable to tourists passing by. It also eliminated a view of Cascade Meadows from the village proper.[58]

Through the early to mid-1950s, while the existing hotel, lodge, tourist cabins, and camping facilities accommodated Canyon's guests, the government continued work on infrastructure a mile north at the new village site. Building the bulk of Canyon Village still remained. Completing this enormous change in a tourist settlement required an infusion of cash—a problem common in many other national parks in need of upgrades. To meet these nationwide funding challenges, Conrad Wirth, then the director of the NPS, established a large-scale, ten-year modernization program in 1956 to upgrade parks and to accommodate postwar tourism. Congress and President Eisenhower supported the program without hesitation and made funds available almost immediately.[59]

Wirth named his new program Mission 66. The name recalled the strategic plans of wartime, with reference to the end of his ten-year program in 1966—the fiftieth anniversary of the NPS. Mission 66 provided funding specifically for projects under the auspices of the federal government—Mission 66 funds were not available to concessionaires for their building expenses. At Canyon, Mission 66 upgraded the remaining infrastructure for visitor services and staff housing (water and sewer systems, roads, sidewalks, landscaping, signage). The program also increased NPS staff and their quarters, upgraded educational materials in the form of interpretive brochures and wayside exhibits, and funded the creation of an entirely new building type: the "visitor center," which through time replaced many ranger stations in national parks. With funding secured and the support of his superiors, Wirth selected the completion of Canyon Village as a kind of demonstration project for his program—a proving ground for Mission 66 to ensure the program's continued political and financial support. This placed a significant amount of pressure on Canyon Village construction, execution, and completion, by both the federal government and the private concessionaires.[60]

It was also at this time that the twenty-year contract for the park's primary concessionaire, the Yellowstone Park Company, was up for renewal. In order to get the new contract, the concessionaire was required to build a significant portion of Canyon Village (lodging, restaurants, gift shops, concessionaire staff housing, &c.) and finance the construction on its own. Committing to this construction was not an easy decision for this concessionaire. The continued shift away from tourists arriving to Yellowstone by rail led to the railroads' diminished interest in funding tourist development as they had since the park's inception. All funding to build the concessionaire structures at Canyon Village would be via private financing with much higher interest rates. Nonetheless, in April 1956 the Yellowstone Park Company signed a new twenty-year contract and bank notes committing them to millions of dollars in construction costs and participation in significant cultural landscape change at Canyon.[61]

With the contract signed and Mission 66 underway, the NPS had a willing private partner and the federal funding they needed to create Canyon Village—Yellowstone's first preconceived place. In order for the business model of concessionaires offering services in national parks to be viable, the concessionaire's success in business is vital. Having endured the lean war years, and facing enormous construction costs at Canyon Village, the Yellowstone Park Company and the NPS's planners abandoned the use of expensive rustic architecture and instead warmed up to employing more cost-effective modern architecture for structures in the village commercial area. With tourist facilities no longer sited along the canyon's rim, Canyon Village could be executed in a modern style without negatively influencing the view of its namesake park feature. There was no need to make the buildings "part of picturesque landscape compositions."[62] Furthermore, the overall layout for Canyon Village had already been "modernized" toward a suburban form, and the term "rustic" had evolved at the time to mean "dated, inadequate, and even unsanitary."[63] Use of modern architecture with federal projects inside and outside national parks was not without precedent. Modern architecture was employed in many federal projects during the Great Depression and World War II. Jackson Lake Lodge in neighboring Grand Teton National Park opened in 1955, presenting a facade of concrete and large expanses of glass.[64]

The shift in Canyon's chosen style meant a change in concessionaire architect from Bozeman's Fred Willson to the Los Angeles firm of Welton Becket and Associates. Welton Becket had contributed to the transformation of Los Angeles's cultural landscape by designing commercial buildings and shopping malls during periods of suburbanization and enormous growth in Southern California. The design firm submitted architectural renderings in

FIGURE 6.18. Welton Becket Sketch of Canyon Village, 1955. This sketch of the planned Canyon Village development emphasizes convenient parking and centralized services housed in modernistic suburban-style structures. Source: Yellowstone National Park Archives, YELL-RG Maps-05.01.667 (courtesy of NPS-YNP).

1955, revealing a new vision for Canyon Village (figure 6.18). Welton Becket envisioned a "contemporary" design focused on meeting the needs of the automobile tourist. McNeil Construction Company, also of Los Angeles, was selected to build the village using Welton Becket's designs. McNeil Construction was also a well-known company, having built the Sun Valley Lodge, Disneyland, and two federally funded guided-missile plants in California.[65]

The plans for Canyon Village, both in its settlement layout and in the details of its architectural design, were dramatic departures from the settlement's earlier look. The shift illustrates geographer Donald Meinig's larger-scale model of regional development in the West. Meinig suggested that in the twentieth century, settlements in the West experienced the strong homogenizing influence of national culture. Enabled by improved communication and marketing networks, the diffusion of national cultural norms influenced how western landscapes evolved and how their settlements grew and intensified. Meinig wrote that only "subcultures with tenacious social patterns (religions, languages, race) can persist as distinct."[66]

Ordinarily, diffusion of new national culture traits might only incrementally influence the evolution of Yellowstone's established cultural landscapes. Indeed, the NPS, with its well-entrenched planners and landscape architects, carefully controlled many aspects of Yellowstone's development. During the first half of the twentieth century, additions to the existing structures and cultural landscape intensification at Canyon followed suit to maintain the rustic character of the original settlement. However, with plans to move Canyon, opportunities arose to create entirely new cultural landscapes.

In moving Canyon's facilities to a new location, the settlement became "disturbed ground" that readily received the invasive "seeds" of postwar American culture. Not surprisingly, the park's planners and concessionaire architects were, as Meinig suggested, influenced by national priorities of efficiency, mass production, convenience, and economic building techniques. Planners thus chose a new kind of tourist development for Canyon over earlier, naturalistic styles strongly associated with more traditional national park landscape elements.

The construction of this new, modern Canyon Village began during the spring of 1956. Construction proceeded with unprecedented speed through the efforts of four to six hundred workers, who maneuvered an enormous army of backhoes, cranes, trucks, and bulldozers across the landscape. When Canyon Village opened to Yellowstone guests during July of 1957, it was the first completed Mission 66 project and it was referred to as the world's largest motel. Promotional marketing described the village as a must-see feature of the park and celebrated its "modern and spacious" look. The commercial area hosted a new Canyon Lodge with a large lounge, dining room, cafeteria, coffee shop, gift shop, and many other visitor services. Most of these services were offered from a mall-like walkway along the Lodge's glass storefront (figures 6.19–6.20). Prefabricated guest cabins were arranged in groups along loop roads and were described as "cottages" or "modern, motel-type units," each with the convenience and comfort of toilets, heat, hot water, and showers.[67] Certainly, this was a significant improvement over prewar cabins stocked with wash basins, pitchers, and chamber pots. Bordering the parking area were two additional stores, and a year later, the government's Canyon Visitor Center completed the

FIGURES 6.19 AND 6.20. Top: The Canyon Registration Building and Lodge, 1957. Visitors arriving at Canyon during the late 1950s might think they were parking their cars in a suburban shopping center. Photograph by E. Jack Haynes. Source: private collection of Tami Whittlesey, Seal Rock, Oregon. Bottom: Canyon Ranger Station / Visitor Center, circa 1958. The Canyon Ranger Station / Visitor Center welcomed visitors at this modern structure located on the west side of Canyon Village. Photograph by Jack E. Boucher. Source: Yellowstone National Park Archives, YELL 38799-05 (courtesy of NPS-YNP).

horseshoe-shaped suburban mall arrangement. Traditionally, pre–World War II national park settlements offered tourists a view of outstanding natural features and vistas from resting places inside. Here, as from most interior tourist structures at the new Canyon Village, visitors looked out tall, plate-glass windows at a parking lot or service area. The actual canyon was more than a mile away.

The new village was described as having a "contemporary-rustic design . . . to match the pine forest setting."[68] The motel registration building and Canyon Lodge at the village were constructed of wood with fieldstone-work as retaining walls. The Lodge's river-rock chimney and periodic rock facings along the front were "definitely an attempt at an expression of rustic."[69] Despite the rustic touches, the asymmetrical gable roof, tongue-and-groove wood siding, window styling, and the seventeen laminated-wood roof beams extending well beyond the building's footprint gave a contemporary feel to the Lodge.[70] The other structures around the commercial area presented a similar look.

The following year, the completion of the Canyon Visitor Center was the first significant federal building executed under Mission 66.[71] Like the other structures around the village parking lot, its design was also modern, though materials were chosen carefully for this national park structure. For the Canyon Visitor Center, designers chose high-quality wood siding, natural finishes, and multitoned, broken-face masonry to provide a "less formal and more rustic" look.[72] The front entryway was constructed primarily of plate glass, providing daylight to the interior of the building and an unobstructed view of the new large parking lot. "Visitor centers," as Director Wirth preferred them to be called, mimicked the popularity and purpose of shopping centers, with "one-stop convenience" adjacent to a large parking lot. These visitor centers offered a new approach to postwar tourism services. Born out of Mission 66, they were a distinct contribution to American tourism, as an entirely new type of building.[73]

From the start, Canyon Village as a whole was the subject of great criticism, influencing the formation of the new settlement's nascent place identity. Broadly speaking, there were two types of protests related to Canyon Village. First, critics were unsatisfied with the quality of the facility. Second, they disliked the design. Eventually, the negative reaction to using a modern design in Yellowstone extended to the entire Mission 66 program.[74] Even before Canyon Village was complete, the new, prefabricated cabins were referred to as "'chicken coop' style architecture" that was odd for a national park.[75] Several years later, a tourist in 1971 complained that the cabins at Canyon Village "can best be described as a shantytown," evidence that, among some visitors, a less-than-affectionate sense of place had taken hold.[76] Welton Becket's structures at Canyon's commercial area were described by Devereaux Butcher, executive secretary for the National Parks Association, as "colossal and of freak design."[77]

Ethan Carr, landscape architect and Mission 66 historian, suggests that Canyon Village met such criticism because "it was stripped of associative ornamentation and was purposefully located to avoid becoming a compositional element of park scenery. By protecting the scenery . . . the new concession areas would never be accepted as part of it, at least not the way an earlier generation of hotels had." However, widespread national reactions to postwar modern architecture's relationship with landscape outside of parks also influenced reactions to Canyon Village. Carr adds, "The increasingly alienated relationship of architecture to the surrounding landscape—arguably a central characteristic of modernist landscape design and planning—had far more influence on the perception of Canyon Village than the style or details of the structures themselves."[78]

The design of Canyon Village paralleled the larger evolution of tourist businesses along the nation's postwar roads. Dictated by the economics of mass-produced architecture, the needs of automobile tourists, and protection of unique park features, the NPS wanted all new overnight accommodations to be "simple, but as comfortable and convenient as possible." These facilities were just a "means to an end," unlike previous rustic hotels that were carefully placed in park scenery and seen as park attractions.[79] This shift at Canyon drew public criticism because the modern look and layout of the area did not meet visitor expectations of a traditional national park experience.

While park managers and the concessionaire absorbed these criticisms, the old Canyon settlement entered a period of striking transition that lasted almost a decade. The concessionaires honored their contractual obligations by removing their structures near the canyon's rims. They relocated smaller buildings such as guest cabins to other park settlements or contracted for the removal of more complex and challenging buildings. Surprisingly, a few of the larger Canyon structures are still recognizable today at their new location outside the park. The Yellowstone Park Company contracted for the removal of Canyon Lodge and its associated buildings during 1959 and

1960. Although these structures could have been burned on-site to facilitate removal, the contractor was able to find a buyer for four Canyon Lodge buildings. Charles Bovey purchased these buildings in the process of rebuilding the historic community at Nevada City, Montana, further infusing this reconstructed western town with Canyon's pioneer-like sense of place.[80]

The Grand Canyon Hotel was also removed from Canyon's cultural landscape early in this transition. Removing the hotel was not part of the master plan for Canyon from the 1950s, but the old hotel was drawing tourists away from its heavily financed neighbor—Canyon Village. The concessionaire turned a critical eye to the high cost of maintaining the hotel, while it slowly slid downhill, taking Canyon Village revenue along for the ride. After going into exorbitant debt with Canyon Village, the concessionaire's commitment to maintaining the Grand Canyon Hotel changed. Indeed, the policies and aesthetics of prevailing postwar "slum clearance" may have played a role in this change. In 1957, the hotel underwent a formal engineering structural assessment to determine if it was financially feasible to repair the hotel and keep it open for tourists. Unfortunately, the engineering report was not encouraging.

The concessionaire chose to abandon the hotel, though it did opt to keep a few of the existing buildings associated with the hotel and reuse them in the new village. In 1959, the hotel was deemed unsafe and closed. The entire building was sold to a salvage company for $25—all valuable elements of the hotel's interior and infrastructure were removed by the contractor through the winter of 1959–1960. In August 1960, during the process of demolition, the center of the hotel caught fire and spread rapidly through the wooden hotel frame that remained. In less than twenty-four hours, what remained of the hotel was gone. The cause of the Grand Canyon Hotel fire was never determined.[81]

Rod Wheaton, a former NPS cultural resources executive, laments the abandonment of the Grand Canyon Hotel as "one of the great architectural losses in Yellowstone National Park."[82] Today, a structure with the history and stature of Robert Reamer's Grand Canyon Hotel not only would be rehabilitated (whatever the cost) but also would be a National Historic Landmark.[83] Perhaps cultural landscape losses such as the Grand Canyon Hotel have contributed to the continued preservation of other structures such as Old Faithful Inn, Lake Yellowstone Hotel, and many other historic buildings inside and outside of national parks.

As portions of the old Canyon settlement were removed, the government and concessionaires reworked these areas to meet the landscape architecture and planning goals established during the Great Depression. Planners intended to return many abandoned sites to a more natural state, and some sites would be reconfigured for day tourists exploring the area after arriving by automobile. Though some of the abandoned buildings were removed right away, others served a new purpose. A few were used temporarily, then later removed. For example, Frank and John Craighead used the abandoned Haynes Photo Shop at the West Rim and, later, a concessionaire mess house near the Grand Canyon Hotel for their thirteen-year-long groundbreaking research on Yellowstone's grizzly bears.[84] Similarly, the new Canyon Village saddle horse concession, still in operation today, inherited two of the older hotel's staff dormitory structures.

The transformation of Canyon's cultural landscape enabled a long-sought-after change in the West Rim's tourism geography. The main touring route to Canyon from the south no longer funneled motorists to the brink of Upper Falls and along Canyon's West Rim and "main street." Tourists could still visit Upper Falls, but they had to turn off the new section of the Grand Loop Road onto a new access road leading to the falls to start their exploration. Tourists turning off the main highway near Upper Falls now navigated the West Rim's two distinctly different geographies that had been gradually interwoven over time. Short segments of treeless, abandoned roadways were evidence of the earlier tourist routes that had been left to reseed naturally. When workers laid a new hundred-car parking lot near the end of the access road to Upper Falls, they erased and overwrote evidence of the Haynes Picture Shop and the Ranger Station, two contributing structures along Canyon's "main street" that had been recently removed.[85] Disturbed sites in this old central business district appeared to tourists as unused, cleared fields with hearty grasses and weeds growing through abandoned obsidian gravel paving. Earlier West Rim routes near the Yellowstone River and Upper Falls were turned into tourist walking and biking paths.[86]

Park managers continued transforming Canyon on the east side of the river during the mid-1960s to meet pre–World War II planning goals. Across the river, the NPS reworked the driveway to the old Canyon Lodge to serve as an access road to a large new parking lot capable of accommodating both cars and buses. The parking lot was laid over the site of the old rustic lodge.[87] Here, tourists in the 1960s likely poured out of vehicles and bustled to overlooks and trailheads unaware they were moving through a place where earlier visitors to Canyon Lodge had been fed and entertained while they vacationed close to Yellowstone's Grand Canyon. Further down the South Rim Road, more adjustments were made for auto tourists. At the Artist Point parking lot, sidewalks and a traffic island were added in the process of separating parking for cars and buses from pedestrian walkways. The changes at Artist Point, sparked by Mission 66 plans, significantly altered the look of this tourist stop by removing much of the rustic architectural signature of an earlier era.[88]

By February 1966, all of the old Canyon settlement on either side of the Upper Falls was gone and merely a memory. Ironically, in that same year, Congress also passed the Historic Preservation Act, which certainly would have influenced decisions on how Canyon's cultural landscape evolved to meet post–World War II tourism. Like so many downtowns across the nation, many historic structures and cultural landscapes at Canyon were lost to forces of modernization and to the migration of "urban" services to more peripheral locations. Today, all that remains of the original Canyon settlement near the Upper Falls are the day-use facilities (trails, overlooks, and their access roads), comfort stations, and artifacts scattered on the ground.

The legacy of the new Canyon Village includes persisting challenges for Yellowstone's administrators and concessionaires. Perhaps more so than any other settlement in Yellowstone, Canyon is a "working" cultural landscape and tourist facility. Yellowstone's managers have continued to upgrade and adjust Canyon Village since the Mission 66 era as moneys were made available. Additional modern cabins were added and the campground was expanded in the mid- to late-1960s. An expansion of the village sewer system followed in the early 1970s and again in the 1990s.[89] Recognizing the quality and style problems with the initial prefabricated cabins at Canyon, the NPS began planning for lodging redevelopment in the late 1980s. The lodging redevelopment plan includes replacing the prefabricated Mission 66 cabins with several individual lodges, the first two of which, Cascade Lodge and Dunraven Lodge, were constructed during 1992 and 1998, respectively. Five additional lodges were completed by 2017. The design of each lodge is intended to return a more traditional park-like feel to lodging at Canyon (figure 6.21). These more traditional replacements contrast with Welton Becket's contemporary-style structures in the commercial area, prompting

planners to consider altering the look of the commercial buildings to provide style consistency.[90]

The NPS replaced the Canyon Visitor Center from 1958 with a new structure that opened to the public in 2006 (figure 6.22). At the start of this project, all of Canyon Village underwent a cultural resource evaluation, as required by the National Historic Preservation Act of 1966. The commercial area was determined to be eligible for listing on the National Register of Historic Places because of its association with Mission 66. This determination encouraged careful attention be paid to the new visitor center's architectural design. Wyoming State Historic Preservation Office officials suggested mitigating the Mission 66 visitor center removal from this historic district by modifying the new building's design. These officials suggested that, instead of a decidedly modern execution like Becket's buildings across the parking lot, the new structure's style should recall the look of the historic Grand Canyon Hotel.[91] Introducing design elements of the Grand Canyon Hotel inside this commercial area, deemed eligible for the National Register due to

FIGURE 6.21. Dunraven Lodge, 2013. The newer upscale accommodations at Canyon include the neotraditional Dunraven Lodge. Photograph by Jody Lyle. Source: National Park Service, Yellowstone National Park, YELL 19634d (courtesy of NPS-YNP). (Original in color.)

FIGURE 6.22. Canyon Visitor Education Center, 2006. The modern Canyon Visitor Education Center combines all the conveniences of a twenty-first-century building with architectural touches that reflect more traditional elements of rustic design. Photograph by Diane Papineau. (Original in color.)

its Modern Mission 66 associations, has begun a process of style mixing at Canyon Village. Indeed, planners intend (when needed) to replace modern-style buildings in the suburban-style commercial area with new buildings in a more traditional style. With the mixing of styles at Canyon Village, the site has become a fascinating example of an increasingly hybridized architectural landscape.

As a national park landscape, today's Canyon tourist settlement is unique. Unlike anywhere else in Yellowstone, Canyon's cultural landscape and sense of place have experienced radical change. The visitor experience at Canyon today has not benefited from the traditions and cultural fabric embodied in Canyon's first effective settlement near Upper Falls. The two Canyon places are like different parts of the same being, though severed in space and time: one part very much alive, the other laid to rest. The existence of these two personalities makes it possible for a granddaughter fresh from her recent visit to Canyon to spark a very lively discussion with her grandfather who honeymooned there decades prior. They each know this place called Canyon, but changing generations of park managers and concessionaires framed the visitor experience of the Grand Canyon of the Yellowstone very differently for each. Grandpa knew the place of Canyon as it came of age, rooted organically in place with all the traditions, charm, bravado, and showiness one would expect of a confident, self-conscious adolescent. His granddaughter returned home recalling a national park place formed with the benefit of hindsight, concern, and preconception—a more managed place influenced by established professionals and by the twentieth-century expectations of modern visitors.

No longer was the Canyon tourist settlement sited adjacent to its namesake. While the earlier settlement was growing organically, park concessionaires gravitated toward building near the canyon's rim, centralizing the business of transportation and basic human needs near the actual Grand Canyon of the Yellowstone. The new Canyon Village settlement pattern couldn't be more different. It mimicked the convenient, decentralized suburban places and the automobile culture that were dominant at that time in the United States. Just as motorized travel increased during the suburbanization of America, an automobile trip to view the Grand Canyon of the Yellowstone became, in the 1950s, the most common excursion from Canyon Village.

At Canyon Village, modern building designs were selected over traditional, more rustic styles strongly associated with national park places. Park concessionaires and their architects selected efficiency, convenience, and economical building techniques over mythic, natural styles intended to blend in with the landscape. Site designers also used trees to screen these new features from the public. By contrast, nearly all of the original organic Canyon settlement structures were designed in styles that became the foundation for "Parkitecture." These earlier buildings were designed to blend with their environment, adding materially to the national park "scene." Pioneer log construction, the primary building style used at Canyon, had fostered the feeling of visiting the American frontier.

As a Yellowstone National Park cultural landscape, Canyon Village today represents a hybrid human place. It reflects American postwar affluence, increases in automobile ownership, and large suburban developments while simultaneously serving national park tourists in a large, western wilderness reserve. The radical evolution of Canyon's cultural landscape has clearly presented two contested visitor experiences of Canyon as a national park place—two very different sets of visual norms, cues, and values through which to experience one of the most sacred features in all of the national parks. As one Canyon staff member in the 1950s noted: "Canyon Lodge cabins now have water and bath rooms, and the souvenir shops are certainly larger, but those warm fuzzy feelings that only pine[-]scented wood smoke on crispy nights could bring are gone."[92]

NOTES

1. For a synthesized description of the formation (and coloration) of the Grand Canyon of the Yellowstone, see Diane M. Papineau, "Transforming Place at Canyon: Politics and Settlement Creation in Yellowstone National Park" (MS thesis, Montana State University, 2008), 3–5. Specific technical treatises describing the geology of Yellowstone's Grand Canyon include Gerald M. Richmond, "Geology and Evolution of the Grand Canyon of the Yellowstone, Yellowstone National Park, Wyoming," in *Centennial Field Guide*, vol. 2, edited by S. S. Beus (Rocky Mountain Section of the Geological Society of America, 1987), 155–60; Robert O. Fournier et al., *A Field-Trip Guide to Yellowstone National Park, Wyoming, Montana, and Idaho—Volcanic, Hydrothermal, and Glacial Activity in the Region*, US Geological Survey Bulletin 2099 (Washington, DC: Government Printing Office, 1994), 36–37; Robert L. Christiansen, *The Quaternary and Pliocene Yellowstone Plateau Volcanic Field of Wyoming, Idaho, and Montana*, Professional Paper 729-G (Reston, Virginia: United States Geological Survey, 2001): G41–G42 and G51.
2. Elaine Hale, Yellowstone Cultural Resources Specialist and Archaeologist, personal communication, 2005.
3. Mack W. Shortt, "Museum of the Rockies Archaeological Research in the Canyons of the Yellowstone," *Yellowstone Science* 9, no. 2 (2001): 16–20.
4. "Canyon Rim Drives, Road Rehabilitation Environmental Assessment / Assessment of Effect, June 2006" (Yellowstone National Park, WY: Branch of Planning, Compliance, and Landscape Architecture), 74–75; "Cultural Landscape Inventory, Artist Point, September 2003" (Yellowstone National Park, WY: Branch of Planning, Compliance, and Landscape Architecture), part 3a, page 10.
5. Aubrey L. Haines, *The Yellowstone Story: A History of Our First National Park*, vol. 1 (Yellowstone National Park: Yellowstone Library and Museum Association, 1977), 38.
6. John Hyde, *Official Guide to the Yellowstone National Park* (1887 issue) (St. Paul, MN: Northern News Co. [W. C. Riley], 1886). Hyde quotes Reverend Hoyt: "Well, we have reached Cascade Creek at last; and a beautiful grove of trees, beneath whose shade sparkles a clear stream, whose waters are free from the nauseous taste of alkali, furnishes a delightful place in which to camp. Now—dismounting, and seeing that your horse is well cared for, while the men are unloading the pack-mules and pitching the tents—walk up that trail winding up that hillside; follow it for a little among the solemn pines, and then pass out from the tree shadows, and take your stand upon that jutting rock—clinging to it well meanwhile, and being very sure of your footing, for your head will surely grow dizzy,—and there opens before you one of the most stupendous scenes of Nature,—the Lower Falls and the awful Canyon of the Yellowstone" (111–13).
7. Holm Transportation Company, 1912, Letter to the Secretary of the Interior, December 6, Box 29, Folder 190 (Holm), Yellowstone National Park Archives.
8. John Pitcher, Report of the Acting Superintendent of Yellowstone National Park to the Secretary of the Interior, 1905 (Bound File, Yellowstone National Park Library), 13; Pitcher, Report of the Acting Superintendent . . . 1906, 13–14; Samuel B. M. Young, Report of the Acting Superintendent of Yellowstone National Park to the Secretary of the Interior, 1907 (Bound File, Yellowstone National Park Library), 8; Ernest Peek, Annual

Report of Chief Engineer, Corps of Engineers Reports, 1906, item 243, box 100 (Yellowstone National Park Archives), 13.

9. This early tent hotel at Canyon was a temporary arrangement—it left little or no archaeological record on the ground, and its exact site is not known. The best location information is provided in Richard A. Bartlett, *Yellowstone: A Wilderness Besieged* (Tucson: University of Arizona Press, 1989; originally published 1985): 51; and George Bird Grinnell, "Through Two Ocean Pass," *Forest and Stream*, January 29, 1885, 22.
10. Bartlett, *Yellowstone*, 48–51.
11. Haines, *Yellowstone Story*, vol. 2, 471; Louis C. Cramton, *Early History of Yellowstone National Park and Its Relation to National Park Policies* (Washington, DC: United States Government Printing Office, 1932), 61.
12. Haines, *Yellowstone Story*, vol. 2, 472 and 476.
13. Papineau, "Transforming Place at Canyon," 58 and 104–16.
14. Joni Louise Kinsey, *Thomas Moran's West: Chromolithography, High Art, and Popular Taste* (Lawrence: University Press of Kansas, 2006), 118; Gail S. Davidson et al., *Frederic Church, Winslow Homer, and Thomas Moran: Tourism and the American Landscape* (New York: Bulfinch Press, 2006), 107.
15. Haines, *Yellowstone Story*, vol. 2, 40 n60, 184–85; Lee H. Whittlesey, "Brief History of the Brink-of-the-Upper-Falls Developed Area in Yellowstone National Park," 2003, unpublished manuscript, Yellowstone National Park Library vertical files, 4–5.
16. George S. Anderson, Report of the Acting Superintendent of Yellowstone National Park to the Secretary of the Interior, 1891 (Bound File, Yellowstone National Park Library), 6.
17. Haines, *Yellowstone Story*, vol. 2, 129; Tamsen E. Hert, "Luxury in the Wilderness: Yellowstone's Grand Canyon Hotel, 1911–1960," *Yellowstone Science* 13, no. 3 (2005): 21–36.
18. Ruth Quinn, *Weaver of Dreams: The Life and Architecture of Robert C. Reamer* (Gardiner, MT: Leslie and Ruth Quinn, 2004), 73–79; Hert, "Luxury in the Wilderness."
19. Haines, *Yellowstone Story*, vol. 2, 265.
20. Lee H. Whittlesey, "Storytelling in Yellowstone: Horse-and-Buggy Tour Guides in the Grand Old Park, 1872–1920," 2005, unpublished manuscript, Yellowstone National Park Library vertical files, 122–23; Lee H. Whittlesey, "Wonderland Nomenclature: A History of the Place Names of Yellowstone National Park," 1988, unpublished manuscript, Yellowstone National Park Library, 959.
21. Papineau, "Transforming Place at Canyon," 149–53.
22. Lee H. Whittlesey and Yellowstone Staff, *A Yellowstone Album: A Photographic Celebration of the First National Park* (Boulder, CO: Roberts Rinehart, 1997), 90.
23. Haines, *Yellowstone Story*, vol. 2, 134–37.
24. Edward H. Moorman, "Yellowstone Park Lodge and Camps Company Manager," 1954, unpublished memoir, Yellowstone National Park Library, 4.
25. Lloyd M. Brett, Report of the Acting Superintendent of Yellowstone National Park to the Secretary of the Interior, 1913 (Bound File, Yellowstone National Park Library), 5.
26. Papineau, "Transforming Place at Canyon," 108–10.
27. Haines, *Yellowstone Story*, vol. 2, 41, 46, and 338.
28. William C. Everhart, *The National Park Service* (New York: Praeger Publishers, 1972), 15–16; Alfred Runte, *National Parks: The American Experience* (Lincoln: University of Nebraska Press, 1979), 89–105.

29. Haines, *Yellowstone Story*, vol. 2, 273–74.
30. David Louter, *Windshield Wilderness: Cars, Roads, and Nature in Washington's National Parks* (Seattle: University of Washington Press, 2006).
31. "Cultural Landscape Inventory, Artist Point, September 2003" (Yellowstone National Park, WY: Branch of Planning, Compliance, and Landscape Architecture), part 2a, 4.
32. Lary M. Dilsaver and William Wyckoff, "Agency Culture, Cumulative Causation and Development in Glacier National Park, Montana." *Journal of Historical Geography* 25, no. 1 (1999): 76.
33. For a detailed description of the evolution of Canyon Camp and Lodge, see Papineau, "Transforming Place at Canyon," 201–8. Quote from Yellowstone Park Camps Company Brochure (1924), author's collection.
34. Ruth Quinn, *Weaver of Dreams*, 73–79; Tamsen E. Hert, "Luxury in the Wilderness," 21–36.
35. Canyon's West Rim development maturation is described in Papineau, "Transforming Place at Canyon," 180–99, 209–12.
36. James E. Vance, *This Scene of Man: The Role and Structure of the City in the Geography of Western Civilization* (New York: Harper's College Press, 1977): 24.
37. Rodd Wheaton, "Architecture of Yellowstone: A Microcosm of American Design," *Yellowstone Science* 8, no. 4 (2000): 17; Linda F. McClelland, *Building the National Parks: Historic Landscape Design and Construction* (Baltimore, MD: Johns Hopkins University Press, 1998), 17–18 and 91–120.
38. Wilbur Zelinsky, *The Cultural Geography of the United States* (Upper Saddle River, NJ: Prentice Hall, 1992), 13.
39. William Wyckoff, *Creating Colorado: The Making of a Western American Landscape, 1860–1940* (New Haven, CT: Yale University Press, 1999), 112.
40. Lee H. Whittlesey and Yellowstone Staff, *Yellowstone Album*, 172–73; Bartlett, *Yellowstone*, 297–302.
41. Willard Kistler to the Commanding Officer, CCC Company 544, March 24, 1937, Yellowstone Historic Center Archives, West Yellowstone, Montana, 1; Leo Kimmett, "Life in a Yellowstone CCC Camp," *Annals of Wyoming* 56, no. 1 (1984): 75 and 76.
42. McClelland, *Building the National Parks*, 234–36.
43. Edmund Rogers, Report of the Superintendent of Yellowstone National Park to the Secretary of the Interior, 1937 (Bound File, Yellowstone National Park Library), 34.
44. Rogers, Report of the Superintendent . . . 1939, 24.
45. Rogers, Report of the Superintendent . . . 1939, 24; Rogers, Report of the Superintendent . . . 1940, 21; Master Plan: Yellowstone National Park, Wyoming, January 1, 1941, National Park Service, Yellowstone National Park Archives.
46. Barry Cullingsworth and Roger Caves, *Planning in the USA: Policies, Issues and Processes* (Boston, MA: Routledge, 2003), 58; John Levy *Contemporary Urban Planning* (New York: Prentice Hall, 2003); McClelland, *Building the National Parks*, 195–200.
47. Master Plan, Yellowstone National Park, Wyoming, October 1, 1933, Yellowstone National Park Archives; McClelland, *Building the National Parks*, 307; Ethan Carr, *Wilderness by Design: Landscape Architecture and the National Park Service* (Lincoln: University of Nebraska Press, 1998), 241.
48. Master Plan, Yellowstone National Park, Wyoming, January 1, 1939, Yellowstone National Park Archives.

49. Master Plan, Yellowstone National Park, Wyoming, January 1, 1939; Master Plan, Yellowstone National Park, Wyoming, January 1, 1941, Yellowstone National Park Archives, text section Canyon Development: General; Fred Willson, architectural rendering of Canyon Lodge Center, Yellowstone National Park, Yellowstone Park Company, December 1940, Yellowstone National Park Archives.
50. Haines, *Yellowstone Story*, vol. 2, 369; Master Plan, Yellowstone National Park, Wyoming, January 1, 1939, Yellowstone National Park Archives; Master Plan, Yellowstone National Park, Wyoming, Jan 1, 1941, Yellowstone National Park Archives.
51. Levy, *Contemporary Urban Planning*, 54; Dolores Hayden, *Building Suburbia: Green Fields and Urban Growth, 1820–2000* (New York: Vintage Books, 2003), 3.
52. Hayden, *Building Suburbia*, 132–38.
53. John Ise, *Our National Park Policy: A Critical History* (Baltimore, MD: Johns Hopkins University Press, 1961), 537; Jerome B. Wood, "National Parks: Tomorrow's Slums?" *Travel Magazine*, April 1954, 14–16; Robert M. Yodor, "Twenty-Four Million Acres of Trouble," *Saturday Evening Post*, July 3, 1954, 32 and 78–80; Bernard DeVoto, "Let's Close the National Parks," *Harper's Magazine*, October 1953, 49–52.
54. Papineau, "Transforming Place at Canyon," 303–4.
55. Photograph (1950) of Grand View under construction (YELL 20622), Yellowstone Museum Collection, Heritage and Research Center, National Park Service; Canyon Rim Drives, Road Rehabilitation Environmental Assessment / Assessment of Effect, June 2006, National Park Service Branch of Planning, Compliance, and Landscape Architecture, Yellowstone National Park, Wyoming, 71.
56. Microfilm copy of plan for 1954–55 overlook reconstruction of Inspiration Point, Office of the Park Engineer, Dept. of Interior—National Park Service, Yellowstone National Park, National Park Service, Maintenance Division, Mammoth Hot Springs, Wyoming; Photograph of Inspiration Point construction (YELL 20623), Yellowstone Museum Collection, Heritage and Research Center, National Park Service; Photograph (1955) of completed Inspiration Point overlook, by Condon, October 2, Yellowstone Photo Collection, National Park Service Division of Interpretation, Mammoth Hot Springs, Wyoming; Yellowstone Weekly News, 6 December 1959, Yellowstone National Park community newsletter, published by the National Park Service, Strempel Collection, copy in author's possession; *Haynes Guide to Yellowstone Park* (St. Paul, MN: J. E. Haynes, 1959), 133; Photograph (1958) of new Lower Falls platform, Yellowstone Photo Collection, National Park Service Division of Interpretation, Mammoth Hot Springs, Wyoming.
57. Master Plan, Yellowstone National Park, Wyoming, February 29, 1952, Yellowstone National Park Archives.
58. Master Plan, Yellowstone National Park, Wyoming, February 29, 1952, Yellowstone National Park Archives.
59. Ethan Carr, Mission 66 Contextual History, Draft US Government Report (Washington, DC: National Park Service, 2004), 112–16 and 202. For a complete history of Mission 66, see Ethan Carr, *Mission 66: Modernism and the National Park Dilemma* (Amherst: University of Massachusetts Press, 2007).
60. Sarah Allaback, *Mission 66 Visitor Centers: The History of a Building Type* (Washington, DC: US Department of the Interior, 2000); Ethan Carr, Mission 66 Contextual History, 190–91.

61. Mark D. Barringer, *Selling Yellowstone: Capitalism and the Construction of Nature* (Lawrence: University Press of Kansas, 2002), 117 and 124–27; Haines, *Yellowstone Story*, vol. 2, 375–76.
62. Allaback, *Mission 66 Visitor Centers*, 23.
63. Allaback, *Mission 66 Visitor Centers*, 22.
64. Allaback, *Mission 66 Visitor Centers*, 9; Mary Shivers Culpin, *"For the Benefit and Enjoyment of the People": A History of Concession Development in Yellowstone National Park, 1872–1966* (National Park Service, Yellowstone Center for Resources: Yellowstone National Park, Wyoming, 2003, YCR-CR-2003-01), 102.
65. Ethan Carr, Mission 66 Contextual History, 193–94; "Canyon Village Construction Is First Park Expansion Job," *Billings Gazette*, May 11, 1956, box D-68, folder Canyon Village 1956, Yellowstone National Park Archives.
66. Donald W. Meinig, "American Wests: Preface to a Geographical Interpretation," *Annals of the Association of American Geographers*, no. 62 (1972): 163.
67. Thomas J. Hallin letter to Newell Gough Jr., dated December 27, box YPC-145, folder Maintenance-Construction, Canyon Village, 1955–1960, Yellowstone National Park Archives; Canyon Village Special, 31 August 1957, public relations newsletter published by Yellowstone Park Company, Yellowstone National Park Library vertical files, Yellowstone National Park, Wyoming, 1, 2.
68. Canyon Village Special, 31 August 1957, public relations newsletter published by Yellowstone Park Company, Yellowstone National Park Library vertical files, Yellowstone National Park, Wyoming, 4.
69. Lemuel A. Garrison memorandum to Chief, Western Office, Division of Design and Construction, March 7, 1957, box D-68, folder Canyon Area Development 1957, Yellowstone National Park Archives.
70. Welton Becket quoted in "Canyon Village Construction."
71. Lemuel A. Garrison, Report of the Superintendent of Yellowstone National Park to the Secretary of the Interior, 1959 (Bound File, Yellowstone National Park Library), section 6.
72. Lemuel A. Garrison memorandum to Chief, Western Office, Division of Design and Construction, March 7, 1957, box D-68, folder Canyon Area Development 1957, Yellowstone National Park Archives.
73. Conrad Wirth memorandum to Washington Office and All Field Offices, February 10, 1956, Box D-68, folder Canyon Village 1956, Yellowstone National Park Archives; Carr, Mission 66 Contextual History, 85; See Allaback, *Mission 66 Visitor Centers*, for a complete history of this building type.
74. Ethan Carr, *Mission 66: Modernism and the National Park Dilemma*, Review Draft, 2005, 372.
75. Barringer, *Selling Yellowstone*, 137.
76. Walter E. Levi letter to Roger Morton, Secretary of the Interior, September 18, 1971, box A-46, file "A3619 Complaints Concerning Concessions November thru December 1971," Yellowstone National Park Archives.
77. Ethan Carr, Mission 66 Contextual History, 252.
78. Ethan Carr, *Mission 66: Modernism and the National Park Dilemma*, Review Draft, 2005, 356.
79. Conrad Wirth, as quoted in Ethan Carr, *Mission 66: Modernism and the National Park Dilemma*, Review Draft, 2005, 345.
80. For removal of Canyon Lodge and the West Rim "main street" settlement, see Diane M. Papineau, "Transforming Place at Canyon," 400–408.

81. Tamsen E. Hert, "Luxury in the Wilderness," 21–36.
82. Rodd Wheaton, "Architecture of Yellowstone," 16.
83. Jim McDonald, historical architect with A & E Architects, Missoula, Montana. Personal communication, 2008.
84. Craighead use of structures at both the Canyon Bus Compound and at the West Rim is chronicled in Diane M. Papineau, "Transforming Place at Canyon," 408–13.
85. Master Plan, Yellowstone National Park, Wyoming, February 1966, Yellowstone National Park Archives, map and narrative, 2, 3.
86. Master Plan, Yellowstone National Park, Wyoming, revised June 1964, Yellowstone National Park Archives.
87. Master Plan, Yellowstone National Park, Wyoming, revised January 1965, Yellowstone National Park Archives; Master Plan, Yellowstone National Park, Wyoming, February 1966, Yellowstone National Park Archives.
88. John S. McLaughlin, Report of the Superintendent of Yellowstone National Park to the Secretary of the Interior, 1966 (Bound File, Yellowstone National Park Library), section 1; Cultural Landscape Inventory, Artist Point, September 2003, National Park Service, Branch of Planning, Compliance, and Landscape Architecture, Yellowstone National Park, Wyoming, part 1, pages 16, 23.
89. Prospectus: A Concession Business Opportunity for Lodging, Food and Beverage, Retail, Camping, and Other Services at Yellowstone National Park (Denver, Colorado: Intermountain Regional Office, 2004): section D; McLaughlin, Report of the Superintendent . . . 1964, section 4; electronic correspondence with Tim Hudson, former National Park Service Chief of Maintenance in Yellowstone, March 21, 2008.
90. Value Analysis Study for Canyon Village Lodging, May 1, 1996, Yellowstone National Park, Management Services Group, Denver Service Center, National Park Service (1996): section Executive Summary-Conclusion; Environmental Assessment: Lodging Redevelopment, Canyon Village, Yellowstone National Park/Wyoming-Montana-Idaho, Branch of Planning, Compliance, and Landscape Architecture, 1988, Yellowstone National Park, Wyoming, 21.
91. Michael V. Finley memorandum to Assistant Regional Director for Cultural Resources and Partnerships, Intermountain Region, January 24, 2000, Canyon Visitor Education Center Administrative History files, Division of Interpretation, Yellowstone National Park, Wyoming; Environmental Assessment: Canyon Visitor Center Rehabilitation, Yellowstone National Park, Wyoming, February 2001, National Park Service, Branch of Planning, Compliance, and Landscape Architecture, Yellowstone National Park, Wyoming, 15; Assessing Major Changes to a Mission 66 Structure: Canyon Visitor Center, no date, Yellowstone National Park, Canyon Visitor Education Center Administrative History files, Division of Interpretation, Yellowstone National Park, Wyoming, 11.
92. Electronic correspondence with Canyon Lodge (1954, 1955, 1956) and Canyon Village (1957) Yellowstone Park Company employee Kurt Strempel, Indianapolis, Indiana, dated October 7, 2005.

FIGURES 7.1 AND 7.2. Top: Roosevelt Lodge, ca. 1927. This Haynes postcard view shows the rustic-style log building appealed to tourists who were in search of an authentic experience in the Old West. Note the traditional "antler fence" in the foreground. Bottom: Camp Roosevelt Interior, ca. 1922. A framed portrait of Theodore Roosevelt was the centerpiece of the rock fireplace in the interior of the main Lodge building. Sources: private collection of Tamsen Emersen Hert. (Originals in color.)

7

Roosevelt Lodge

Tamsen Emerson Hert

A stop at Camp Roosevelt will not appeal to everybody. It is well to understand that there are no rooms with bath, or other service elements of an elegant or luxurious nature. It is well to know, also, that there is little opportunity for "dressing up" and formal entertainment. Camp Roosevelt is a comfortable western camp surrounded by a wilderness. Its primary appeal is to visitors who delight in (or who need) foot trails, saddle-horse trails, trout fishing, exploration, nature study or relaxation.[1]
—YELLOWSTONE PARK CAMPS

TUCKED AWAY in the northeastern corner of Yellowstone stands rustic Roosevelt Lodge. Built during 1919 and opened in 1920, it is one of the few original lodges remaining in the park today. Compared to the large, expensive, full-service hotels that had become common to national park landscapes early in the twentieth century, Roosevelt, as well as the other five lodges constructed in Yellowstone between 1917 and 1925, offered inexpensive alternative accommodations for visitors who were touring the park. While similarly styled lodges at Mammoth Hot Springs, Old Faithful, Canyon, Lake, and Sylvan Lake emphasized casual accommodations, it was Roosevelt Lodge, with its remote location far removed from the park's highlighted features, that created a distinctive cultural landscape in Yellowstone that remains even today solely oriented around a truly rustic experience.

Roosevelt's origins can be traced to Yellowstone's earliest camp concessionaire, William Wallace Wylie. Wylie introduced his moveable-camping tours through Wonderland in 1883. At that time, the traditional five- to six-day hotel tour averaged fifty dollars, which made Wylie's six- to seven-day tour of the park for thirty-five dollars an inexpensive way for a middle-class

https://doi.org/10.5876/9781646427697.c007

clientele to see the wonders of the region. As the popularity of his tours grew, and thus his business, he petitioned the Department of the Interior for permission to establish permanent camps, which he believed would make his operation more efficient and more appealing to his patrons.[2]

Wylie's proposals, however, were contingent on the approval of a long-term lease that would have to be granted by the Department of the Interior. After enduring several years of refusals for the requested lease, Wylie decided to erect his permanent camps in 1896, based on a mere promise from government officials that his annual permits would be renewed.[3] By 1898, the renamed and incorporated Wylie Permanent Camps had established four permanent camps: one each at Apollinaris Spring (Willow Park), the Upper Geyser Basin, Lake Outlet, and Grand Canyon. In addition to the camps, two lunch stations were also added, with one at Gibbon Canyon and the other at West Thumb.[4] Beginning in 1899, the Wylie operation witnessed a steady increase in the number of budget-minded visitors choosing to stay in the camps.[5]

The success of Wylie's permanent camps did not sit well with the Northern Pacific Railroad or with Harry W. Child, owner of the hotel and transportation companies. According to Mark Barringer:

> Wylie constantly irritated the wealthy and snobbish Child because the tourists who used his camps were a different sort, not at all like those who stayed at the posh hotels; his guests paid low prices for Spartan accommodations and dust-plagued stagecoach tours.[6]

Consequently, Child and the Northern Pacific Railroad (Child's financial backer) tried anything and everything to disrupt Wylie's camp operation, even violating the Interstate Commerce Commission ruling that prohibited discriminatory price tactics. One effective technique was to bundle the purchase of a railroad ticket with discounted hotel accommodations but not allow Wylie a similar opportunity to offer a favorable deal for camp patrons. Denied his fair share of Yellowstone's tourism boom during 1904—a result of travel to and from the World's Fair in St. Louis—Wylie's tolerance of those tactics finally came to a head.

Ed Moorman, a long-time employee of the Camping Company, recalled that business at the Wylie Camps was very slow in 1904, but:

> the hotels, however, did a good business that year. . . . The railroads, too, made discriminating rates against the Camping Company. If I recall correctly, a round[-]trip ticket could be purchased to Gardiner including stage

> and hotel accommodations at a good saving as against buying a rail ticket to Gardiner only and then buying locally the ticket for the Camps tour of the Park. It was this problem that led W. W. Wylie to go to Washington, D.C.[,] in the spring of 1905 to appear before the Interstate Commerce Commission, in the hope to have this discrimination discontinued.[7]

In 1905, Wylie teamed up with George Lamar, an attorney from Washington, DC, and took on the biggest challenge of his life, suing the Northern Pacific Railroad. The Interstate Commerce Commission decided in Wylie's favor, citing that in addition to interfering with free and fair competition of an authorized concessionaire, the railroad was also restricting the freedom and opportunity of tourists to select their conveyance and entertainment.[8] Though victorious in the suit against the Northern Pacific Railroad, Wylie wearied of what was later termed "bureaucratic process fatigue" and sold the Camping Company to Harry Child and to Arthur W. Miles, a businessman from Livingston.[9] Not surprisingly, Child and Miles were issued a ten-year lease for their newly acquired camping operation. With the financial backing of Child and the methodical management of Miles, the renamed Wylie Permanent Camping Company became quite successful through the following decade.

Miles expanded the business in 1906 by adding two new camps. The first, Swan Lake Camp, located just south of Mammoth Hot Springs on panoramic Swan Lake Flat, replaced Wylie's earlier camp near Apollinaris Spring. The second, Camp Roosevelt, was erected near Tower Fall and represented an entirely new addition to the company operation and, perhaps most importantly, a completely new tourist experience. In contrast to the hustle of the complete Yellowstone tour, Camp Roosevelt offered an excursion into a quieter world of wholesome relaxation. Just three years earlier, President Theodore Roosevelt spent nearly three weeks in the park, relaxing and camping just above Rainy Lake in the Tower Fall area. Miles and Child capitalized on that event and established Camp Roosevelt at the Cooke City and Tower Fall junction, approximately one and a half miles from Roosevelt's actual campsite, in commemoration of the president's visit in April 1903.

Once completed, the 1907 Wylie Permanent Camping Company brochure announced "The New Roosevelt Camp Trip" and described Camp Roosevelt's setting as:

> the most perfectly ideal location for a camp in the Park. . . . A beautiful little meadow with majestic fir trees encircling it on three sides and a grove of quaking-aspen screening it from the road on the fourth, a

> crystal ice-cold mountain stream coming from the forest and skirting one side of the meadow; . . . and a most superb view of the serried . . . crags of the Absarokas on the East and Northeast; surely Nature has done everything possible to make this a perfect spot to enjoy outdoor life.[10]

Indeed, visitor Frederick Dumont Smith agreed with the promotional literature and found the location of Roosevelt to be enchanting. In his *Book of a Hundred Bears*, Dumont remarked, "We reached Camp Roosevelt in time for a late lunch. The camp is set in a charming grove, with tent houses and tents for cooking and dining."[11]

Over the next few years, the fame of the Wylie Permanent Camping Company spread throughout the country, and visitation to Yellowstone via the "Wylie Way" increased substantially. In 1909, the Wylie Way, as it was known through the promotional acumen of the company's publicist Howard Hays, hosted a record number of 7,717 guests.[12] Camp Roosevelt's tranquil location and relaxed ambience proved to be a powerful draw. Miles's and Child's booming camping business caught the attention of other astute entrepreneurs, who soon followed the successful Wylie Way model. By 1913, two additional permanent camping companies vied with the Wylie operation for Yellowstone's increasing volume of tourist traffic: the Shaw and Powell Camping Company and Hefferlin's Old Faithful Camping Company. While the Old Faithful Company remained rather small, the Shaw and Powell operation grew quickly and became the chief rival of the Wylie operation. In direct competition with Camp Roosevelt and the Wylie Way, Shaw and Powell established a camp within walking distance of Tower Fall and touted their tour as the "Modern Way."

As visitor expectations and park management practices changed, the "modern way" would come to all of the national parks' facilities. With more than twelve national parks and monuments to administer by 1916, the Department of the Interior removed park oversight and control from the hands of the Department of War and the United States Army and created a new agency, the National Park Service (NPS), which would now protect and preserve Yellowstone and the other parks in the system. This administrative shift coincided with the admittance of the automobile to Yellowstone (beginning in 1915). This ushered in a new era of automobile-oriented tourists who needed facilities for their vehicles and who often desired the convenience and affordability of more casual accommodations. For example, a Yellowstone Park Camping Company brochure from 1918 stated, "In addition to the accommodations already mentioned, the Yellowstone Park Camping Company has an enclosure for private automobiles, where cars may be stored free of charge."[13] Likewise, the automobile brought greater numbers of tourists and increased mobility that resulted in adjustments to the length of the standard park tours offered by all concessionaires.

One of these adjustments was the closure of certain facilities, such as the Fountain Hotel, that were deemed obsolete. On the other hand, a selective expansion of camps was also promoted to meet the demands of the automobile-touring public.[14] Ideally, these camps would be about "a day[']s travel" apart. By 1920, the company was highlighting their services to automobile visitors, including the issuing of a brochure titled *In Your Own Automobile*, in which Hays described the park as a "motorist's paradise."[15]

With the creation of the NPS in 1916, Stephen T. Mather was appointed director of the new agency, with Horace M. Albright serving as assistant director—both in charge of all business in the national parks. Their primary concern was the consolidation of the Yellowstone transportation, hotel, and camping concessions: "They believed that the competition among franchisees was detrimental to the traveling public and that monopolies for each major facet of the operation—hotels, transportation, and camping—would simplify administration and increase visitation."[16]

The restructuring of the transportation and lodging concessions resulted in several changes, including Harry Child maintaining ownership of both the hotel and transportation companies; photographer F. Jay Haynes, who previously owned and operated the Monida and Yellowstone Stage Company, continuing to operate his photographic franchise; and A. W. Miles and John D. Powell, owners of the two major camping companies, joining together in the consolidation of all the camping companies and becoming the principal operators of the new Yellowstone Park Camping Company.[17] Ed Moorman recalled this episode in the park's history:

> Many of the former operators were not pleased with the new set-up, but in reality it was very good for the tourists as they were free from the annoyance of being solicited by many outfits if they had not heretofore purchased their Park tickets elsewhere.[18]

With the onset of World War I, railroads were no longer allowed to run excursion trains for mere pleasure, which limited visitation to Yellowstone. Likewise, wartime restrictions on gasoline and other automobile supplies curtailed much of the private vehicle traffic to the park. Most of the park's hotels were closed, and while the camps remained open, they lost money.[19] It is no surprise that following the war, in 1919, A. W. Miles and J. D. Powell decided to sell the Yellowstone Park Camping Company to Howard Hays.

In an effort to resume the prewar volume of tourism to Yellowstone, Hays began rebuilding camp operations with the construction of more substantial facilities and promoting the "camps way" in Yellowstone. He began by changing the name of the company to the Yellowstone Park Camps Company. During the fall of 1919, construction began on a rustic lodge building at Camp Roosevelt, which was selected as the site of the first lodge building in a new system of accommodations designed to meet the new mobile lifestyle of the automobile tourists. Horace Albright, superintendent of Yellowstone, was pleased with the idea of the new lodge system, believing that the rustic log construction would provide a "dude ranch appearance." Brochures for the camp emphasized its informal and friendly atmosphere, referring to it as "Out-West Americanism."[20]

Construction began in fall 1919, with the lodge opening in the spring of 1920. The dimensions of the one-story log building were approximately ninety feet by fifty feet, with an "L" extension that was twenty-nine feet by fifty-nine feet. The exterior log walls were unpeeled and saddle-notched, which gave the building its signature rustic appearance. It is interesting to note that the front porch originally wrapped around the southeast corner of the building. This wraparound porch prominently appears in a Haynes postcard from 1920 (figure 7.1). According to various sources, this extension was removed around 1947. The floor of the porch was constructed of matched and dressed pine flooring atop log joists.

The lodge's interior was designed to provide a lounge and dining area for the campers. This room featured two stone fireplaces with concrete hearths and log mantels, as well as a log rail twenty-five feet in length that separated the lounge from the dining room. The furnishings were of a rustic design and included "an eleven-inch diameter enameled-iron drinking fountain, a Bradford upright Grand piano, pine tables, a 'rustic' hat rack, log settees with loose cushions, 110 maple folding chairs, and assorted bookcases."[21]

The dining room was furnished with fourteen pine tables in various sizes, pine serving stands, and ninety-three black and yellow dining chairs with bar backs and cane seats. Striped linen curtains hung on wrought-iron rods, and hangers decorated both lounge and dining room. In commemoration of the lodge's namesake, a framed print of Theodore Roosevelt hung over the mantel in the lounge (figure 7.2).

Between 1921 and 1923, Camp Roosevelt served as the headquarters for the Yellowstone Park Forest and Trail Camp, a program aimed toward providing an outdoor educational experience for teenage boys. Professor Alvin G. Whitney, from the Roosevelt Wild Life Forest Experiment Station at New York State College of Forestry in Syracuse, served as director. The purpose of the camp was stated in a publication from 1921:

> The Forest and Trail Camp is a summer nature school designed for boys between twelve and eighteen years. Its basic principle is that of character-building through the hardy pastimes of woods and trail, through self-discipline, and through helpfulness in a cultured camp community.
> The celebrated wonders of the Yellowstone, with its geysers and hot springs, its vast forests and mighty canyons, as well as those other varied recreational interests,—the herds of big "game," the marvelous trout fishing, the scenic trail trips afoot or on horseback, and for the more adventurous the climbing and exploring among remote lakes and mountain gardens,—appeal alike to all who visit the great Park; but it is to the growing boy that they are most fascinating.[22]

Ed Moorman recalled building a small swimming pool for the Camp, along with an "assembly house" in 1920.[23] The assembly house served as the camp's headquarters or council building beginning in 1921, but meals for the campers were provided at the Lodge. Whitney charged $500 per camper for the nearly six-week-long camp. Even though Whitney brought out a number of boys, Moorman noted that it was not sufficient to pay the Company for the operating expenses. All told, Moorman believed that the Company lost $4,000 in this venture.

Ever the advertising and promotional expert, Howard Hays, the president of the Yellowstone Park Camps Company, continued to publicize and market Camp Roosevelt, which was not included as an overnight stay in the basic tour package. In 1923 he published a brochure titled "Yellowstone Vacations, Camp Roosevelt":

> *In General*
> A stop at Camp Roosevelt is not included in the standard four and one-half days' sightseeing tour of Yellowstone Park. . . . Many travelers who are using the regular service of the Yellowstone permanent sum-

> mer camps, or the Yellowstone hotels, go to Camp Roosevelt for an extra day or an extra week in the Park. Almost all regular tours pass the camp, thereby eliminating any extra transportation charges; on the three regular tours which do not pass the camp, the side-trip to Camp Roosevelt is made for an extra transportation charge of five dollars.[24]

Hays used every angle to promote the camping company. Just as Wylie used testimonials in the beginning, Hays continued the tradition. Dr. Henry Van Dyke described the Roosevelt area in the 1922 brochure:

> And now as we rest at the Roosevelt Camp, in the northeast corner of the Park, looking out across the canyon of the Yellowstone, between Hellroaring Mountain and Specimen Ridge, up the long, wild, lovely valley of the Lamar River, with its open, golden pastures and meadows and its dark, hanging woods of pine and spruce and Douglas firs and its silvery groves of quaking aspens, we are ready to report that the Yellowstone is distinctly not spoiled.[25]

In 1924, Hays developed serious health problems and sold the company to Harry W. Child, owner of the boat, hotel, and transportation companies, and Vernon Goodwin, a California hotelier. Through the next several years, the Yellowstone Park Camps Company evolved from a simple tent-camping operation to a system of lodges with cabins and modern kitchen and dining facilities, including the setup at Roosevelt. During this time the term *lodge* became commonly used in association with the camps company, but the name did not officially change to the Yellowstone Park Lodge and Camps Company until 1928 when Child became the sole owner of the enterprise.[26] By 1929, Roosevelt Lodge offered accommodations in thirty-seven rustic tourist cabins and twenty-six wood-framed and tent-topped cabins located on both the east and west sides of the main lodge (figure 7.3). As more Americans drove their own automobiles to and through the park in the 1920s, Yellowstone witnessed a substantial increase in tourism, partially spurred on by the wartime call to "See America First." With Yellowstone at the top of everyone's list, the camps and lodges, including Roosevelt, experienced a flurry of business during the 1920s.

Following the onset of the Great Depression, because of a lack of funding, no services were provided at Roosevelt Lodge from 1932 to 1933, and it was closed again from 1943 to 1946 due to the labor shortage brought on by World War II. With the end of the war, tourism resumed its momentum, and with that increase came the need not only to reopen the camps and other facilities but also to upgrade them. Roosevelt would, however, have to wait because, in 1947, the United States Public Health Service determined that the lodge required a new kitchen, so the camp remained closed.

FIGURE 7.3. Camp Roosevelt Cottages, ca. 1922. Camp Roosevelt readily adjusted to the automobile era in the park. In this Haynes postcard, cars are parked out front of the main lodge and nearby cottages. Source: private collection of Tamsen Emerson Hert. (Original in color.)

Upon Child's death in 1931, his son-in-law, William M. Nichols, became president of the Yellowstone Park Company.[27] Now overseeing the camping company, he proposed abandoning the Roosevelt area and relocating all assets to Fishing Bridge. The reasoning behind this was that the operation of Camp Roosevelt was never profitable and the Fishing Bridge area required an increase in accommodations. However, the camp's removal was stayed when, during 1947, the company decided to remodel and upgrade the kitchen at Roosevelt Lodge.[28] It is likely that during this renovation the wraparound portion of the front porch was removed; otherwise, few modifications have been made to Roosevelt Lodge itself, with the exception of the relocation of camper cabins to Roosevelt from other areas of the park.

Today, Roosevelt Lodge still offers a quiet, rustic getaway in Yellowstone's northeast corner. It remains the most casual lodging in the park, and the Old West theme still dominates the experience. Visitors can ride horses, take a stagecoach ride, enjoy a steak cookout, and have a sing-along with cowboys. The lodge has found its niche in providing precisely the "pioneer" landscape that many visitors have desired to see and experience, for more than a century.

The story of Roosevelt Lodge illustrates several larger themes in the evolution of Yellowstone's cultural landscape. First, it demonstrates that park managers, concessionaires, and visitors all saw the appeal of an affordable lodging alternative to the grand hotels being developed at other park attractions in the early twentieth century. Second, the successful marketing of Roosevelt Lodge to the early automobile-touring public suggested the power of that constituency in shaping later park landscapes, both in Yellowstone and in other park settings. This group of visitors demanded affordable lodging, flexible accommodations, and convenient automobile-oriented services, and Roosevelt Lodge demonstrated how that could succeed in providing an enduring alternative to more traditional hotels and packaged tours. Third, the enduring rusticity of Roosevelt Lodge (both in architecture and in activities) reflected the persistent appeal of having a simple "frontier experience" in Yellowstone, far from the spectacles of geysers and waterfalls. Such an experience resonated well with the flowering of dude ranches in nearby Montana and Wyoming. Ironically, Roosevelt Lodge allowed visitors to relive that pioneer experience in a western setting where it never actually happened (because of the park's early creation in 1872). Still, visitors seem to enjoy sitting in one of the oversized rockers on the lodge's broad front porch and simply absorbing the quiet ambience of Roosevelt's idyllic setting. No doubt it harkens many a visitor back to an earlier, less harried era.[29]

NOTES

1. *Yellowstone Vacations: Camp Roosevelt* (Yellowstone Park Camps Co., 1923), 3.
2. Elizabeth A. Watry, *More than Mere Camps and Coaches: The Wylie Camping Company and the Development of a Middle-Class Leisure Ethic in Yellowstone National Park, 1883–1916* (MA thesis, Montana State University, April 2010), 39.
3. Filed December 11, 1897, by James A. Blanchard and George H. Lamar, *In the Department of Interior, Washington, D.C., Before the Secretary. In the Matter of the Application of William W. Wylie for a Lease in the Yellowstone National Park, with the Privilege of Furnishing Camping Accommodations. Amended Application and Reply to Report of Acting Superintendent*, 10.
4. Watry, *More than Mere Camps and Coaches*, 42, 59. In 1896 Wylie Camps were located at Willow Park, the Upper Geyser Basin, Lake, and Canyon.
5. The growing popularity of the Wylie camps can be followed in *Reports of the Acting Superintendent of Yellowstone National Park to the Secretary of Interior* (Washington, DC: Government Printing Office, 1899–1909); 1899: 975 visitors, p. 5; 1900: 802 visitors, p. 4; 1901: 1,371 visitors, p. 14; 1902: 1,870 visitors, p. 15; 1903: 1,767 visitors, p. 9; 1905: 3,668 visitors, p. 11; 1906: 1,745 visitors, p. 10; 1907: 2,146 visitors, p. 9; 1908: 3,446 visitors, p. 5; and 1909: 7,717 visitors, p. 5.
6. Mark Barringer, "When Harry Got Taken: The Early Days of the Yellowstone Park Camps," *Annals of Wyoming* 69, no. 4 (1997): 4.
7. E. H. Moorman, *Manuscript*, Hays Collection #3151, Box 6, Moorman Manuscript folder, American Heritage Center, University of Wyoming, Laramie, Wyoming.
8. "Decisions of the Interstate Commerce Commission of the United States, April, 1905 to August, 1906," *Interstate Commerce Reports*, vol. 11 (Rochester, NY: Lawyers Co-Operative Publishing Company, 1906): 154–55.
9. Watry, *More than Mere Camps and Coaches*, 77–78. A. W. Miles operated a dry goods business and a grocery and provided supplies to Wylie. Mark Barringer, *Selling Yellowstone: Capitalism and the Construction of Nature* (Lawrence: University Press of Kansas, 2002), 50.

10. Wylie Permanent Camping Company, *Yellowstone National Park* (Chicago, IL: Poole Bros., 1907), 21.
11. Frederick Dumont Smith. *Book of a Hundred Bears* (Chicago, IL: Rand McNally and Company, 1909), 197.
12. *Report of the Acting Superintendent of Yellowstone National Park to the Secretary of the Interior* (Washington, DC: Government Printing Office, 1909), 5. In an effort to maintain the hotel concession, Child sold shares in the camping company to Haynes. Barringer, *Selling Yellowstone*, 61.
13. *Yellowstone Park Camping Company, 1918* (Livingston, MT: Yellowstone Park Camping Company, 1918), 6.
14. Barringer, *Selling Yellowstone*, 61.
15. *In Your Own Automobile* (Yellowstone Park Camps Co., 1920).
16. Barringer, "When Harry Got Taken," 7.
17. Watry, *More than Mere Camps and Coaches*, 102; Barringer, *Selling Yellowstone*, 65.
18. Moorman, *Manuscript*, 16.
19. Barringer, *Selling Yellowstone*, 61 and 69.
20. James Mote and Berle Clemensen, *Historic Structures Report, Historical Data Sections, Lake Hotel, Lake Lodge, Roosevelt Lodge, Old Faithful Lodge, Yellowstone National Park, Wyoming* (Denver, CO: Denver Service Center, Historic Preservation Branch, National Park Service, US Department of the Interior, 1981), 77; Barringer, *Selling Yellowstone*, 61; *Yellowstone Park Camps* (Yellowstone Park, WY: Yellowstone Park Camps Co., 1926), 2.
21. James R. McDonald Architects, *Roosevelt Lodge, Yellowstone National Park, Historic Structures Report* (Missoula, MT: James R. McDonald Architects, 1993), 15.
22. *Yellowstone Park Forest and Trail Camp for Boys and Young Men* (New York: Merrill Press, 1921), 9.
23. Moorman, *Manuscript*, 18; The buildings were likely built the previous year in anticipation of the camp beginning in 1921.
24. *Yellowstone Vacations: Camp Roosevelt*, [2].
25. *Yellowstone Park Camps* (Yellowstone Park Camps Co., 1922), 19.
26. The history of the Yellowstone Park Company is complicated and is best explained in *Selling Yellowstone*, by Mark Barringer, and Mary Shivers Culpin's *"For the Benefit and Enjoyment of the People": A History of Concession Development in Yellowstone National Park, 1872–1966* (Yellowstone National Park, WY: National Park Service, Yellowstone Center for Resources, 2003).
27. All of Harry Child's properties, the Yellowstone Park Hotel Company, the Yellowstone Park Transportation Company, the Yellowstone Park Boat Company, and the Yellowstone Park Lodges and Camps Company were merged in 1936 into the Yellowstone Park Company.
28. James R. McDonald Architects, *Roosevelt Lodge*, 31.
29. Special thanks to Elizabeth Watry for reviewing this text for accuracy.

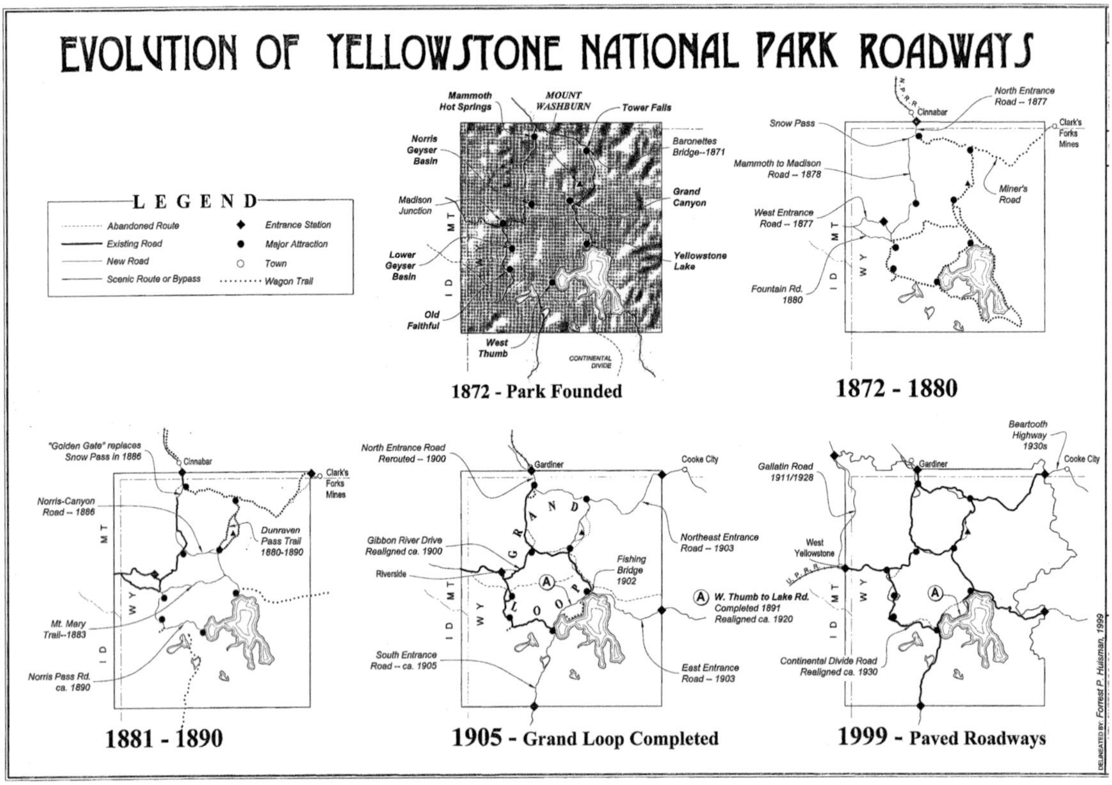

FIGURE 8.1. Evolution of Yellowstone National Park Roadways, 1872–1999. The construction of Yellowstone's road system played a fundamental role in fulfilling the congressionally mandated goal of transforming a remote region of natural wonders into a "public park and pleasuring grounds for the benefit and enjoyment of the people." Source: adaptation by Timothy Davis of Forrest Huisman, "Evolution of Yellowstone National Park Roadways, Addendum to Yellowstone National Park Roads and Bridges, HAER No. WY-34-3," 1999, Library of Congress, Washington, DC.

8

Yellowstone's Evolving Roads

Timothy Davis

Yellowstone's road system exemplifies the long-overlooked role of cultural landscapes in shaping the past, present, and future of America's national parks. As the primary means through which visitors encounter Yellowstone's wonders, roads have exerted an inordinate impact on the park experience. Not only do these carefully crafted corridors frame the park experience both literally and figuratively—determining what most visitors see and how they see it—but the commingling of technological, aesthetic, and ecological attributes underscores the inadequacy of conventional approaches to national park research and management. A brief history of Yellowstone's roads reveals their centrality to popular and professional perceptions of the park while underscoring the value of cultural landscape-based approaches to management and preservation.[1]

One of the primary benefits of the cultural landscape approach is its ability to provide fresh insights into environments that are overlooked or undervalued by conventional authorities or the public at large. Along with elucidating physical characteristics that are ignored, misunderstood, or actively disparaged, the cultural landscape approach explicates the range of forces

https://doi.org/10.5876/9781646427697.c008

involved in their creation. This interdisciplinary emphasis guards against the tendency to reduce complex interactions between human and natural factors into narrowly framed assertions about environmental impacts, aesthetic merits, or pragmatic imperatives. The goal is not to elevate one aspect over another but to illuminate the ways in which landscapes embody evolving social practices, environmental factors, and cultural concerns. The cultural landscape approach also emphasizes the human experience of place, underscoring the ways in which natural and human-made spaces are endowed with form and meaning by those who use them, either in person or through memories, imagination, and representations in various media. A final advantage of the cultural landscape approach is its insistence on going beyond description, categorization, and prescription to show how the built environment plays an active role in the construction and contestation of cultural values.

Yellowstone's road system—like national park roads in general—affords an ideal illustration of the cultural landscape approach's ability to shed new light on underappreciated environments. For the majority of today's visitors, the park's roads are simply utilitarian corridors affording access to scenic highlights and travel services. Their existence is taken for granted, as are the ways in which they wind in graceful curves, showcase signature features, and employ rustic design elements to blend with natural surroundings. In this sense, Yellowstone's roads are victims of their own success, melding engineering, landscape architecture, historic preservation, and natural resource management to minimize their impact and lead visitors through a seemingly fortuitous succession of sensorial delights. When park roads enter the visitor's consciousness, it is usually in a negative way in the form of traffic congestion, deferred maintenance, or sharp curves, narrow pavements, and other attributes that demand more attention than conventional highways. Park managers have often focused on these practical aspects instead of pursuing more holistic policies, with unfortunate consequence for both natural and cultural resources.

The rising tide of ecological awareness and wilderness ethics has also impacted the physical fabric and cultural connotations of park roads. For much of the past fifty years, environmental advocates and a significant portion of park personnel have cast park roads as unwarranted intrusions requiring remediation or elimination. From this perspective, whatever value park roads might have as artistic achievements or engineering accomplishments remains secondary to their status as environmental encroachments and relics of outdated policies that ostensibly prioritized the provision of public access over the protection of natural resources. The controversies generated by these evolving perspectives underscore that park roads are not just utilitarian structures but active participants in debates about the nature and meaning of America's national parks.[2]

When Yellowstone was established in 1872, it was widely accepted that road development was a top priority. Safeguarding scenic features was an important prerequisite, but improved access was required to fulfill Congress's directive to transform Yellowstone's natural wonders into "a public park and pleasuring ground for the benefit and enjoyment of the people."[3] Contemporary audiences saw no contradiction between scenic preservation and road construction. Intrepid travelers might follow the primitive trails assayed by early adventurers, but the majority of visitors had neither the time nor the inclination for such strenuous endeavors. With eastern tourist regions and municipal parks as the primary precedents, visitors expected to travel by wagon or stagecoach along attractively designed roads affording convenient access to principal features. Park administrators shared this goal, though they were challenged by meager appropriations and Yellowstone's imposing size and challenging topography.

Nathaniel Langford, Yellowstone's first superintendent, highlighted the importance of road development, both to attract visitors and to encourage concessionaires to provide tourist facilities the government was ill-equipped to construct or manage (figure 8.1). Exemplifying contemporary conceptions of the appropriate form and function of a national park, he professed it a certainty that "the march of civil improvements will reclaim the solitude, and garnish it with all the attractions of cultivated taste and refinement." Having created the park, Langford proclaimed, the government was obligated to make it accessible to the American people. Langford called for a circuit drive that would tie into the privately constructed roads leading to the park's west and north entrances and allow visitors to experience Yellowstone's major attractions without retracing their route. This was both a logical outgrowth of nascent tourist practices and a classic means of moving visitors through public parks and private estates. Congress declined Langford's requests for funding, leaving it to his successor Philetus Norris to initiate construction on what would eventually become Yellowstone's Belt Line, or Grand Loop.[4]

Modest appropriations enabled Norris to undertake this ambitious effort in 1878. Beginning at Mammoth Hot Springs, he worked south in a counterclockwise direction, reaching the Lower Geyser Basin at the end of the first year and completing slightly more than one hundred miles by the end of his appointment in 1881. Norris's most storied achievement was the so-called Glass Road around the base of Obsidian Cliff, a promontory between Mammoth Hot Springs and the geyser basins. When his workmen discovered that horse-drawn scrapers, picks, and shovels made little impact on the hardened volcanic material, Norris had them build bonfires on the intended roadbed and douse the superheated rock with cold water. The resulting contractions fractured the surface so they could gradually work down to a passable grade. This innovative solution became part of the lore and legend of the park. The rest of his work was less charitably received. The inherent challenges of difficult terrain, primitive technology, and paltry funding were exacerbated by Norris's lack of professional expertise and desire to open up Yellowstone's attractions as quickly as possible. The resulting combination of steep grades, poorly cleared stumps and boulders, mud wallows, and bone-jarring "corduroy" cross-logs, was widely condemned by early tourists, who often had to forsake their wagons and proceed on foot or horseback. Key attractions like the Grand Canyon of the Yellowstone and Lower Falls remained beyond the reach of wheeled vehicles. Concessionaires complained that the abominable reputation of Yellowstone's roads imperiled their efforts to develop appealing accommodations.[5]

Widespread dissatisfaction with travel conditions resulted in the transfer of road-building responsibilities to the US Army Corps of Engineers in 1883. The first engineering officer assigned to the park, Lieutenant Daniel Kingman, emphasized the need to improve not just the extent but the quality of Yellowstone's road system. Good roads were needed not only to benefit travelers and concessionaires, Kingman claimed, but to do justice to Yellowstone's status as a pioneering federal institution. Along with pleading for enhanced appropriations, he drew up design standards aimed at enhancing both the functionality and appearance of park roads. Main routes should be eighteen feet wide with gravel surfaces equipped with crowns and ditches to improve drainage. Trees should be cleared to a width of thirty feet. Dry-laid stone retaining walls should shore up raw and unstable embankments. Where roads crossed streams and swamps, substantial timber bridges and plank causeways would replace crude log bridges and the loathsome corduroy. Most importantly, engineers should devote ample time to scouting and surveying alignments that balanced practicality and scenic appeal. If these dictums were followed—and Congress provided sufficient funding—Kingman proclaimed, the result would be "a highway into Wonderland that will surpass the famous Appian Way."[6]

Kingman may not have achieved this lofty goal, but his improvements greatly enhanced the tourist experience and, by extension, Yellowstone's status as the prototypical embodiment of the national park idea. Mindful of the problems caused by his predecessor's rush to open up new territory with hasty and slipshod construction, Kingman devoted most of his four seasons in the park to improving existing roadways. His forces constructed new bridges; widened, graded, and resurfaced roadbeds; and realigned sections deemed poorly located or beyond repair. Along with relocating the northern entrance road along the Gardner River to eliminate hazardous grades, he completed a major realignment of the route between Mammoth Hot Springs and Swan Lake Flat. The existing route through Snow Pass was steep, tortuous, and as its named suggested, subject to heavy accumulations that delayed opening in the spring and produced treacherous mudholes after the snow melted away. Kingman replaced it with a more direct alignment that reached the Swan Lake plateau via a picturesque canyon known as the Golden Gate.

The shorter and more scenic route was clearly superior, but surmounting the final ascent required more funding and technical expertise than Norris could muster. Benefiting from increased appropriations and engineering acumen, Kingman directed his forces to blast and cut their way up the canyon wall. Enormous quantities of rock were excavated and an imposing cliff was bypassed with an elaborate 228-foot-long wooden trestle supporting a 16-foot-wide plank roadway. At the lower end of the trestle, Kingman's workmen cleared a space for wagons to squeeze between the cliff and a charismatic stone column. The pragmatic engineer wanted to eliminate the outcrop to provide safer and more convenient passage but acquiesced to suggestions that tourists might enjoy the experience of passing through the seemingly natural gateway. Both the stone pillar and thrilling passage across the rickety trestle were soon celebrated as highlights of the Yellowstone tour.

Of equal importance to many travelers, Kingman's improvements shortened the standard trip by a full day. This was achieved in part by constructing a cutoff between Norris Geyser Basin and the Grand Canyon, so visitors could travel directly by wagon instead of laboring over the rough and circuitous bridle trail around the tip of Lake Yellowstone. Public appreciation for the Army Corps efforts was reflected in reduced complaints and rapidly rising visitation. Remarking on the changing conditions, a travel writer in 1886 proclaimed "so many improvements have been made, particularly during the last year, that whatever may have been the case heretofore, the park is now traversed by the best roads I have ever seen in a mountain country."[7]

This flattering assessment belied the amount of work remaining to realize the vision of a full-fledged loop of high-quality roads linking the park's major features. Not only did Kingman's crossover require visitors to retrace their path to the geyser basins, but most of the bottom half and northeast quadrant of the park remained inaccessible to wheeled vehicles. Kingman's successor, Captain Clinton Sears, repeated his insistence that more and better roads were required for Yellowstone to perform its intended function. "The National Park is a great national trust," he remonstrated, "which should be carefully guarded and preserved, while, at the same time, made readily, safely, and cheaply accessible throughout its extent." Sears's emphasis on balancing preservation and access anticipated the fundamental tenet of the National Park Service's founding legislation by thirty years. While this "dual mandate" has generally been attributed to the rediscovery of Frederick Law Olmsted's long-lost 1864 report to the Yosemite Board of Commissioners, the unlikelihood that Sears would have encountered the uncirculated document suggests that the challenges of Yellowstone's road system elicited similar sentiments about the appropriate form and function of America's national parks. Congress was not moved by prescient pronouncements, however, as penurious appropriations produced limited improvements over the next few years. The most impressive accomplishments were the construction of an 86-foot-long trestle in Gibbon Canyon and a 115-foot span across a tributary of the Yellowstone River.[8]

There was a brief uptick in road building in 1891–1892 due to enhanced funding and the arrival of Lieutenant Hiram Chittenden, an energetic engineer whose vision and enterprise played an outsized role in the development of Yellowstone's transportation system and the park in general. During his initial two-year stint, Chittenden replaced Norris's rough trail from the Upper Geyser Basin down to Lake Yellowstone and up to the Grand Canyon with a bona fide wagon road tying into Kingman's cross-park cutoff. While the northeastern quadrant remained inaccessible, this allowed visitors to make a circuit of the park's major southern and central attractions, though they still had to backtrack between Mammoth and the geyser basins.

Chittenden was transferred to Louisville, and meager appropriations over the next few years limited improvements to bridge replacement and a few minor connections. In some years, the allotments were insufficient to cover basic maintenance. Renewed complaints prompted superintendent James B. Erwin to declare: "If Congress intends to ratify and make good its dedication of the park to the people of the United States as a pleasuring ground for its benefit and enjoyment, it should yield to the demands of the people and make additional appropriation for the construction of new roads, which will add to their pleasure and benefit by opening new and wonderful phenomena and scenery."[9]

When Chittenden returned to the park in 1899, he pursued an ambitious agenda that led to the completion of the Grand Loop in 1905. Benefiting from increased appropriations stemming from Yellowstone's growing popularity and concomitant complaints about travel conditions, Chittenden turned first to the improvement of the road through the Golden Gate (figures 8.2–8.4). Along with fine-tuning grades

FIGURES 8.2 AND 8.3. Top: Workmen with "Pillar of Hercules," ca. 1885. When Lt. Daniel Kingman's forces carved a passageway around this stone pillar during the construction of the Golden Gate Viaduct in 1885, they created a beloved roadside feature that blurred the distinction between natural and cultural landscapes. Source: detail of stereographic view, Yellowstone National Park Archives, YELL 36977 (courtesy of National Park Service–Yellowstone National Park; hereafter NPS-YNP). Bottom: Entrance to Golden Gate, no date. The "Pillar of Hercules" continued to be a fascinating roadside feature as the road through the Golden Gate saw continued improvements. Photograph by F. Jay Haynes. Source: Yellowstone National Park Archives, YELL 7621 (courtesy of NPS-YNP).

FIGURE 8.4. Golden Gate Viaduct, 1885–1977. Relocating the stone pillar during upgrades to the Golden Gate Viaduct blurred the distinction between natural and cultural features while underscoring the appeal of road-related features and cultural landscape preservation. Source: adapted by Timothy Davis from Jill Caouette, "Golden Gate Viaduct, 1885/1900/1933/1977, Golden Gate Viaduct, HAER No. WY-46-1," 1999, Library of Congress, Washington, DC.

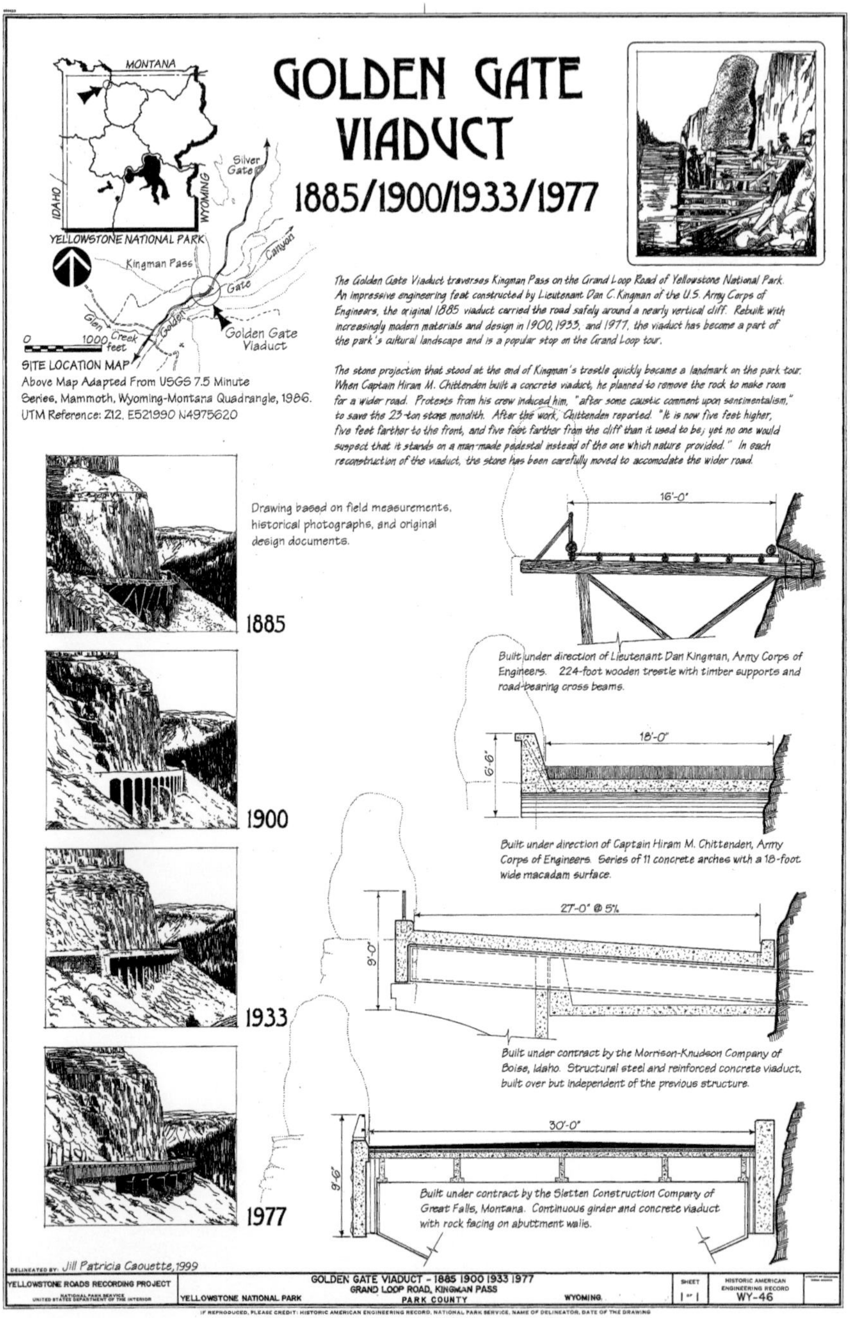

and alignments, he replaced Kingman's timber trestle with a more substantial, concrete viaduct that was easier for stagecoaches to negotiate and more reassuring for travelers unnerved by the original construction's rickety appearance. Chittenden initially intended to eliminate the stone pillar, which posed an even greater obstacle given the wider roadway and increased traffic, but succumbed to what he characterized as the "sentimentalism" of those who insisted the feature had become an integral component of the Yellowstone experience. In what could be considered the first act of cultural landscape preservation in Yellowstone or any other national park, Chittenden directed his forces to move the twenty-three-ton monolith to the edge of the widened roadway, concealing the concrete pedestal on which it rested, to retain the illusion of a "natural" stone gateway. This blurring of the line between natural and cultural landscapes was repeated during subsequent upgrades in 1933 and 1977.[10]

Chittenden oversaw the construction of two more significant structures in 1903. To emphasize that visitors were not simply passing through pretty scenery but entering a grand civic institution, he marked the Gardiner gateway with an imposing stone arch bearing the inscription "FOR THE BENEFIT AND ENJOYMENT OF THE PEOPLE." Constructed of rough-hewn basalt to echo the rugged appearance of the Northern Pacific Railway's newly completed train station nearby, the majestic structure set the precedent for iconic portals marking the entrances to America's national parks. President Theodore Roosevelt laid the cornerstone, underscoring the significance attributed to the gesture and engendering its sobriquet the Roosevelt Arch.

Adopting a radically different aesthetic, Chittenden spanned the Yellowstone River above the Upper Falls with an elegant neoclassical arch seemingly more suited to an urban park or English landscape garden than the rough-hewn Western frontier (figure 8.5). Chittenden was well versed in these precedents and believed national parks merited equally sophisticated treatments, especially in such signature settings. Since traditional stone construction would have been inordinately expensive, he employed the newly developed Melan method of reinforcing concrete with steel beams laid lengthwise during the construction process, which had to be completed in a single pour for maximum strength. Accomplishing this task in the Wyoming wilderness was a monumental achievement. Coordinating with the full moon to augment a generator borrowed from the Yellowstone Park Hotel Company, Chittenden's forces worked in multiple shifts for

FIGURE 8.5. The Chittenden Bridge, no date. The impressive 1903 Melan-arch "Chittenden Bridge" combined advanced technology with classical elegance to span the Yellowstone River above the Upper Falls. Photographer unknown. Source: National Park Service, Historical Photograph Collection.

seventy-four hours straight. The delicate profile and graceful proportions of the Chittenden Bridge afforded a striking contrast to previous utilitarian spans and the rustic stone-faced bridges generally associated with national park development.[11]

While Chittenden's monumental structures garnered extensive praise and engendered enduring appreciation, his contributions to the broader park landscape had even greater impact on Yellowstone's landscape and the national park system as a whole. Along with dramatically improving the tourist experience by completing the Grand Loop, he articulated an approach to road development that influenced national park policies for decades to come. At the broadest level, he expounded on the need to ensure both preservation and access. Yellowstone's legendary attractions alone could not guarantee its success as a national park. "If the roads are bad, the hotels ill-kept, or the transportation uncomfortable," he contended, "no amount of grandeur of natural scenery can compensate for these defects." At the same time, he insisted the park should be preserved in its natural state to the full-

FIGURE 8.6. Dunraven Pass section of the Grand Loop Road, ca. 1906. The Dunraven Pass Road's graceful curvature epitomized Hiram Chittenden's advice that national park roads should harmonize with their surroundings with minimal excavations and gracefully winding curves. Source: private collection of Timothy Davis. (Original in color.)

est degree possible. "The true policy of the government in dealing with this problem," he declared, "should therefore be to make the roads as limited in extent as will meet actual necessities, but to make such as are found necessary perfect examples of their class."

Building on his familiarity with municipal parks and the writings of prominent landscape architects such as Olmsted and Andrew Jackson Downing, Chittenden laid out a series of precepts aimed at maximizing scenic potential while minimizing the visual impacts of road construction. While it was important to secure good grades and safe locations, engineering criteria should not trump scenic concerns. Following natural contours rather than mathematically precise alignments would reduce the need for unsightly excavations and produce graceful curves that were attractive in their own right. When cuts and fills were necessary, they should be supported by well-constructed retaining walls. Dangerous sections should be outfitted with rustic wood or stone safety barriers. An eighteen-foot-wide surface would accommodate two-way traffic and allow vehicles to pass each other safely.

To alleviate the monotonous straightaways encountered on many older sections, Chittenden called for new alignments employing sinuous curves to provide visual interest and prevent visitors from having to view extensive stretches of roadway. He insisted that the purpose of park roads was to enhance the tourist experience and make park travel as enjoyable as possible (figure 8.6). Straying from the shortest path to create compelling views was worth the additional expense and occasional deviation from engineering standards, as was the protection of natural features such as the Golden Gate and another picturesque passage known as the Silver Gate. While heavy-handed engineering should be avoided, carving precarious paths around precipitous promontories could provide memorable thrills. Clearing away downed timber and encouraging grass to grow along roadsides would improve appearances and attract grazing animals. "In these and other ways," he enthused, "the roads will themselves be made one of the interesting features of this most interesting region."[12]

Chittenden implemented these strategies while constructing the final segment of the Belt Line between the Grand Canyon and Tower Falls. The relatively straightforward end sections were completed in 1903, but an additional two years were required to cross Dunraven Pass and construct a spur to the summit of Mount Washburn, the highest peak in the park. While the gently curving Dunraven Pass Road laid lightly on the landscape, the Mount Washburn Road required considerable blasting and extensive retaining walls to scale the rocky summit, making it the most dramatic drive in the park. Adventurous tourists who opted for this detour were treated to what Chittenden characterized as a "kaleidoscopic effect" as glimpses of distant scenery alternated with dizzying chasms and jagged cliffs. As with the Golden Gate, they thrilled to the frisson of danger and embraced the combination of natural beauty and engineering prowess. The top of the mountain was graded to provide a parking area for wagons so visitors could enjoy the panoramic views.[13]

The East Entrance or "Sylvan Pass" Road was completed in 1905, affording access from Cody, Wyoming. The route's most notable engineering feature was the "Corkscrew Bridge" or "Loop-Over," which employed earthen ramps and a curving span to cross back over itself and maintain an acceptable grade while ascending a steep incline. A more modest southern entrance led to Jackson, Lander, and Dubois. Chittenden also constructed a towering 410-foot-long steel truss bridge across the Gardner River and relocated a mile-long section of the North Entrance road. When he left the park in 1906, Chittenden proclaimed that Yellowstone's road system was essentially complete. Maintenance would continue to be a challenging proposition and additional improvements might be required to accommodate evolving demands, but he expressed confidence that subsequent managers would maintain the policy of balancing scenic preservation with a comprehensive but carefully limited road system constructed to exacting technical and aesthetic standards. His predecessors' remarks were generally buried in government reports, but Chittenden's ideas gained greater currency through publication in road-building periodicals and his popular history of Yellowstone National Park.[14]

While it has become popular to malign motorists and blame the automobile for visitors' reliance on roads, stagecoach-era tourists rarely strayed from the primary circuits and preferred grand hotels or commercial tent cabins to roughing it in the wild. Many appeared to be as enamored of the travel experience as the park's natural attractions themselves. Road-related features like the Golden Gate, Chittenden Bridge, Roosevelt Arch, and the Loop-Over were celebrated in souvenirs ranging from postcards and stereo views to playing cards, silver spoons, and Dresden china. Stagecoaches joined bears and geysers as icons of the Yellowstone experience, appearing in postcards, tourism brochures, and a wide range of souvenirs. Guidebooks and travel writers recounted road-construction feats, detailed the various vehicles, and described the typical multiday tour at length, narrating the passage along Yellowstone's Grand Loop and marveling at the scope and complexity of Yellowstone's staging operations, which employed hundreds of coaches and over a thousand horses, along with barns, blacksmith shops, and other support structures. Even John Muir was impressed, though he lamented that the hurried pace and rigid schedule of the standard tours prevented visitors from experiencing nature more fully. The identification of Yellowstone with the stagecoach transportation was so strong that sentimentalists cited the preservation of the traditional travel experience as a justification for prohibiting motorized vehicles. Calls to retain this stagecoach system as a romantic vestige of the Old West and integral component of the park experience underscore the degree to which Yellowstone's status as a cultural landscape was firmly established by the turn of the twentieth century (figure 8.7).[15]

The stagecoach companies ardently opposed the admission of automobiles. This stance was undoubtedly rooted in financial rather than sentimental concerns, given their considerable capital investment and the income generated by carrying approximately twenty thousand visitors a year. Concessionaires would also suffer, since motorists could bring their own provisions and engage in the rapidly growing fad of auto camping. Yellowstone Park Transportation Company President Harry Child preferred to present the prohibition of automobiles as a matter of public safety. Motorists would not only endanger themselves on roads that were barely adequate for

FIGURE 8.7. *The Land of Geysers*, 1906. This Northern Pacific Railroad brochure exemplifies the extent to which visitors, concessionaires, and park managers considered roads and vehicles to be integral components of the Yellowstone experience. Note Roosevelt Arch (center left). Source: Yellowstone National Park Archives, YELL 109805 (courtesy of NPS-YNP). (Original in color.)

horse-drawn vehicles, he claimed, but threaten the health and well-being of stagecoach passengers, a considerable portion of whom would be killed, maimed, or otherwise traumatized when horses panicked on encountering the contraptions.

A US Army Corps of Engineers study in 1912 considered various options for resolving the conflict, including a separate loop for automobiles, a light-rail system, and the improvement of existing roadways coupled with regulations aimed at reducing interactions between the two modes of transportation, with the understanding that the stage companies would gradually transition to motor buses. Department of the Interior Secretary Franklin Lane endorsed the plan in 1915. Motorists were required to proceed in the counterclockwise direction employed by stage drivers and follow strict schedules designed to minimize conflicts. Speeds were limited to twelve miles per hour on hills, eight miles per hour on sharp curves, and twenty miles per hour in other locations. Drivers were instructed to defer to horse-drawn vehicles when contacts occurred. This arrangement proved as unsatisfactory to motorists as to stagecoach passengers, for whom plodding along behind horse-drawn conveyances rapidly lost its appeal. Within two years, the stagecoaches gave way to gaily painted touring cars, specially designed for park travel. These bright yellow "auto stages," rapidly assumed iconic status on their own, as the Yellowstone Transportation Company's fleet swelled to over a hundred vehicles to accommodate visitors arriving by train to avoid the rigors of cross-country motoring on marginal roads.[16]

Yellowstone was the last major park to allow automobiles. Mount Rainier led the way in 1908, followed by Crater Lake in 1911 and Glacier in 1912. Yosemite and Sequoia succumbed to intense lobbying by automobile advocates in 1913. While park administrators expressed concern about the ability of park roads to accommodate automobiles safely, there were few objections on philosophical grounds. Despite former British ambassador James Bryce's oft-cited analogy between the admission of automobiles to Yosemite and the fall of Eden, the Sierra Club not only embraced the decision but partnered with National Park Service director Stephen Tyng Mather and motoring organizations to purchase and improve an abandoned mining road through the park's high country. "We think the automobile adds a great zest to travel," Sierra Club secretary William Colby proclaimed, "and we are primarily interested in the increase of travel to these parks." Muir himself appeared unperturbed, reasoning that motorists would stick to existing routes with

FIGURE 8.8. "Welcome! To Cody Wyoming the Home of 'Buffalo Bill' and the Scenic Entrance to Yellowstone Park," 1917. The National Park Service joined conservation organizations such as the Sierra Club, automobile interests, and local boosters in promoting recreational motoring as a means of making national parks accessible to a broader spectrum of the American public. This vintage advertisement promoted Cody, Wyoming, as a scenic gateway to the park. Source: National Archives, Record Group 79, Entry 9, Box 368, Suitland, Maryland.

little impact on untrammeled wilderness (figure 8.8). At this point in history, Muir and other conservationists believed the primary threat to America's national parks was not too many visitors but too few. Given the time and expense of the train-, stagecoach-, and grand hotel-based paradigm, many dismissed national parks as elite retreats of little value to the broader American public. Without a strong constituency, parks were vulnerable to both private and public incursions, as demonstrated by the diminution of Yosemite's borders in 1905 and the decision in 1913 to inundate the majestic Hetch Hetchy Valley to create a reservoir for the city of San Francisco. Low visitation also made it harder to secure funding for existing parks or justify additional reservations.[17]

This view was shared by the growing coalition of interests advocating for the establishment of a permanent federal bureau devoted to the preservation, management, and expansion of the national park system. The common thread running through a series of conferences, proclamations, and congressional hearings leading to the establishment of the National Park Service in 1916 was that outdated roads and inadequate accommodations prevented Americans from enjoying their priceless heritage of natural wonders. "Our national parks are practically lying fallow," declared Mather, "and only await proper development to bring them into their own." Upgrading outmoded carriage roads would be an expensive and time-consuming proposition, but Interior Secretary Lane embraced the effort, proclaiming, "Parks without people are a burden, not a benefit." Mather made it clear that the NPS was not abandoning its commitment to balancing preservation and access. "It is not our plan to have the parks gridironed with a system of roads," he assured, "we want to keep a large section of each park a wilderness that will only be covered by trails, so the natural wild character will be maintained." A directive was issued under Lane's signature in 1918 underscoring the importance of minimizing scenic impacts and harmonizing roads and other improvements with their surroundings. Rather than rely on private enterprise or the Army Corps of Engineers, the NPS established its own engineering and landscape architecture divisions, pointedly granting the latter authority over the former in all but the most technical considerations. The basic engineering functions were shifted to the Bureau of Public Roads (BPR) in 1926 to keep up with the growing workload and ensure the highest technical standards, with strictures in place to ensure the continued emphasis on scenic development and landscape preservation.[18]

While Yellowstone possessed the most comprehensive and well-designed road network in the national park system, considerable work was required to accommodate automobiles. Motor roads had to be wider and straighter than wagon roads, with lower and more consistent grades. They also had to be more substantially constructed, with stronger subgrades, better drainage, and more durable surfaces. Bridges had to be wider and stronger. Guard walls and guardrails afforded reassurance for those unaccustomed to mountain roads. Motorized visitors required additional facilities, as well, from entrance and gas stations to campgrounds, housekeeping cabins, and cafeterias. With stage drivers no longer serving as de facto tour guides, the NPS became more heavily involved in education, building museums and constructing interpretive panels at key locations. Various types of scenic pullouts were developed so motorists could stop safely to enjoy the views. NPS landscape architects took the lead in minimizing the impact of road construction and harmonizing structures with the park environment (figure 8.9). Though they were often constructed with new materials, bridges, buildings, and other structures were generally designed in the rustic style, with heavy timbers and handlaid stone veneers. Along with conforming to longtime traditions in landscape architecture, the log-cabin look and rugged masonry aligned Yellowstone's cultural landscape with popular conceptions of the American frontier.[19]

More powerful machinery and advanced construction techniques allowed road builders to accomplish tasks beyond the means of their predecessors, as did the influx of funding that began in the mid-1920s and burgeoned with the Depression-era relief programs of the 1930s. Civilian Conservation Corps (CCC) crews contributed significantly to the motorization of Yellowstone's roadside landscape. The ample though relatively low-skilled manpower was particularly useful for labor-intensive tasks like rehabilitating construction scars, building guardrails, and effacing segments rendered obsolete by improved alignments. Private financing came into play, as well. During the 1920s, Yellowstone Superintendent Horace Albright convinced John D. Rockefeller Jr. to fund a roadside improvement campaign aimed at removing downed timber and other detritus cast aside by earlier road crews more concerned with efficiency than aesthetics. The positive response to this program led to similar efforts in other parks, and its continuation by NPS and CCC forces.[20]

FIGURE 8.9. Entrance Checking Stations and Waysides and Pullouts. Accommodating motorists entailed the construction of additional features employing rustic architecture and naturalistic landscaping to harmonize with their surroundings. Source: adapted by Timothy Davis from Jill Caouette, "Entrance Checking Stations, Addendum to Yellowstone National Park Roads and Bridges, HAER No. WY-34-6," 1999; and Caouette and Meredeth Mitchell, "Waysides and Pullouts, Addendum to Yellowstone National Park Roads and Bridges, HAER No. WY-34-9," 1999, Library of Congress, Washington, DC.

When the NPS took control, Yellowstone had zero miles of hard-surfaced roads (figure 8.10). Some sections were only wide enough for a single car, and sharp turns and steep grades abounded. By 1939, nearly half the park's 347 miles of roads had been paved with asphalt mix or high-pressure oil treatments, including 96 of the Grand Loop's 123 miles. In 1926, the NPS and BPR agreed on an eighteen-foot-wide paved surface with three-foot shoulders. BPR engineers deemed this inadequate by the mid-1930s, prompting considerable debate until NPS officials acquiesced to widening the Grand Loop to twenty feet with four-foot shoulders and a twenty-six-foot total width on entrance roads.

FIGURE 8.10. The challenges of road building in Yellowstone, ca. 1920. NPS road builders adapted this section of the Grand Loop Road to automobile traffic while preserving the rustic ambience and thrilling proximity to the towering basaltic cliff. Photographer unknown. Source: National Park Service, Historical Photograph Collection.

The demand for wider and straighter roads resulted in yet another revision to the Golden Gate Viaduct. A structural steel framework carried a twenty-seven-foot-wide reinforced-concrete deck over Chittenden's eighteen-foot-wide iteration. The "natural" stone pillar was relocated once again. BPR engineers tried to eliminate a sharp curve above the viaduct by tunneling through a rocky outcrop. When the unstable formation collapsed, the entire bluff was cleared away, leaving a wide parking area from which visitors could view the viaduct and surrounding scenery. The Silver Gate, another feature of Yellowstone's historic cultural landscape, was preserved by constructing a bypass to accommodate larger vehicles and hurried motorists. In another indication of the reverence accorded Yellowstone's historic transportation landscape, NPS officials insisted on preserving the Chittenden Bridge even though it fell well below revised guidelines. A sturdier but less picturesque concrete span replaced the legendary Loop-Over in 1919, but the constricted arrangement was ill-suited to automobile traffic. Improved construction techniques and enhanced appropriations allowed the NPS to construct a more gradual, automobile-friendly roadway higher on the mountainside, leaving the abandoned structure as a testament to the early days of motor travel. The most heavily engineered new structure was a towering five-span steel bridge over the Gardner River between Tower Junction and Mammoth Hot Springs. While the exposed steel was a departure from NPS practice, it allowed motorists to soar across a deep canyon, replacing several thousand feet of steep, dangerous, and scenery-scarring roadway. Many obsolete spans were replaced by modern reinforced bridges clad with rustic stone veneer in typical NPS fashion.[21]

Park officials quickly realized that new facilities were required to meet changing needs and expectations. With more visitors traveling on their own instead of taking prepaid tours, rustic entrance stations were constructed on the major approach roads. The diminutive North Entrance station was completed in 1921 (reconstructed in 1936), followed by the West Entrance Station in 1924, the South Entrance Station by 1932, and the Northeast Entrance Station in 1935. Museums designed in the same rustic idiom were constructed at Fishing Bridge and Norris and Madison junctions, along with additional educational exhibits at wayside pullouts, including a particularly notable example at Obsidian Cliff that became known in NPS circles as the "Nature Shrine." Concessionaires operated gas stations with modest mechanical services, along with stores combining traditional tourist paraphernalia with sundries for motorists and campers.

The exploding popularity of auto camping exerted a profound impact on Yellowstone's cultural landscape. By 1917, the NPS had established free campgrounds for motorists at Mammoth Hot Springs, Old Faithful, Lake, and Canyon. Along with fireplace grates, picnic tables, water, and pit toilets (eventually replaced with modern flush units), these facilities originally included hulking, open-sided garages to shelter the open or canvas-topped touring cars predominant into the 1920s. Realizing that the initial practice of allowing campers to park at will within designated areas was both inefficient and environmentally destructive, the NPS shifted to more systematically planned and sustainable arrangements, with main driveways, parking spurs, and other elements articulated by judiciously arranged plantings, rocks, and other rustic barriers. With the heaviest camping load in the park system, Yellowstone played a pioneering role in this regard. Drive-through designs that eliminated the need to back up became popular in the 1930s as cars and camping trailers grew in size. Amphitheaters with rows of log benches centered on a fire ring, stage, and log-framed projection screen hosted nightly ranger talks that fostered comradery and advanced the NPS's educational mission. Community halls and central washing facilities afforded additional spaces for socializing. Most campgrounds were augmented by concessionaire-operated housekeeping cabins equipped with beds, stoves, and minimalistic furniture for visitors unwilling or unable to fend completely for themselves. So-called lodges occupied a higher niche between auto-camp cabins and full-service hotels. Generally located at sites vacated by stagecoach-era camping companies, operations like Roosevelt Lodge consisted of wood or canvas-topped cabins grouped around a rustic central lodge offering meals and other amenities.[22]

NPS officials hailed the automobile's impact on the Yellowstone experience. When a lowly Model-T laden down with camping gear became the first automobile to legally enter the park, NPS publicist Robert Sterling Yard proclaimed the dawning of a "new and greater Yellowstone." Along with making the national park experience accessible to a broader cross-section of the American public, free campgrounds (figure 8.11) and increasingly affordable automobiles allowed visitors to come and go where they pleased and tarry as long as they wanted, instead of being rushed through on hurried and inflexible packaged tours. Mather credited the freedom and cost-savings afforded by auto camping with fostering a more sustained and meaningful park experience. Asserting that hurried stagecoach-era tourists had treated national parks as "stupendous natural spectacles, to be seen (or we might say *done*) in a short time, as one might view an art exhibit or a pageant," Mather maintained that the NPS's embrace of the automobile produced a new paradigm in which "people turned to the national parks as places to *live* during their vacations and 'get next to Nature.' "[23]

Mather may have overestimated the public's appetite for extended communes with nature, but the agency's auto-friendly policies dramatically increased visitation in Yellowstone and the National Park System as a whole. Yellowstone received 20,250 visitors in 1914, the last year of auto-free operation. By 1917 there were 37,408 visitors, 21,268 of whom arrived in 5,700 private cars. The national parks and monuments as a whole received 468,268 visitors and 54,692 cars. Mather rejoiced when total visitation topped the million mark in 1920, assisted by 128,074 cars. Yellowstone's 1920 admissions numbered 79,777, with 49,491 arriving in 13,586 private automobiles and the rest taking advantage of the transportation company's yellow cars. Map-

FIGURE 8.11. Lake Campground in Yellowstone National Park, 1928. The Park Service provided free public campgrounds in popular locations such as Lake Yellowstone, Old Faithful, and Fishing Bridge to accommodate the burgeoning interest in auto camping. Photographer unknown. Source: National Archives and Records Administration, National Park Service Photographs.

makers and guidebook writers incorporated advice for motorists and auto campers, while official NPS photographs, postcards, and other souvenirs celebrated the Yellowstone's motorization. The park's visitation hit 260,697 in 1929 before dropping during the initial years of the Depression and rebounding to 579,696 in 1941. NPS-wide visitation topped 20 million that year due to dramatic improvements in road conditions and a significant increase in the number of parks and monuments. Auto camping experienced an even more dramatic surge. By 1920 Yellowstone's major campgrounds were hosting over a thousand visitors on busy summer nights, more than double the combined total of nearby hotels and lodges, for a seasonal tally of 40,000. The yearly total reached 125,000 by 1926 and continued to rise until World War II drastically reduced national park visitation and domestic travel as a whole.[24]

While a few critics condemned the improved roads and crowded campgrounds, Mather and his colleagues celebrated the motoring throngs as evidence of the agency's success in transforming national parks from elite retreats into quintessential components of contemporary American life, with the attendant increase in political capital for protecting and expanding the National Park System. Like Frederick Law Olmsted and other predecessors, they saw national parks not simply as wilderness preserves but as civic institutions affording multiple social, economic, personal, and political benefits. Along with exposure to nature and healthful outdoor recreation, national parks stimulated regional economies, underscored the value of government action, and brought together what was considered for the time to be a diverse array of citizens in shared appreciation for America's scenic and historic treasures. Extolling the ability of campground life to rejuvenate harried urbanites and foster comradery across traditional social, economic, and sectional divides, Albright proclaimed, "It is a thrilling sight to visit any of the camps in the national parks on a midsummer evening and see from five hundred to a thousand city folks busy around their little fires, the evening air filled with odors from a hundred coffee pots and a hundred frying pans."[25]

NPS officials insisted the decision to accommodate automobiles did not entail a retreat from preservationist principles. In Yellowstone and other older parks, the emphasis was on improving existing roads, not imposing new ones. Where existing alignments could not be updated, the old sections were restored to natural conditions, with little change in net mileage. Some observers maintained that the automobile actually reduced the human imprint on Yellowstone. According to Albright, doing away with stagecoaches and reducing travel time between major features led to the elimination of four hotels and twenty-five additional lodging compounds, along with barns, blacksmith shops, and other support structures. Meadows were no longer subjected to grazing by thousands of horses in the summer or by livestock supplying hotels with fresh meat and milk. The paving program eliminated the long-lamented "dust menace" that plagued horse-drawn and motorized visitors alike, which made travel miserable and coated park roadsides with an unsightly and unnatural layer of pulverized soil. During the 1920s and 1930s the NPS warded off multiple attempts to construct additional entrance roads to serve outlying communities eager to capitalize on Yellowstone-bound tourists. Albright, who succeeded Mather as NPS director in 1929, warned that increasing the number of entrances would put undue pressure on existing facilities and insisted that the 90 percent of Yellowstone yet untouched by roads remain undeveloped in perpetuity. Montana interests overrode these objections to secure congressional support for the Beartooth Highway, which connected Cooke City with Red Lodge and Billings, creating a new North-

FIGURE 8.12. Traffic Jam, Upper Geyser Basin, 1956. In 1956, the combination of dramatically increased demand and inadequate facilities, as shown in the photograph, taken at Old Faithful, prompted the National Park Service to initiate a major redevelopment plan known as Mission 66. Photographer unknown. Source: National Park Service, Historical Photograph Collection.

east Entrance when the road opened in 1936. As predicted, the increased traffic resulted in calls for expanded visitor services.[26]

The pressure to upgrade roads and associated facilities reached new heights in the decade after World War II. Years of budgetary neglect combined with postwar prosperity and improvements in cross-country highways to create a nationwide outcry about travel conditions in Yellowstone and the National Park System as a whole. By 1956, reports of slum-like campgrounds, overflowing parking lots, and congested and dangerously outdated roadways prompted Congress to fund a ten-year, $1 billion improvement campaign called Mission 66 in reference to the stated goal of rectifying perceived problems in time for the NPS's Golden Anniversary. According to the original vision, improved roads would not only accommodate the dramatic increases in visitation but further preservation efforts by allowing the NPS to shift new and existing facilities to less sensitive locations, away from key attractions or beyond park boundaries (figure 8.12). Yellowstone's Canyon Village development epitomized this strategy, along with trends toward modern architecture and shopping center–style visitor complexes that critics condemned as incompatible with park values. The NPS had little success convincing concessionaires to forsake profitable locations steeped in tradition for remote outposts with architecturally unappealing offerings. The old

Canyon Hotel was eliminated with assertions of structural shortcomings and a remarkably well-timed fire, but the developments at Old Faithful, Lake, and Mammoth stayed put. Canyon Village and the long-delayed Grant Village were the primary legacies of this well-intentioned but imperfectly realized policy.[27]

NPS officials were even more frustrated by reactions to the road-building component of Mission 66. While mainstream publications and the general public welcomed the improved roadways and expanded parking facilities, the Sierra Club, Wilderness Society, and similar organizations accused the NPS of prioritizing motorized recreation over resource protection. NPS officials repeated earlier assurances that they were largely upgrading existing roads, not constructing new ones, but critics contended that the heightened visitation and ever-present automobiles compromised a park's ability to serve as an escape from the pressures of modern urban life. They also observed that wider, straighter roads were more destructive of scenery and encouraged speeds that were incompatible with traditional park values. The NPS insisted it was maintaining a balance between preservationist sensibilities, the public's right to enjoy its parks, and federal highway engineers' attempts to impose even more intrusive design standards, reminding wilderness advocates that the greater portion of major parks remained undeveloped and largely unvisited.[28]

Yellowstone's Mission 66 road program was relatively uncontroversial, since much of the Grand Loop had been upgraded to the highest prewar specifications. Major work included the reconfiguration of junctions at Madison and the Grand Canyon to facilitate traffic flow, the widening and straightening of several troublesome segments, and the construction of bypasses at Firehole Canyon and Virginia Cascades, where adequate upgrades would have been too costly and destructive of scenery. The original segments were designated scenic one-way drives, retaining the slow speed and intimacy with surroundings characteristic of traditional park roads. The tortuous Mount Washburn Road was declared off-limits to private vehicles, though concessionaire-operated shuttle-bus service was offered from 1959 to 1975. While not identified as such at the time, these measures acknowledged the importance of preserving transportation-related cultural landscapes.[29]

The legendary Chittenden Bridge was the most prominent casualty of Mission 66. Along with being too narrow for modern traffic, the aging concrete structure had deteriorated to the point that BPR engineers ruled it unsafe for vehicular traffic. When the NPS announced plans for a new span, Chittenden's son-in-law asked if the original could be preserved as an exemplar of American bridge-building and a memorial to the illustrious engineer. NPS officials weighed options on practical, aesthetic, and historical grounds. Reinforcing the crumbling structure and widening the deck were deemed undesirable, since remedial measures would compromise historic appearances. The option of retaining the original as a pedestrian crossing and constructing a modern bridge nearby was rejected as too destructive of surrounding scenery, the preservation of which, it was noted in a prescient application of cultural landscape history, had prompted Chittenden's innovative design. The NPS regional historian characterized the bridge as "one of the major historical features of Yellowstone National Park" and observed that there was growing appreciation for the significance of cultural features in parks managed primarily for their natural qualities, but maintained that despite its outstanding technical and aesthetic attributes, association with one of the most prominent figures in Yellowstone's history, and longtime service to the traveling public, its national significance was insufficient to outweigh pressing practical concerns. He called for thorough engineering and photographic documentation prior to demolition, along with the construction of a roadside exhibit chronicling the bridge's history and Chittenden's broader contributions to the Yellowstone story. Suggestions that the new bridge emulate Chittenden's design in both form and technique, with a wider and stronger Melan Arch accommodating two-way traffic, were dismissed with the argument that a progressive engineer such as Chittenden would have eschewed such an outmoded approach. Dedicated in 1963, the ensuing reinforced-concrete open-spandrel arch Chittenden Memorial Bridge paid homage to the original design without slavish imitation and accommodated two thirteen-foot-wide travel lanes flanked by sidewalks (figure 8.13).[30]

Yellowstone's next major road improvement campaign was a more dramatic demonstration of the challenges of balancing pragmatic concerns, natural and scenic resource protection, and historic preservation in iconic American landscapes. By the 1980s, there was widespread agreement that Yellowstone's road system was struggling to accommodate the two-million-plus annual visitors arriving in ever larger vehicles, elongated RVs, and mammoth tour buses. Along with structural issues such as cracking pavements, ragged shoulders, and sunken subgrades, the curves and road widths considered overblown by 1920s traditionalists struck modern engineers,

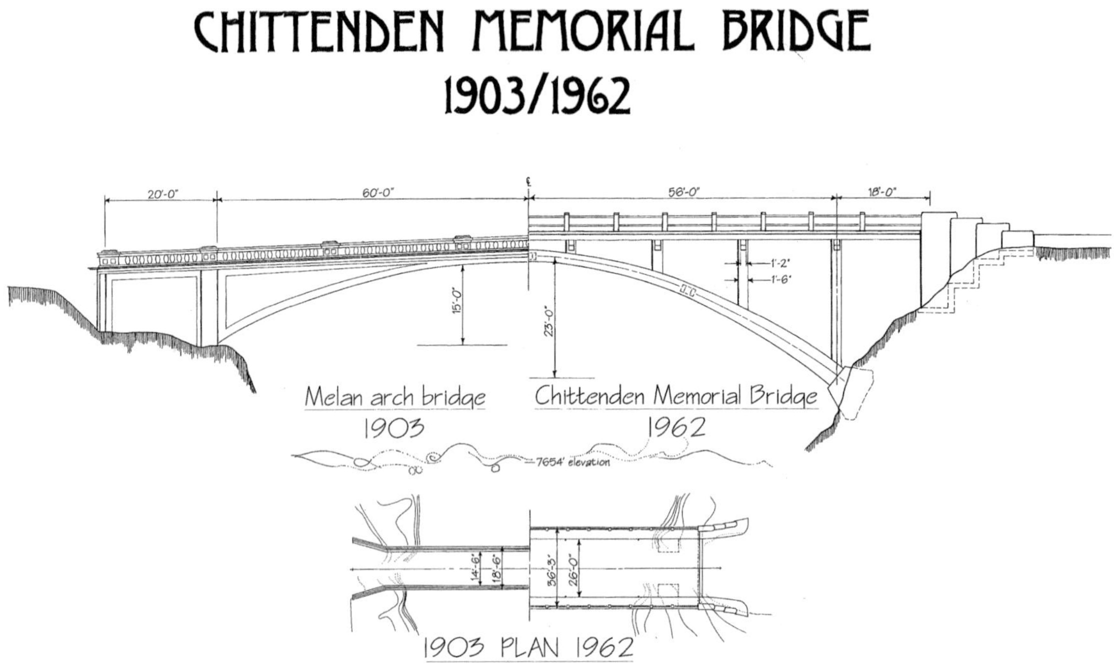

FIGURE 8.13. The Chittenden Memorial Bridge, 1962. This diagram shows how the new bridge reinterpreted its constricted and structurally unsound predecessor in modern forms and materials. Source: adapted by Timothy Davis from Jill Caouette, Chittenden Memorial Bridge 1903/1962, Chittenden Bridge / Chittenden Memorial Bridge, HAER No. WY-88, Library of Congress, Washington, DC.

park managers, and many visitors as outdated and unsafe. The combination of aging roadways and accelerating demands exacerbated long-standing complaints about congestion at entrances, major features, and along the roadways themselves. At the same time, the National Historic Preservation Act of 1966, National Environmental Policy Act of 1969, and internal NPS policies mandated procedures to mediate against ill-considered overdevelopment. Nascent ideas about cultural landscape preservation were gaining academic and institutional credence, as were concerns about road-related resources in particular. Even the most efficiency-minded Yellowstone road-improvement advocates had little interest in replicating the controversial 1970s bypass at Old Faithful that drew universal condemnation as more appropriate for an interstate highway than America's oldest national park. Renewed reverence for NPS rustic architecture led to the listing of Northeast Entrance station, the Obsidian Cliff Nature Shrine, and several other road-related structures on the National Register of Historic Places. With the possible exception of federal highway engineers, all parties recognized the importance of preserving other aspects of Yellowstone's roads to the greatest extent consistent with contemporary traffic demands and safety standards (figures 8.14 and 8.15).[31]

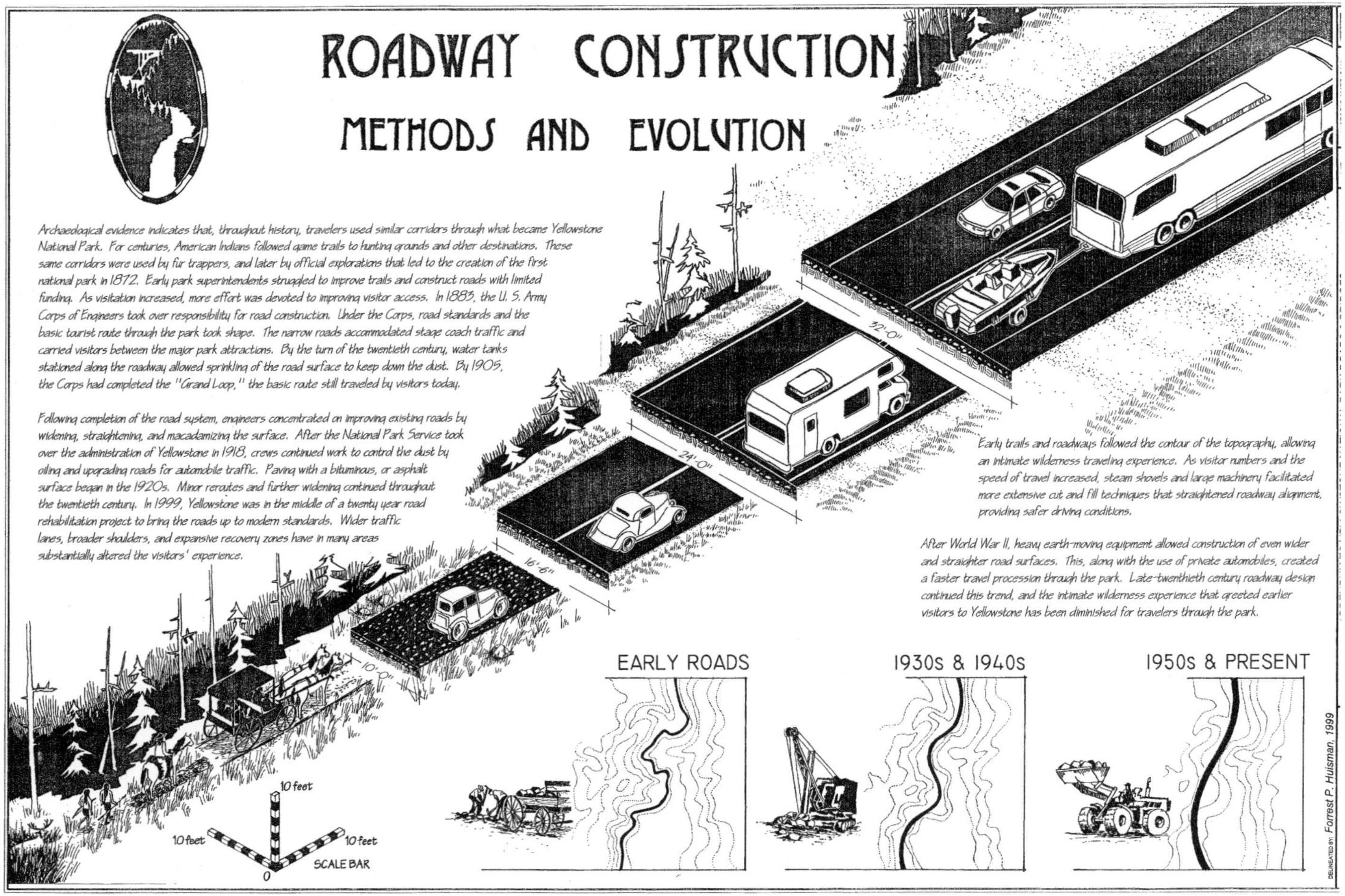

FIGURE 8.14. Roadway Construction Methods and Evolution. This diagram shows how methods of national park road construction and design have evolved over time and suggests that Yellowstone's roads are historically significant cultural landscapes that embody evolving social, natural, and technological factors. Source: Forrest Huisman, "Roadway Construction Methods and Evolution," HAER No. WY-24, 1999, Library of Congress, Washington, DC.

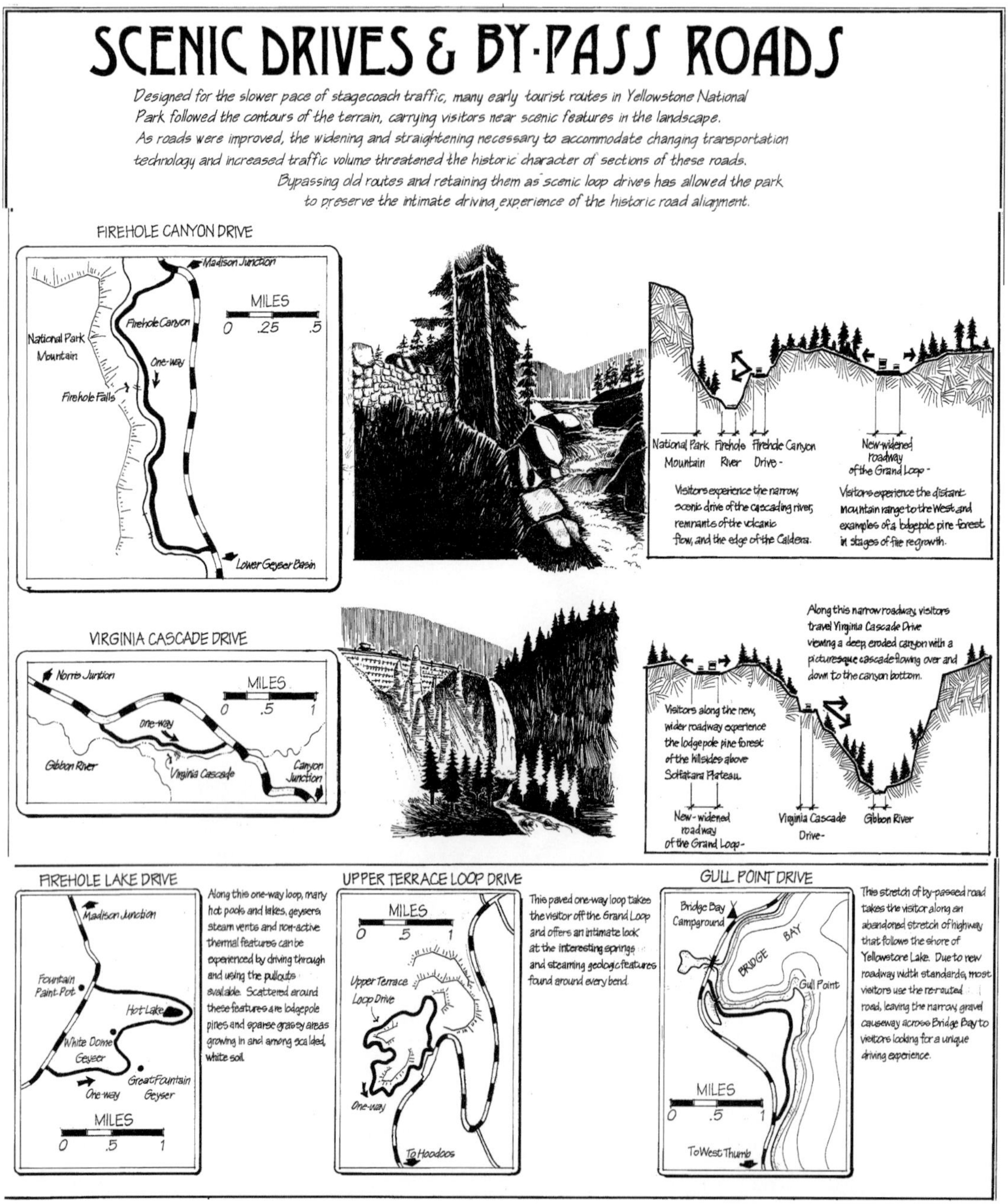

FIGURE 8.15. Scenic Drives and Bypasses of the Grand Loop. Bypasses and one-way drives preserved cultural landscapes and the traditional park road experience. Source: Forrest Huisman, "Scenic Drives and Bypasses of the Grand Loop, Addendum to Yellowstone National Park Roads and Bridges, HAER No. WY-34-8," 1999, Library of Congress, Washington, DC.

In order to guide the proposed improvements and comply with relevant statutes, Yellowstone personnel collaborated with NPS regional staff, the NPS's Historic American Engineering Record (HAER), and associated state historic preservation offices in an ambitious and innovative effort to research the history of Yellowstone's roads, evaluate their national significance, document existing conditions, and identify the individual features and overall design aspects that endowed the park roads system with a unique and irreplaceable historic character. This multipronged program resulted in voluminous documentation, listing of the Grand Loop and other resources associated with the history of Yellowstone's roads and bridges on the National Register of Historic Places, and extensive recommendations aimed at accommodating modern environmental and engineering concerns while retaining the historical integrity of individual elements and the system as a whole. These included the retention and repair of innumerable culvert headwalls, the dismantling and reassembly of masonry veneer on expanded bridge abutments, and broader directives asserting that in order to maintain historic character, improved roads should continue to lie "gently on the landscape," exhibit "grace in alignment," and be accompanied by "architecturally pleasing structures" compatible in scale and appearance with the natural environment. Signifying the ascendancy of the cultural landscape concept, the National Register nomination asserted that the fundamental determinant of historical character was that "the road must evoke a feeling that it is a park road and an image that is distinctive from those found outside the boundary of the park."[32]

While Yellowstone's Parkwide Road Improvement Plan garnered considerable acclaim for its attention to historic values and cultural landscape concerns, it represented a transitional and, in some corners, controversial stage in the evolution of NPS cultural landscape management and historic road preservation (figures 8.16 and 8.17). When the primary research and analysis was conducted in the late 1980s and early 1990s, historic roads were regarded primarily as engineering artifacts. While the HAER documentation, National Register nomination, and treatment recommendations invoked broader landscape concerns, these were not addressed with the same specificity as engineered features such as bridges and culverts. The technical drawings and preservation measures for the latter elicited considerable praise, but critics contended that broader landscape characteristics and experiential qualities could have received better protection through more

FIGURES 8.16 AND 8.17. Top: Improved Roadways, 1996. This view illustrates how improved roadways were characterized by longer curves and paved shoulders. Yellowstone's Parkwide Road Improvement Program in 1992 engendered debate about efforts to balance modern traffic demands with historic preservation concerns. This view shows a portion of newer, reworked highway in the park. Bottom: Older Road Landscape Along Dunraven Pass, 1996. This portion of the Grand Loop near Dunraven Pass illustrates the older style of road construction in the park. Photographs by Timothy Davis. (Originals in color.)

detailed exegesis and greater attention to the cumulative impact of seemingly incremental improvements such as the addition of four-foot-wide shoulders, which were lower than mainstream engineering standards but significantly increased the amount of pavement in view, especially in concert with longer, more gradual curves. Terms such as "grace in alignment" and "gently on the landscape" afforded considerable latitude for interpretation, while directives to "evoke a feeling that it is a park road and an image that is distinctive from those found outside the boundary" seemed similarly vague and insubstantial. While the design team earnestly endeavored to apply these principles, the decision to employ wider pavements, longer curves, more expansive clearances between the road and surrounding features elicited complaints that the traditional park road ambience was being sacrificed for the sake of speed and efficiency. The Historic American Engineering Record conducted additional research to add a cultural landscape dimension to earlier technical documentation, while the NPS's Park Historic Structures and Cultural Landscape Program advocated more restrictive preservation policies such as those being developed simultaneously in Glacier National Park. Both the Yellowstone and Glacier programs reflected growing tensions between historic road preservation and traditional engineering priorities throughout the country that led to numerous publications and national conferences during the 1990s and early 2000s.[33]

Yellowstone officials defended their approach, emphasizing the lengths to which they had gone to address historical concerns and noting that both the overall plan and individual components were approved by preservation authorities at the state, regional, and national levels. The Federal Highway Administration honored several segments with prestigious design awards. The program's leaders questioned both specific accusations and the intellectual underpinnings of critics' complaints, maintaining that advocates of more stringent preservation measures failed to understand the history of Yellowstone's roads and the dynamic nature of cultural landscapes in general. Given that the park's roads and associated landscapes had undergone frequent changes over the course of history, attempting to freeze the evolutionary process at a particular point in time was not just intellectually arbitrary and functionally unrealistic but a repudiation of the underlying tradition of park road-builders to employ the best means available to balance the competing demands of preservation and access.[34]

FIGURE 8.18. Auto Stages at Sylvan Lake, no date. Traveling Yellowstone's roads became an integral part of the visitor experience. This Haynes postcard view shows early travelers sightseeing at Sylvan Lake, not far from the East Entrance to the park. Source: private collection of Timothy Davis. (Original in color).

While similar arguments could be mustered for all manner of "improvements," from the replacement of Old Faithfull Inn with a LEED-certified postmodern Lincoln Log extravaganza along the lines of the recently reconstructed visitor center, to the creation of a jetport in Hayden Valley, they raise important questions about the unique challenges of cultural landscape preservation. Whether or not one agrees with the underlying reasoning or end results, the Parkwide Road Improvement Program dramatized the degree to which Yellowstone's landscape has always been as much a cultural construction as a natural fact, embodying evolving social, technological, and political concerns as well as baseline ecological conditions. While they are often taken for granted, roads exemplify both the evolving nature of the park experience and the intersection of natural and cultural realms (figure 8.18). Yellowstone's founders hailed road development as the fundamental prerequisite for converting natural wonders into an innovative cultural landscape henceforth known as a national park. By conceiving and completing the Grand Loop, Norris, Kingman, Chittenden, and their colleagues transformed the national park idea from an intellectual construct to a physical fact, applying long-held ideas about scenic tourism and public park development to the unique exigencies of the American West. Stagecoach-era travelers celebrated these achievements, joining concessionaires and park officials in embracing the expectation that roads and vehicles afforded the primary means of experiencing America's national parks. The NPS adapted these design and visitation practices to the automobile age, extensively reshaping Yellowstone's infrastructure to accommodate changing social and technological factors and extending the national park experience to an increasingly broad spectrum of the American public. Throughout this process, roads served as the primary means of balancing preservation and access, channeling visitors into discrete development corridors while employing picturesque landscaping and rustic design to elide distinctions between natural and cultural environments. Reconciling competing concerns became increasingly complex during the second half of the twentieth century as visitation expanded dramatically and considerations such as historic preservation and ecologically based environmental protection vied with traditional emphases on visitor services and scenic values.

The relocation of the Gibbon Canyon stretch of the Grand Loop exemplified the practical and conceptual challenges confronting twenty-first-century park managers. Nestled along the winding river at the bottom of a rugged canyon, flanked by mud pots and boiling springs, and culminating in the spectacle of Gibbon Falls, this segment had long been regarded as one of the most picturesque portions of the Grand Loop and a masterful illustration of the ability of park roads to showcase spectacular scenery. During the early 2000s, concerns about environmental impacts, combined with the desire of federal highway engineers to alleviate safety and maintenance issues, led to its replacement with a more commodious roadway located in a less ecologically disruptive manner through a prosaic pine forest above the canyon rim. The new segment employed the expanded serpentine curvature of other reconstructed sections of the Grand Loop, and the associated bridge and waterfall-viewing platform exhibited similar evocations of traditional NPS rustic design, but the historic views and intimate connection with the Gibbon Canyon landscape were lost, along with the physical fabric of the road itself. Extensive efforts were taken to restore the canyon as accurately as possible to conditions predating the road's construction. A discreet trail allowed physically capable visitors to enjoy the canyon's charms in what was deemed a more appropriately park-like manner (figure 8.19).

FIGURE 8.19. Old and new highway alignments, Gibbon Canyon, 2014. The relocation of the Grand Loop in Gibbon Canyon and rehabilitation of the historic roadway underscores the complex relationship between natural and cultural resource protection along with value of the cultural landscape approach for addressing such concerns. Note the newer highway above the river (upper right). Photograph by Jim Peaco. Source: Yellowstone National Park Archives (courtesy of NPS-YNP). (Original in color.)

For those familiar with internal NPS power struggles, the Gibbon Canyon relocation could be viewed as a characteristic example of pragmatic imperatives and natural resource agendas trumping cultural resource concerns. From a broader perspective, the project underscores the value of the cultural landscape approach as a means of challenging artificial distinctions between natural and cultural resources while promoting interdisciplinary analysis of places and processes that are highly politicized or taken for granted as natural and inevitable. Regrettable as the loss of the historic roadway might be, future landscape historians will undoubtedly view the relocation project as an equally illuminating embodiment of evolving cultural concerns. The rehabilitated river bottom, meanwhile, is at once an ecologically appropriate "natural" environment and the product of dramatic human intervention—a cultural landscape by any definition of the term. By calling attention to the ways in which individual localities, broader resource types, and the park as a whole are holistic entities embodying complex and evolving interactions between natural and social spheres, cultural landscape research affords invaluable insights about the nature and meaning of Yellowstone and other national parks.[35]

NOTES

1. For a broad overview of national park road development, see Timothy Davis, *National Park Roads: A Legacy in the American Landscape* (Charlottesville: University of Virginia Press, 2016); key sources on the development of Yellowstone National Park include Hiram Chittenden, *The Yellowstone National Park, Historical and Descriptive* (various editions, 1894–present); Aubrey Haines, *The Yellowstone Story*, vol. 1 (Niwot, CO: Yellowstone Library and Museum Association, in cooperation with Colorado Associated University Press, 1977); Aubrey Haines, *The Yellowstone Story: A History of Our First National Park*, vol. 2, rev. ed. (Niwot, CO: Yellowstone Association for Natural Science, History, and Education, in cooperation with the University Press of Colorado, 1996); Richard Bartlett, *Yellowstone: A Wilderness Besieged* (Tucson: University of Arizona Press, 1985); and Mark Daniel Barringer, *Selling Yellowstone: Capitalism and the Construction of Nature* (Lawrence: University Press of Kansas, 2002). In her National Park Service reports, Marcy Shivers Culpin chronicled the evolution of Yellowstone's road system in minute detail. See "Yellowstone National Park Roads and Bridges, Historic American Engineering Record (hereafter HAER), No. WY-24," "Grand Loop Road, HAER WY-55)," and *The History of the Construction of the Road System in Yellowstone National Park, 1872–1966, Historic Resource Study, Vol. 1* (National Park Service, Rocky Mountain Region, Division of Cultural Resources, 1994); information on individual roads and bridges can be found in the HAER's online archive, accessed through the Library of Congress's website.
2. Davis, *National Park Roads*, 227–81; Richard Sellers criticized the NPS's emphasis on recreational development and chronicled the rising influence of natural science–based management in *Preserving Nature in the National Parks: A History* (New Haven, CT: Yale University Press, 1997); these shifting perspectives were advanced and embodied in Edward Abbey, *Desert Solitaire: A Season in the Wilderness* (New York: Random House, 1968); US Department of the Interior, National Park Service, *Park Road Standards* (Washington, DC: Government Printing Office, 1968); US Department of the Interior, National Park Service, *Yosemite General Management Plan* (Denver, CO: NPS Denver Service Center, 1980).
3. "'An Act to Set Apart a Certain Tract of Land Lying Near the Headwaters of the Yellowstone River as a Public Park,' Approved March 1, 1872 (17 Stat. 32)," in *America's National Park System: The Critical Documents*, 2nd ed., edited by Lary M. Dilsaver (Lanham, MD: Rowman and Littlefield, 2016), 20.

4. Haines, *Yellowstone Story*, vol. 1, 180–215; Culpin, "Yellowstone National Park Roads and Bridges, HAER No. WY-24," 1–5.
5. Haines, *Yellowstone Story*, vol. 1, 240–46; Culpin, "Yellowstone National Park Roads and Bridges"; Chittenden, *Yellowstone National Park* [1895], 130–31; William Thayer, *Marvels of the New West* (Norwich, CT: Henry Bill, 1892), 68; Carrie Adell Strahorn, *Fifteen Thousand Miles by Stage. Vol. 1, 1877–1880* (New York: Knickerbocker Press, 1911; repr., Lincoln: University of Nebraska Press, 1988), 254–86.
6. Culpin, "Yellowstone National Park Roads and Bridges," 22–24; Haines, *Yellowstone Story*, vol. 2, 209–11; Bartlett, *Yellowstone*, 75–77, Kingman quoted on 77.
7. Accounts vary, but Chittenden maintained that Assistant Superintendent G. L. Henderson dissuaded Kingman from removing the rock; Chittenden, *Yellowstone National Park* [1918], 245; Haines, *Yellowstone Story*, vol. 2, 212–15; Bartlett, *Yellowstone*, 75–79; Culpin, "Yellowstone National Park Roads and Bridges," 22–27; George Wingate, *Through the Yellowstone Park on Horseback* (New York: O. Judd, 1886), quoted on 12.
8. Haines, *Yellowstone Story*, vol. 2, 216–17; Culpin, "Yellowstone National Park Roads and Bridges, HAER No. WY-24," 29–33, Sears quoted on 29–30; Olmsted, "Preliminary Report upon the Yosemite and Big Tree Grove" [1865], in *The Papers of Frederick Law Olmsted. Vol. 5, The California Frontier, 1863–1865*, edited by Victoria Post Ranney (Baltimore, MD: Johns Hopkins University Press, 1990), 488–516.
9. Haines, *Yellowstone Story*, vol. 2, 217–22; Culpin, "Yellowstone National Park Roads and Bridges," 34–38, Erwin quoted on 38.
10. Chittenden, *Yellowstone National Park* [1918], 244–46, "sentimentalism" quote on 246; Haines, *Yellowstone Story*, vol. 2, 222–30; Davis, *National Park Roads*, 50–51; Culpin, "Yellowstone National Park Roads and Bridges, HAER No. WY-24," 38–39; Culpin, "Golden Gate Viaduct, HAER No. WY-46," 2–3.
11. Chittenden, *Yellowstone National Park* [1918], 243–48; Haines, *Yellowstone Story*, vol. 2, 229–44; Davis, *National Park Roads*, 51–52; Culpin, "Yellowstone National Park Roads and Bridges," 43–46; Nancy McClure, "Chittenden Memorial Bridge, HAER No. WY-88," 1–12.
12. Chittenden, "Roads in the Yellowstone National Park," *Good Roads*, no. 5 (January 1894), 3–23; Chittenden, *Yellowstone National Park* [1895], "defects" on 201; Chittenden, *Yellowstone National Park* [1918], 237–67, "true policy" on 237; Chittenden, "The Government Road System of the Yellowstone National Park," in US Department of Agriculture, Office of Public Road Inquiries, *Bulletin No. 21. Proceedings of the International Good Roads Conference held at Buffalo, New York, September 16–21, 1901*, 71–78, "interesting features" on 77; Haines, *Yellowstone Story*, vol. 2, 254–55; Davis, *National Park Roads*, 53–56; Culpin, "Yellowstone National Park Roads and Bridges," 40–67.
13. Chittenden *Yellowstone National Park* [1918], 247–48, 306–17, "kaleidoscopic" on 311.
14. Chittenden, *Yellowstone National Park* [1904], 264–67; 323–31; Chittenden, *Yellowstone National Park* [1918], 247–48, 306–17; McClure, "Addendum to Yellowstone National Park Roads and Bridges, HAER No. WY-24," 187–89, 216–32; McClure, "Corkscrew Bridge, HAER No. WY-86," 1–7; Haines, *Yellowstone Story*, vol. 2, 244–55.
15. Davis, *National Park Roads*, 45–57; Haines, *Yellowstone Story*, vol. 2, 100–59, 256–60; Barringer, *Selling Yellowstone*, 34–58; Reau Campbell, *Campbell's New Revised Complete Guide and Descriptive Book of the Yellowstone Park* (Chicago: Rogers and Smith, 1914 edition), 95–140; Jack E. Haynes, *Haynes Official Guide: Yellowstone National Park* (St. Paul, MN: F. J. Haynes,

1915 edition), 12–106; Charles Taylor Jr., *Touring Alaska and the Yellowstone* (Philadelphia: George W. Jacobs and Co., 1901), 296–388; John Muir, *Our National Parks* (Boston: Houghton Mifflin Company, 1905), 39 and 51; Robert Sterling Yard, *The Book of the National Parks* (New York: Scribner's Sons, 1921), 209; for additional insights about Yellowstone's stagecoach era, see Lee Whittlesey and Elizabeth Watry, eds., *Ho! For Wonderland: Travelers' Accounts of Yellowstone, 1872–1914* (Albuquerque: University of New Mexico Press, 2009); and Lee Whittlesey, *Storytelling in Yellowstone: Horse and Buggy Tour Guides* (Albuquerque: University of New Mexico Press, 2007).

16. Davis, *National Park Roads*, 67–70; Haines, *Yellowstone Story*, vol. 2, 256–75; F. J. Haynes, "Transportation in the Yellowstone National Parks," in *Proceedings of the National Park Conference Held at the Yellowstone National Park* (Washington, DC: Government Printing Office, 1911), 21–29; *New Roads in Yellowstone National Park*, Senate Document No. 871, 62d Cong, 2d sess. (July 1, 1912).
17. James Bryce, "National Parks—The Need of the Future," *Outlook*, December 14, 1912, 811–16, quoted on 813; Colby's remarks recorded in *Proceedings of the National Park Conference Held at Yosemite National Park* (Washington, DC: Government Printing Office, 1912), 139; John Muir, *The Life and Letters of John Muir*, vol. 2, ed. William Bade (Boston, MA: Houghton Mifflin, 1924), 378–79; Alfred Runte's *National Parks: The American Experience* (Lincoln: University of Nebraska Press, 1979) prominently highlighted Bryce's quote as a prescient prognostication of future problems, as did many subsequent accounts.
18. Davis, *National Park Roads*, 70–87; Mather's "fallow" comment appeared in "The National Parks on a Business Basis," *American Review of Reviews*, no. 51 (April 1915): 430; Mather's additional remarks in US Congress, House Committee on Public Lands, *Construction of Roads, &c. in National Parks and Monuments: Hearings before the Committee of Public Lands . . . on* H.R. 524, 68th Cong., 1st sess. (February 7, 8, 12, and 14, 1924), p. 6; Lane quoted in *Proceedings of the National Parks Conference* (Washington, DC: Government Printing Office, 1917), 12; Lane memorandum reproduced in Dilsaver, *America's National Park System: The Critical Documents*, 35–39; Davis, *National Park Roads*, 62–70. NPS landscape design policies and achievements during this period are covered in depth in Ethan Carr, *Wilderness by Design: Landscape Architecture and the National Park Service* (Lincoln: University of Nebraska Press, 1999), and Linda McClelland, *Building the National Parks: Historic Landscape Design and Construction* (Baltimore: The Johns Hopkins University Press, 1997).
19. Davis, *National Park Roads*, 88–107; McClelland, *Building the National Parks*, 201–33.
20. Davis, *National Park Roads*, 110–51; Horace Albright and Robert Cahn, *The Birth of the National Park Service: The Founding Years, 1913–1933* (Salt Lake City, UT: Howe Brothers, 1985), 158–63; Albright, "Preserving Wilderness Beauty Along Forest Roads," *American Forests and Forest Life*, no. 31 (January 1925), 36–37; Culpin, "Yellowstone National Park Roads and Bridges," 82–83.
21. Haines, *Yellowstone Story*, vol. 2, 346–56; Davis, *National Park Roads*, 148–49; Culpin, "Yellowstone National Park Roads and Bridges," 68–116; Culpin, "Grand Loop Road," passim.
22. Haines, *Yellowstone Story*, vol. 2, 299–311, 358–66; *Annual Report of the Director of the National Park Service*, 1917–39; for a contemporary overview of rustic visitor facilities in state and national parks, see the reprint edition of Albert Good's 1938 *Park and Recreation Structures* (New York: Princeton Architectural Press, 1999), with Yellowstone structures appearing vol. 1, 29, 37, 191, 195, and 197; vol. 2, 175–78.

23. Yard, *Book of the National Parks*, 209; Mather, "The Ideas and Policies of the National Park Service Particularly in Relation to Yosemite National Park," in *Handbook of Yosemite National Park*, edited by Ansel Hall, (New York: Putnam's Sons, 1921), 80; Haines, *Yellowstone Story*, vol. 2, 347–54. The classic account of the rise of auto camping is Warren Belasco, *Americans on the Road: From Autocamp to Motel, 1910–1945* (Cambridge, MA: MIT Press, 1979).
24. Visitation statistics from *Annual Report of the Director of the National Park Service*, 1917–39, and official online sources: https://www.nps.gov/aboutus/visitation-numbers.htm and http://www.yellowstone.co/stats.htm.
25. Albright and Frank Taylor, *Oh Ranger! A Book About the National Parks* (New York: Dodd and Mead, 1934), 26–48, quoted on 43; Aldo Leopold expressed some of the earliest critiques in "Conserving the Covered Wagon," *Sunset Magazine*, March 1925, 21 and 56; and "The Last Stand of Wilderness," *American Forests and Forest Life*, November 1925, 599–604; US Forest Service Chief W. B. Greeley criticized Yellowstone's automobile-oriented development policies in "What Shall We Do with Our Mountains?" *Sunset Magazine*, December 1925, 14–15 and 81–85; Davis, *National Park Roads*, 62–81; Paul Sutter called attention to rising concerns about the automobile's impact on national parks in *Driven Wild: How the Fight Against Automobiles Launched the Modern Wilderness Movement* (Seattle: University of Washington Press, 2002).
26. Albright, "The Everlasting Wilderness," *Saturday Evening Post*, September 29, 1928, 28, 63, 66, and 68; according to Haines, only two hotels were closed (Norris and Fountain), along with twelve camps and lunch stations (*Yellowstone Story*, vol. 2, 355); Davis, *National Park Roads*, 154–85.
27. Davis, *National Park Roads*, 222–28; Haines, *Yellowstone Story*, vol. 2, 366–86; for a broad overview of Mission 66, see Ethan Carr, *Mission 66: Modernism and the National Park Dilemma* (Amherst: University of Massachusetts Press, 2007).
28. Davis, *National Park Roads*, 229–43; Carr, *Mission 66*, 255–89.
29. Culpin, "Yellowstone National Park Roads and Bridges," 127–32; McClure, "Addendum to Yellowstone National Park Roads and Bridges," 193–95, 207–10, 221–22, 228–30; Haines, *Yellowstone Story*, vol. 2, 366–88.
30. Details of Chittenden Bridge replacement based on copies of records from Yellowstone Research Library provided to author on June 13, 2012; quote is from page 8 of Regional Historian's memo accompanying letter from Regional Director to NPS Director (July 8, 1960).
31. For insights into the growing appreciation for America's historic roads see Timothy Davis, "Looking Down the Road: J. B. Jackson and the American Highway Landscape," in *Everyday America: J. B. Jackson and Recent Cultural Landscape Studies*, edited by Paul Groth and Christopher Wilson (Berkeley: University of California Press, 2003), 62–80; Paul Daniel Marriott, *From Milestones to Mile-Markers: Understanding Historic Roads* (Duluth, MN: America's Byways Resource Center, 2004); David Louter, *Windshield Wilderness: Cars, Roads, and Nature in Washington's National Parks* (Seattle: University of Washington Press, 2006).
32. National Park Service, *Parkwide Road Improvement Plan: Yellowstone National Park: Wyoming/Montana/Idaho* (Denver, CO: NPS Denver Service Center, 1992); the HAER documentation included the studies referenced above along with additional reports on individual roads and bridges, with associated drawings and historic photographs; selections from the HAER Yellowstone documentation can be seen in Timothy Davis, Todd Croteau,

and Christopher Marston, eds., *National Park Roads and Parkways: Drawings from the Historic American Engineering Record* (Baltimore, MD: Johns Hopkins University Press, in association with the Center for American Places, 2004), 144–67; National Park Service, National Register of Historic Places, *Multiple Property Listing: Historic Resources of Yellowstone National Park, Associated with Construction of the Road System in Yellowstone National Park, 1872–1966*, prepared by Marcy Culpin, 1995, quoted on 43.

33. The author was a participant in these discussions and the historic road preservation more generally. Davis, *National Park Roads*, 266–73; Davis, *Landscape Line 16: Historic Roads* (Washington, DC: US Department of the Interior, National Park Service, Park Historic Structures and Cultural Landscapes Program, 2005); Davis, "Documenting America's National Park Roads and Parkways," in *Transportation Research Record: Journal of the Transportation Research Board, No. 1981* (Washington, DC: Transportation Research Board of the National Academies, 2006), 148–59; US Department of Transportation, Federal Highway Administration, *Flexibility in Highway Design*, [1997]; Paul Daniel Marriott, *Saving Historic Roads: Design and Policy Guidelines* (New York: John Wiley and Sons, 1998); US Department of the Interior, National Park Service, *Going-to-the-Sun Road Rehabilitation Plan / Final Environmental Impact Statement* (April 2003); Amy Vanderbilt and Steve Moler, "Saving a National Treasure," *Public Roads* 70, no. 3 (November/December 2006): 22–31.
34. Draft letter, Yellowstone Superintendent Suzanne Lewis to NPS Chief Historical Architect Randall J. Biallas (May 11, 2005) (author's files).
35. Davis, *National Park Roads*, 276–81.

FIGURE 9.1. Campers at Yellowstone Lake, 1936. These campers prepare for their evening meal at Yellowstone Lake in the summer of 1936. The young man in the white cap (second from right) is William V. Wyckoff, father of co-editor William K. Wyckoff. Photographer unknown. Source: private collection of William K. Wyckoff.

EPILOGUE

Reflections on an Evolving Cultural Landscape

Karl Byrand and William K. Wyckoff

The natural wonders and fantastic landscapes of Yellowstone have made it one of the most famous national parks in the world. Most visitors to the park undoubtedly seek out its scenic canyons, thermal features, wildlife, lakes, and rivers. What the contributors to this book have explored is how the park's cultural landscapes—pieced together over time in bits and pieces in different settings within the park—have slowly become an integral part of experiencing Yellowstone (figure 9.1). This cultural landscape is, for the most part, off the average visitor's radar, even though visitors spend much of their time navigating through its midst. When in the park, visitors eat in the restaurants, sleep in the hotels and campgrounds, shop at the numerous concessionaire stores, spend time in the museums and other interpretive facilities, drive on the park's roads, and hike on trails and boardwalks. Even so, much of that landscape fades into the background amid the bison, geysers, and waterfalls.

https://doi.org/10.5876/9781646427697.c009

As the authors have demonstrated, in various portions of the park there are several compelling reasons for considering these cultural landscapes more carefully. First, cultural landscapes are important because they frame natural landscapes. They remind us that experiencing nature in a setting such as Yellowstone is a product of culture and history just as much as it is a product of natural processes. Simply put, how we see Yellowstone's Grand Canyon and waterfalls is very much influenced by the kinds of experiences we have there. How do we anticipate the visit? What trails and viewpoints take us to the Canyon? How do we spend time at nearby lodges and hotels? What do museums, trail brochures, and ranger walks tell us about the setting? Our authors explore how culture shapes what we see through the windshield and along the trails, and they demonstrate that Yellowstone's built environment is a critical window into the natural world.

Second, cultural landscapes are important because the stories of their creation make visible different historical processes at work in the park. We believe there are plenty of valuable lessons to be learned by looking at these historical signatures. As the different development areas in the park reveal, the cultural landscape offers a visible record of how people have shaped Yellowstone in different ways since 1872. Some of that record remains on the present-day scene, but other parts were destroyed, particularly before the late 1960s and early 1970s. Since then, changing national park policies have recognized the importance of cultural resources, a shift that has had enormous implications for managing Yellowstone's cultural landscapes. But, as our contributors have shown, even vanished features can tell many stories when they are reconstructed through archival documents and images.

And what does that record show? It demonstrates how Yellowstone was part of a much larger world, a world of railroad promoters, changing visitor needs and expectations, huge technological transformations, and government entities that evolved over time to make the park what it is today. The detailed case studies in this collection illustrate how those agents of change have played out differently at various centers of development since the park's creation.

As Yellowstone's cultural landscape matured, we have seen how *park visitors* drove many changes, a function of their evolving needs and expectations as they toured the park. For many visitors, accommodations that were acceptable in 1885 proved inadequate three decades later. As automobiles became the norm for western touring, the park's visitors demanded roads and accommodations to meet their itinerant habits. Later, when wildlife viewing ascended in importance, the visitors helped drive the infrastructure and policies that made such encounters possible. In addition to visitors, the *park concessionaires* were key agents in the production of Yellowstone's cultural landscape. How were tent camps and development areas laid out? What were seen as important activities at a rustic park lodge versus one of its fine hotels? How were rooms and dining halls decorated? What kinds of stories would be told by park bus drivers, boat captains, and lodge employees? In myriad ways, concessionaires shaped the answers to these questions. Finally, *park managers*—in the form of the US Army and, later, the National Park Service—also played a significant role in determining cultural landscape development. In many situations, the park's overseers had veto power over what could be added to the cultural landscape by concessionaires. They also had the power to shape and constrain the activities of park visitors. Park managers produced their own cultural landscape features as well, from visitor centers and entrance stations to boardwalks and interpretative roadside displays.

Third, cultural landscapes are important because they can add a great deal to the richness and diversity of experiencing the park today. One of the key reasons for creating this collection of essays was the hope that Yellowstone's future managers and visitors would make its cultural landscapes a more central, visible part of experiencing and enjoying the park. We argue that cultural landscapes of national parks in the American West are legitimate features that need to be recognized, respected, and interpreted. In the past, the National Park Service has often done its best to downplay the visibility of Yellowstone's cultural landscapes in order to highlight the park's spectacular natural features. Making that human signature successfully blend in with a larger natural ambience has often been a priority. Yellowstone's complex human history suggests, however, that much of its unique identity as a place is anchored in how nature and people have in fact crafted a common world within its borders.

YELLOWSTONE'S SETTING: ONE PARK, MANY PLACES

Yellowstone remains the "Crown Jewel" of the national park system. The cultural landscapes created there since 1872 reflect a long record of human activity, changing patterns of tourism, and evolving philosophies of park management and planning. As the authors demonstrate, the length of Yellowstone's tenure as a park, as well as its size and internal complexity, make it an outstanding setting to explore cultural landscape change. They also illustrate the unique value of the park's archival record that has preserved an amazing array of superintendent reports, correspondence, concessionaire literature, travel narratives and diaries, maps, and photographs. The authors have been able to draw from that enormous collection of primary source materials to reconstruct the detailed changes that have occurred within each of the park's development areas.

The authors also illustrate how diverse those areas were and how their evolution helped define and complicate Yellowstone's identity as a place. Part of Yellowstone's majesty is its internal diversity with so many distinctive features protected within the park's boundaries. In fact, each development area capitalized on one or more of these unique attractions in the park's physical landscape. Our respective journeys through Yellowstone show how the cultural landscapes that were produced in each of these localities reflect this close marriage to their respective natural settings. Thus, as lodges, cabins, and hotels came and went, for example at Lake, Canyon, or Mammoth, the cultural landscapes they helped create contributed to the overall character of these natural settings. Indeed, the authors depict how these cultural features became integral parts of each setting (figure 9.2).

At the same time, they share how many common forces have shaped the entire park's evolution and how these larger-scale elements have imparted homogenizing influences across all of the park's cultural landscapes. Changes in American politics, economics, and technology generated broad yet similar changes across the park. In that sense, all the authors tell similar stories; thus, a common narrative emerges. As we know, during Yellowstone's early years, the majority of visitors to the park were people from nearby areas. They traveled through the park along rough roads and camped at any site deemed suitable for an overnight stay. A few modest lunch stations and primitive lodges appeared, but demand for visitor facilities was modest, and cultural landscape developments were minimal.

As better rail connections to the park were established, wealthier, long-distance travelers arrived in greater numbers. These new visitors demanded more services and more organized touring experiences. Basic camping sites were supplemented with formal tent company facilities, such as those estab-

FIGURE 9.2. Henry Soffe Thompson Jr. is pictured at a viewpoint in the Grand Canyon of the Yellowstone River in 1926. He is the grandfather of publisher George F. Thompson. Photograph (2022) by George F. Thompson and used by permission.

lished by Wylie and Shaw and Powell. Large hotels, such as Old Faithful Inn and the hotels at Mammoth Hot Springs and Canyon, offered new lodging choices. As park roads improved and as transportation companies created standardized stage routes and schedules, visitors were all exposed to similar narratives about the park and its features. For example, visitors who traveled the "Wylie way" largely made the same stops at the same park features on the same schedule. This homogenization of the visitor's experience helped frame the park in ways that endure to the present.

As time passed, visitor demands continued to change. Yellowstone's cultural landscape became a more visible and encompassing part of a park visit. People wanted swimming pools and dance halls, and they enjoyed attending ranger talks, taking guided walks, and watching bears feed on garbage behind the hotel. Park managers and concessionaires were willing participants in this effort. After all, they wanted to encourage park visitation. Adding infrastructure, concession services, and recreational activities was seen as making good investments to increase the park's popularity. Clearly, a central part of this strategy was to allow and then encourage automobile use in the park, a policy that fundamentally and irrevocably transformed Yellowstone's cultural landscape. The National Park Service improved roads, viewpoints and bridges, created and enlarged parking lots, and established

FIGURE 9.3. Overlook, Upper Falls of the Yellowstone River. Source: Photograph (2010) © Janet L Pritchard, from her book, *More than Scenery: Yellowstone, an American Love Story* (George F. Thompson Publishing, 2022), 66. Courtesy of the artist.

automobile campgrounds (figure 9.3). Concessionaires followed suit by adding fueling stations and automobile repair shops and by selling goods better suited to this new type of visitor. The automobile also reframed how people experienced the park and what they saw.

While the Depression and World War II disrupted elements of park development, postwar visitation boomed, prompting another round of landscape changes broadly associated with the National Park Service's Mission 66. The resulting cultural landscapes were quite unlike those seen before within national parks. The style of the facilities and infrastructure that the National Park Service and concessionaires added between 1955 and the early 1970s was modern in appearance and strikingly different from earlier periods. In addition to infrastructure that often looked more suburban than rustic, the National Park Service also made new additions to the interpretive landscape that served further to homogenize the Yellowstone visitor experience. New museums, visitor centers, roadside exhibits, and park pamphlets carefully laid out what people were expected to see and experience as they navigated the park's Grand Loop Road.

Then things changed: Following this period of large-scale development, the National Park Service reassessed the impact of a hundred years of cultural landscape evolution on Yellowstone. Specifically, the NPS was concerned with how a century of development had allowed the cultural landscape to encroach on sensitive physical landscapes such as the park's thermal basins. As a result of this managerial and philosophical shift, the Park Service set a goal to reduce and remove many cultural landscape features that were deemed invasive to the park's threatened natural wonders. During this period, campgrounds were removed, other overnight facilities such as housekeeping cabins were significantly reduced in number, earlier developments at Fishing Bridge were scaled back, and plans were laid to eliminate all overnight facilities at the Upper Geyser Basin. While not all of these plans came to fruition—Old Faithful Inn, Old Faithful Lodge, and the Snow Lodge still serve overnight guests—the National Park Service successfully initiated a policy shift that continues to shape planning at every development node within the park today.

FIGURE 9.4. Yellowstone in Postcards. Vintage F. Jay Hayne's postcards and real-photo cards of Yellowstone, American Antiquarian Society, Worcester, Massachusetts (2010). Photograph © Janet L. Pritchard, from her book, *More than Scenery: Yellowstone, an American Love Story* (George F. Thompson Publishing, 2022), 87. Courtesy of the artist.

INTERPRETING YELLOWSTONE'S CULTURAL LEGACY

In important ways, this collection reflects a much larger transformation that is occurring within the National Park Service itself. The past forty years have seen a growing awareness of cultural resources, even in the West's great "natural" national park units. Certainly, the Vail Agenda's (1992) recognition of the importance of preserving these types of landscapes prompted a growing set of mandates and procedures that made their removal or alteration a more thoughtful, careful process. Still, many park managers have been slow to embrace the definition or importance of what a "cultural landscape" is in the first place.

Our hope is that this book marks an opportunity for park managers and the visiting public to reflect on the value of Yellowstone's cultural landscapes and to see them as integral parts of what makes Yellowstone the special place it is. We also hope that the varied stories told here demonstrate that such interpretations need to include both an appreciation for the uniqueness of each of these development areas as well as how they exemplify larger processes at work. Finally, we hope that, years from now, visitors to all of these areas within the park will find a growing diversity of written materials, exhibits at visitor centers, and ranger-led talks and walks that acknowledge, celebrate, challenge, and ponder the importance of the park's cumulative cultural landscape and all it entails. Indeed, it is the cultural as well as the physical landscape that truly shapes what visitors see and how they will see it when they journey through the park. Yellowstone, since its inception in 1872, remains a landscape made magical by its natural wonders. But that magic is everywhere framed and shaped by the people who came to see and understand it. Their signatures also help make Yellowstone the unique place it is, both today and for future generations to enjoy (figure 9.4).

Acknowledgments

Many people and institutions made this collective effort possible. As with any large and complex project, this book evolved through time, and the editors wish to especially thank Lary M. Dilsaver, Terence Young, Geoff Buckley, Lee Whittlesey, and additional anonymous reviewers for looking over various chapter drafts and outlines as our initiative unfolded. We also wish to acknowledge the wisdom and patience of all of our contributing authors. Each one of them developed a special relationship with Yellowstone's landscape and history that is reflected in every page of this book. More broadly, the editors wish to acknowledge other scholars in history and geography that paved the way for our efforts. We learned a great deal from so many individuals who knew the park well and shared it in their work. In particular, our appreciation goes to the fine scholarship of Richard Bartlett, Ethan Carr, Mary Culpin, Aubrey Haines, Linda McClelland, Judith Meyer, Kiki Rydell, Paul Schullery, Elizabeth Watry, Lee Whittlesey, Michael Yochim, and Randall Wilson.

Financial support also made this book possible, and the editors especially thank the Foundation for Landscape Studies for its generous funding with

https://doi.org/10.5876/9781646427697.c010

a David R. Coffin Publication Grant. In addition, both Montana State University and the University of Wisconsin–Sheboygan contributed funding and institutional support to the project, and we gratefully acknowledge our respective home institutions.

So much of this research emerged directly from original archival sources, and the editors and authors depended greatly on the expertise and generosity of archivists, librarians, and experts in historical photography. The archivists and historians at the Yellowstone National Park Archives, now housed in the beautiful Yellowstone Heritage and Research Center in Gardiner, Montana, were pivotal in opening the doors to so much of the material that helped bring to life the cultural landscapes that are the focus of this book. For much of this project, Lee Whittlesey served as the park's historian and chief archivist, and every one of our contributors depended on Lee's knowledge of the park and its archival riches. We appreciate his enduring support. We also thank Katrina Shafer, Erin Smerage, Lena Muldoon, and Hayley Tuggle for helping explore and finalize image selections for the book. Their enthusiasm for the project and for finding the right photographs and maps to illustrate the park's evolving cultural landscape contributed greatly to the visual riches of this book.

Elsewhere, Kim Scott (Special Collections Library Archivist at Montana State University) and Lory Morrow, Heather Hultman, and Patricia Davis (Photo Archivists at the Montana State Historical Society) helped identify important material and images for the project. For other photographs in the book, we also thank Rob Park at the Yellowstone Gateway Museum (Livingston, MT), Matt Nelson at Yale University's Beineke Library, and Traci Baetz at the Department of the Interior Museum. We also acknowledge generous private collectors such as Michael Francis (Billings, MT) and Tami Whittlesey (Seal Rock, OR), who made available images from their personal archives. We appreciated the assistance of the National Archives, the National Park Service, the Library of Congress, and the United States Geological Survey. Special thanks to Janet L. Pritchard for allowing us to use the wonderful images from her book *More than Scenery: Yellowstone, an American Love Story* (George F. Thompson Publishing, 2022).

The editors also acknowledge the inspiration and continuing contributions of our publishing friends at GFT Publishing. Our publisher, George Thompson, carefully shepherded the project from beginning to end, and his energy and expertise made this book possible. Our eagle-eyed editor,

Mikki Soroczak, also offered excellent editorial guidance every step of the way. Similarly, our publishing partners at the University of Wyoming Press were unfailingly helpful and enthusiastic as the project reached its later stages. Special thanks to our editor, Darrin Pratt, and to Laura Furney, Beth Svinarich, Laura Walker, Tina Kachele, Dan Pratt, and Carolyn Elerding for all of their guidance and expertise in putting the book together.

Finally, we wish to thank our families for their ongoing patience and encouragement. Thanks to Linda, Tom, Katie, Sherri, and Kade for all of your love and support over the years as this project moved toward publication.

Index

Page numbers followed by f indicate figures, page numbers followed by n indicate notes, and page numbers followed by t indicate tables.

About the Contributors

TIMOTHY DAVIS long served as a historian for the National Park Service specializing in cultural landscape research and preservation. He is the co-editor of *National Park Roads and Parkways: Drawings from the Historic American Engineering Record* (Johns Hopkins University Press, in association with the Center for American Places, 2004) and the author of *National Park Roads: A Legacy in the American Landscape* (University of Virginia Press, 2016). During his more than two decades with the National Park Service, Davis has directed numerous documentation projects on roads for the agency's Historic American Engineering Record (HAER) program. Recently retired, Davis looks forward to spending more time in the parks he has spent his career writing about.

TAMSEN EMERSON HERT, now retired, oversaw the operation of the Emmett D. Chisum Special Collections at the University of Wyoming Library, which includes an extensive collection of material on Yellowstone National Park and the Greater Yellowstone Ecosystem. First smitten with a love for Yellowstone in 1967, Hert has spent her career researching and publishing on the park's history and cultural landscapes. She is also a Past President of the Wyoming State Historical Society and a recipient of the University of Wyoming's Agnew Milstead Distinguished Librarianship Award.

DIANE PAPINEAU is a geographer who spent considerable time in Yellowstone as a seasonal employee before turning her academic attention to the story of the Grand Canyon of the Yellowstone and its associated development area. Writing as a real Yellowstone insider, Papineau is able to draw on her experiences from actually living in the park. She also knows many of the workers and park managers who shaped the Canyon landscape and the visitor's experience there. After completing a masters thesis on Yellowstone's Grand Canyon development area at Montana State University, Papineau moved to Helena and helped develop the State of Montana's GIS capabilities. She recently retired and enjoys life in Helena.

LANGDON SMITH, recently retired, served as a professor in the Department of Geography, Geology, and the Environment at Slippery Rock University in Pennsylvania. His research focus on public lands and parks was inspired by the time he spent exploring Yellowstone National Park and its surrounding wildlands. While at Slippery Rock, Smith enjoyed taking students on field trips to many national parks around the American West, including Yellowstone. He was also been instrumental in developing the university's Master of Science in Sustainable Systems program.

LEE H. WHITTLESEY is retired Park Historian for Yellowstone National Park, serving in that position for twenty-five years. He has spent much of his forty-year professional career working in the park and writing more than a dozen books and twenty-five journal articles on the park's history, geography, and wildlife. Recently, Whittlesey received the Forest History Society's Blegen Award for his coauthored article in *Montana: The Magazine of Western History* entitled "Abundance, Slaughter, and Resilience of the Greater Yellowstone Ecosystem's Mammal Populations: A View of the Historical Record, 1871–1885" (Spring 2020).

YOLONDA YOUNGS is a professor in the Department of Geography and Environmental Studies at California State University, San Bernardino. She specializes in environmental geography, cultural-historical landscapes, geospatial methods, and national parks and protected lands. She co-edited, with Geoffrey Buckley, *The American Environment Revisited: Environmental Historical Geographies of the United States* (Rowman & Littlefield, 2018). She is also the author of *Framing Nature: The Creation of an American Icon at the Grand Canyon* (Lincoln: University of Nebraska Press, 2024). *Framing Nature* earned her the 2024 J. B. Jackson Prize in Geography for the best book on the American cultural landscape.

About the Editors

WILLIAM K. WYCKOFF is a cultural and historical geographer of the American West who taught at Montana State University—just up the road from Yellowstone National Park—between 1986 and 2020. Today, he remains an Emeritus Professor of Earth Sciences. He is a co-editor, with Lary Dilsaver, of *The Mountainous West: Explorations in Historical Geography* (University of Nebraska Press, 1995) and is the author of numerous books on the American landscape, including *Mac McCloud's Five Points: Photographing Black Denver, 1938–1975* (University of New Mexico Press, 2023), *Riding Shotgun with Norman Wallace: Rephotographing the Arizona Landscape* (University of New Mexico Press, 2020), *How to Read the American West: A Field Guide* (University of Washington Press, 2014), *On the Road Again: Montana's Changing Landscape* (University of Washington Press, 2006), *Creating Colorado: The Making of a Western American Landscape, 1860–1940* (Yale University Press, 1999), and *The Developer's Frontier: The Making of the Western New York Landscape* (Yale University Press, 1988). In 2016, he received the Aubrey Haines Award from the National Park Service and in 2023 was awarded the Lifetime Achievement Honor of the American Association of Geographers. Bill and his family live in Bozeman, Montana.

KARL BYRAND is a cultural and historical geographer whose passions for Yellowstone and its Upper Geyser Basin were kindled during his time at Montana State University, where he completed a master's thesis on the park. After receiving his PhD in geography from the University of Maryland, Byrand taught geography for many years as a professor and department chair at the University of Wisconsin–Sheboygan. Recently retired, Karl lives in Los Angeles, California.